Vladimir Nemirovich-Danchenko and the Moscow Art Theatre

This is an authorized translation of *Nemirovich-Danchenko* (Moscow, 1979) by Inna Solovyova, historian, author, and senior researcher of the Moscow Art Theatre Archives.

Untranslated before now, it is the only comprehensive account of the life and work of Vladimir Nemirovich-Danchenko (1858–1943), co-founder with Konstantin Stanislavsky of the Moscow Art Theatre and one of the pioneers of the art of directing. Nemirovich-Danchenko was one of the few prominent theatre practitioners who lived and worked from Russia's Tsarist period through the inception and consolidation of its Soviet period. Thus, it is also a story about the development of Russian society and culture during the last half of the nineteenth century and the Soviet half of the twentieth century. Additionally, it explores the Moscow Art Theatre's interpretive and production work on the plays of Chekhov, Shakespeare, Ibsen, Dostoevsky, Leo Tolstoy, Maxim Gorky, and many others. The central theme of the book focuses on the contingent dialectical relationship between artists and their changing socio-political realities.

The author's narrative is stylistically informal and based on archival documents, most of which are referenced here for the first time in English and will be of great interest to students and scholars in theatre and performance studies.

Inna Solovyova (1937–2024) was one of Russia's most prominent theatre historians and critics with expertise in the history of the Moscow Art Theatre.

James Thomas is a Professor in the Maggie Allesee Department of Theatre and Dance in the College of Fine, Performing and Communication Arts at Wayne State University.

Routledge Advances in Theatre & Performance Studies

This series is our home for cutting-edge, upper-level scholarly studies and edited collections. Considering theatre and performance alongside topics such as religion, politics, gender, race, ecology, and the avant-garde, titles are characterized by dynamic interventions into established subjects and innovative studies on emerging topics.

Performing Corporate Bodies
Multinational Theatre in Global India
Sarah Saddler

The Phenomenology of Blood in Performance Art
Edited by T J Bacon and Chelsea Coon

Contemporary Performance and Political Economy
Oikonomia as a New Ethico-Political Paradigm
Katerina Paramana

Consent in Shakespeare's Classical Mediterranean
Women Speak Truth to Power
Artemis Preeshl

Navarasas, Autoethnodrama & DIY Immersive Theatre
An Interactive Book for Adventurous Readers
Nandita Dinesh

Vladimir Nemirovich-Danchenko and the Moscow Art Theatre
Inna Solovyova, Translated and edited by James Thomas

For more information about this series, please visit: www.routledge.com/Routledge-Advances-in-Theatre--Performance-Studies/book-series/RATPS

Vladimir Nemirovich-Danchenko and the Moscow Art Theatre

Inna Solovyova
Translated and edited by James Thomas

Figure 0 Vladimir Nemirovich-Danchenko. By permission of the Moscow Art Academic Theatre.

LONDON AND NEW YORK

First published in English 2025
by Routledge
4 Park Square, Milton Park, Abingdon, Oxon OX14 4RN

and by Routledge
605 Third Avenue, New York, NY 10158

Routledge is an imprint of the Taylor & Francis Group, an informa business

© 2025 Inna Solovyova and James Thomas

The right of Inna Solovyova and James Thomas to be identified as author of this work has been asserted in accordance with sections 77 and 78 of the Copyright, Designs and Patents Act 1988.

All rights reserved. No part of this book may be reprinted or reproduced or utilised in any form or by any electronic, mechanical, or other means, now known or hereafter invented, including photocopying and recording, or in any information storage or retrieval system, without permission in writing from the publishers.

Trademark notice: Product or corporate names may be trademarks or registered trademarks and are used only for identification and explanation without intent to infringe.

Published in Russian by Iskusstvo Publishers (Moscow, 1979)

British Library Cataloguing-in-Publication Data
A catalogue record for this book is available from the British Library

ISBN: 9781032781136 (hbk)
ISBN: 9781032781174 (pbk)
ISBN: 9781003486282 (ebk)

DOI: 10.4324/9781003486282

Typeset in sabon
by codeMantra

Contents

Translator's Preface	*vii*
1 The Long Beginning 1858–1886	1
2 Everything Is Nearby 1886–1896	32
3 Opening 1896–1899	63
4 In the Theatre from Ten to Seven 1899–1904	88
5 First Farewells 1904–1905	114
6 Returning to a New Place 1905–1906	143
7 At Home 1906–1909	159
8 Russian Tragedy 1908–1910	179
9 Options for an Ending 1910–1914	198
10 Fifth and Sixth Life 1914–1919	209
11 Chapter from another Book 1919–1943 (The Soviet Years)	226
Index	*251*

Translator's Preface

The name of Vladimir Nemirovich-Danchenko (1858–1943) is always associated with Konstantin Stanislavsky due to their collaboration in founding and leading the Moscow Art Theatre in 1898. In the Anglo-American theatre world, however, Stanislavsky's name has been more prominent because of the extensive writings by him and his followers.

Nemirovich-Danchenko's life remains somewhat enigmatic since he left little written about himself, resulting in limited awareness about him in the Anglo-American theatre world. However, in his home country, researchers have ensured his significant role in the study and practice of theatre. Among these researchers, the author of this biography, Inna Solovyova, who headed the commission for studying and publishing the creative legacies of Stanislavsky and Nemirovich-Danchenko, stands out. She has published works like *Nemirovich-Danchenko* (1979) and *K. S. Stanislavsky* (1980–1994) in six volumes, comprising the director's manuscripts, along with many other works related to the history and creative heritage of the Moscow Art Theatre. Recognizing her contributions, the Russian Government awarded her the Order of Merit for the Fatherland in 2008 and the Order of Alexander Nevsky in 2018.

This translation offers a comprehensive overview of Nemirovich-Danchenko's life and work. It covers key themes such as the turbulent era of late tsarism, the Russian Revolutions, and the changing relationship between the artist and shifting socio-political realities. It explores the role of women in Russian theatre, the impact of avant-garde movements, and the political climate of the Soviet Union, including the establishment of socialist realism. The work of prominent playwrights and directors and the Moscow Art Theatre's relationship with the fields of literature, film, and music are also explored. Not least of all, it provides a myriad of insights into the Moscow Art Theatre's day-to-day workings and relationship with the broader theatre community. Overall, this translation offers a comprehensive and in-depth exploration of Nemirovich-Danchenko's life and the socio-political context in which he lived and worked, making it an invaluable resource for anyone interested in Russian theatre and culture.

viii *Translator's Preface*

Vladimir Nemirovich-Danchenko and the Moscow Art Theatre is an archival biography that delves into researching and analyzing primary materials such as letters, diaries, and photographs. Solovyova's aim was to construct an accurate portrayal of Nemirovich-Danchenko based on these primary sources. Notably, the narrative presented in her work lacks substantial scholarly citations. Throughout the original 400-page text, there are relatively few such citations, with references to other sources often labeled as "notebook," "director's plan," "letter," or simply omitted altogether. Her approach, which is largely followed in this translation, ensures a smooth reading experience and enhances the biography's accessibility to a broader audience.

However, archival biographies often face challenges with information gaps and incomplete records, leaving readers with unanswered questions. To address this, Solovyova fills these gaps by providing essential background information and historical context from her own storehouse of expertise. Furthermore, she skillfully employs foreshadowing and retrospection to suggest what might have occurred during these gaps or what the future might hold.

It is important to acknowledge that the current translation is semantic, focusing on delivering the meaning of the original text, with some scope for paraphrasing. Accordingly, it may contain some residual gaps and transitions due to language, cultural differences, and length constraints. To mitigate these limitations and enhance clarity and flow, I have implemented several approaches. First, I have included plot summaries to provide context for unfamiliar plays. Second, I have included supplemental text for clarification. Lastly, I have added a limited number of chapter endnotes. Despite some loss of content and narrative continuity, however, it is equally important to underscore that a substantial amount of valuable material and story development has been preserved.

Readers are encouraged to seek out additional information about the intriguing story of Nemirovich-Danchenko's life. His *My Life In The Russian Theatre* (Little, Brown and Company, 1936) contains a panoramic survey up to the beginning of the Soviet era and covers Anton Chekhov, the birth of the Moscow Art Theatre, the early European tours, and the influence of Leo Tolstoy. Elizabeth Reynolds Hapgood's *Chronology* at the end can be a helpful companion to the present translation. Also valuable is Laurence Senelick's comprehensive *Historical Dictionary of Russian Theatre* for information and facts that cannot be found in this work.

The complete version of Solovyova's archival biography in Russian can be found at theater-lib.ru, Solovyova I. N. *Nemirovich-Danchenko*. Moskva.: Iskusstvo, 1979. Lyubov Friedkina's day-by-day chronology of Nemirovich-Danchenko's life and work can be found in Russian at theater-lib.ru, Fryeydkina L. M. *Dni i guodi Vl. I. Nyemirovicha-Danchenko: Lyetopis zizni i tvorchyestva*. Moskva: VTO, 1962 (*Days and Years of Vl. I. Nemirovich-Danchenko: A Chronicle of His Life and Work*).

1 The Long Beginning 1858–1886

Personal Revelations and Professional Legacy

Vladimir Nemirovich-Danchenko rarely discussed his personal life. His autobiography, titled *From the Past*,[1] does not delve into his emotions, despite the implication of the title. Instead, it provides a straightforward and concise narrative that lacks everyday details. It functions more as an informative account rather than a personal exploration.

Even in an early questionnaire for *Wenger's Biographical Dictionary of Russian Writers*, which was never published, his responses were laconic. Birthdate: 1858. Location: The Caucasus, Ozurgeti, near Poti.[2] Parents: Father, a retired lieutenant colonel and landowner in Chernihiv Province. Mother, née Yagubova, Armenian. Ancestry: Indefinite. For which Nemirovich added a reservation: "If I am not mistaken." Asked about any outstanding people in the family, he replies, "I do not know of any."

The questionnaire asked for Significant Life Events. Answer: "I prefer to remain silent." The questionnaire asked him to describe himself. He answers: Know thyself? Looking back, I can say that I grew up alone and lived 'with might and main' early, around age 16. I began working on myself late, around age 25, and I hope for the strength to continue this most important work of a person until the end of my days."

> My friends say that I have great stamina and a hidden temperament. Others say that I am lethargic and only have occasional bursts of energy. Maybe, I don't know. There was a period of melancholy, and I got over it. I have a great reserve of cheerfulness in me.

Throughout his life, Nemirovich-Danchenko rarely contributed new information to what the biographical dictionary already contained. It seems as though his memory only awakened when asked about his early experiences and then closed up again. Later in life, when prompted by others, he shared stories that were typical of any artist's biography influenced by a love for the stage. He resided in an apartment near a park with a summer theatre, purchased tickets with borrowed money, and attempted to mimic his favorite

DOI: 10.4324/9781003486282-1

2 Vladimir Nemirovich-Danchenko and the Moscow Art Theatre

actors by draping his mother's black shawl like a cloak over his shoulders, reminiscent of a provincial tragedian playing Hamlet. He also ventured into writing and authored a drama called *Poor Noel Rambert*, which was inspired by French life.

Nemirovich-Danchenko always felt deeply connected to society as a whole. He considered himself a part of the broader human experience. He was a man of his time, belonging to a specific generation and profession. Despite changes in society, he embraced them naturally but was not defined by them. The Moscow Art Theatre Museum houses a significant collection of personal documents and papers attributed to Nemirovich-Danchenko. These artifacts provide valuable insights into his life beyond the realm of arts. Some of these items were neatly stored in a large box under his name, while others were initially unboxed and unidentified but later sorted out. When arranging the ephemera in chronological order, the birth certificate should be placed first, followed by the registry book from the church of the 32nd Caucasian Battalion of the Assumption of the Blessed Virgin Mary. The birthdate recorded in the book is December 11, 1858, and the baptism occurred on January 18, 1859. The ceremony was conducted by battalion priest Johann Shmenev, with witnesses Pyotr Gladky and Alexei Popov. The document was signed by Father Shmenev of the Caucasian Linear Battalion № 32. Other witnesses included Podkolzin, son of the Ozurgeti district governor and an army captain, as well as cavalier Alexander Nikolaev and Maria Tsulukidzeva, wife of Ozurgeti city police warden Prince Tsulukidze. The last item in chronological order is a medal titled "For the Defense of the Caucasus," which was awarded by decree on May 1, 1944. Nemirovich-Danchenko would have received this medal on April 20, 1945. However, he passed away on April 25, 1943.

In the intervening years, various identification cards, membership cards, and passes are included. These items consist of a red cloth book titled Friend of The Children with the number 225325, an Auto-Club membership card, and a Theatre Workers' Union card with a leather cover embossed with a lyre. The union card, issued in 1941 (with membership since 1919), lists his primary workplace as the Moscow Art Theatre of the Union of Soviet Socialist Republics, with the position of Director. Dues were paid until March 1943.

Bank papers related to the mortgage of Neskuchnoye, his country house in Ukraine, along with related bills marked as Paid, are also present. There is a summons to a meeting in the city of Batum on February 28, 1913, where Nemirovich-Danchenko was called as a witness in a case involving the defendant and Alexander Mgebrov, who were accused of the first part of Article 102 of the criminal code. He was arrested as an actor of the Moscow Art Theatre for participating in an armed uprising in 1905. The collection also includes publisher's contracts. One contract is an agreement with A. F. Marx to acquire the rights to the works of Vl. I. Nemirovich-Danchenko up until January 28, 1904.[3] The agreement specifies a quantity of 144 pages, each containing 35,000 characters, with a payment rate of 125 rubles

The Long Beginning 1858–1886   3

per page. Unfortunately, this work was never published. There is also an agreement with Academica Publishing House, stating the author's address as Bolshaya Nikitskaya, 50, Apt. 1, and a receivable amount of 17,920 rubles. Furthermore, there are purchase records from Wolf's Bookstore, located near Kuznetsky Bridge. On January 26, 1907, Nemirovich-Danchenko made several book acquisitions, which included the third volume of Alexander Kuprin's literary works, the 14th collection of *Znanievtsy's Book of Facts*, Muther's comprehensive history of art, a French novel titled *The Garden of Epicurus*, Vyacheslav Ivanov's masterpiece *Eros*, Valery Bryusov's notable work *Earth's Axis*, another piece by Valery Bryusov, and a publication by Stanislaw Przybyshevsky. In 1933, he purchased books titled *Sevastopol*, *Hydrocenter*, The *Desert*, and *Tsushima* from the Writers' Bookshop on Mokhovaya Street.

Other notable items include:

- A certificate titled Royal Edict of the Emir of Bukhara, signed by Emir Seyid-Alim on January 24, 1914, bestowing the Bukhara Order of the Silver Star of the second degree upon him for the benefit and peace of the people and the friendship between Bukhara and the Russian Imperial Government.
- A doctor's note from March 23, 1921, recommending daily heating of the liver region using an electric heating device for Vladimir Nemirovich-Danchenko, due to his liver ailment.
- A document titled People's Artist, signed by Soviet Minister of Education Anatoly Lunacharsky in April 1924.[4]
- A letter of commendation for patronage work for the Armed Forces.
- A pass card for the Kremlin Hospital, with a receipt for funeral expenses and a stay at Barvikha Health Spa in 1938, following the death of Nemirovich-Danchenko's wife.
- A lunch pass for the Kremlin cafeteria.
- An order for pastries, roast beef, ham, Swiss cheese, red caviar, English cake, grapes, apples, cookies, and tangerines from the Yeliseyev Hotel, billed to Nemirovich-Danchenko Street, 5/7.
- Parade passes for various events on Red Square, including May 1, 1935, June 19, 1936 (Gorky's farewell), June 20 (his funeral), November 7, 1937, and November 7, 1938 (for the anniversaries of the Russian Revolution).
- An invitation to the elections for the Supreme Soviet of the USSR on December 12, 1937.
- An honorary lifetime pass to the racetrack.
- A pass for the All-Union Agricultural Exhibition of 1939, showcasing champion beef cattle.

Despite being eighty-one years old in 1939 and feeling good that summer, he was unable to attend the exhibition due to being too busy. He had to open his new production of *Three Sisters* at the beginning of the season. About

Figure 1.1 Konstantin Stanislavsky and Vladimir Nemirovich-Danchenko, co-founder directors of the Moscow Art Theatre. By permission of the Moscow Art Academic Theatre.

which one spectator who attended the dress rehearsal would write: "I don't know which of the world's blessings could compare with this blessed day at The Moscow Art Theatre."

But first, a long life had to unfold (Figure 1.1).

Journey Towards Education and Independence

Georgian Prince Alexander Sumbatov was a classmate of Nemirovich-Danchenko's in high school in Tiflis. They were close friends, and both shared a passion for the theatre. They even came up with stage names in case their dreams of becoming actors came true. Sumbatov became the renowned Maly Theatre actor Alexander Yuzhin,[5] while Nemirovich-Danchenko aspired to be an actor named Nikolai Severov, although he eventually did not pursue this path. Both also had plans to pursue a university education.

In 1877, Sumbatov went to St. Petersburg to study law at the university. Along the way, he made several stops, including Vladikavkaz, Kharkiv, Orel, Yelets, Voronezh, and Tula. Each stop had a purpose for Sumbatov, such as seeing specific actors or visiting family. However, these names and places

Figure 1.2 Vladimir Nemirovich-Danchenko (~1877). By permission of the Moscow Art Academic Theatre.

may not be familiar to readers, and their significance lies within this circle of friends and their shared love for the theatre, particularly in Tiflis (Figure 1.2).

Many years later, the great actor Yuzhin (formerly known as Sumbatov) reflected on these earlier times, describing a younger generation for whom theatre and literature were central to their lives. They viewed personal matters through the lens of art, while others in their cohort identified themselves through politics, social issues, science, or religion. It would be unfair to judge someone for their affiliation with a particular group, just as it would be unreasonable to expect fish to fly or birds to swim.

Unlike Sumbatov, Nemirovich-Danchenko did not make any detours on his way to Moscow. He obtained the necessary certificate for university admission on August 16, 1876, and ten days later submitted a petition stating his intention to join a higher educational institution in the Russian Empire. The petition described Nemirovich-Danchenko as a nobleman who had successfully completed the science curriculum at Tiflis High School and had no obstacles preventing his departure from Tiflis.

Even if the Police Department of the 1st Mountain Division had behaved less officiously, they would still have no doubts about Nemirovich-Danchenko's

6 Vladimir Nemirovich-Danchenko and the Moscow Art Theatre

case. Few of his high school classmates violated the law, even by reading the wrong books. You might have heard a rumor about a student who brought Karl Marx's *Capital* to class, but Nemirovich-Danchenko had only glanced at it. If there was one thing that stood out about young Nemirovich-Danchenko, it was not his interest in politics. At one point, he had experienced a passionate love affair and even went so far as to rent an apartment for their rendezvous. However, the relationship ended abruptly and tumultuously. On another occasion, he had gifted an actress with an extravagant bouquet costing twenty-eight rubles. He had obtained the money by tutoring since the tender age of thirteen. As a high school senior, he was already teaching evening classes.

However, all of that belonged to the past. Now, he was on his way to Moscow. Passengers packed the trains, and neighbors dozed off against one another. Most were not headed to Moscow but rather further on to St. Petersburg. They were not students, but rather individuals with families and promising new positions awaiting them. There were plenty of new job opportunities available that were too good to pass up. However, the passengers had their concerns as well. There was uncertainty surrounding the reliability of these new positions and whether they would end up having to relocate yet again. Their worries were absent back home, but now everyone was on the move.

The final destination and whether it was truly worth it remained unclear, but the general rhythm of life had everyone on edge. Eyes were alert, observing every detail amidst the chaos of the train stations. The scent of coal, locomotives, smoke from the bustling samovar at the station, the smell of new leather luggage, and the aroma of cabbage soup in the station's cafeterias. It was the smell of time, the smell of travel. Each person had their own matters to attend to. In times like these, individuals tried to focus on their personal goals, as still and determined as a pole star.

Attending university was a necessity, and based on the advice of his high school director, Nemirovich-Danchenko chose the Department of Physics and Mathematics. First, there were scholarships available for students from the Caucasus. Second, there seemed to be a growing interest among young people in the natural sciences. A friend from the Tiflis school once commented that if she were to attend school, she would not choose the arts and humanities, deeming them nonsensical. Of course, she was mistaken, but the question lingered as to whether resolving personal matters through the lens of theatre and literature was wise. Pursuing this career path felt like an extension of his childhood, carrying on the games he used to play on the windowsill until his final year of high school. It involved hanging posters and using playing cards to act out the roles in *Hamlet* and *A Mother's Blessing*. It may not have been actual childhood, but rather a sense of romanticism at an ill-timed moment. While this approach might have suited someone like Sumbatov, who hailed from the Caucasus and came from an aristocratic family involved in battles for ancestral lands and hiring assassins, Nemirovich-Danchenko knew he

The Long Beginning 1858–1886   7

needed to be more realistic. He needed to stay focused and avoid any romantic detours. His ultimate destination was Moscow. Most of his fellow travelers were heading to St. Petersburg, where the changing times seemed to move with more energy. In addition, if he was genuinely interested in mathematics, St. Petersburg boasted Pafnuty Chebyshev, the founder of the School of Mathematics, whereas Moscow was not particularly known for this subject.

If he chose St. Petersburg, he wouldn't be a lonely seventeen-year-old because his brother Vasily lived there.[6] Despite the fourteen-year age difference between them, they had recently reconnected when Vasily, a well-known writer, visited the family in Tiflis. However, why choose St. Petersburg? First, if rumors were true that the fighting in the Balkans would soon resume on a larger scale (which they were), his brother would be away from St. Petersburg for the next few months, serving as a war correspondent. Therefore, the younger sibling wouldn't have the protective presence of his brother. Second, the younger sibling wasn't eager to depend on anyone. While he wouldn't refuse offered help, he desired independence. He was determined to make it on his own. That was the prevailing trend, and it was his natural inclination.

It might be challenging, but he wouldn't burden others with his troubles. He didn't recognize the pride of an artist that he concealed within himself. Failure was shameful because it meant he couldn't perform as well as others and lacked talent. It was even more embarrassing to not endure failure privately. We need to understand the mental rule that the seventeen-year-old brought from home and upheld throughout his life. We shouldn't be embarrassed by the self-centered tone of his letters, in which he talks about his successes, generous payment, respectful treatment, positive feedback, and the failures of his rivals' intrigues. He had the right to report those things. However, he found it not only unpleasant but also impossible to complain. When things were troubling, it was better for him to stay silent.

"After completing the science course at Tiflis High School, I kindly request Your Excellency's permission to enroll in the physics and mathematics department of the university under your supervision." Sergei Soloviev, the rector, approved the application on August 26, 1876.

And so, Moscow began.

Balancing Intellect, Theater, and Societal Expectations

Moscow is hilly; even a casual walk can take you to a place with a panoramic view. The houses that would obstruct that view still needed to be built; however, something else was obstructing it. At that time, *The Alarm Clock* magazine began a comic, multi-issue fact-finding tour of Moscow. So here it was, the famous Moscow: giant billboards concealing outdated building facades, smelly back alleys, sidewalks that were either broken or freshly repaired, and broken street pavement (they had just asphalted one block of Tverskaya Street, which became the source of a joke about the Duma sending one of its members to the Sierra Nevada—isn't that where

8 *Vladimir Nemirovich-Danchenko and the Moscow Art Theatre*

asphalt comes from? At least they should properly install cobblestones in front of the governor-general's house, so passengers would not tumble out of their carriages and sleighs).

The magazine's column was not for tourists but for people looking to rent an apartment, to know how to get to the office more conveniently, where to send servants for shopping, and where to have a meal. Nemirovich-Danchenko's fellow passengers on his trip in 1876 were concerned about settling into their new jobs. Would they be given a good salary and would they be trustworthy, or would they quickly disappear? Newcomers only wanted to settle down, not conquer the city. This was one reason the column did not provide a "bird's-eye view" of the city from somewhere like Sparrow Hills, where a panorama of Moscow lay below, glittering with golden onion domes, ready to belong to anyone who could conquer it. But in the pages of another excursion, the tour guide for *The Alarm Clock* warned readers not to go to Sparrow Hills. You could not get there since its slope collapsed into the Moscow River when they tried to erect the Church of Christ the Savior there. The entire hillside, with all its oaks and pine trees, had collapsed into the water below. There was only a cliff there now, crumbling and barren. The city built a horseback road, but it was long and treacherous, and coach drivers avoided it. There were barracks for bricklayers from before the slope's collapse, which later became a prison transfer facility. Somebody eventually dismantled them, but the location remained unwelcoming. Thus, another project without any limits or oversight.

Children played, and horses loaded up with water barrels around the fountain in Theatre Square, the site of the Bolshoi and Maly Theatres. Water carriers did not have time to stop and wonder at the bronze charioteer controlling the four mighty horses atop the roof of the Bolshoi Theatre. Nearby was the Nikolaev Parade Ground: an earthen field surrounded by ropes on posts and gas lamps at its corners. The area was already being developed, destroying the symmetry of its nearby buildings. The new facilities were barracks-like and bureaucratic, and the public did not like them. The rundown state of the renowned Maly Theatre disappointed visitors from the provinces who had heard so much about it.

Imperial Moscow University was surrounded by old houses and rows of bookstores with furnished rooms. In Chekhov's *A Dreary Story* (1889), one of the characters passed through this area and observed,

Here are the gloomy, dilapidated university gates, a bored janitor in a sheepskin coat, a broom, and a pile of snow. For a young boy fresh from the provinces, who imagined that the temple of science was an actual temple, such a gate did not make a strong impression. The shabbiness of the university buildings, the gloominess of the corridors, the soot on the walls, the lack of light, and the dull appearance of the steps, cloakrooms, and benches were among the initial reasons for the inclination towards pessimism in Russian history.

The observer did not have the opportunity to appreciate the architecture of the magnificent Kazakov building, including its overall design, dome, gently curved wing overlooking Nikitskaya Street, and charming portico-balconies.

Nearby grocery shops were quick to extend credit to students. If the shopkeeper was also a homemaker, she showed particular sympathy toward the buyers: "Each of them has a mother." Sometimes, she would jot down the purchase of cigarettes or tea without asking for the buyer's name. However, when it came time to pay, the laid-back shopkeeper had only recorded "the handsome student" or "the merry student." Fortunately, Nemirovich-Danchenko did not have to rely on the kindness of shopkeepers. He had received a scholarship from Tiflis (Chekhov also received a scholarship from his hometown of Taganrog), and his living arrangements were satisfactory.

Nemirovich-Danchenko's archives include letters from his early years in Moscow, signed by Boris Sezenevsky. When Sezenevsky's wife fell ill and passed away, Nemirovich-Danchenko covered the expenses of her burial. He regularly sent money, considering it a loan. The drawings beneath Sezenevsky's signature and other papers in the MAT museum exhibit similar examples of Nemirovich-Danchenko's tendency to think with a pencil, adding flowers around the corners in a mechanical manner. He wrote to the seventy-three-year-old Sezenevsky in 1932. He remembered Sezenevsky's house, where he had lived as a student while helping Sezenevsky and his brother Volodya with their studies. During the First World War, Volodya served as a general officer in charge of sanitary trains but did not disclose what had happened to him.

Tutoring the Sezenevskys provided him with an apartment, a desk, and spending money. This arrangement was more sustainable than the "lessons with lunch" that his classmates used to have there. The warm coziness of the place suited him perfectly. He was not very involved in student life, choosing not to wear a university uniform or the fashionable attire of the time, which typically consisted of a Russian-style shirt tucked into a belt, a wide-brimmed hat, and blue-tinted glasses "for better vision," indicating his student and socialist identity. Soon after arriving in Moscow, he appeared in a photograph with his friend Gribov. He had a firm, cheerful mouth, and thick hair. A meticulous retoucher added red and blue embroidery to his linen shirt collar and corded hem: a young man who wore a plain jacket, like everyone else on a summer day.

In 1918, Yuri Sobolev published a monograph about Nemirovich-Danchenko, whose youth in Moscow coincided with the peak of revolutionary sentiments. Nemirovich-Danchenko remembered hearing arguments and rumors about a specific room off Sretenka Street. And a discussion group, like Land and Will,[7] where a young woman spoke passionately, dismissing all objections. Something from these impressions may have surfaced when MAT produced *The Cherry Orchard* a quarter-century later. Looking at Peter Trofimov, "the eternal student," the audience could have imagined cheap rooms, gray with dampness and tobacco smoke, and voices hoarse from arguing. (The custom of the time was not so much argument as strident ideological

10 *Vladimir Nemirovich-Danchenko and the Moscow Art Theatre*

monologues, just as Trofimov gives the impression of listening to himself more than others.) Or, on the contrary, something Nemirovich-Danchenko imagined for the production may have influenced his response to the biographer's questions, clouding his memory of reality.

This wealthy Sezenevsky family, where Nemirovich-Danchenko taught the sons how to color eggs during Passion Week of 1878, was not concerned with what they did on Sretenka Street in those years. Societal insulation covered specific aspects of their everyday life. However, sometimes tremors penetrated the insulation. Terrorists mistakenly blew up a train; it was not the one in which the tsar was traveling. *New Times*, required reading, raised the "either/or" question: either make bombs like the revolutionaries or decorate the ham with frilly paper for the first meal after the Lenten fast. This imposed choice was misleading, as life was not polarized in this way.

Nevertheless, if not this choice, some other choice still needed to be made, and for Nemirovich-Danchenko, it was a serious matter. He was a good student; he might have become a teacher if he didn't become a mathematician. He also audited and passed a few courses in law school. Thus, he didn't feel like an amateur when writing about criminal proceedings to make extra money. He had a way with words, had some understanding of psychology, and could reason and persuade. All of this would be useful if he chose a legal profession. But he found neither course of study enjoyable. He could see that Moscow was filled with intelligent people who only saw their jobs as a means to an end. Doctors mainly treated patients for money; officials in state institutions (banking, railroad, judicial, clerical) served their time without joy; high school teachers lost interest after teaching the same thing year after year. Nemirovich-Danchenko later said, "To be constantly engaged in one's chosen work is the exceptional happiness of a human being." In his youth, he also formed an opinion about where people can find such work-related pleasure: "In this sense, actors are the happiest people."

The joy of individual creativity, the work of a writer, is constantly tested in solitude. If one were to lose faith in oneself, the desire would surely be lost as well. In the theatre, however, each person involuntarily infects others with creativity, even if the actors cannot stand each other. Some may feel gloom and doom, but it is never seen as a hateful burden. He always loved the spirit of camaraderie, the openness of personalities, the theatre's similarity to a large and eccentric family, the enjoyment of working in a talented company, and the absence of arrogant silence and empty talk. Later on, director Anatoly Efros said, "Actors are like a feminine part of creative humanity and they need understanding and affection."[8] Nemirovich-Danchenko loved actors throughout his life, much like an ideal man loves women: passionately, even embracing their shortcomings.

Everything that comprised the theatre's essence intoxicated him: the smell of gas lights, the fresh paint on new posters, and the sound of music in the park where the summer theatre performed. His intoxication surpassed that of a mere spectator, yet the joys of amateur acting were not sufficient for him

The Long Beginning 1858–1886 11

either. Granted, those were good times when Sumbatov wrote down the text of a vaudeville from memory because they didn't have a copy of their own. They rehearsed it in an empty apartment, and Sumbatov performed with them upon returning home for his first student holiday. The production was presented to the public (the ticket revenue going to needy students) at the same summer theatre in the park, where the music had once come to Nemirovich-Danchenko in his dreams. In the fourth act, Nemirovich-Danchenko's character delivered a passionate monologue, concluded it, fell to his knees, and earned applause. In such situations, someone always said, "You have real talent, and you should pursue the stage." This time, it was said to him by a leading actor at The Korsh Theatre, where he was performing in Chekhov's play *Ivanov*.

After another year of amateurism in Moscow, he signed a contract with Kazantsev, the impresario of the Rostov-on-Don Theatre, and prepared the roles of Chatsky and Molchalin. He almost killed off the budding mathematician, Nemirovich-Danchenko, and allowed the budding actor, Severov, to take over. He would not be alone: his brother Ivan gave up military service to become the actor Mirsky. And his sister Varvara became the actress Svetlanova, initially in operetta and later in a dramatic troupe. His mother, Alexandra, led a nomadic life with her military husband for thirty-six years in cities where people rarely spoke the word "theatre." However, in her later years, she became an avid theatregoer and a devoted "stage mother," traveling throughout the provinces with her actress-daughter.

Nevertheless, despite everything, he went back on his decision. Nemirovich-Danchenko never explained why he changed a career choice that was already decided upon. He mentioned eye problems, but this did not prevent him from quickly settling down in newspaper editorial offices, where reading galleys was more harmful to one's eyesight than footlights. Now he had to abandon the preparation of the roles of Chatsky and Molchalin for their debuts in Rostov.

Theatrical Journalism and Evolving Ideals

Nemirovich-Danchenko spent every evening in Moscow at the theatre, starting in the fall of 1877. However, he would only go backstage if his current benefactor had good relationships with the newspapers and could get him in. At that time, he was known as "the Press." Anyone can write and get published in a local tabloid. It's easy to summarize a play and say one actor was "divine," another was "okay but a bit young for the role," and a third was "bad." This is why one can only become a professional journalist if someone influential recommends them. In Nemirovich-Danchenko's case, it was Osip Pravin, an actor who remembered their acquaintance in Tiflis, who helped him out. (As a student, Nemirovich-Danchenko often visited Alexander Yablochkin's home to tutor his son and eagerly listened to conversations about the theatre.) Through Pravin, he was introduced to Alexei Alexandrov of *Russian News*, where he eventually worked as a journalist.

12 *Vladimir Nemirovich-Danchenko and the Moscow Art Theatre*

In the 1930s, researchers became interested in Nemirovich-Danchenko's earliest work as a critic. An article by Lyubov Freidkina in *Theatre* magazine caught his attention,[9] leading him to want to revisit his past reviews. He requested copies of pages from *The Russian Courier* from the Lenin Library (invoices for photocopies, dated July 3, 1940, are still in the archive box). They printed his theatre reviews from 1877 onwards. But before that, there was St. Petersburg's *The Alarm Clock*, a weekly satirical literary and artistic magazine. Although Nemirovich-Danchenko wasn't on the staff, he regularly contributed pieces to the newspaper's "Mailbox" section (featuring a devil in a dashing skirt and a mail carrier's cap with horns as its logo). As the staff got used to him, a new column called "Nicks and Kicks" was introduced. The column was a collaboration between Nemirovich-Danchenko and Nikolai Kicheev and was called "Notes of Theatrical Rogues." The logo they used was always the same: a naked devil sitting under an umbrella trying to cover up with a banner titled "Onstage and Backstage."

Under this logo, you obviously couldn't write an article titled "*Hamlet*, the drama by William Shakespeare: Mochalov in the role of Hamlet." They also didn't ask if they loved the theatre as you did. Readers of *The Alarm Clock* simply[10] enjoyed the theatre and reading about it. They wanted to know the plot of new plays, so summaries were necessary. They also wanted to know about successful actors, so their names had to be included. Readers were also interested in tributes and gifts, such as the benefit performance for actress Sophia Akimova. Subscribers to *The Alarm Clock* appreciated it when a journalist criticized impetuous newcomers. In a recent incident, newcomer Mr. Yuzhin was criticized for lacking judgment in taking on the role of *Uriel Acosta*, considering his unsuitable figure and voice. There were rumors that he would also portray *Hamlet* for laughs, as well. Some believed he should have been more self-aware of his youth and not overstep his abilities. Competing with favorite celebrities was not wise. Subscribers also appreciated it when famous people were called out. Glikeria Fedotova, a well-known figure,[11] was openly criticized for her role in Ostrovsky's new play. The review remarked that she would have been better suited for the role of Larissa ten years ago, and now it was time for her to play older women. Maria Yermolova's habit of pulling at her elbows was also mentioned as a bad mannerism. Anton Chekhov wrote about Yuzhin, while "Nicks and Kicks" covered Fedotova and Yermolova.

This biographer would have been interested in finding letters where young Nemirovich-Danchenko reprimanded his co-contributor for frivolous reporting, but such letters do not exist. It is important to note that Nikolai Kicheev was not a lively coffee-house reviewer. He was a serious university man who spoke quietly, laughed sparingly, and adhered to the newspaper's accepted style. The writing style of the 1870s was influenced by a close relationship with the public, many of whom had a disrespectful attitude toward art. This public was described by Stanislavsky as arrogant and sophisticated in their tendency to criticize everything. They believed they were always right and were free from the inferiority complex inherited from critics who mocked them for not understanding art. According to them, it was the artists' fault for not making themselves more understandable. Saying "I don't like it" did not imply a lack of understanding but rather a high standard.

The journalism of the 1870s was also characterized by a temperance craze and a distaste for idols. Equally significant was the liberation of people from the influence of officialdom and the practice of deference toward authority figures. They preferred to be rude rather than submit to authority. These characteristics explain why the theatre reviews of the 1870s lacked enthusiasm. It seemed that surrendering to the power of artistic expression and conveying it was no longer considered necessary for writing about theatre. These attributes were associated only with "aesthetes" and "old-timers." The theatre reviews of the 1870s lack individual voices and instead reflect the voice and tone of the publication. Identifying the authorship of Nemirovich-Danchenko's work would be impossible without the help of a journalism expert and Masanov's Dictionary of Pseudonyms. Even Chekhov's newspaper articles, which were printed without a signature, cannot be identified.

Nemirovich-Danchenko frequently wrote short pieces, often without signing them, for commissioned works. Two St. Petersburg newspapers, *Modern Times* and *The Voice*, commissioned him to write about local theatrical affairs for their entertainment sections. In his first article, "The Provincial Theatre" (*Russian News*, 1877), he dryly and pretentiously stated that "Dramatic art in Russia is, as we know, far from reaching a high level of development." However, he did provide mentoring to his readers and spoke out about the theatre's troubles. He correctly identified bureaucracy as the issue in the capitals and ignorant impresarios as the problem in the provinces. These impresarios exploited actors in the same way as laborers, and actors cared more about their own success than the success of the theatre. The author hoped for the establishment of an actor's association, though they had not yet taken root in Russian life.

He discussed the experience of creating such a society in Tiflis, but he did not exaggerate the talent of his Tiflis acquaintances or compare them to the actors at the Maly Theatre. He found Tiflis's Sergei Palm to be unbearable when he attempted serious roles and imitated Sergei Shumsky from the Maly Theatre, who truly deserved his fame.[12]

Unsurprisingly, the fate of the two young men from Tiflis was ultimately determined by the Maly Theatre, though they had differing opinions about their future relationship with it. Sumbatov-Yuzhin hoped the Maly Theatre would always be a standard for excellence and remain an unchanging treasure, while Nemirovich-Danchenko did not believe in such preservation. The heritage of the Maly Theatre did not interest him. His only goal was to maintain a flexible, changeable, and lifelike representation of artistry and acting. However, thoughts about all of this were still distant. For now, Nemirovich-Danchenko only had daily reports of current performances, one after another, and the editorial office awaited his work.

14 *Vladimir Nemirovich-Danchenko and the Moscow Art Theatre*

Liberalism's Struggle and Compromise in Oppression

The editorial offices of *The Russian Courier* were located on Stoleshnikov Lane, with printing taking place on Petrovka Street in the same building as a credit company. The head office was at Nikolai Lanin's home near the Moskvoretsky Bridge. Both the locations and the logistics posed challenges for Nemirovich-Danchenko, the newspaper's secretary, reflecting the complexity of the business itself. In terms of official roles, E. Seleznev was the publisher, V. Seleznev signed the editorials, Lanin provided the funding, and Philip Nefedov served as the literary head. [i] Initially, the editorial office lacked distinct selling points. As a result, they began with a certain level of confusion, stating, "Issuing the first number of our new newspaper today, we must say a few words about its tasks, direction, and content." However, the only concrete point they could make at the time was that they charged less than their competitors. From its first issue, however, the newspaper showed that it intended to be liberal. It was verbose, with lengthy discussions about the weather and entertaining anecdotes for its readers. For example, one story recounted an incident at a particular factory where an English engineer asked a clerk to "Get me Xenophon [Ksenofonta]." Due to the engineer's poor Russian, the clerk heard this as "Get me a pound of hay [funt sena]." Consequently, he brought in the hay but could not find the engineer who supposedly requested it. As a result, the clerk was fired, prompting *The Russian Courier* to question why and speculate about factory conditions. The newspaper also regularly featured the obligatory topic for all Moscow journalists: the condition of the streets, particularly highlighting the potholes in front of the Chief of Police's house on Tverskaya Boulevard. As time went on, a different mindset would emerge. But for now, Nemirovich-Danchenko said, the newspaper was created by "young professors" who collaborated on its writing, and their unwavering liberalism could be relied upon (Figure 1.3).

For readers seeking "special explanations" at the editorial office, they would encounter a young man of short stature with blue eyes, dark brows, combed-back hair, and a promising "captain's beard." In his youth, the editorial secretary was deeply serious. Photographs from that time show him in poses of reading or looking up from a book. In one picture, he can be seen sitting behind a book, displaying a starched collar and cuffs. Twelve years later, Nemirovich-Danchenko would publish the story *Literary Bread* (1891), not an autobiography but rather a portrayal of a lifestyle he might have led at the time. The story begins,

> Almazov entered the editorial office of a fledgling newspaper. A desk with drawers, a cabinet, and a few beechwood chairs stood in a small room with two windows. Here, at least, the coming and going of his writing brethren will not disturb him.

He wrote realistically, describing wooden chairs and the energized, slightly elevated tone of a daily newspaper. He also talked about the cowardice of

Figure 1.3 Vladimir Nemirovich-Danchenko (~1879). By permission of the Moscow Art Academic Theatre.

the "chief" and the stupidity of censorship, as well as subscriptions, rival publications, the hurry of messengers and copy editors, and the happy days of receiving fees. He captured the hustle and bustle of a closed world. "He entered it firmly, calmly, continually watching and scrutinizing," the author wrote about the protagonist. He quickly joined in and got along. Of course, Almazov was not evidence of the author himself, but there are no diaries or similar materials available.

Nemirovich-Danchenko worked at *The Russian Courier*, with interruptions, from 1879 to 1883. In modern terms, he was a freelancer, department head, and executive secretary. The newspaper business is addictive and motivates a person, and employees become accustomed to the demanding nature of compiling daily newspapers as a 24/7 job. Naturally, he neglected his university studies and eventually abandoned them altogether. In the fall of 1880, however, Nemirovich-Danchenko still applied to the university's Rector. He took exams but did not finish his courses; he had decided on a life as a journalist.

He not only wrote about the theatre but also wrote about it constantly. There was not a notable stage event in Moscow during those years that he did not respond to, just as his full-time colleagues in other editorial offices did. Prominent theatre critic Sergei Flerov started working at the same time, and his reviews were published in Mikhail Katkov's conservative *Moscow Gazette*, putting him in an antagonistic relationship with the liberal press. Flerov wrote calm, politically independent articles that paid attention to art, and they were worth reading, regardless of readers' opinions about his

16 Vladimir Nemirovich-Danchenko and the Moscow Art Theatre

newspaper. In any case, "aesthetes" and reactionaries were bound to be in close proximity. There is a conversation in *Literary Bread* between Almazov, the protagonist, and Trostnikov, an impoverished liberal journalist from the reformist 1860s, who criticized him. Almazov asked uncertainly, "I still don't quite understand. How can you not appreciate the beauty of literature?" Trostnikov responded sharply, "Well, there you go! All the young people are like that today." People like Trostnikov captured Nemirovich-Danchenko's imagination. He considered himself lucky to have fallen in with a group of liberals. He once said to Semyon Wenger, "The first employees of *The Russian Courier* understood my point of view, and I have held onto its main ideas ever since." The junior professors who created newspapers impressed him with their clarity of position and demand for progressive ideas in every work. He himself refused to back down if he didn't find liberal ideas in a play he reviewed. He argued that Turgenev's *A Month in the Country* was unsuitable for the stage. His verdict was decisive: "If it were more serious than an ordinary love story, it would not be so tiresome despite its obsolescence. However, it lacks social interest, and even its details have little connection to public life."

He was even stricter about an Ostrovsky play that had just opened, *Guilty without Guilt*. "Imagine a melodrama of the most sensational variety, tickling the nerves of the frivolous spectator, without living characters, without distinctive features, without evidence of social observation." He found the play's wandering viewpoint and whimsical subject choices alarming, as well as the superfluous characters who enjoy nature's whimsy. Similarly, he believed *The Heart is Not a Stone* could have succeeded if the author had removed the motley and frivolous character, the clowning and eloquent thief Innokenty.

Nor did he have any tolerance for Nikolai Leskov, for example. Liberals considered it mandatory to criticize Leskov, not forgiving his politically ironic novels, *No Way Out* and *Daggers Drawn*, just as they did not forgive Dostoyevsky for parodying leftists in *Demons*. "Plays like Nikolai Leskov's should never be included in the repertoire of a serious theatre." However, he was willing to overlook shortcomings if a play had a social aim. He tolerated a particular comedy that, while not standing up to strict literary criticism, had some social and educational value.

As a reviewer for *The Russian Courier*, he did not specifically write about what he cared about as a liberal or as someone who merely conveyed what he had seen. He developed his own style, not very desirable for a newspaper concerned about its small number of subscribers, but organic for him. He did not intend his reviews for the audience, but for the stage and "behind the scenes." He would mentally reassign roles differently from the production itself. He did this for *Maria Tudor*, Victor Hugo's 1833 play at the Maly Theatre. He didn't want to give the role of the Queen to Yermolova, but to Fedotova, and he wanted Nikulina to play the role of Jeanne, which she couldn't handle. However, there was no one in the company to play Fabiano, so the reviewer examined this problem separately from his role as a reviewer. "We

The Long Beginning 1858–1886   17

need to update the troupe and replace many of them." He even intervened in matters about which he had no authority to speak about, such as comparing Yermolova's salary with Alexandra Yablochkina's and insisting they increase Yermolova's. His review was like the performance log of a production:

> A few words about the makeup. The stage of the theatre near the Push-kin monument is quite bright, but the actors don't seem to mind. Out of all the actors in *The Old Master*, only Struzhkin and Shumilin succeeded in their makeup; Chatsky's was too dark, and Vasilyev's was too light. Barlak's makeup was too obvious.

His ability to notice small details while also having a holistic view was remarkable. Therefore, when he saw the actress Polina Strepetova, he uncharacteristically felt compelled to share an account with the audience: "I can still hear her saying, 'Mommy, what have you done to me?' This phrase continues to haunt me and prevents me from simply reporting. It left a powerful impression on me!" And he was right, just as he was right when he wrote about Strepetova in *The Poor Bride*. Her mix of tears, delicacy, and the ability to express a character's entire world in a single moment fascinated him. He captured those moments that theatre exists for. He believed that the highest level of talent was reached when those moments accurately portrayed the role, summed up the entire work, and elevated the results to a magical level.

Nemirovich-Danchenko believed that all the great theatre he and Stanislavsky created revolved around moments like when Anna Karenina, played by Alla Tarasova at MAT in 1937, expressed agonizing confusion, saying, "What shall I do, Annushka, what shall I do?"

> These are the special moments that an actor's creativity brings to the stage. These moments make up the essence of theatre; this is why we exist. That's why the theatre building, the associated arts, and the entire administration exist. These moments bring joy to art. However, this joy would not be complete without the support of everyone involved in the arts, who appreciate and encourage the exhalations of true artistic genius and creativity.

It's tempting to search through the everyday records and reviews of the young reformist critic "V" for a draft of the plan that took his entire life to implement. This plan began with the desire for socially significant plays of high literary quality and ended with ethical concerns. For instance, the young reviewer repeatedly discussed Griboyedov's play, *Woe from Wit*, which MAT would produce four times. ("Whether we will ever see it in its desired form remains a secret of the executive board, which pays little attention to my ideas.") He criticized the conventional dramatic model that used self-imposed rules to create a "workable" play from a novel. He aimed to liberate the stage for Dostoevsky and Tolstoy while preserving the novelistic structure of their

18   *Vladimir Nemirovich-Danchenko and the Moscow Art Theatre*

plays. He also criticized the unnecessary crowd of extras in Othello's Cyprus scene and the "peasant" costumes worn by the even more awkward extras in the Manasseh Ball scene in Uriel Acosta. These opinions came from someone who appreciated the artistry of the crowd scenes in *Othello* and *Uriel Acosta*, directed by Stanislavsky, and who himself created an impressive image of the power-hungry Roman crowd in *Julius Caesar.*

Even the most detailed list of complaints, however, still needed more creative thought. For example, in the list of criticisms Nemirovich-Danchenko had about *Woe from Wit*—"Famusov's costume is a mix of the 1820s and the 1870s." "Tugoukhovsky as well. Skalozub wears a costume from the 1820s. Zagoretsky wears a mustache and beard from the 1820s and dresses in modern clothes." "Chatsky has mutton chops from the 1850s and dresses in contemporary fashion." He concluded his critique with a rhetorical question: "Is it really so expensive to costume the play as it should be? Five or six thousand rubles more," and the actors "could have prepared their roles more thoroughly. All it requires is a good, intelligent, energetic manager and nothing more."

He also criticized a production of *Othello*:

> What has this theatre shown us? The production is stingy. Let's say Othello arrives. There should be an entourage, a crowd, and music to greet him. What did they show on this small stage? A military chorus came out and took up half the stage: no entourage, not a single person....

Still, it was still only a minor issue: why was it so difficult to invite extras and properly costume them? The bigger questions about Cyprus (which had just escaped a maritime assault) and Othello's storm-tossed ship (which had barely reached shore and should have been met with crowds and music), not to mention how to stage it—all of this did not even occur to *The Russian Courier*'s reviewer. He only focused on the theatrical representation of an "entrance," without considering the scene's meaning and its place in the production.

Nemirovich-Danchenko's reviews often highlighted the shortcomings of the ensemble and the actors' failure, which their colleagues' work did not compensate for. The concept of ensemble was crucial for this critic and connected to the artistic whole. However, in his reviews, he acknowledged the play's aesthetic integrity but only acknowledged a portion of the effort required to create it. When did the concept of considering a stage production as a work of art come about? Critic Vissarion Belinsky, when describing Pavel Mochalov's revolutionary performance of Hamlet at the Maly Theatre in 1837 did not view a stage production as equivalent to artistic creation. No one discussed an "impressive production," "brilliant production," "controversial production," or "meaning and poetry of the production." The reviewer for *The Russian Courier* did not mention this either.

The Long Beginning 1858–1886   19

Although he was critical of the theatre of his time, he also lived within it. He wrote like everyone else at that time, quickly, for "the next edition." In the evening, the play; in the morning, the review in the newspaper. His articles do not reference what he does aside from his purely theatrical interests. After stating the review's title, the author included an informal outline:

> The production of Turgenev's *A Month in the Country* at the Maly Theatre on March 5, 1881: Turgenev's comedy in its first and second editions. The stage value and longevity of the play. 'Picturesque' plays from the Maly Theatre's repertoire. Overall execution of the plays staged at the Maly Theatre.

The resulting article includes everything mentioned here but does not reveal the writer's unique perspective. They published the review the next day.

It is difficult to determine whether Nemirovich-Danchenko's detachment was part of his job or whether he was troubled by liberal Alexander II's assassination in St. Petersburg that week and its promt conservative backlash (a response to the increasing radicalization and revolutionary activities in Russia during the late nineteenth century).[13] In his memoirs, MAT actor Vasily Luzhsky described how his Moscow household was frozen in fear upon receiving a telegram about the events in St. Petersburg.[14] They were afraid to go out, fearing a pogrom. In this family of wealthy native Russians, who would come after them, and why would they want to harm them? They were afraid even though nothing happened. Shortly before his death, Dostoevsky feared a similar massacre: "the massacre of educated people by the masses." Sumbatov-Yuzhin remembered the event: "I will never forget the icy indifference with which the middle class reacted to the murder of the tsar," he wrote, who witnessed all this personally on March 1 and the following days. "The scene in Petersburg is terrible. Everyone is on edge; there are patrols, scavengers, despair, and complete societal collapse everywhere." He recalled Vasily Averkiev's "disgraceful article" published the day after the execution of anti-Tsarist People's Will members (whose modus was terrorism).

> Frolov, the executioner, paces back and forth on the scaffold; he looks like the owner of a low-end pub. He is accompanied by a small, frail assistant who acts like a waiter in a cheap pub. The police also sent five burly prisoners in sheepskin coats with prison brands on their backs to assist the hangman. Frolov carries out his task calmly and sensibly.
>
> Drumbeats and music suddenly erupt; a patriotic Russian song is played. Of course, I was far from saying what the police officer beside me said about the executed criminals: 'What, jerking your legs now? Well, go on, jerk your legs. You'll never do it again.' Nor did his words shock me or sound insensitive to me.

20 *Vladimir Nemirovich-Danchenko and the Moscow Art Theatre*

The authorities did everything correctly. It was not pleasant, but it was the correct thing to do.

All the productive thoughts then emerging—the fact of their eruption, the disputes about the legal and moral justifications for the murder of a person who stands above the law (the tsar), along with the possibility of a lawful trial—all this productive thinking *The New Times* removed with an ageless response as a coarse rhetorical question: "What's wrong with them? Why do they want more than everybody else?"

"A reactionary time had arrived in the history of Russian public life." That's how Nemirovich-Danchenko would talk about this period when he rehearsed *Ivanov* twenty years later. He would say, "I remember...." But before it became the memory of a historical period, the actor had to live through it. To see the shameless joy of those only waiting for the command to turn back the clock. To see the sordid and rapid collapse of a liberal society that had carelessly forgotten to stipulate that free thinking was free only as long as there were no contrary instructions from above. But now the state had caught liberal society unprepared for a crackdown. You witnessed the liberals' attempts to hold out for more concessions, on the offensive, waiting, while in the end, the authorities still forbade free thinking, even though there was nothing left to forbid. It was already ground into dust.

Some people did support beliefs for which the authorities could imprison or deport them. Nemirovich-Danchenko admired those who invariably raise their voice, radiate sarcasm, appear to be begging for arrest, and yet remain untouchable. For most, however, the term going around was "marking time," which is what it was: a time that did not exist for you, that you did not live in, but only waited for it to pass. Once all these new government crackdowns and restrictions began, no one could say when they would be over. Something like this had happened before and ended. Wait a little. Someone figured out a law of pendulum oscillation to the left and right. Let's not interfere for now. Was this book being censored now? No kidding! Let's talk about it tomorrow, not literally tomorrow, but when this other, different day comes. In six months, they will "allow" it once again. A year goes by, and you wonder how you ever hoped to print it. You felt proud of unpublished books. Then you felt proud of unwritten ones. (What could you write beneath a sword?) You stiffened in defense of what you did not even do. Or what it was already too late to do, even if they allowed it. Because time, waiting patiently with clenched teeth, ignored, objectively passes while changing many things in its course.

How long would it take for this phenomenon to go away? Only three months had passed since March, and the liberal *Russian Courier* was already desperate: "We have become destitute. Even essential foodstuffs have become scarce due to their high prices. It's not particularly reassuring! It's hard to find good manners and honesty these days! Even innocent children are turning out to be bad-tempered now." Meanwhile, government surveillance increased. *The Russian Courier*, previously an uncensored publication, had already received a warning and was shut down again upon publication for some time. From

September to November 1881, the newspaper did not appear. Temporarily, Nemirovich-Danchenko worked at a branch of the Tula Land Bank. In December 1882, the authorities suspended the publication again for three months. If there were another "foul-up," they would completely shut down the publication. The owner, Nikolai Lanin, dismissed the editorial team and personally took over the editorship. However, Nemirovich-Danchenko did not remain with the newspaper after its resumption and the new owner-editor's conservative change of direction. He left, as they said, "to nowhere" and could be proud of the fact. All the same, he interpreted the same plot motive for quitting a job less heroically in *Literary Bread*. So, we'll turn to this early story of his once again.

The protagonist Almazov worked in a decent but unprofitable newspaper, whose owner secretly envied the circulation and popularity of a mediocre rival newspaper. At some point, the owner changed the tone of his publication, so Almazov quit the paper and tried to make a living as a novelist. Then came monetary difficulties, promissory notes, the failure of a new story he counted on borrowing against, and family frustrations. There were no positions at the publications where he wanted to work. The only promising prospect was the *Daily Gazette*, which had always been a sign of literary and public failure for him. Conversely, they would publish his story. Then followed Almazov's revolt, his loud mutiny against the prospect of becoming a writer for hire. The story concluded with three sentences of pure information: Almazov agreed with everything, did not have to part with his wife, and published his story where it was accepted. The traditional story of the idealist's surrender to banality, the selfless man to commercialism, was displaced from within, which loosened and revitalized its meaning. The biography's unsentimental accuracy and cold, sad objectivity dissolved any potential conflict. For it didn't revolve around choosing between good and evil, honor and dishonor, or social conscience and the commercial press, but rather that the flow of life eliminated the choice. The world lost its polarity and became demagnetized. You were willing to starve rather than collaborate with a terrible newspaper, but if you placed these two newspapers side by side in front of a stranger, you wouldn't notice the difference between the one you despised and the one that represented your entire life. One was irritating, the other was gloomy, but both were lifeless and as dry as dust.

Passion and Responsibility

Meanwhile, consistent earnings were of utmost importance to him as he was no longer living alone. On March 14, 1883, just before *The Russian Courier*, with its newly conservative stance, was published, Nemirovich-Danchenko wrote a letter to Pavel Pchelnikov, the Moscow office manager of the imperial theatres.

> Dear Pavel: I would like to remind you once again of my request regarding my wife's [sic] (Kuzmina) stage debut.[15] I am reminding you because

22 Vladimir Nemirovich-Danchenko and the Moscow Art Theatre

> I understand that you have other responsibilities at the moment and might easily forget about such a request.

He was anxious: "Please excuse me for not waiting until the date you had set, but I assure you that my motivation is not driven by financial or family considerations, but solely by a sense of indignant injustice."

The public became aware of Kuzmina through reviews signed by "V," which introduced her to Moscow after her performances in private theatres in 1880.

> Mrs. Kuzmina, who was known in the provinces, does not possess the most exceptional qualities for the stage. She is of small stature, not conventionally beautiful, her eyes lack expressiveness, and her voice is slightly harsh. However, it is well-known that the public often relies too heavily on initial impressions. It is no wonder that they were initially unfriendly toward Mrs. Kuzmina. After the first act of *Wandering Fires*, there were some barely restrained hisses. The audience's reaction was a grave mistake. She passionately delivered the monologues in the second act, captivating both herself and the public.
>
> Mrs. Kuzmina is an actress who performs with great emotional intensity and is likely to achieve remarkable success in various roles. It's unfortunate that her debut roles failed to reveal her stage talent or education, and that she should perform in dramatic roles that require a more serious treatment.

Her "provincial fame" led to her lack of focus on stage and her tendency to gaze painfully toward the audience. On the other hand, she was able to completely immerse herself in the circumstances of her role with "deep feelings" and display extremely natural crying ("her tears extended beyond the boundaries of artistic performance," one reviewer noted). Nemirovich-Danchenko had been thinking about Mrs. Kuzmina for a long time, observing and almost studying her. She had the ability to portray a "modern young woman" without any artifice, and she could also convey the bitterness accumulated from unpleasant unavoidable contacts with unpleasant people. For her benefit performance, she chose to play *Parasha, the Siberian Girl*, a character that had guaranteed tears in the auditorium for half a century.

When Nemirovich-Danchenko was almost eighty, he would attend a rehearsal of *Woe from Wit* at MAT and discuss the character of Sofia in the play: the daughter of the elderly patriarch Famusov, a member of his social circle, and the future wife of General Skalozub. Perhaps her husband's adjutants would become her lovers? Nevertheless, she developed charmingly. A "tea rose." One actor objected, "She is more substantial than that; she stands out from the others. Otherwise, why would Chatsky love her so much?" This response surprised Nemirovich-Danchenko. "Has a woman you loved never disappointed you? You are a lucky man. They have disappointed me throughout my entire life."

The Long Beginning 1858–1886   23

He had a deep affection for Mrs. Kuzmina and recognized her undeniable talent, although his sentiment resembled that of a teacher more than an admirer. Her acting instilled in him fundamental ideas about the contagious nature of acting, its direct connection with the nervous system, spontaneity, and simplicity. Nonetheless, he believed that simplicity without characterization and complexity was too easily attainable.

Kuzmina was in her thirties, while he was not yet twenty-three. She was not free, and a church marriage was impossible. Therefore, he felt an even greater responsibility for their union, a responsibility that was not imposed upon him but willingly taken on. They would not rely on her for financial support.

What could he expect after leaving Lanin's newly conservative *Russian Courier*? He had made a name for **himself** in the literary and theatrical world, not a celebrity, but still....

Self-Improvement Through Continuous Effort

He was still working at the editorial office of *The Russian Courier* when his first play, *Wild Rose* (1881) by Vladimir Ivanov (pseudonym), opened on October 5, 1882. *Wenger's Biographical Dictionary* quoted him as saying, "I wrote a trivial farce that was produced at the Maly Theatre. It ran for ten performances with some success." *The Russian Courier* responded negatively to *Wild Rose*, with the author himself writing the review anonymously. He was as critical of his own debut as he was of others.

In the protagonist's debut piece in the fictional work *Literary Bread*, Almazov is confronted by antagonist Trostnikov's tough questioning about his writing. He asks Almazov what he is writing for, what message he wants to convey to society, and what he hopes to achieve. Almazov responds by saying, "I wrote the story; what can I say? I just wanted to start somewhere, and I didn't want to stay at a small newspaper forever." The motivation behind writing *Wild Rose* was the same—he needed to start somewhere.

In *Wild Rose*, a young widow, who is also the aunt of an adult nephew, discovers that he has chosen an extremely unsuitable bride. She takes it upon herself to change his mind and prove that his affection is not serious. The plot follows the rules of a vaudeville trifle, but the author attempts to add more detailed "coloring of social life" (as described in Nemirovich-Danchenko's review). This is evident when the young woman, whom they don't even know, is present, and the aunt and her friend say terrible things about her, as if they knew her well:

- "She is a dangerous person, a nihilist!"
- "What makes you think she is a nihilist?"
- "Come on! She works at the library, reads Ferdinand Lassalle, and hides in the middle of nowhere."
- "Have you read Lassalle yourself?"[16]
- "What! Like I would ever read him!"

24 Vladimir Nemirovich-Danchenko and the Moscow Art Theatre

Everyone is embarrassed when the young woman reveals her true identity and declares, "Are you surprised that I'm not wearing blue glasses and don't have short hair [like a socialist radical]?" Unsurprisingly, reviewers in the 1880s could only summarize the plot of *Wild Rose*. But what else was there beyond the plot and "recent trends" in plays of that kind? There was a good reason for staging a new play in just one week, or even after only one rehearsal, which was the norm at the time. In one of his reviews, Nemirovich-Danchenko noted that the actors already understood the characters in most new plays before they even began. They didn't need to create the characters but rather just act out the text. Anything beyond that was unnecessary. This insight is evident in Nemirovich-Danchenko's review of *Maria Tudor* at the Maly Theatre on October 19, 1879:

> Mr. Muzil played his role cleverly and sensibly, attempting to make this Jewish figure a typical caricature of the time, but this was completely unnecessary. The role serves only as an introduction to clarify what will happen. He has no character, so he should have just delivered the lines and nothing more.

The temptation to add imagination was pointless, lacked dramatic value, and was firmly rejected.

Initially, it was difficult to determine who had influenced "Vladimir Ivanov," later known as Vladimir Nemirovich-Danchenko, and eventually by his full name. It was natural to look for the influence of Ostrovsky, the great playwright who wielded control, charmed, and used his status in Russian theatre as a workshop in the Italian tradition, where the master applies the life-giving brush to the students' assignments or even their "finished" works. For instance, the young playwright Nikolai Soloviev faded into insignificance under the influence of "Ostrovsky's theatre." Sumbatov-Yuzhin remembered how his own play, *Sergei Satilov*, had caught Ostrovsky's attention. Ostrovsky praised it, annotated the margins, and offered to complete it himself. "I didn't want that," said Sumbatov-Yuzhin, and neither did Nemirovich-Danchenko.

Nemirovich-Danchenko was initially influenced not so much by an individual's personality but more by the theatre of the time and the impact of the average repertoire play. Breaking free from this influence was more challenging than escaping the magic of someone else's individuality. In some ways, Nemirovich-Danchenko was not entirely free, while in other ways, he had a degree of freedom—capturing the essence of the times, the sound of the moment, and being attuned to the societal typologies of that era. In both *Wild Rose* and *Our Americans* (1882), which followed his moderately successful debut at the Maly Theatre, it was clear from the beginning which actor the author had in mind for certain roles. Who could be better suited to play the lazy gossip Nedomekov in *Wild Rose* than Maly Theatre comic actor Ivan Samarin and who could bring more sincerity and humor to the coquette's role, shedding tears on behalf of the suffering she caused her

The Long Beginning 1858–1886   25

nephew's bride, than Fedotova (affectionately known by her colleagues as a bucket of inexhaustible tears)?

But another entertaining aspect emerged in *Our Americans*. The author wrote "for the actor," but he also wrote something more. Initially, his protagonists were comical, but a drama soon unfolded about people who were too small or too large for their designated social roles. However, these characters willingly embraced their public images and found themselves unable to escape them. In Nemirovich-Danchenko's plays, the survival of absolute swindlers relied on "false appearances," as indicated by the character list for *Our Americans*, particularly the aging and handsome Zolotov-Dvorzhevich. He posed as an engineer from the newest school, challenging a factory owner while advocating for women's emancipation in front of the owner's daughter. His diploma was counterfeit, and his beliefs were even more so, with the entire plot centering around his public exposure. In another play, the handsome but destitute Tumanov pretended to be a prince. However, the heart of the play was not the traditional comedic deception of the hero pretending to be someone else. Instead, it delved into the genuine, painful, and sometimes ridiculous struggles of these characters as they tried to fit into their chosen positions.

In *Our Americans*, humor arose from a millionaire manufacturer's desire to portray himself as an enlightened American and encourage his daughter's freedom ("You can even marry an American Indian tomorrow if you want to."). He despised his role as a manufacturer and attempted to act like a benevolent and intelligent ruler. When the censor banned his 1885 play *Without Love*, which Nemirovich-Danchenko later reworked into *Dashing Force*, the rich protagonist, Khamovnikov, was no longer pretending to be his chosen social role. Instead, he became entirely submissive to it, unable to experience anything beyond its demands. The character was consumed by his role, and his story was told in an amusing manner, accompanied by references to Schopenhauer and discussions on our inclination to quote others: "The landlords seem to be more afraid of Diderot than of the governor." In *Dashing Force*, this anecdote developed into a full-fledged drama. The protagonist eagerly embraced the role of a "new man" in the 1880s, openly acknowledging the power of money, his desire for wealth, and, most importantly, the opportunity to become a capitalist (including engaging in philanthropy). He was willing to enter into a strategic marriage, and the revised version of the play offered him that chance. The updated version added a mother with a heart condition, the heroine's suicide attempt, a mysterious lover, and the possibility of turning a transactional marriage into a happy one. None of these elements were present in the original version, which depicted a confused, unhappy, and foolish life. Once a decision was made or a path chosen, it would take control and throw you into a whirlwind. Everything would culminate in chaos, with things being rearranged and turned upside down, and a fear of forgetting something, which inevitably happened. The carriages would depart loudly, with those left behind yelling after them. But it wasn't over yet: the protagonist Zhdanovich promptly shot himself, without uttering a monologue or any words at all.

Dashing Force premiered at Korsh's Theater on November 20, 1886, as part of a benefit performance. The melodrama that the public became familiar with emerged in this version. Nemirovich-Danchenko was fully aware that what he created had limited lasting value. He didn't anticipate a future in which banned manuscripts would resurface and regain relevance or importance. It is said that Ivan Goncharov kept manuscripts on his desk for ten years.[17] In today's fast-paced world, a work loses its significance entirely in just ten years. And one more thing. The writer-baron Ivan Turgenev claimed that a "let it sleep" attitude was possible because he had enough leisure time. Chekhov had to support himself with his earnings, however, so he couldn't afford such a romantic attitude. "I was cold and hungry. And for every ruble, ten mouths were open!"

This is where our young author's work ethic originated. He did everything in his power to have his plays staged in the present moment, as he believed that what he wrote today would lose its life on the stage by tomorrow. *Our Americans* had some modest success at the Maly Theatre. After that, he corresponded with Alexei Potekhin,[18] who oversaw the repertoire at the Alexandrinsky Theatre in St. Petersburg. Initially, the response was unfavorable, but eventually they agreed to produce his play when it became apparent that this Muscovite knew the ins and outs of the stage and demonstrated it. The structure of Nemirovich-Danchenko's early plays adhered to tradition, whether it was a vaudeville like *Wild Rose* or a melodrama like *Dark Forest* (1884), which revolved around the love of a future stepmother for a future stepson, whose mother she had driven to her grave. However, the characters' attitudes were psychologically fresh. The protagonist always transitioned between social positions, moved around, and struggled to adapt to new circumstances. These characters were untimely and out of place. The protagonist of *Dark Forest*, Mamadyshev, was an aging and jealous man, out of his time. He would have been better suited as a noble gentleman letting his estate go to ruin to satisfy his wife's whims, rather than working as an ill-timed bank director of *Falcons and Ravens* (1885) (co-authored with Sumbatov-Yuzhin). Tormented by his actual job, Mamadyshev committed embezzlement and blamed the bank's cashier.

Ancestry and character did not align, and neither did character and position. The typical settings in Nemirovich-Danchenko's plays were "walk-through locales" that were open and equalizing, such as public gardens, rooming houses, or private homes with diverse societies where everyone was welcome. Misalliances occurred at every step, not only in marriage but also in character and situation. In his plays, Nemirovich-Danchenko explored characters who were willingly or unwillingly displaced, hastily assimilated, or powerless to assimilate, moving from "rags to riches" or back again. Characters were not secure in their environment, as the environment itself was unstable and

The Long Beginning 1858–1886 27

diverse. For example, in Natasha's role in *Without Love* (1885), the author's note states,

> They had clogged her head with knowledge devoid of a system. Her milieu is always wildly diverse: merchants, elected officials, professors, hangers-on, gossips, pilgrims, schoolchildren, etc. Everything holds her back: she wants to talk, thinks it is better to be quiet; she wants to have fun, but some worry grabs hold of her.

The more intense the characters, the less forthright they were. Their weak inner impulse made them entirely at the mercy of subjective beliefs or barely glimpsed desires. For instance, Zhdanovich lived strictly according to a principle, while his wife mistook a flicker of passion for love that would change her entire life.

"Displacement" caused characters to question their routine ideas. In *Without a Position* (1886), the protagonist Varvara shocked her conversation partners by stating,

> What is a lie? What is the truth? These are only words invented by people. Mind, power, and energy: this is truth. And ideals, honor: these are only words. You understand these things differently from me. Nowadays, there is a specific set of ideals, but it will be different in a hundred years. Instinct is the eternal truth. Society demands you be honest according to its laws. Look like you are honest, and that will be enough.

In *Lucky Man* (1887), the protagonist Bogucharov lived by a similar principle. He lacked a conscience, taking whatever pleased him and benefiting himself with audacious artistry. One of his discarded mistresses attempted to shoot him when he confessed his selfishness, but the bullet missed, and he pulled it out of the wall, once again proving his luck.

All these peculiar, free-spirited people, who are both conditioned and driven by forces beyond their control, were products of their time. In *Without a Position*, Varvara described her generation as being swept along by the current of life, while still believing they have control over their own actions. Nemirovich-Danchenko's plays reveal a different style of drama, one that incorporates the active participation of "the flow of life" in the conflicts. However, this idea was not something the author consciously expressed but rather an unconscious implication. For instance, in *Without a Position*, there is a conversation about the theatre. Varvara loves the stage, but she believes it does not reflect real life. She observes people laughing as if everything is fine while tragedy lurks nearby. Each family has its own hidden drama, which unfolds amidst a general sense of cheerfulness. Just like Chekhov later explained, "People eat lunch, their happiness grows, and yet their lives fall apart." Similarly, Nemirovich-Danchenko's dramas explore the "flow of life," although his plots do not confine themselves to dining or

28   *Vladimir Nemirovich-Danchenko and the Moscow Art Theatre*

living room settings. Instead, they revolve around familiar theatrical events such as suicides, murders out of jealousy, fatal illnesses like consumption, the hysterics of abandoned women, public outcries, revelations of deception, acts of selflessness, and moments of repentance.

There are instances where the playwright attempts to deviate from this type of theatre. One such example is found at the beginning of the fourth act of *Without a Position*: a woman anxiously awaits her lover-guest for dinner at her home, fearing he has left her. She is not alone; her aunt and a young relative are also present at the table. She is restless, and the others are concerned for her, though they do not address the main issue. They read the newspaper aloud and discuss the day's events. In the background, the sound of the cook sleeping behind a partition can be heard. Eventually, the others disperse, leaving behind a heavy silence. The passage of time is marked by the sound of a passing carriage and the call of a cuckoo, signaling the late hour. "The cricket and I are the only ones awake. Another hour has passed."

Without a Position is the most inconsistent among the early plays, both awkward and thrilling. Reflecting on his work from 1882 to 1887, Nemirovich-Danchenko admitted, "I wrote it without much consideration for the meaning of theatre or the social responsibilities of art." However, remnants of his focus on issues of indecision can still be found in the essence of those years. Despite perplexing managers and never reaching the stage, the author did not hastily make any changes. If he hesitated to trust the character types he created, he also hesitated to leave those same characters without commentary or correction. He diminished his sympathy for the "displaced person" to instead critique him. Rather than making statements that support social change, he compared today's conservatism to an old house in disrepair, with cracked boards, crumbling wallpaper, and insects crawling out of the cracks, but with the promise of renovation and the eventual demise of the insects. His characters made poignant statements, such as "There will be others better than you and me. There will be nothing to confuse them. They will deeply believe in the ultimate triumph of the ideal. That's why I envy you." In the story *Lucky Man*, Bogucharov's rival, who is modest but persistent in his pursuit of the ideal, receives public appreciation, while the egotistical admirer of all things beautiful, strong, and original gets punched in the eye. Was this a concession to "commonplace" morality? Yes and no. Nemirovich-Danchenko devoted much thought to Bogucharov's enlightened way of life.

However, when he brought this idea to the stage, someone with liberal-minded views, like Trostnikov from *Literary Bread*, was constantly hovering over him. This liberal-minded individual irked Nemirovich-Danchenko with his dogmatic thinking and disregard for pure literary artistry. He declared,

> Conservative-minded authors take some vulgar person, some scum they should hang from the nearest tree, and take a fancy to him, and write a

The Long Beginning 1858–1886 29

psychological novel about him. Why does a reader need to know how one fool fell in love with another fool, and what came of it?

Liberals criticized Tolstoy similarly when they mockingly wrote about his "epic about the love of the wife of a high-ranking official, the beautiful Anna Karenina, for the equally beautiful aide-de-camp Vronsky." However, what was considered unfair when it came to Tolstoy was deemed fair for Nemirovich-Danchenko. He could choose to ignore the demands of the nearby voice, but the voice persisted. Was he weary of the voice's proclamations that the artist should serve the greater good and address sensitive social issues? Okay, but how?

Almazov, the character in *Literary Bread*,

felt utterly confused. He understood that this constantly irritated person blamed him for the sweetness of literary bread, that he expected him to take on additional responsibilities, and Almazov wanted to comply. But how could he fulfill the desires of his unsatisfied soul? By being honest? Did he ever write anything that went against decency, conscience, or the oppressed, the poor, or the wretched? What other kind of honesty did this liberal high priest require from him? He wrote a story. Where was the shame in that? They would pay him four hundred rubles, and there was no shame.

Traces of this confusion and a willingness to adhere to the creature's demands often surfaced in our playwright's works. For instance, he depicted the workers' strike at the factory, where they were given "swamp water with boiled frogs instead of soup" by the owners. Another line highlighted the pointlessness of conventional charity, stating that the region had "a hospital, a school, and Sunday readings, but all this was without a program, merely for show and praise." And in addition to Sunday readings, there were thirty taverns. Did the voice desire this? Was he vengeful, or were you skillfully shaping the essence of his desires as if dutifully fulfilling them? It was possible to ignore him. His influence was fading. Conservatives were already chastising him for his deafness to innovation and his lack of interest in art for art's sake. And yet….

"He demands some form of commitment." It was crucial to comprehend these obligations, but it was also crucial to know oneself. Despite having the external advantages and skills of a talented journalist, he should not have had to adapt foreign plays for the local stage. (The Russian Drama Theatre staged his adaptation of the French farce, *Bankrupt in France* (1885), for a charity performance on January 21, 1885, in the same building later reconstructed for MAT.) While these successes and skills were gratifying, they also left wounds.

This path could continue indefinitely, but he needed to do something significant to move forward. Perhaps in playwriting (admittedly, there was little prestige in mastering this profession in the woeful form shaped by the dreadful experience of *Falcons and Ravens*). Maybe in prose (he initially started as

30 *Vladimir Nemirovich-Danchenko and the Moscow Art Theatre*

a prose writer as well). Or perhaps there was a latent potential in a gift that had not yet discovered its name. Since his youth, Nemirovich-Danchenko had led a life that hardly allowed for introspection. First, it was the life of a journalist, governed by the rhythm of daily publications. Then came the carousel of theatrical affairs. No fixed personal perspectives. Even his departure from *The Russian Courier* was indefinite. He left, and then in the summer of 1883, he informed Potekhin that he had returned to the newspaper: "I am back after a change in the editorship. They will forward your letters to me." In his notebook, when he later attempted to recount the events of his career, he made a note: "Returned to Goltsev's editorial staff; edited at *The Russian Courier* since September 4. Finally left after Lanin's new role as editor."

There were no sudden breakthroughs in Nemirovich-Danchenko's life story. However, someone comparing what he accomplished in 1880 with his achievements ten years later would be astonished: here was a different person with a different temperament. It was natural in such situations to look for some general changes or a nearby personality. In many biographies of Nemirovich-Danchenko's generation and environment, meeting a person from a different social group or encountering fresh ideas and culture were crucial influences, though not necessarily involving a famous person. For Chekhov, contact with author Dmitry Grigorovich was significant.[19] Likewise, for art critic Igor Grabar,[20] the home of magnate Dmitriev provided an environment where he felt comfortable as a guest, and no one made jokes about the lowbrow witticisms guiding his work in the commercial press.

During his early years in Moscow, Nemirovich-Danchenko had many meetings with remarkable people. While there is no need to list every theatrical name, he briefly encountered them all. He also knew Ostrovsky, saw Turgenev, and heard Dostoevsky at Pushkin celebrations. Additionally, it is worth mentioning Pushkin's close friend and biographer, Anna Kern, who was living her final years in Moscow. He fondly remembered her as a "dear little older woman." However, these meetings needed to have greater significance in order to bring about change or resolution. There were no significant days in Nemirovich-Danchenko's youth, no milestones, only slow, continuous, directed forward movement. He paved his own path and belonged to a group of individuals who ardently and rigorously pursued self-improvement. He did not leave behind a list of mental complaints about himself, as Sumbatov-Yuzhin did. Nor did he compile a catalog of things a civilized person should not do, like Chekhov did in one of his letters. However, he was adept at self-examination without illusions and identified the entrenched flaws of his environment within himself. He understood the effort required to detach oneself from this stubbornness and work through issues independently. "Continuous day and night work, perpetual reading, study, willpower ... Every hour is precious...." These were Chekhov's words.[21] Though Nemirovich-Danchenko may not have read them, he came to the same conclusions himself. "I began working on myself very late, at age 25, and I hope that my strength will guide me in continuing this most important work of a person until the end of my days."

Notes

1 *From the Past* (*Iz Proshlovo*, 1935) was published in English by Little, Brown and Company as *My Life in the Russian Theatre* in 1936.
2 The Caucasus is an area between the Black Sea and the Caspian Sea and is mainly occupied by Armenia, Azerbaijan, Georgia, and Russia. It is home to the Caucasus Mountains. Ozergeti is the capital of the western Georgian province of Guria. Poti is a port city in Georgia on the eastern coast of the Black Sea.
3 Adolph Marx (1838–1904) book publisher, teacher, folk song collector, and publisher of Field magazine.
4 Anatoly Lunacharsky (1875–1933) was a Russian Marxist revolutionary and the first Bolshevik Soviet People's Commissar responsible for the Ministry of Education. He was also a playwright, critic, essayist, and journalist throughout his career.
5 The Maly Theatre (Small Theatre) is the oldest operational theatre in Russia and, until the birth of the Moscow Art Theatre, widely considered Russia's preeminent theatre.
6 Vasily Nemirovich-Danchenko (1845–1936) was an author, essayist, journalist, and memoirist.
7 Land and Will was a clandestine revolutionary society formed in Russia in the early 1860s.
8 Anatoly Efros, *The Joy of Rehearsal* (New York: Peter Lang, 2006), 19.
9 Lyubov Freidkina (1858–1943) was a journalist and historian specializing in Russian theatre.
10 Pavel Mochalov (1800–1848) was a famous actor of classic Russian Romanticism.
11 Fedotova, Glikeria (1846–1925) was a famous leading actress associated with the Maly Theatre.
12 Sergei Palm (1849–1915) was a theatre and operetta actor, director, and organizer of troupes in Odessa, Tiflis, and St. Petersburg.
13 On March 13, 1881, Tsar Alexander II was killed by a revolutionist's bomb, an act blamed falsely on the Jews. Pogroms started across Russia in the days and months following.
14 Vasily Luzhsky (1869–1931) was an actor and director associated closely with MAT.
15 Mrs. Kuzmina was not his legal wife, and it is mentioned later that she was already married.
16 Ferdinand Lassalle (1825–1864) was a leading spokesman for German socialism, a disciple of Karl Marx, and one of the founders of the German labor movement.
17 Ivan Goncharov (1812–1891), novelist whose realistic works are considered classics of Russian fiction.
18 Alexei Potekhin (1829–1908) was a playwright and novelist, a member of the Society of Russian Literature Lovers and the Academy of Sciences Fine Arts Division.
19 Dmitry Grigorovich (1822–1900) was among the first Russian writers to portray rural life realistically and openly condemn the serfdom system.
20 Igor Grabar (1871–1960) was a post-impressionist painter, publisher, restorer, and historian of art.
21 Chekhov, Anton Pavlovich. *Letters of Anton Chekhov to His Family and Friends* (Cleveland, OH: Good Press, 2021), 51–54.

2   Everything Is Nearby 1886–1896

Marriage and Creative Fulfillment

In August 1886, Nemirovich-Danchenko married the daughter of Baron Nikolai Korf, a well-known public figure and educator.[1] Fate brought him and his close friend Alexander Sumbatov together when not one, but three weddings took place that turned friends into cousins. Three women, Lydia, Ekaterina, and Maria, all with the maiden name Baroness Korf, got married. The first married actor Alexander Lensky,[2] the second married Nemirovich-Danchenko, and the third married Sumbatov. All three remained true to their choices until the end. The Korf family was natural and relaxed at home, showing polite and friendly tolerance toward people from different social circles. After the wedding, the newlyweds went to St. Petersburg, where Nemirovich-Danchenko's mother, Alexandra, and sister Varvara lived. His brother Vasily had just returned there from his travels as an author. A new sense of family emerged, which was unusual for Nemirovich-Danchenko. "I spend entire days with Ekaterina. We live in peace and friendship, cheerfully. As good as anyone could wish for." For someone like Nemirovich-Danchenko, who was primarily focused on himself ("I've sailed alone all my life…"), Ekaterina was an educated, sensitive, and coquettish beauty according to the standards of the 1880s. She was raised beyond the norms of her time. Her cheerfulness, respect for her husband's concerns, confidence in his freedom, and effortless self-control satisfied them both for a lifetime. Their marriage lasted for over half a century, endured many hardships, and in the end, both could echo what he said on their honeymoon: "As good as anyone could wish for."

He was only twenty-eight, yet it felt like he had to hurry because time passed so quickly in those days. Soon he would be in his thirties, then past his thirties. "Goodbye, dear nickname: young and promising. Much worse would be 'old and failed to live up to expectations.'" Sometimes he was angry with himself, as he wrote to his constant conversational partner Sumbatov-Yuzhin: "You are smarter than I, and you know you cannot come up with a play better than the one you write. And I dream of writing one better than the one I will write anyhow."

DOI: 10.4324/9781003486282-2

Vivid Realism in Storytelling

Baron Korf built a modest manor house, which he named Neskuchnoye [cheerful], in the heart of the steppe during the mid-nineteenth century. In 1887, Nemirovich-Danchenko arrived at the estate, a year after marrying Korf's eldest daughter. For nearly thirty summers thereafter, he and his family regularly visited the property. It was understandable to seek refuge from the hustle and bustle of the city. The house was surrounded by untouched wilderness, however, and by the end of each summer, even the owners grew so tired that they would celebrate the sight of the first telegraph pole on the way back to Moscow.

Nemirovich-Danchenko was always highly impressionable. In this region, he encountered what he referred to as the "peasant kingdom"—a strong and conscious community with a distinct identity. Immersed in the sensations of the steppe, he understood why the inhabitants revered the land as an essential element of life. He experienced the same vibrancy as the surrounding wilderness, which teemed with life as much as it contained remnants of the past. The land evoked a magnificent feeling that demanded expression, necessitating communication. And that's where the struggle began.

> While writing stories or novels, I could create something. But when I thought about theatre, even the esteemed Maly Theatre, it seemed as if all originality had vanished. How could I convey to the spectators in Moscow and St. Petersburg the excitement I felt from the dark depths of the grounds at dusk or the shimmering heat over an ancient burial mound? What techniques could actors like Alexander Lensky, Sumbatov-Yuzhin, Sadovsky, Yermolova, and Fedotova use to capture the melancholy or peculiarity of the silent Russian countryside?

The question remained: was prose writing his true calling? Even in his early novels, he focused on depicting the setting, though not as everyone else perceived it. In his story *The Textile Worker* (1881), a village had grown into a town due to the presence of a factory. However, it remained rooted in its village characteristics and occupations, lacking the attributes of an industrial city. Nemirovich-Danchenko portrays the factory yard on a sunny, empty Sunday. The paved square is desolate, with employees closing their windows to escape the heat. The sober and somnolent workers reside in factory-provided barracks. In the middle of the day, an older man and woman, both intoxicated, enter the barracks in single file, much to the disdain of their teetotaling son. Unsteady footsteps resonate on the cast-iron staircase and the cast-iron tiles in the barracks corridor (wooden tiles are deemed unsafe due to frequent fires, and nightly fights pose a risk of knocking over kerosene lamps).

In his earliest works, Nemirovich-Danchenko effectively captured the rhythm of the action. For instance, he depicted the bustling scene of changing

34 *Vladimir Nemirovich-Danchenko and the Moscow Art Theatre*

stations while waiting for a train's late arrival, causing congestion of wagons and carriages in the parking spaces. Despite this chaos, everyone at the station maintained a sense of philosophical peace. Trains were always running late, and the employees at the station buffet, with their green unwashed tea cups and stainless-steel appliances, were lazy and stuck-up. Meanwhile, the passengers languished beside their luggage. However, as soon as the train whistle blew, the tempo changed. Noise filled the air as people pushed and shouted, fearing they would be left behind.

Nemirovich-Danchenko also explored clichéd and stereotypical events in his writing. One example is seen in *Porcelain Dolls* [n.d.], where he incorporated the clichéd excursion to a resort, complete with geological outcroppings adorned with travelers' carved names. The story inevitably led to the Temple of the Aeolian Harp, Lermontov's Cave, and Failure Lake, where travelers would humorously exclaim clichéd expressions such as "What if you fall in?" or "If I ever want to drown myself, I will come here."

As Nemirovich-Danchenko's writing developed, he became more accurate in depicting the characters' psycho-physical state and their interdependence on emotions and physicality. In *The Mist* (1894), for instance, he opened the story with a surprising scene where the eldest son, wearing boots and visibly exhausted from the heat, strode angrily past visiting women in corsets and men in fresh summer suits. He made his way through the shaded veranda into the house and emerged with a rifle, later using it to shoot himself. Additionally, Nemirovich-Danchenko's prose was notable for its meticulous attention to the timing, atmosphere, and events that preceded and surrounded the story. For instance, in *A Good Case* (n.d.), he vividly described the lingering smell of food in the rooms in the middle of the night. It was 3:00 a.m., and the maid had to clean up after guests while trying to sleep on the go. The tension was high due to a conversation that had taken an inappropriate turn, resulting in hurtful words being exchanged. Everyone had to maintain silence to avoid disturbing others. In *The Blusher* (n.d.), Nemirovich-Danchenko depicted the lethargy one experiences after a nap, the arrival of early winter twilight when darkness fell at 6:00 p.m., and the soft glow spreading across the ceiling as streetlamps were lit.

Although Nemirovich-Danchenko's plots were predictable, his strength lay in his remarkable creativity in developing the characters. An example of this can be found in *The Goldfish* (1886), where a retired military officer with side whiskers defied expectations by being a pleasant and free-thinking individual, rather than a reactionary as one might assume. His pages are filled with numerous incidents and characters that are not essential to the plot, yet they are always depicted with precision and keen observation. In *The Gold fish*, Nemirovich-Danchenko describes the older man's love for his newspaper. It brings him joy to receive it every day and carefully unfold it, ensuring he doesn't miss a single issue he subscribed to. He becomes nervous when the newspaper is not delivered and upset when he learns that its publication has been suspended. The retiree with whiskers is a loyal reader of the liberal

Everything Is Nearby 1886–1896 35

newspaper, *The Voice.* The absence of his newspaper not only upsets him but also disrupts his habitual routine.

Nemirovich-Danchenko excels in vividly portraying action, such as the scene of a man who rises early at four in the morning and has been in the scorching heat all day. His lower lip trembles, and he holds his rifle with the muzzle pointing down toward the ground. He shoots a peasant's horse that has repeatedly strayed into the field for the umpteenth time. In *A Good Case*, the suicide scene takes place in a cozy, cramped apartment filled with shelves and display cabinets. As the shooter collapses, he has time to observe how everything slowly falls onto him.

Even in his earliest works, it is remarkable how meticulously Nemirovich-Danchenko describes the "scenery." In the juvenile drama *At the Postal Station* [n.d.], the windows are adorned with red calico, adding to the everyday nature of the setting. In contrast, a red glow illuminates a potential crime scene. A traveler lies in a small room with a wooden ceiling, on which a large cross is drawn from the soot of a candle. Through these descriptions, Nemirovich-Danchenko conveys the real as both ordinary and metaphorical. Sound also plays a significant role in his stories. The murmur of a brook accompanies an impending murder, lulls a child to sleep, captures the sluggishness of life, and echoes the call of a cricket. In *A Good Case*, the protagonist suffers from a painful headache, intensifying his sensitivity to sounds, ultimately leading to the fateful climax.

> The dining room clock chimed four o'clock. Victor Sergeyevich went to the weapons cabinet, retrieved a revolver, examined the barrel attentively, and locked the door between the office and the corridor. He then approached the desk, placed the barrel in his mouth, and pulled the trigger.

The precise depiction of this process holds its own undeniable power. Nemirovich-Danchenko writes to ignite the reader's imagination, as though his words are waiting to be embodied and completed through non-verbal means. As though this has yet to be acted out, but in the meantime, here are explanations of the setting and internal conditions. Here is the setting for a scene from the short story *At the Graveyard Cross* (n.d.): drought, a thunderstorm, and only a dusty wind, appears but does not break. In the house, they are dining, having shut themselves off from the heat. The protagonist's thoughts become entangled; his nerves become strained and disturbed by the monotonous sound of "a bee that flew between the shutters and the window glass and struggled there for a long time." Here are the internal conditions:

> Inside, I felt as if I were smashing all the dishes, shouting at Kirill Vasilyevich in an inhuman voice, shooting at him with pistols. And I only clenched my jaw, tightened my cheekbones, and looked at a jar of mustard, which I had forgotten to cork.

36 Vladimir Nemirovich-Danchenko and the Moscow Art Theatre

It is easy to say this was an intuitive imagining of the theatre. Maybe such imagining exists. But there was no such theatre.

Struggle with Tradition and Modernity

Nemirovich-Danchenko thoroughly studied the theatre that was available to him. His involvement with Moscow's Maly Theatre and later St. Petersburg's Alexandrinsky Theatre happened quickly and naturally. In a letter to Sumbatov-Yuzhin in 1881, it was evident that he had established his authority in the theatre: "Let me handle the casting. I have a good relationship with Grekov, the Stage Manager at the Maly Theatre, and he will ensure the play is well-performed." The writer eagerly uses theatre jargon to emphasize his influence and connections. Although this enjoyment will soon fade, Nemirovich-Danchenko would retain his managerial skills. He would no longer be the finicky amateur who boasted about his clumsiness in dealing with bureaucratic matters. First, he recognized that ordinary people worked there, some intelligent, some not, some kind-hearted, and some not. Second, the state was a reality and a necessity; there was no way around it, only getting through it. Nemirovich-Danchenko was familiar with the behind-the-scenes workings of the theatre, both in terms of management and artistic aspects. As a playwright, he cherished his right to attend rehearsals of his plays and intervene if necessary, even leading them if required. Over the years, he became the one to teach others.

He presented his play *Lucky Man* (1887) at the Alexandrinsky Theatre, commenting, "St. Petersburg is freezing; it's not as comfortable as being backstage at the Maly Theatre." However, he had no reason to complain thus far: "Aleksey Potekhin, the playwright in charge of the repertoire, gives me full freedom to choose and order new scenery for my productions." While in St. Petersburg, he expressed concerns about the Moscow performance of the same play: "Tell Chernevsky and Geltser that I want them to make the fourth act as impactful as possible.[3] We should have a real studio or an artist's study with a piano, desk, etc." He instructed Sumbatov-Yuzhin, "Keep me informed about all production details." He took charge of those details with authority. Eventually, people grew accustomed to his persistent nature and took it into consideration. In the following season, he presented *Last Will* (1888) in St. Petersburg, stating,

> The actors knew their roles by heart from the first rehearsal. I sent all the sets made according to my instructions to Fedorov two weeks ago. The Stage Director's Office is meticulously working on the production and accepting everything. There are very few cuts in the play.

Previously, he was dissatisfied and believed that every little thing was worth the effort: more enthusiasm, more expense, more time. Now he realized that time is more valuable than money. The Alexandrinsky Theatre was currently staging *Gold* (1895) with resident stars Maria Savina and Vladimir Davydov. The title was already on the poster when the tsar passed away, and all performances stopped for official mourning until the end of the year. Rehearsals for the play could continue during the theatre closures, but despite this, the artistic result remained unchanged. Instead of hoping for something different, everything repeated itself in rehearsal.

However, if he requested a piano on stage, they provided it. They would complain and mention budget difficulties if he asked for new scenery, but they still provided it. They would build it from scratch, just as they always had, but with a fresher look.

As a young reviewer, he noticed that the audience loved to see the actor perform in the same way he did yesterday, albeit in a new play. Many years later, he would attend a play at the Alexandrinsky and smile knowingly, saying, "Davydov is still Davydov, and the audience is delighted that he remains the same." How could you not love this feeling? It was so easy to love the old theatre forever. To love its brilliance amidst its routine: the orchestra led by the first violin, Albert Jungmann's melodies before the show, the warm heating system, and the doorkeepers calling out at the entrances—"Programs! Programs!" To love the completeness of this feeling that emerged when you were no longer annoyed for the hundredth time by the forest and garden scenery ("approved by the highest authority," the staff proclaimed). But it wouldn't be the same if you took away the orchestra playing Jungman's music and changed the scenery. But as the twentieth century approached, Nemirovich-Danchenko began to yearn for the traditional feelings of theatre that he cherished. However, a creative revolution in the arts was beginning to unfold. One of the key figures in this revolution was the choreographer and dancer Mikhail Fokine,[4] who famously proclaimed that in order to accomplish something in ballet, one must also have a certain level of disdain for it. Nemirovich-Danchenko now understood the significance of that "also." Beyond all other emotions and feelings, one had to hate ballet.

It wasn't just the monotonous routine that bothered Nemirovich-Danchenko. Although that was the first thing he noticed, it was also the display of self-assured skill and the egos of the actors that required them to stick to traditional stage positions. Additionally, there was the humiliating expectation for playwrights to write roles specifically tailored to an actor's persona. Writing with Yermolova in mind may have been enjoyable, but it also felt limiting because he had to write for the performer rather than the role. Moscow's private theatres had recently adopted this demand as well. Nemirovich-Danchenko had been receiving matter-of-fact requests from the new actor-manager, Maria Abramova, which angered him, likening it to placing an order with a tailor.[5] However, Nemirovich-Danchenko himself was like a literary tailor. His play, *The Last Will* (1888), had obediently catered to predetermined roles: Fedotova played the "fashionable society woman," and Yermolova played her "long-suffering rival." The *Last Will* was his first widely acclaimed success. *New Business* (1890) solidified that success, and *Gold* deepened it. Yet, these customized plays did not instill much self-confidence in the author.

While these plays aligned with the theatre's established aesthetic system, they did not capture Nemirovich-Danchenko's essential thoughts and creative goals. The Maly Theatre was struggling, but it persisted, hopeful that the difficult days would pass. They relied on the influential voice of the great Yermolova to support this prophecy. They entrusted the openings of their repertoire to popular playwright Viktor Krylov, allowing him to have fun and make a living. Friedrich Schiller's plays examined the present, while Krylov's plays catered to it. However, the present remained artistically undefined, lacking an authentic voice in the theatre.

Naturally attuned to the movement of ideas and life itself, Nemirovich-Danchenko initially expressed this gift in a mentally unfavorable situation. Acknowledging the changes, as well as their inevitability and artistic consolidation, felt like a betrayal. Nonetheless, the concept of "hard times" was palpable. These hard times didn't repeat themselves explicitly in historical events, but rather in the persistence of the same problem. How could one manage such times with dignity if the opportunity presented itself? Or, the fact that spiritual losses would occur regardless of the chosen path, given the difficulties of the times. In any case, forging ahead unthinkingly would be a death sentence.

The characters that caught Nemirovich-Danchenko's attention were caught in this "displacement," in the turbulence of instability and fear of stability. "Now, something new and nauseatingly boring has arrived." For the protagonist of the novel *Under the Wife* (n.d.), the monotonous routine of his life coincides with his wife's "hopeless routine" of performing in Meyerbeer's opera *The Huguenots* for the fifty-seventh time.

There was not a single gesture he did not anticipate. She will now glance at the conductor to show her experience and begin her aria. Just before a beautiful high note, she will step forward on stage and coyly smile at the audience; then comes her roulade and a long fermata. The audience will applaud; she will shuffle in a boyish manner because she plays a pageboy. Then "he" will be friendly to the women in the chorus because Urban, her character, is mischievous and well-liked.

The protagonist of *Under the Wife* also foresees everything that will happen to him or has the ability to foresee it. As his wife returns, she is flushed and rejuvenated, with traces of makeup still visible on her face. "I had to repeat the ballad three times! Three times!" Then they will argue because he says he can no longer travel around Europe with her. And why won't she try to establish herself with an imperial stage in Moscow or St. Petersburg? She will cry, saying she won't ask for a debut unless they invite her, but he can ask on her behalf if he wants to. And he will not leave because she loves him and he loves her, and love is one of those forces that bind a person to routine and a lack of freedom. He gazes down the street: lights flashing, shops illuminated, muddy and wet roads. Umbrellas, raised trousers, chatter, someone rushing and yelling at others.

Loneliness and a lack of freedom accompany a fragmented, chaotic, and urbanized life. This situation serves as a constant background to the story, summarizing the action. Another backdrop is presented: the powerful, alienated world of the steppe, incredibly incomprehensible and causing anxiety for those who enter its confines. A carriage moves further away from the last rest stop, and the passengers feel like strangers, at the mercy of the indifferent elements. The scent of burning lingers—the estate they are visiting has been set ablaze. The horses are charred in their stables, their skulls exposed. In *The Mist*, the characters fear arson, and coals smolder in the story *In the Steppe*, while the village burns down in *In Dreams* (1901). The author skillfully establishes the lighting: the night after the fire scene, dark silhouettes against the twilight sky; flames erupt from smoldering heaps, casting crimson reflections on faces and linen shirts; water is poured onto the flames, and once again, everything is cloaked in darkness. One of the burned-out huts emits a light—a lamp is illuminated, and a piece of bread rests on the table; a peasant stands and prays fervently, with no roof above him. The young scientist living on the farm next door berates himself. It makes him sick when he remembers how he shouted at the fire brigade in an unsteady commanding voice. Doubting whether he ordered correctly at the very moment of command, not knowing what to order, not knowing anything. Incompetence can manifest in different ways: confusion, reflection, or audacity. It haunts Nemirovich-Danchenko's characters regardless. People entrust them with responsibility, but they don't know how to carry it out and curse themselves for undertaking it.

In one of his summer letters to Sumbatov-Yuzhin, Nemirovich-Danchenko mentioned writing a story called *Dilettantes* [n.d.]. It's challenging to determine which of his future works he had in mind here. It could apply to any of them since the word "dilettante" could describe each. Vitaly Vilenkin, the leading Nemirovich-Danchenko scholar, observed that his characters "die from corrosive amateurism, which spreads from professional activities to the very essence of the character and paralyzes his powers. This far-reaching amateurism worried the writer most of all." In *The Brothers Karamazov*, Alyosha Karamazov has a conversation with Nikolay Krasotkin. He recalls reading somewhere that if a Russian boy is given a star map he's never held before, he'll return it corrected the following morning. According to Dostoevsky, this attitude is an eternal characteristic of youth and a sign of the times. Nemirovich-Danchenko captured these conceited star-map-correcting boys in their forties and beyond. He understood the influence of an idea on such individuals. If practicality and "business" became the idea, he infused the play with tragicomedy. However, the idea remained unchanged. He took the characters at the end of their lifecycles, outliving their hour and full of inexhaustible, unnecessary energy. This is Stolbtsov,

40 *Vladimir Nemirovich-Danchenko and the Moscow Art Theatre*

the protagonist of *New Business*. This is Solntsev, the protagonist of *In the Steppe*, whom the author calls

> a Russian Don Quixote of the second half of the 19th century, a man who considers himself a great practical man and a man of action. At the first thought of any new enterprise, he quickly develops all the details and compiles a grand project with estimates down to the smallest detail. He spends the shortest amount of time on all this—not even enough time for his fellow landlord to write a simple letter to his tenant—and presents the project to wealthy sponsors, to the government offices of St. Petersburg, the specialists.

Nemirovich-Danchenko's dilettantes also bother him in another way: they are immersed in eternal problems, revealing what can be called a dilettantism of the spirit. Narcissistic and helpless, like amateurs. In the presence of the powerful materialism of the steppe, amidst the ominous silence that some claim resembles the sound of a distant threshing, and others liken to the cry of a night heron, the significance of this dilettantism of the spirit emerges. *Police Inspector Stanovoy* (1896) finds his position unbearable and possesses artistic inclinations. He is drawn to the works of the astronomer Camille Flammarion: *Popular Astronomy, The Starry Sky and Its Wonders*.[6] Here, we have a star map in the possession of an aging Russian boy destined to become a police officer.

While amateurism may become the subject of mockery, it still remains a source of dramatic tension. In the broadest, most philosophical sense of the term, the inability to truly live is both dramatic and shameful. However, the capacity to live, in the particular way it may manifest, is also dramatic and shameful, albeit with shades of primal baseness. Nemirovich-Danchenko does not contrast skilled individuals with dilettantes, but rather with his peculiar and persistently preoccupied "refuseniks": Andrei Kalguyev in *New Business*, Valentina in *Gold*, and Vasily Onisimovich in *In Dreams*. The first two are fools threatened with forced guardianship, embodying a remarkable and innate "incompetence." The third is as capable as can be, yet deliberately abandons his skill because it disgusts him. The advantages and disadvantages of "declining" do not determine the final outcome; these roles have "open endings" that defy the conventions and norms of the existing theatre. Actress Iya Savina believes there was a mistake in the fourth act of *Gold* when Valentina agrees to marry someone to whom she feels no connection. She desired a different resolution, failing to recognize that the irony of the marriage was precisely what made it effective.

The established rules of the theatre demanded a fully developed, satisfying progression of the dramatic events, accompanied by a moral motive. It was necessary to clearly state who was right, who was wrong, and what action should be taken; the strength and directness of the answers were considered crucial in a play. Discovering material that refrained from assigning

Everything Is Nearby 1886–1896   41

blame or prescribing a course of action, finding moral motives that were not predetermined but gained power through their unresolved nature—these challenges were only half the battle. The true test lay in confronting and manipulating them artistically, without violating the established laws of the stage or succumbing to its conventions. Nemirovich-Danchenko was envious of playwrights who didn't have to face such challenges. He longed to come home after a season of hard work and

> read whatever you come across, with your feet up, gaze at the moon with meaningless philosophizing, observe the ants and spiders, search for serious drama in every person's face, sometimes cursing but never getting angry. And when all of this becomes boring, write a new play in 10–12 days.

Sumbatov-Yuzhin wrote whatever play he had in mind. "And me—I dream of writing one better than the one I will write anyhow."

Evolving Artistic Vision and Encounters with Chekhov

"The most important thing to teach yourself is that if you set a goal for yourself, stick to it, do not waste time on anything else, and never relax your vigilance because you know that what you want will likely appear completely unexpectedly, and probably not where or when you expected it." This quotation is from a letter to Sumbatov-Yuzhin. Both friends are purposeful, goal-oriented individuals. Here's how the critic Nikolai Efros sketched a portrait of Sumbatov-Yuzhin: "Happy are those who know their way Happy are those steadily moving in a known path toward clearly set goals."[7] You could say the same thing about Nemirovich-Danchenko by adding one more property, a changeable one: the ability to understand your goal is moveable and has its own celestial motion, its own mysterious orbit. The "known path" changes course as it pleases because it is not the singleness of the goal that is important but the willingness to recognize that a goal has shifted, appeared suddenly, and was not where you expected it.

It's curious that Nemirovich-Danchenko, a playwright who pursued his task with such persistence for so many years, worked so hard on a play "better than the one he would write anyhow" and ultimately found this play written by someone else. He was jealous of others' success and did not believe anyone could be "without that horrible feeling that arises in every author regarding the success of another." When that feeling arises in him regarding the plays of Sumbatov-Yuzhin, a lifelong friend,

> we suppress it in ourselves with sincere, rather than fake honesty. Frankly, I am pleased with myself in this sense. This play is your 3rd or 4th where my appreciation of your success has not cost me the slightest tension.

42 Vladimir Nemirovich-Danchenko and the Moscow Art Theatre

He wrote this in 1898, and in December 1896, he refused the Griboyedov Prize for his play *The Price of Life* (1896) because Chekhov's *The Seagull* came out the same year.

"Chekhov is the talented me." That is an unusual turn of phrase. Having said this, an ambitious person might blame himself, hate the lucky man who did what you unsuccessfully tried to do yourself, or even resign in failure and defeat. However, his relations with Chekhov developed smoothly from the start. They persisted without "drama," even increasing in closeness, that is, to the extent possible between two reserved persons of their social circle and generation. Nemirovich-Danchenko couldn't remember exactly when or where he first met Chekhov, but it seemed almost impossible that they hadn't become acquainted. They had both studied at the university around the same time (and it wasn't like thousands of students were accepted back then), and they both worked part-time at the same editorial offices. Nemirovich-Danchenko was particularly interested in everything his friend wrote for the stage. Although Chekhov hadn't mentioned anything to him about producing *Swan Song* (1887), Nemirovich-Danchenko was willing to handle the arrangements for the work at the Maly Theatre. He said to Chekhov, "If you don't want to offer it yourself, just give me a copy. I'll introduce it for you and connect you with anyone you need." Chekhov appreciated Nemirovich-Danchenko's intelligence and kindness. In his humble way, he described his new acquaintance by saying,

> Nemirovich-Danchenko is a very pleasant person who will become an original playwright in due time. Every year, his writing gets better. I also like him as a person; he is decent and tries to be tactful. It seems like he's working on himself.

Their conversations were honest, but they didn't happen frequently. They lived in different parts of the city. Chekhov's address was easily remembered since Dr. Korneev, whose guest house the Chekhov family rented on Sadovaya-Kudrinskaya Street, printed monthly advertisements in *The Russian Courier*. Nemirovich-Danchenko, on the other hand, had settled in Chudov Lane off Myasnitskaya Street after getting married. Once, Chekhov went there to deliver a reprint from the March 1889 issue of *The Northern Herald*, which had published his latest play, *Ivanov* Nemirovich-Danchenko felt embarrassed that his guest went out of his way and couldn't find him at home. "I read it and understood it." That was his response to the message his guest left. "I believe it's not the first time you've been told that you're the most talented among us, and I agree with that opinion without any sense of envy." However, Nemirovich-Danchenko didn't consider the play a masterpiece; rather, he saw it as an opportunity for one. It seemed to Lensky that the author disregarded stage requirements too much (Lensky had noticed the same thing in Chekhov's play, *The Wood Demon*). Did he not know these requirements? Were they even necessary to know?

Everything Is Nearby 1886–1896 43

"Personally," Nemirovich-Danchenko wrote, "I'm not an ardent defender of these requirements. In fact, I'm completely indifferent." He maintained this indifference, much like Chekhov. For example, while working on *Ivanov* (which was written hastily in ten days but took a toll on him afterward), he was fully aware of the constraints on his freedom as a playwright. In fact, few people remember Chekhov's famous words in a letter about working on *Ivanov* and gradually freeing himself from bondage—it was a continuation of their discussion about the vital freedom for a playwright, which Chekhov had not yet achieved. "What a shame that we live on opposite sides of Moscow!" Yes, it was indeed a pity. Nemirovich-Danchenko respected personal boundaries and maintained harmonious relationships with others. Although Nemirovich-Danchenko admired Chekhov, he didn't believe this obligated Chekhov or required his awareness.

It took a long time before Nemirovich-Danchenko allowed himself to express his feelings in a letter to Chekhov, stating, "Your songs will end, and it seems to me that my literary and spiritual life will also come to an end. I may write this loftily, but you know that it comes from the heart." The connection between Nemirovich-Danchenko's own literary and spiritual life and someone else's "song" burdened him heavily whenever he wrote prose or drama. No matter how clearly he saw the connection between himself and nature, there was often room for an intermediary, a distorting lens. This becomes painfully obvious in his early works—the scandalous short story *Bad Habit* (n.d.) echoes Gogol's *Mirgorod*, while *Drama at the Postal Station* (1881) suggests Lermontov's *A Hero of Our Time*. Eventually, Nemirovich-Danchenko would free himself from this dependence, but the presence of an intermediary between the subject and the writer always seemed to persist. Considering Nemirovich-Danchenko's reluctance to be influenced by others or swayed by their perspectives in everyday life, his willingness to merge his opinions with those of others, particularly Chekhov, becomes even more striking.

A connection with Chekhov can be seen in everything Nemirovich-Danchenko did from the early 1890s. One could easily categorize this as the influence of a brilliant writer on a lesser one, but it's not that simple. Furthermore, Nemirovich-Danchenko's contact with Chekhov may have impacted his memory, inspiring him to view his younger years as a treasure trove of images and adaptations for directing Chekhov's plays in the future. In his memoirs, Nemirovich-Danchenko recalls visiting his neighbors, including a young scientist who inherited a large estate. This scientist was initially described as lazy and fond of entertaining guests and drinking. They engaged in spirited discussions, sometimes even arguing passionately about lofty matters. These were the types of characters one might find in Chekhov's stories. While the Neskuchnoye community offered valuable insights, the young scientist in question was likely Nikolai Karyshev.[8] However, Karyshev's true nature differed greatly from Nemirovich-Danchenko's memories. Karyshev was an active and hardworking professor at Tartu University in Estonia,

44 *Vladimir Nemirovich-Danchenko and the Moscow Art Theatre*

specializing in economic statistics. It's worth noting that even Vladimir Lenin held Karyshev's statistics in high regard, though not his theories. Nevertheless, it was Chekhov who influenced Nemirovich-Danchenko's perspective and angle of refraction, making it essential for him to remain loyal to this viewpoint. Nemirovich-Danchenko was independent and ambitious, enabling him to appreciate the hyper-sensitivity of his writing to external rhythms, structures, and inspirations. While this characteristic could hinder a writer, it could also provide freedom for him. However, he also acknowledged something different: his talent for self-dissolution, responsive creativity, and insightful-creativity was a unique and previously irrelevant gift.

He was destined to be a director. It was an unfortunate calling, as if he were born a pilot with no airplanes and all that remained was to create one.

Dedication to Theatre and Cultural Collaboration

We should write about his busyness. Additionally, we should note that we have arbitrarily divided his occupations. First, he was a critic and a journalist, then a playwright, then a prose writer, and finally a teacher at the Philharmonic School (since we have to begin this topic now). This plan made for a convenient presentation, but we should also mention that he did not give up one occupation while pursuing the others. For example, his reviews (which were no longer in *The Russian Courier* but now in *The Russian Gazette* and *News of the Day*) continued to be published, although not as frequently as before. He also did not ignore subjects outside the theatre—in *News of the Day*, he led the "Today" section. He also continued writing short stories, despite receiving criticisms from colleagues for remaining with the popular press. Those who criticized him did not offer to lend him money, and serious magazines were not generous with advances, but *The Moscow Illustrated Gazette* was.

Because he was a man of society, he had many meetings and conferences. He was a remarkably efficient person burdened with many tasks. It is well known that if you want anything done, you should ask a busy person to do it. According to his memoirs, his days in Neskuchnoye were long and expansive, requiring work related to his commitments in Moscow and local obligations. For example, he visited public schools and the nearby vocational school in memory of his late father-in-law. Perhaps Nemirovich-Danchenko thought of Korf when he gave one of his stage characters a line about the only asset of the intelligentsia inherited from the nobility: "We were born bearing within ourselves certain assumptions and principles, which others still need to achieve through the work of entire generations. Wherever fate has guided you, this legacy of your fathers will remain with you." If you do not squander it, that is.

The principles of the nobility would then become tangible in MAT; let this be its first introduction. Nemirovich-Danchenko's responsibilities extended beyond the workday, but he meticulously planned his schedule, leaving no

Everything Is Nearby 1886–1896 45

free time. Every year (less frequently as time passed), his plays premiered at the Maly and Alexandrinsky theatres. This not only brought excitement to the author but also required a great deal of effort. In particular, he had to collaborate with the Literary and Theatrical Committee of the imperial theatres, a position he was appointed to in September 1891. This work involved conscientiously reading numerous plays. He also engaged in projects aiming to reform the imperial theatres, presenting detailed plans that were never implemented. Additionally, he corresponded with those in charge of these efforts in Moscow and St. Petersburg. A review of these meetings reveals a busy and eventful life.

In the 1880s and 1890s, there was a resurgence in open conversation, enabling people to discuss previously forbidden topics. This led to a revival of camaraderie and the formation of discussion circles, where individuals could converse about their impossible dreams and find like-minded companions. Ideas were exchanged in the hopes of forming possible alliances. Nemirovich-Danchenko attended a continuous series of theatrical evenings, never missing a performance. He would attend shows at various theatres, including the Maly Theatre, as well as emerging theatres like Anna Brenko's and Fyodor Korsh's.[9] He also watched touring companies, notably the Meiningen Company, as well as amateur performances. In fact, Nemirovich-Danchenko praised one amateur actor in Aleksey Pisemsky's play *Self-Governance*,[10] produced by the Society of Art and Literature. It is worth noting that one of the amateur actors in the society adopted the stage name Stanislavsky, though his role was only in a crowd scene.

It is intriguing to observe how people's paths cross long before they formally meet. The amateurs from the Society of Art and Literature would perform on Sofiyka Street, which was situated across from the Philharmonic School, a renowned gathering place for many visitors, including actors from the Maly Theatre, Stanislavsky, and Nemirovich-Danchenko himself. They would also perform at the Hunting Club on Vozdvizhenka Street, which was later reconstructed as the Kremlin Hospital. However, let us not dwell on the future. It is worth mentioning that in a few years, the building where they performed would become the venue for the first rehearsal of *The Seagull*, and it is there that Chekhov would first notice Olga Knipper,[11] a young woman who had recently graduated from the Philharmonic School. Conveniently, the Philharmonic School was located close to everything.

Transforming Theatre Through Education

In 1883, the Society of Amateur Music and Drama in Moscow changed its name to the Moscow Philharmonic Society. By 1891, when Nemirovich-Danchenko began teaching at the school, it was in its fourteenth academic year. The school's rights were officially recognized as equal to those of the conservatories of the Russian Imperial Musical Society. While talented and financially needy students could receive exemptions or scholarships, instructional

46 *Vladimir Nemirovich-Danchenko and the Moscow Art Theatre*

fees were still required for classes. The majority of the approximately 300–400 students were aspiring instrumentalists and singers.

From the beginning, the school's director, Pyotr Shostakovsky, who had studied under Franz Liszt, served as both conductor and pianist. He organized ten annual showcases that brought vibrancy to Moscow's music scene, and the student musicians gained a reputation for excellence. However, the drama classes did not achieve the same level of acclaim. Admission to the drama program was less competitive than at the Imperial Theatre School, and it carried a different reputation.

If Shostakovsky had placed more emphasis on the drama program, he would not have agreed for Sumbatov-Yuzhin and Nemirovich-Danchenko [a non-actor] to share the teaching duties of the course, which involved three years of study. Despite the playwright's renown and his undeniable taste and knowledge of theatrical work, an actor would have been a better fit for teaching acting. Fortunately, Shostakovsky didn't mind, and Sumbatov-Yuzhin was able to convince him. The newly appointed teacher would teach four classes per week, each lasting two hours.

The students were generally uninspiring, and their skill level was minimal. It is not surprising that Nemirovich-Danchenko expelled many of them. Given the discouraging circumstances, it is remarkable that he himself didn't leave. Nemirovich-Danchenko wasn't enthusiastic about any of his students among the first and second cohorts, but he was passionate about teaching and the enigmatic nature of the craft. If one were to identify Nemirovich-Danchenko's most significant activity from 1891 to 1897, it would be these classes.

During the 1890s, Nemirovich-Danchenko's thoughts about theatre occupied only a small portion of his mind, although he would later return to this subject as a novelist and author of theatre criticism and articles. His novel, *The Mist*, delves into the intertwined yet distinct fates of the children of a noble family. A young cavalryman quarrels with his father, forsakes a military career for the theatre, and ultimately takes his own life because of an actress. This theme of rupture and emancipation reemerges in his novel, *The Last Meeting* (1894), set on a steppe farm. The plot revolves around a couple who unexpectedly cross paths, despite both desiring and planning the encounter. The woman is tense, struggling to maintain composure. "Let me see you. What are Russian actors like? I have never seen them up close." While he may provide solace in her misfortune, he himself remains unhappy and dissatisfied. Nevertheless, he refuses to renounce the theatre.

He: I will achieve my goal.
She: For fame, is it?
He: Yes, whatever that means.
        And so, he departs for Novocherkassk.

What does provincial Novocherkassk offer? Is it any different from provincial Yelets or provincial Vologda? The world does not require rediscovery.

Nemirovich-Danchenko hastens to identify its indicators in a few words, to name the very thing everyone knows about actors: the narcissism compensating for the bitterness of a nomadic existence, the clashes of starving egos, the priesthood of the stage, who excels at what, the disdain for a foolish audience whom actors impudently mistreat, the frayed nerves, the smell of gasoline emanating from cleaning old garments.

The story does not challenge or romanticize the qualities for which respectable society reproaches bohemian life; it does not present them in a different, poetic light. His *Drama Behind the Scenes* (1896) astounds readers with its elderly, wrinkled characters, decayed teeth, and dreadful hair, worn out by coughing; their rented abodes differ from the poetic and carefree hangouts play-actors. This is destitution devoid of sentiment, cruel to the point of starvation (the protagonist notices the stench of vomit backstage. She doesn't need money herself since she lives on an allowance). This is what they call fame: everyone rudely eyes you on the street; everyone passes judgment.

In *The Last Meeting*, Nemirovich-Danchenko scarcely maintains the conversational tone until the end and barely concerns himself with the events transpiring between the two characters. Instead, the protagonist delivers a monologue about society's bias against actors: "The reason is their liberty, and that's what you can't tolerate. Their lives are separate, and they have no interest in your principles and morals." The monologue is intriguing, but the issue is more complex than that. It's worth considering why, in the nineteenth century, the desire to become an actor gained such passion and energy and became a widespread concern. Anyone who chose the theatre profession, whether earlier or later, would undoubtedly hesitate and consider the obstacles. Relatives would discourage this ambition just as they would discourage a son who wanted to be a sailor or a mercenary: travel is not safe, the income is uncertain, and the separation is long. Yet, from time immemorial, acting has been a profession of both charm and risk. In the nineteenth century, theatre stood apart from other occupations, acquiring a particular meaning and capabilities.

The drama of alienation characterized the nineteenth century, as work and practical activity ceased to express the individual. Many people languished, feeling unfulfilled in their daily lives. This lack of fulfillment is evident in characters like Sorin in The *Seagull*, who holds the position of a state councilor but does not feel like one. Similarly, estate manager Shamrayev and doctor Chebutykin do not feel fulfilled in their respective roles. They, along with others, merely serve as interim actors, unable to fully embrace their true callings. It is increasingly common for individuals to turn to the theatre after trying their hand at more conventional paths in life. For example, Nemirovich-Danchenko's brother and sister did not pursue acting until later in life. Olga Knipper and Margarita Savitskaya also did not decide on a theatrical career until the age of twenty-seven. Savitskaya, in particular, contemplated the choice between the theatre and the convent, vowing that she would rather die than not become an actress. In daily life, people often find themselves trapped in monotonous

48 *Vladimir Nemirovich-Danchenko and the Moscow Art Theatre*

social roles that do not allow them to be their true selves. This is where the allure of the theatre lies. On stage, one can express their true self and immerse themselves in their roles. As one character puts it,

> I am a prince on stage. I live his life; his thoughts torment me; I cry his tears over poor Ophelia and love her as forty thousand brothers cannot love. And you! You are young and attractive; you have fire in your eyes, music in your conversation, and beautiful movements. You will enter the stage like a queen and exit the stage like a queen and stay that way.

Furthermore, the theatre offers something that often goes unnoticed and unappreciated in daily life: personal experience. The audience may not respond to one's powerful emotions outside the theatre, but within its walls, personal experiences are valued. As one character observes, "Only in the theatre! Oh, if you offer even half of these treasures to the public, the theatre will erupt with applause." However, the theatre, despite its potential, may not always meet expectations. It may struggle to attract an audience and fail to inspire its actors. Yet, even in its most desperate moments, the theatre secretly waits for individuals seeking self-realization through the stage. This is exemplified by the character in *Drama Behind the Scenes*, who flees from a merchant's family to join a hungry and ill-mannered theatre troupe from Lutsk. The stage offers him the salvation he craves, a way to escape his unfulfilling life.

While the promise of the theatre is real, it is not without danger. It attracts individuals who desire salvation, but many are ill equipped to handle it. The stage is crowded with people who seek, revel in, and even find happiness in it, but who ultimately prove unfit for its demands. After establishing himself as a successful theatre-maker, Nemirovich-Danchenko maintained a compassionate fondness for aspiring actors and actresses who longed to take the stage and never lose that feeling. These individuals, who had no desire for anything else but to wear the crown of theatrical royalty every night, fervently sought recognition and adoration. Numerous letters were sent expressing their desires, often seen as amusing, pitiful, and embarrassing from an outsider's perspective. Rather than ridicule those who wrote the letters, we should be ashamed for invading their privacy by reading them. They were never intended for our eyes; rather, they were meant to be read by someone who truly understood and empathized with their dreams. Nemirovich-Danchenko, despite his tough demeanor, was that someone. He comprehended the sentiments expressed in those letters and sympathized with the writers. One letter that received no mocking was from an office worker in Morshansk who posed the question of whether someone with physical challenges could enter the stage, specifically mentioning a noticeable gap tooth. The writer even included a drawing of a face with an arrow pointing to the tooth.

Nemirovich-Danchenko promptly expelled a disrespectful young man who arrogantly stated that he joined the theatre with the intention of taking advantage of the abundance of women for free, simply because he had the means and spare time. However, the student quickly changed his tune as Nemirovich-Danchenko knew how to enforce his rules. Nemirovich-Danchenko dedicated significant time and effort to working with individuals who may have been considered lost causes. His writings about the students in his early classes evoked a range of emotions, from laughter to tears. Some students faced challenges such as lisps, accents, squeaky voices, or hearing loss. Nevertheless, speaking candidly with them was easy, knowing their unwavering dedication to the stage. "I cannot imagine my life without the stage," one student firmly expressed. As an educator, Nemirovich-Danchenko felt the weight of individuals who were willing to sacrifice everything for the stage, driven by their burning desire for self-expression. In this position, he had the opportunity to contemplate the advantages and risks associated with such fervor.

While reflecting on himself and others who shared his passion for the theatre, Nemirovich-Danchenko likely recognized that its allure extended beyond being an escape from unfulfillment, It also offered the enchantment of unity and the satisfaction of collaborative work. The idea of a collective of workers, a commune, or a phalanstery was familiar in this context, particularly to the generation of the 1890s. The protagonist of *The Last Meeting* attributes society's prejudice against actors and the appeal of the acting profession to participants' freedom to engage in their chosen craft. However, Nemirovich-Danchenko himself seemingly did not emphasize the same aspect as the protagonist. To him, theatre primarily presented an opportunity for unrestricted creative expression.

When Nemirovich-Danchenko started at the Philharmonic School, he had no official guidelines or manifestoes. Instead, he created notebooks that contained schedules for lessons, meetings, conversations, rehearsals, reviews, and exams. These detailed notebooks included students' names on the left side, along with names from previous years, plays, and various other names at the top. Educational plans were developed by combining titles and surnames, both in general and for each student individually. Additionally, there were lists, calendars, grading, roles, and exercises. Throughout his life, Nemirovich-Danchenko used these large yellow sheets of paper with ruled lines to plan his upcoming day, week, and year. The examples were numerous, but every hour had narrow and precise lines that needed to be filled with activities. Nemirovich-Danchenko understood the destructive power of negligence, especially when it came to managing significant projects. He had a favorite phrase, "I would rather give up the project than the organization of it."[12] However, he still enjoyed creating projects and had a talent for it. Therefore, the word "Projects" should be capitalized to emphasize their importance. When referring to the art he served, Nemirovich-Danchenko always wrote the word "Theatre" with a capital letter. Hence, during Nemirovich-Danchenko's time at the Philharmonic School, the theme of dilettantism became increasingly significant in his writing. It represented the organic connection to Russian life as well as its destructive impact. This theme

50 Vladimir Nemirovich-Danchenko and the Moscow Art Theatre

found expression in his work, *The Governor's Inspection* (1896). Chekhov's response letter delighted the author, as Chekhov praised the story for its subtlety, clarity, and overall impression. Chekhov acknowledged the author's deep knowledge of life and noted an improvement in their talent over the years. The story depicted ill-fated amateurishness, a foolish and awkward existence, and an inspection that ended in suicide. Its beauty lay in its "clarity of finish." Chekhov recognized the effort and success of a person refining their art and understood the struggles of everyday life, the choice between amateurism, self-centered skill, or refusal to work. Thankfully, art rewarded the effort invested in it, but the value of skill was different here: higher and more fundamental.

In autumn 1891, when Nemirovich-Danchenko began working at the Philharmonic School, he expressed gratitude for Lensky's suggestion to teach him about makeup and wigs. He acknowledged that his personal experience would help him quickly assimilate Lensky's advice. This last sentence demonstrated that Nemirovich-Danchenko was not completely inexperienced, even in matters as specific as makeup (Lensky was renowned for his creative makeup, making it a valuable opportunity to learn from him). The fear of amateurism remained, though, along with the concern of being seen as inexperienced. He would teach higher skills and understand the movements of the soul and the subtleties of an author's style. However, he would also insist on training in voice, dance, flexibility, and fencing. He placed his hopes on young people and demanded a lot from them. Of course, Nemirovich-Danchenko was not the only one who believed that the theatre's revival would come from the young. Nor was he alone in his passionate dedication to teaching. Alexander Lensky, who taught drama classes at the Imperial School, understood Nemirovich-Danchenko's passion. And although he was often more interested in working with young people than even his own roles, he could hardly do anything about it. That is the disadvantage of theatrical longevity. You cannot refuse admission to the son, nephew, or daughter of your former colleague's best friends. Lensky's list of students contained the same surnames that had always graced theatrical posters. Young people who had grown up with the theatre. They had seen it all and could already do most of it. That is how tradition is maintained, but also how it is preserved and stagnant. They prepared understudies in advance, actors who had "Jr." attached to their surnames, and it was almost symbolic. Despite their kinship, everyone wanted the "Juniors" to faithfully and skillfully reproduce what had been done before.

A person who listens to dozens and hundreds of applicants every year, at some point (it's impossible to tell when), notices that those coming in are different from those who took the exam the year before and the year before that. Something has changed in the atmosphere. (It's not true that young people are always unique by their same age—not always, and novelty is not linked to age.) This changed atmosphere permeates the newcomers. They convey something beyond talent through their presence, rhythm, and breathing. It is important not to overlook this, especially when others do.

Everything Is Nearby 1886–1896 51

However, he is also afraid to trust too much that the new and strange sound will emerge naturally. It is necessary to have a specific "transmitting apparatus"—both external and internal.

The teacher highly values perceptive and dedicated students. However, he checks whether they might be too absorbed in the role and themselves, enjoying what they are given to experience there "for themselves."

Recalling his earliest teaching, Nemirovich-Danchenko believed that he, like everyone else, made mistakes by overestimating his students' talent. But if he did, it was only privately. The evaluations he wrote every year were strict, his hopes were restrained, and he was reserved in his recommendations. In 1895, impresario Alexei Suvorin asked Nemirovich-Danchenko to recommend young actors for his newly created theatre in St. Petersburg. Nemirovich-Danchenko responded with a detailed letter, stating that presently he had graduated over thirty students and could recommended three or four, but without much enthusiasm. Chernov was talented in the role of a household simpleton and was currently in provincial Zlatoust. Additionally, in Zlatoust, Kraft was a decent actress for minor roles, described as elegant, intelligent, and conscientious. He also mentioned the "Grand Dame," Kraft, as someone "imposing, with a beautiful voice and good diction, suitable for the roles often played by opera stars. I would take all of them into my company." Whether Nemirovich-Danchenko considered the possibility of creating "his own company" is hard to say. However, he knew how to form such a company. He suggested that he could recommend someone if Suvorin wanted an actress like his own Abarinova or Zhuleva. Nevertheless, he was generally skeptical. "You have approached the question from the wrong angle."

First, it was necessary to understand what roles Abarinova could not play and find fresh faces for those roles. Next, he advised postponing thoughts about specific roles.

It would be best to choose the plays first—at least three or four "show-stoppers." For example, obtain permission for two of the most exciting plays in Russian drama: *The Power of Darkness* and *Tsar Fyodor Ivanovich*. Then, rather than looking for lovers, ingenues, Grande dame, etc., you would be searching for actors and actresses for these plays.

"New faces, well-suited to the play." Everything that fame can bring to the stage already belongs too much to the established theatre, seen too often through the lens of the established theatre. Therefore, fresh faces, along with newcomers performing Tolstoy's play, for example, would blend with the novelty of the author's thoughts, and the newness of life and art would harmoniously merge. Famous actors who overshadow the author's work with their own "authorship" were unsuitable.

He expressed these ideas firmly, but they weren't entirely clear. Where do we place older actors who have lost their novelty? What should we do with

52 *Vladimir Nemirovich-Danchenko and the Moscow Art Theatre*

new actors once they become well-known? Could the charm of their novelty wear off once they have played the role the manager hired them for? Even in this letter's outline, you can discern the beginnings of the MAT project, and it provokes contemplation.

Remember the conviction expressed here that nothing lasts forever. Nemirovich-Danchenko will later find in Ibsen's *An Enemy of the People* an idea he recognizes as his own: "Truths are not the tenacious Methuselahs people take them for. Normally, a truth lives, let's say, seventeen to eighteen years, twenty at most, rarely longer. And elderly truths are always horribly anemic." "Truths are like last year's stale provisions: That's what makes for moral malnutrition." Ideas and faces grow old and weary. If and when they become exhausted, they are so widely embraced and beloved that you cannot tear them away. (Of all the people to receive this information, it was Suvorin! This newspaper magnate and administrator of public consciousness thrived on presenting his readers with tired, old truths. He believed that anything—whether true or initially false—could transform into an unquestionable platitude.)

We should also consider another individual: this teacher, who seemed to possess an innate ability to understand and predict the actions of actors, forever enamored with their craft. This teacher, with a special gift for comprehending artistic personalities, valued the cause more than individual fame. He recognized how much individuals could contribute to the theatre, bringing their unique perspectives and experiences to a new world. He understood the importance of personal expression, the essence of the soul, in art. However, he viewed all of this as a means to an end. Yes, self-expression and individuality are important, but only in service of something greater—the role, the play, the production, the theatre, art, life. Similarly, the use of imagination, attention to detail, and the ability to create strong associations on stage were all valuable to Nemirovich-Danchenko as long as they served an external purpose. Even the pursuit of perfection itself was not immediately embraced by Nemirovich-Danchenko. The aspiration for perfection had to align with something external—the work itself. This goal held more significance than achieving perfection. The specifics of what it meant to fulfill this crucial external purpose could change, but the recognition of its importance remained constant. Before the work even began, Nemirovich-Danchenko developed a necessary steadfastness, an unwavering commitment to his principles. He was prepared to refuse, to disappoint. He understood that the theatre was not a sanctuary for those seeking a respite from unfulfilled lives.

Since Nemirovich-Danchenko began teaching at the Philharmonic School, the dropout rate had been high. This necessitated telling unqualified stu-dents the truth, without deluding themselves into thinking that they should guide their decisions. Instead, the focus must be on protecting the integrity of the theatre, which would suffer if these students were allowed to participate—either through subpar performances or through the toxicity of resentment and joylessness. Nemirovich-Danchenko is required to report the acceptance and graduation rates for the school years from 1891 to 1897.

Everything Is Nearby 1886–1896 53

In the first year, he worked with Sumbatov-Yuzhin and taught seventeen students in the first-year cohort and fourteen in the second. In 1892–1893, he taught all three levels, including the third level with Sumbatov-Yuzhin. They again accepted seventeen students. The following year, sixteen students were accepted, with ten passing from the first level and four more from the opera class. Twelve students graduated. They established a system of preparing several full-length plays to showcase the graduates' skills. In 1893/1894, Nemirovich-Danchenko led all three levels and took over the general management of drama classes. Sumbatov-Yuzhin was replaced by Nikolai Rybakov, a well-known actor from the Maly Theatre.

The first-year course covered the theory of poetry, readings of poems and fables, and classical verse. Nemirovich-Danchenko chose *The Iliad*, poems by Afanasy Fet, and *Ondine*, a romantic fairy tale with an unorthodox meter intended as "a middle-ground between verse and prose." The second semester's syllabus included more scenes and prose. There was no attempt at explication, only questions like "Have you read the prose passages? Have you tried to act prose, to embody it on stage as prose?" Nemirovich-Danchenko credited himself with strengthening the teaching of general education subjects and creating a library of dramatic works.

During the reporting period, he worked with 170 students and graduated forty-four, including twenty-seven actresses and seventeenth actors. He listed the times and places of all the classes and exam performances. Nemirovich-Danchenko had a rule that successful younger students would participate in the performances of older students. For example, the program for *Thunderstorm* shows that a first-year student, Ivan Moskvin, played the role of the older man.[13] Nemirovich-Danchenko prepared this report thoroughly and followed a strict methodology. However, the daily affairs and specific details of his lessons were not included in the accounts. As a result, there are no examples of his teaching in Nemirovich-Danchenko's records or his students' memoirs. We know that he discouraged students from relying on ready-made models and instead taught them his unique approach to understanding a role. He also taught them to analyze the literary and psychological qualities of a play, to delve into it as a living character, and to create art in a particular direction and genre. Additionally, his lessons incorporated discussions on morality, everyday life, and philosophical questions. However, Nemirovich-Danchenko's teaching methods remain unclear to us since there is no proper description of them. This lack of clarity extends to his rehearsals as well. Nemirovich-Danchenko did not intend for his teaching to be valuable in itself; instead, he expected his students to internalize and apply his teachings to breathe life into their performances.

Nemirovich-Danchenko may have been offended when the Philharmonic School accepted students whom the Imperial Theatre School had rejected. For instance, actor Ivan Moskvin later recalled feeling saddened and resentful after failing the exam at the Imperial Theatre School, even after achieving fame. The examiners at the Imperial Theatre School were knowledgeable and

54 *Vladimir Nemirovich-Danchenko and the Moscow Art Theatre*

talented, observing everything. Unfortunately they only selected individuals who resembled their own faces. They rejected others, presumably because they did not fit standard Russian physiological types, and the imperial theatres primarily focused on performing Ostrovsky plays. (At the Philharmonic School, many students with German, Polish, Jewish, and Caucasian surnames were accepted.) Moskvin was the most "Russian" of them all: he was from Moscow and the son of a housemaid. No one disputed his Russian identity, but he was too distinctive and did not fit the mold for the imperial stage, as he did not embody the "Russian type" showcased there. Nemirovich-Danchenko recognized the inherent value of his students and the enigmatic qualities they possessed. He sought and accepted those who were not necessarily the best or the most perfect, but rather the ones who were unique in their own way.

Unresolved Ideals and Existential Struggles

Many things have remained unresolved for Nemirovich-Danchenko throughout the challenging past year. Progress with his new play has been difficult. The setup is intriguing, starting with a suicide, which typically marks the end of a play. However, this play moves forward to explore the reasons behind the suicide, which are not criminal but rather spiritual and philosophical. It delves into the investigation of a heart that has become dried up and empty and is now rebelling against this emptiness. The play begins with a suicide and concludes with a powerful statement: "Live! Live! We don't know why or for whom, but we need to find out!" The story shares similarities with a motif that will be present in *Three Sisters* "If only we knew..." "Know what you are living for, or else everything is nonsense, rubbish...." However, *The Price of Life* (1896) exhausts its author. Nemirovich-Danchenko did not finish it during his stay at Neskuchnoye over the summer. He had to return to Moscow with an incomplete manuscript, to a city where everything followed a strict schedule on the same narrow-lined paper that we are already familiar with. On September 6, he attended a review of selections prepared by students over the summer.

Nemirovich-Danchenko completed *The Price of Life* in the guest rooms of Gethsemane Priory near Trinity-Sergius Monastery. He found solace in the silence of this place, appreciating the opportunity to escape and leave everything behind. In fact, these respites were somehow incorporated into his schedule, and nothing would disrupt them. They granted him the solitude to be alone with his thoughts and organize them, allowing him to finish the play. He completed it in November 1896, and the initial readers praised it highly.

With a desire to share his thoughts with Chekhov, Nemirovich-Danchenko set the groundwork for a much-needed conversation in a long letter.

> I'm waiting for an appointment with you. Unfortunately, our appointments often pass without leaving a trace. I don't know why. Because

Everything Is Nearby 1886–1896   55

appointments are inconvenient for meaningful exchanges of ideas, we must meet ten times as simple pleasure-seekers before the mood arises for a pleasant conversation. Could it be because of your reclusive nature? I feel so small in comparison to you, and your talent overwhelms me. Even initiating a conversation feels daunting.

1896 was a challenging year all around. The century was coming to an end, burdened by unresolved, persistent, and festering questions. New questions had sprung up and piled upon the old ones, stagnant at their roots, untouched. Those who aligned with the liberal principles of the 1860s could argue that none of the demands made during that time had ever been met, and therefore, the original demands remain unchanged. However, there is now more emphasis on "ideals" rather than "demands," and thus, discussions on ideals are taking place. In 1896, Nemirovich-Danchenko wrote in *In Dreams*, in which a man from that era refers to himself as "the men of the 'sixties" and criticizes the current generation of young intellectuals. It is disastrous for a society when its problems remain unresolved (and it is merely an empty gesture for the state to declare them resolved); the more the authorities prohibit discussion of these problems, the more closed off public thinking becomes. However, life does not wait for problems to be resolved—it continues on, accumulating additional problems that are distorted in advance because they depend on the still unresolved ones. Both old and recent problems intersect and are tightly intertwined in opposition. This leads to anger and unresolved conflicts among people, with accusations being thrown back and forth. One side blames the other, and the other retaliates. The young assistant professor from *In Dreams* states,

Your main complaint is that we do not blindly trust your 'sixties generation, do not take to the streets with your banner, and do not recite your ideals. But do not forget that we have not ignored your legacy and now we must also address the problems you have left us. They have turned out to be much greater than you may realize.

The man from the 'sixties responds, "You have not yet experienced all the challenges of life. But soon, you will have to." The assistant professor counters,

Your ideals fought against the violence of the powerful against the weak, which outraged you, while our ideals fight against the shallowness that exists within all of us, which also deeply offends us. And excuse me, but that is no small matter.

However, it is worth noting that the assistant professor who speaks these words has no more faith in the fight against *poshlost* [complacent mediocrity and moral degeneration] than in the ideals of his conversation partner. He dismisses

56 *Vladimir Nemirovich-Danchenko and the Moscow Art Theatre*

the dreams of someone nearby who hopes for "a fairy tale life where there is no *poshlost* in a derisive manner. That person is mistaken. Life will harshly and mercilessly disappoint them because even if you are an angel in human form, there will always be a bit of *poshlost* in the world around you. It seeps through your pores like fine dust particles, leaving a bitter taste in your mouth.

It is important to recognize that this play does not aim to classify characters as solely positive or negative (the assistant professor may be cold and dishonest, but he is more intelligent than his overconfident interlocutor). Furthermore, the dispute does not occur within the confines of a room but rather against the backdrop of distant fires. If Nemirovich-Danchenko's letter to Chekhov is any indication, it is evident that he is highly agitated, and there are valid reasons for his feelings. It is not easy to resume a routine after enduring what he had to in the recent spring.

Reflections on the Khodynka Tragedy

In the spring of 1896, preparations for the coronation of Nicholas II got underway in Moscow. The editors of *The Field* printed the ceremony for the royal entry in advance, with ornate gold lettering, promising an entertaining spectacle. Muscovites paid large sums of money to secure a seat by a window or balcony overlooking Tverskaya Street, where the procession would parade for three miles from Petrovsky Palace to the Kremlin. If sightseers from St. Petersburg or visitors from the provinces couldn't see the promised team of golden horses, the foreign princes, Asian delegates under Russia's control with their distinctive hats and horses, court footmen, royal guards, and Moors in grand livery, or properly recognize which regiment the Life Hussars, Life Lancers, Cuirassiers, or Horse Guards belonged to, as well as the Minister of the Court's top equestrians, the commander of the Imperial Headquarters, or the tsar himself, they could count on someone to explain it all to them. *The Field's* editor arranged for Nemirovich-Danchenko to provide this service by writing a series of essays about Moscow during the coronation, tailored to the local readers of the magazine. So, let's find out what was happening in the city.

Nemirovich-Danchenko's essays remain interesting to this day. They are lively and unbiased in their descriptions, portraying a city excessively adorned like a gingerbread house, but always enjoyable. The city seems unconcerned with the true meaning of the holiday, focused solely on the festivities themselves. The main guests have not yet arrived, and it still resembles a bustling workshop, with whitewashed boards, the smell of paint, the sound of hammers, and numerous pavilions and decorative displays being constructed. Nemirovich-Danchenko struck the right tone for his essays, avoiding any extreme enthusiasm for the tsar while simultaneously maintaining a level of restraint as a liberal. He successfully captures the festive atmosphere and the mingling of different social classes. Remarkably, he wrote these essays without knowing how events would unfold. The common theme throughout is one of overcrowding, of a space becoming increasingly filled with people,

Everything Is Nearby 1886–1896   57

both open and seemingly impossible to escape. It all began within the walls of the Kremlin, where people gathered to admire the festive lighting. "Not only am I not afraid of the crowd, but I love it." At first, it was enjoyable, feeling the presence of others and being carried along by the lively crowd. "Around me were the cheerful faces of factory workers, artisans, and students." However, there was still darkness; it was only partially lit, and then suddenly became completely dark. "Cheering, noise, laughter, screams, and squeals filled the entire Kremlin area, becoming deafening and creating an eerie atmosphere. They pushed us from the right one minute, then from the left, and then from behind, causing me to bump into someone's back. It became difficult to figure out where we were going and where we were. Finally, we reached what turned out to be the entrance at Spassky Gate.[14] The crowd became even denser at the narrow gate, "and the screams grew even louder under the archway."

"I heard the desperate scream of a child and the scream of a woman. I feared for my life." While the author wrote these lines comically and joked about his own cowardice, he maintained a suitable tone for the action while still being amusing. The townspeople cleared the way for the carriages, and our correspondent boyishly rode out into Red Square on the back of one. The author would not have written in this manner if they had known the tragic ending beforehand and needed to gradually prepare for it.

The first description of the area where the disaster would occur also appeared in the author's essays about other notable places in Moscow for spectators to visit. Beyond Tverskaya Gate,[15] across from the Petrovsky Palace, lies a vast square known as Khodynka Field,[16] about seven miles northwest of Red Square. It serves as a military camp during the summer and was the site of the All-Russian Exhibition in 1882, with buildings initially used for the French Exhibition. The state had also declared it a national holiday venue for the recent coronation. The working classes of Moscow, along with many people from surrounding counties and other provinces, flock to Khodynka Field. Everyone receives a commemorative mug and a bag of candy. Over 400,000 people [sic].

The area is filled with swings, poles, fair booths with theatrical performances, and barrels of beer in wagons. The organization of the national holiday is entrusted to the provincial entrepreneur V.L. Forcatti. Heralds on horseback announce and distribute a proclamation about the coronation at the gates of the Kremlin, Kitay-Gorod,[17] and the main markets. The term "souvenir" was not commonly used at that time, but everyone was eager to obtain a copy as a keepsake. The horsemen struggled to navigate through the crowd, resembling a rehearsal for a stampede. The next essay portrays another scene of congestion, where crowds gather to observe the decorative lighting but face difficulty in passing through. Countless hours are spent crowding at the Arbat Gate, which is adorned with decorative lights. The theme of the crowd, presented in a comical and playful manner, unfolds once again. Once more, the protagonist manages to escape unharmed, but not

58   *Vladimir Nemirovich-Danchenko and the Moscow Art Theatre*

before scolding a disgruntled woman and continuing his search for a subject to captivate the reader's attention. He hopes to engage in conversation with some provincial village leaders, which initially seems promising. However, an obstacle arises as all the elders have gone to the zoo.

The correspondent from *The Field* diligently follows every detail, striving to coordinate the story with the photographer as instructed by the editor. We catch glimpses of tall pillars decorated with enormous Monomakh Hats, vibrant kiosks displaying patriotic flags, the Duma building, and the governor's house adorned with illuminated signs. Additionally, we witness the incessant rain and the mud on the platform where the tsar's train is scheduled to arrive. Moreover, we observe "wooden houses painted green, blue, and brown" on the outskirts of the city beyond the tracks.

Now, imagine composing an essay in which you were already aware of the events at Khodynka. In such a case, this locale would be ideal, encompassing the conveniently located Petrovsky Palace across the street. It is at this palace where a serenade for the tsar's couple is organized under the balcony, in accordance with protocol. Furthermore, it includes a procession stretching all the way to the Kremlin, complete with numerous carriages and the thirty-two adjutants-general assigned to carry the canopy. On either side of this scene, we have chimneyed suburban houses in one direction and the vast horizon with its pristine forest in the other. Even if you knew the eventual outcome, there is no reason to omit passages that express the author's affection for the bustling crowds, the delightful scent of freshly cut wood, the vibrant gingerbread decorations, and the intriguing characters encountered along the way. For example, the author's carriage getting stuck next to a landau with liveried footmen:

> A short distance away, there is a large coach occupied by an elderly merchant wearing glasses, accompanied by a merchant's wife draped in a shawl, their children, and maids—a total of twelve individuals. Behind us lies an even more fascinating sight—an unconventional tilbury gig that cannot be categorized as either a tilbury gig or a carriage, but resembles a simple Russian cart. Seated in the driver's seat is a pleasant and stout figure with a landlord-like air, skillfully guiding the horse.

The essayist is embarrassed by the fact that he, like everyone else, is so captivated by the decorative lighting. It feels like a fairy tale, even though they are just electric light bulbs. He questions why he becomes so carried away and reflects on the challenges that come with aging. Nevertheless, he can still surrender to his dreams, which feel like fairy tales but have substance. He illustrates this by describing how he envisions complete satisfaction, modest material wealth for workers, a clear conscience, justice, and individual freedom. He acknowledges that the dream of individual freedom may be nothing more than a fairy tale, but he is still willing to spend hours gazing at the

Everything Is Nearby 1886–1896 59

beautiful lighting amidst the crowd. Nemirovich-Danchenko, however, does not look down upon simple amusements. He understands the pleasure that comes from being in a crowd and is intrigued by the emerging psychological characteristics in people.

On the night of May 18, after a grand performance, Moscow's leading actors appeared on stage in an epilogue called "Life of the Tsar," representing the Russian people. A correspondent from *The Field* witnessed this performance and reported that "Tomorrow is a national festival at Khodynka Field." Upon sending this report off to St. Petersburg, Nemirovich-Danchenko went to see what was happening at 1:00 a.m. Khodynka Field looked picturesque with scattered tents, campfires, and people sleeping in groups. The writer was tempted to join the crowd and spend the night, witnessing the start of the holiday the next day. However, he ultimately decided to go home.

The writer aimed to make the reader experience the events with him and live through the perspective of an ordinary citizen who had the opportunity to go everywhere. To gather information, the writer decided to take a common approach of talking to ordinary people, such as cooks, coachmen, and water carriers. The writer mentions a cook who had gone to *The Field* but returned empty-handed, warning the writer not to go due to overcrowding. The cook then began sharing unbelievable stories. The water carrier also returned from Khodynka recounting a terrifying incident where a giant keg of beer fell and caused casualties. Despite the chaos, the water carrier managed to fulfill his duty without spilling any water. On the sidewalk, a janitor passes by without a hat, sobbing, and waving his hands. He explains that he's all right but his wife is missing. They went to Khodynka together, and he fears not returning with a royal mug.

He takes a cab to the national celebration, where he meets people coming and going.

> There are a lot of empty spaces, hilly, overgrown with grass, covered here and there with logs. On the hills is a group of ordinary people resting and sleeping. Although he does not ask them, they did indeed come from Khodynka Field.

Nemirovich-Danchenko believes he saw 200,000 or 300,000 people on the way.

> Some correspondents describe the faces of the returnees as exhausted and oppressed. I did not find that to be true. I did not see any fun, true, but the idea that the ordinary Russian has an oppressed and tortured face is a fiction of cheap sentiment. It's much deeper than that. He is so hardy, patient, and able to restrain his feelings for a long time that he seems indifferent even in the tragic moments of his existence. You and I are nervous and quickly express our feelings on our face, but the ordinary Russian is more elusive.

60 Vladimir Nemirovich-Danchenko and the Moscow Art Theatre

He can listen to what they have to say but admits he does not share the ordinary passion for stories "that make your hair curl"—a phrase invariably used in such cases.

Disaster may have struck at Khodynka, but why exaggerate... (The habit of self-preserving skepticism).

I saw some trucks normally used to transport furniture, and I thought: On a holiday when all the workers are free, who wants to transport things, not just from the city to somewhere outside, but from somewhere to the city. I did not realize they were carrying corpses from Khodynka.

Trucks come and go. But also coaches and baby carriages; people have still bought tickets for the stands; nothing has been canceled.

Across from Khodynka Field, the tsar is staying at Petrovsky Castle. After half an hour, he enters the balcony. Hooray. "Glory." The choir sings under the baton of an eminent musician-composer-conductor. Finally, delegations arrive in order. Among them are actors from the imperial theatres, craft masters from Kolyvan, delegations of Moscow cab drivers, and representatives from the society of horse race enthusiasts. Hurrahs for Tsar Nicholas's speech followed a strict order of presentation, which included specific icons from cathedrals that the tsar's family would touch. The tsar's office had prepared an address in advance, which did not mention the Khodynka disaster. The tsar remained faithful to the prepared text. His sorrow over the incident would be addressed later, with visits to hospitals and attending a memorial service for the trampled dead.

Nemirovich-Danchenko crossed the road from Petrovsky Castle. The grandstands were not very full. A Roma chorus and a restaurant were set up on *The Field*. Durov the clown performed and released a balloon. Someone sold ice cream, while another sold "sour soup" (similar to kvass). Many people were there all night. Nemirovich-Danchenko moved from group to group, listening to their faces and stories. Gradually, the events of what happened became clear, but it was also crucial to understand how it could have happened. It was not greed that caused people to trample one another, despite their hunger for sausages and rolls. The shock was not only about what could have happened to an individual, but also about what an individual could become in a crowd. "Each of us is a human being, like all human beings, but when we gather in such large numbers without crowd control, something happens to us. We become like beasts."

Someone recounted standing next to a woman, a dressmaker wearing a hat.

She fell as people ran for safety. I wanted to help her up but knew I would fall too if I turned to assist her. And what do you know? I was the first one to trample over her, with everyone else following my lead. I tried my best not to hit her head with my heel.

Everything Is Nearby 1886–1896   61

Another group of people was tightly packed together.

> I managed to push my way through a little, only to discover a pile of fifteen corpses stacked on top of each other. Their faces were dark red or blue, their eyes already closed. Their hair was disheveled, stained with dusty blood around their nostrils and mouths.

Their clothing was torn, which made the victims appear as beggars, although they were not. Among the corpses, scattered copper and silver coins glistened, payment for their journey to the "other world." The sounds of the orchestra and the shrieks of the Roma choir were audible, while the May heat became stifling for the first time. He spotted another pile of bodies a little further away, and then, with each step, he encountered more corpses along the entire field. An entire mile? Yes, a whole mile. Finally, he descended to the adjacent ravine. "Watch your step, sir," someone softly warned him. Luckily, he avoided stepping on another lifeless body.

Earlier, Nemirovich-Danchenko had sent a diagram of the festival area to *The Field*, and it had now been published. It detailed the locations of stands, kiosks, tents, gift distribution points, and Petrovsky Palace. Someone was directly at fault. Someone neglected to cover the well tops and created narrow passages where people suffocated and lost consciousness even before the stampede began. Inexperienced public servants collected their salaries without understanding the impact of gathering hundreds of thousands of people in one place and how to manage them. (A few Cossacks stood near their tents to maintain order; later, they were found dead in a ditch.)

Khodynka shocked everyone with the extent of the disaster, but it had familiar elements: mismanagement by some and a submissive tendency in others to accept mismanagement. However, in his essays about Khodynka, Nemirovich-Danchenko aimed to explain something that was highly familiar in the context of the unfamiliar. He sought to comprehend the behavior of crowds, which had manifested in such a deadly, vivid, and horrifying manner for the first time. The actions of individuals within a crowd differ significantly from their personal characteristics.

This is where the age-old question of whether incompetent and foolish officials govern Moscow gives rise to a genuinely new problem. "Unforeseen circumstances in a crowd of hundreds of thousands of people have no limits," although Khodynka Field is the least suitable place to discuss this in philosophical terms. Nemirovich-Danchenko conveys his thoughts through documentation rather than philosophy or fear-mongering.

He intended to conclude his articles there, but the editorial office discreetly advised him otherwise. "You are correct that writing about the beauty of the dresses at the balls is inappropriate now. However, we still need a concluding piece from you. Abruptly ending the articles at the Khodynka disaster would be very awkward."

He apologized to readers for the delay and for writing a little more. The readers understood. The final essay contains no outraged exclamations. The Austrian Embassy canceled their ball due to the coincident death of Archduke Karl-Ludwig in his home country, but no one saw a reason to cancel other balls. "The women's faces radiated contentment and happiness that only those who know how to wear luxurious attire and can sense the delightful aura can display."

The orchestra played "The Flight of the Valkyries" as the royal train departed. Someone instructed the editorial boards and offices: "Make every effort to forget about Khodynka as soon as possible." Nemirovich-Danchenko shrugs. For him—and for many others—it *happened* and it is already a part of him and will continue to resonate. The essay concludes with a general summary: "A long series of images from the coronation period reflect the Russian people and their future as in a mirror."

Notes

1 Korf Nikolai (1834–1883) was a public figure, educator, public advocate, and organizer of the country's provincial schools.
2 Alexander Lensky (1845–1910) was an actor and playwright and later Head Director of the Maly Theatre.
3 Sergei Chernevsky (1839–1901) was a stage director. Anatoly Geltser (1852–1918) was a stage designer.
4 Mikhail Fokine (1880–1942) was a groundbreaking choreographer and dancer.
5 Maria Abramova (1865–1892) was an actress and manager who formed her own theatre company in Moscow.
6 Camille Flammarion (1842–1925) was a French astronomer and popular author of more than fifty books on astronomy.
7 Nikolai Efros (1867–1923) theatre critic, journalist, editor, screenwriter and playwright, film critic, translator, theatre historian, and historiographer of MAT.
8 Nikolai Karyshev (1855–1905) was an economist, statistician, zemstvo activist, and journalist.
9 Anna Brenko (1848–1934) was an actress and manager who founded a company of her own in Moscow in 1879. Fyodor Korsh (1852–1923) was an entrepreneur, playwright, translator, and lawyer who formed his own company, a commercial operation, with former members of Benko's troupe.
10 Aleksei Pisemsky (1820–1881) was a playwright with a social justice agenda.
11 Olga Knipper (Olga Knipper-Chekhov, 1868–1959) was a leading MAT actress and Chekhov's wife.
12 *My Life in the Russian Theatre*, 46.
13 Ivan Moskvin (1874–1946) actor and charter member of MAT.
14 Spassky Gate, also translated as Savior Gate, is the main gate on the eastern wall of the Moscow Kremlin that faces Red Square.
15 Tverskaya Gate was once one of the main gates to the city of Moscow. It was located on Tverskaya Street close by what is now Pushkin Square.
16 Khodynka Field was a large open space in the north-west area of Moscow at the beginning of the present-day Leningrad Prospect. It takes its name from the small Khodynka River which used to cross the neighborhood. See *Russia Beyond*. "The Khodynka tragedy: A coronation ruined by a stampede." https://www.rbth.com/history/332466-khodynka-tragedy-coronation.
17 Kitai Gorod [China Town] was a trading and business area of Moscow.

3 Opening 1896–1899

Founding Meeting of MAT

The meeting of MAT's founders took place on Wednesday, June 22, 1897.

The history of MAT, which henceforth becomes Nemirovich-Danchenko's life for the next forty-six years, is well known. Even if people haven't read the books, most well-informed Russians remember much of what happened in MAT's early years. Specifically, they remember how the actors lived in a commune at Pushkino,[1] rehearsed in a barn, and traveled to different cities in search of objects and impressions useful for their inaugural production, Alexey Tolstoy's play *Tsar Fyodor Ivanovich*. They remember how six actors auditioned for the title role, and Ivan Moskvin, who eventually played the role, was the least expected to get it. They remember how Nemirovich-Danchenko studied with him individually at the gatekeeper's lodgings. Nemirovich-Danchenko remembered the evening of the first performance: like Stanislavsky before the beginning, when the music had already started, drowning out Nemirovich-Danchenko's send-off speech, he began to dance to encourage his colleagues. He remembered how the assistant director told him to leave the stage, and how he cried in the wings from the insult. And how the production was a triumph. And how it was an even greater triumph when *The Seagull* opened two months later, and the actors did not immediately understand the meaning of the silence, and the audience was numb, shocked. And then they kissed and hugged each other on stage. People remembered all this too quickly and consistently to dismiss it as a theatrical legend. Instead, it has become part of "a Russian family's traditions," a legacy of the nation's home-grown memory.

But almost nothing remains from the meeting at the Slavic Bazaar. Nor is there a "long, long" letter Nemirovich-Danchenko allegedly prepared but did not send to Stanislavsky about everything said at the meeting. Nemirovich-Danchenko remembered that at Lubimovka,[2] where they went after spending many hours at the restaurant, Stanislavsky armed himself with pen and paper to record everything they agreed on and continued talking about. But no one has found these records. There is a note from Stanislavsky to one of his closest comrades in the Society of Art and Literature, Luzhsky. "Dear Vasily! I'm back and would very much like to see you. I was hoping you

DOI: 10.4324/9781003486282-3

64 *Vladimir Nemirovich-Danchenko and the Moscow Art Theatre*

could write and tell me how to arrange it. We must talk about many things."
It is natural to assume that Stanislavsky would bring Luzhsky into negotiations with Nemirovich-Danchenko. There is also a business card with the
capital letters V. I. N-D, a crossed-out address, "Myasnitskaya, Chudovsky
Lane, Scherbakov house," and a handwritten new address: "Granatny Lane,
Stupishin House." In pencil on the back: "I will be at the Slavic Bazaar at one
o'clock. May I see you there?" While sorting the archive, someone saved this
card in an envelope that Stanislavsky wrote: "The famous first meeting with
Nemirovich-Danchenko. The first moment of the Art Theatre's foundation."

MATs First Season

On July 7, Stanislavsky read *Tsar Fyodor Ivanovich* to the troupe; the scenery models were already prepared.[3] No one seriously considered the work
schedule in which *Tsar Fyodor's* rehearsals interspersed and overlapped with
Chekhov's play. Stanislavsky moved forward with his director's copy of *The
Seagull* while they prepared the historical drama, which centered around
the theme of "awakening the earth to life and the movement associated
with it." They felt a little uneasy about juggling two plays—shouldn't they
focus on one thing at a time? Were these transitions causing unintentional
distractions?

At first, the organizers thought it made sense for Stanislavsky to direct
Tsar Fyodor with the help of Alexander Sanin, and *The Seagull* with the
help of Nemirovich-Danchenko. In May, he wrote to Chekhov about this
arrangement, describing the sound score and lighting:

> In the foreground, it will be completely dark. In the depths of the stage
> on the right, the moon will rise, first red and large, then whiter and
> smaller. By the start of the performance, the stage will be flooded with
> moonlight.

- The sounds of a returning herd of cows and sheep.
- Distant ringing of bells.
- Distant sound of a watchman's clapper.
- Shouts of individual voices from behind the house.
- Distant singing of *Do Not Tempt Me* from across the lake.
- Piano playing in the house.
- The clapper of the night watchman. Several times the sharp cry of a
  seagull.
- A corncrake or brown creeper on the lakeshore.
- A herd of cows and goats passing by during the line, "But try to
  praise Duse in front of her! Oh, no!"
- In the third act, there's an atmosphere of pre-departure confusion,
  with the main door wide open. So, when Trigorin crosses the terrace
  to retrieve his book, he must jump over many travel items.

Opening 1896–1899 65

While Stanislavsky worked on the director's plan for *The Seagull*, Nemirovich-Danchenko suggested that rehearsals for *Tsar Fyodor* could start in his absence: "Begin and coordinate it as you see fit." However, they couldn't maintain their strict division of duties (one doing this, the other doing that, and so on). At Neskuchnoye, Nemirovich-Danchenko repeatedly read *Tsar Fyodor* out loud. "A fantastic play! It's a gift from God." He was already living through this beautiful play. He eagerly agreed with Stanislavsky so that he, not Luzhsky or Sanin, but he ("me" is underlined twice in the letter) could work with the actors and convey to them the infectious happiness he had derived from the play.

Later, Nemirovich-Danchenko wrote about other aspects that *Tsar Fyodor* brings to light:

- "The seed" [fundamental subject] is "Russian truth." Contrasting thoughts: their origins and variations, from engaging with European truth to bankruptcy and future transformation. What are the intriguing features of this captivating Russian truth that interest the West?
- Clashing with Reason: Pushkin's Boris Godunov ("The sacred temple is a rationalist Russia") and political bankruptcy.
- How Russian poetry and art also evoke sentiment.
- The fusion of East and West.
- The virtues of a woman: humility, integrity, and heartfelt wisdom.
- The femininity of the Slavs.
- The darker side of the national genius, its exhaustion, and the conflicting forces:

  - Religiosity vs. hypocrisy
  - Bravery vs. rudeness
  - Anarchism vs. robbery
  - Idealism vs. ruthless cruelty
  - Perceptiveness vs. trickery
  - Sensitivity and tolerance for the present vs. laziness
  - Meekness vs. slavery

- Intuition instead of rationality. "We must know the heart of man." Then Dostoevsky … An understanding of honor and freedom, and tolerance for weakness.
- No castles, no constraints, no walls."

The following statement refers to Alexey Tolstoy himself, not the play, but it highlights what MAT could learn from him.

- The ultimate goal: the desire to transform Russian truth.
- Through dreams, through art. It's no coincidence that Tolstoy says, "This supreme, free, pure truth is the artist, John of Damascus."[4]

66 *Vladimir Nemirovich-Danchenko and the Moscow Art Theatre*

Curious notes. But this was just one of the ideas Nemirovich-Danchenko "transferred" from himself to the production.

According to the First Season Report, Nemirovich-Danchenko conducted eighteen rehearsals for *Tsar Fyodor* (no one specified the number of one-on-one sessions or the additional hours rehearsing with Moskvin). Stanislavsky named Sanin as co-director of *The Seagull*. The credits hardly mattered. Everyone knew who directed *Tsar Fyodor* and *The Seagull*. It wasn't one or the other, not even both together, but "the perfect innovator," "someone formed from a strange merger of you and me," as Nemirovich-Danchenko would later write to Stanislavsky. The contributions from each can be deduced. You can hear the longing of the steppe's night bird from Neskuchnoye in *The Seagull*'s sound score. You can also recognize elements taken from the Khodynka disaster in the next season's scene from Alexei Tolstoy's *The Death of Ivan the Terrible*, where everyone pushes into one another, creating an image of enclosure, waiting in cramped quarters, a spectacle of violent instincts in masses packed together. But more important than identifying initial contributions was the logic behind their transformations.

There is a special joy in sharing at a high level, when memories and desires are infectiously transferred to another, and then separated from both of you into the automatic power of a stage image created by both and yet neither of you. It was fortunate that they didn't make ends meet in the first year and instead mainly lived with the happiness that comes from self-fulfillment. The dry Report of the First Season was surprisingly cheerful, stating, "It will be difficult to determine where our personal, private life ends and our official, communal, business 'service' begins. Our cause is precious because this so-called 'service' is our life."

When someone suddenly experiences such a happy change in their life and circumstances, it's natural to search for the person responsible and without whom it would be impossible. Meyerhold, who was initially Nemirovich-Danchenko's student, associated this joy with the "transformation" of all his previous possibilities based on what he learned from Stanislavsky. The Philharmonic School seemed dull and weak, causing him to cool off toward his teacher. Similarly, Luzhsky found his years in the Society of Art and Literature to be difficult and joyless. Stanislavsky's classes were merely exercises in stage technique for him. He learned the "craft" by trying to deliver his lines fluently and faithfully. However, now he was able to "create." What can he attribute this miracle to if not the arrival of Nemirovich-Danchenko? These unfortunate comparisons lingered with Stanislavsky and Nemirovich-Danchenko, even beyond the grave, as they were, in fact, one creative entity. They were a happy "someone."

The Hermitage Theatre, which was recently converted from a warehouse, was damp and cold, and nothing was prepared. The floors were bare, and candles had to be used for lighting. They even had to wear their overcoats in the auditorium.

We were rehearsing the scene of Prince Shuisky's reconciliation with Boris Godunov, and it was thrilling to hear the sounds of our voices in that dark, damp, cold space where we couldn't see the ceiling or the walls, with melancholic, gigantic shadows creeping around. It was inspiring to feel that the "soul" we all loved was seated there in the empty dark stalls, listening to us.

Chekhov attended a rehearsal of *Tsar Fyodor* in September 1898.

In 1921, Olga Knipper reminisced about when everything was ahead of her: youth, homeland, and lifework. This memory painted the past in a rosy hue and helped her experience it as a double happiness. But it was also an absolute joy to the touch, just like the fabric of the green stage curtain, the streaks of wax on the dark glass bottles, the white cloth covering the table in the auditorium—where icons rested and water was prepared for prayer blessings—on a sunny day.

The Foundation and Early Trials of MAT

"It was fortunate that we did not know everything and did not have high expectations because if we had foreseen it, we probably would not have proceeded." This ironic statement from Nemirovich-Danchenko's memoirs refers to more than unforeseen organizational difficulties. The initiator of the Slavic Bazaar meeting likely did not have a precise plan for what he wanted to say: "We are starting a revolution in the theatre; would you lend me a hand?" Nemirovich-Danchenko was forty years old when MAT opened (Figure 3.1). It is an age when individuals typically solidify their established lives. Who begins as a revolutionary at forty? He was simply looking for someone to help him complete and enhance his previous work.

He had a rough idea of the repertoire for the future theatre: Henrik Ibsen, Gerhart Hauptman, and Chekhov, none of whom had been produced on the Russian stage yet. It was clear who would join the troupe and the advantages of having a company of actors who shared the same ideas. Nemirovich-Danchenko attempted to involve entrepreneur Fyodor Korsh in his plans, but the proposal did not interest him. He had a similar conversation with actor and director Alexander Fedotov with no results.[5] It was only natural to continue searching, and that's when Stanislavsky's name came up. Nemirovich-Danchenko may have been aware that Stanislavsky was seeking a partner to embark on a professional career. At one point, Stanislavsky assumed that his partner would be Mikhail Lentovsky, a famous and adventurous impresario. Stanislavsky had staged Hauptmann's play *The Ascension of Hannele* with a company Lentovsky had assembled and in premises he had rented. Critic Nikolai Efros praised the performance in *News of the Day*. Newspapers interviewed the director, who spoke about his plans for a Public Theatre in Moscow and his intention to continue working with the same actors. He mentioned the need to "discipline our future actors, wean them from provincial and stage habits, and instill in them a sense of the high seriousness of their work." However, it was naive to expect great seriousness from Lentovsky,

68 *Vladimir Nemirovich-Danchenko and the Moscow Art Theatre*

so it was not surprising that things did not work out with him. There were also rumors that Stanislavsky intended to professionalize the amateurs who performed with his Society of Art and Literature.

Preliminary conversations between Nemirovich-Danchenko and Stanislavsky most likely took place at the First Congress of Stage Actors in March 1897. They both participated in the meeting and heard several speakers discuss the idea of a public theatre (not sponsored by the government) from the podium, so the idea was in the air. It was only natural for them to meet. And each one could safely assume that the other would assist in achieving a specific and sufficiently firm goal. But the goal will still shift and transform beautifully.

Think about the year that separated the June meeting at the Slavic Bazaar from another day in June. On that day, the young actors of the Partnership for the Establishment of the Moscow Public Theatre called out to one another at the Pushkino train station. They hired taxis for a ride to their summer cottages or walked straight to the theatre-shed in the parkland of the neighboring estate, where the owner had provided space for rehearsals. Now, imagine this year as if it were lived and photographed as a double exposure. The surface layer showed plans, goals, and considerations, but beneath that layer, another layer materialized.

At first glance, everything seemed to go haywire. Plan after plan ended in frustration. They had envisioned starting performances at the Paradise Theatre in the winter of 1897/1898, but it did not happen. They informed the theatrical press that the idea of a Joint Stock Company of Public Theatres and Audiences was well underway, when in reality, only Stanislavsky's printed plans for the project existed. They had planned for famous actors like Kondrat Yakovlev, Nikolai Roshchin-Insarov, and Ivan Shuvalov to participate, but their involvement was still uncertain. The budget was also uncertain. Eventually, they spent an entire day together in November and made a detailed estimate of expenses. However, the question of where all the money would come from remained. They sent a proposal to the City Duma, but even the most intelligent Moscow Duma members couldn't understand the rationale. They even discussed subsidized performances for low-income people, but none of the proposals received a subsidy or even a prompt refusal.

Eventually, they raised money from acquaintances and wealthy patrons who supported the Society of Art and Literature and the Philharmonic School. The gesture had a touch of status-seeking, not from becoming famous with the start-up, but from pride in supporting a new idea. Konstantin Ushkov was the first to sign up, emphasizing that he was the first. When they published the Report on the Activities of the First Year (June 14, 1898–February 28, 1899), they would highlight the names of thirteen members of the unofficial Association for the Establishment of a Public Theatre in Moscow. These names were K. S. Alexeev; Sav. T. Morozov; D. P. Vostriakov; Sergei. T. Morozov; A. E. Hennert; V. I. Nemirovich-Danchenko; K. A. Gukhale; K. V. Osipov; N. P. Koznov; I. A. Prokofiev; I. A. Lukutin; K. K. Ushkov; W. K. Figrang.

Even with careful planning, things did not go smoothly. When undertaking projects like this, there is always the worry that someone else will adopt and take your idea to the public while you face delays. They had initially hoped to lease the Shelaputinsky Theatre in Theatre Square, but their plans were delayed, and the Maly Theatre quickly set up a branch there. As a result, they had to open at the Hermitage Theatre on Carriage Row, which was located some distance from the city center. Unfortunately, this location came with its drawbacks—there was a noisy public garden nearby and a pervasive smell of alcohol, which did not align with their desire to create an attractive and sophisticated atmosphere for their theatre. Additionally, the intense public interest surrounding their venture was not in line with their intentions. There were rumors that Stanislavsky planned to present his own students at a new theatre, and people expected experimental productions and reforms. The press also fueled the rivalry between Nemirovich-Danchenko and Alexander Lensky of the Maly Theatre, adding to the excitement.

They had envisioned preparing a repertoire of ten or fifteen productions and intended to debut in Moscow since an attempt to enlist provincial theatres for tryouts did not work out. Rehearsal was of utmost importance to them, but they faced a challenge—they had nowhere to rehearse since the unheated barn at Pushkino, which they had hoped to use, was unavailable until fall, and the theatre's owner was unwilling to release the venue early. Nemirovich-Danchenko often remarked, "I would rather resign from the entire project than have disorder within it." Despite this, changes in their plans did not bother him, and he didn't rush to get back on track with their original plan. He understood that the enterprise had already gained its own momentum and significance, providing him with the freedom to move forward with his own, albeit unclear, planning.

A busy year passed, during which he dealt with negotiations, calculations, and countless unanswered reports. He sought answers in various offices, constantly worried about time and money running out. Nonetheless, everything continued to progress, and by the year's end, the deeper layers of the project began to reveal themselves. He experienced this period just as he should have, recognizing that even the delay proved beneficial. They now knew what they didn't know before.

Nemirovich-Danchenko had been aware of Stanislavsky prior to singling him out in his writings about theatre. However, he still harbored doubts about wealthy individuals involving themselves in something that was a source of livelihood for others. Nevertheless, he couldn't help but notice the complete dedication that Stanislavsky had for his work, even if it occasionally turned into a whim. Being a man of action, Nemirovich-Danchenko was naturally cautious around people who indulged in their whims. Despite holding a popular opinion of Stanislavsky's productions, Nemirovich-Danchenko had a profound discovery when he experienced them firsthand. It's easy to admire something upon initial encounter, but much more challenging to overcome preconceived notions and change one's perspective and emotions. Like most

70 *Vladimir Nemirovich-Danchenko and the Moscow Art Theatre*

audiences, he was familiar with Stanislavsky's crowd scenes and consistently praised their cohesiveness. However, Stanislavsky's work offered more than just crowds and cohesiveness. For instance, take the festival scene in *Uriel Acosta*.[6] This scene featured visually diverse compositions on a variety of stage platforms, beautiful costumes, ceremonial bows from the cavaliers, dance-like movements, and a dramatic expansion of space around the title character. In a moment of panic, the rabbis and guests emerged from beneath the stage, donning black and yellow prayer shawls over their multi-colored costumes, all in response to a sinister trumpet call from below.

Stanislavsky was known as well for his fondness for using real weapons and antiques on stage. The public either praised this aspect or grumbled about the cost and historical accuracy. One notable example was Stanislavsky's portrayal of Othello, where he brought a nervous dynamism to the character, making him relatable to modern audiences. Regardless of whether the sword at his hip was an authentic weapon for a Venetian Moor or a samurai sword, what mattered was the skill and fright-factor with which he wielded the antique weapon that seemingly appeared in his hand. And wasn't Stanislavsky correct in his appreciation for real objects on stage? These objects held value because they were authentic, devoid of clichéd staging or the obligatory placement of a sofa on stage right for the tenth consecutive play. Everyone knew where it belonged and that the love scene would inevitably take place there. Likewise, a table and two chairs were expected on stage left. Therefore, it was understandable for this talented director to collect rarities—fabrics, clothing, weapons, household items—even without knowing which production they might benefit, simply because they were fascinated by their symbolic energy. However, symbolic life can also be found in ordinary objects. Take, for example, *The Seagull's* worn-out carpet spread on the grass in the garden, the summer hammock that everyone had at their dacha, the croquet mallets, the broken glass in the old greenhouse, the old magazines endlessly read in the summer, and the flapping curtain on the homemade stage in the garden. These were not the typical stage properties, but rather representations of practical life, promising a fresh "stage life" instead of a stale "stage scene." It was about faithfulness not to theatrical replica, but to the reality these recognizable objects represented. Everyone knew that Stanislavsky possessed a rare imagination and the unique ability to find the stage means to bring it to life. However, the recurring themes in his productions, such as the piercing sound of a trumpet breaking the silence, were not as obvious. This sound would reappear throughout Stanislavsky's directing career, even in Byron's play *Cain*, where it would return from heaven. Equally persistent was the festival motif, where the world seemed to overflow with itself.

One example of this overflowing world can be seen in Stanislavsky's direction of Hauptman's play *The Sunken Bell*. Here, the world gushed, echoed, and ran over itself, creating an elusive and captivating mist of materiality followed by a fantastic, luminous evaporation. In Stanislavsky's productions, rhythm, light, sound, and subjectivity combined to create their own

Opening 1896–1899 71

self-activating, plot-forming effects and a poetic atmosphere. The directorial plot emerged from these elements, separate from the play's literary plot, and possessed its own distinct system and power.

It was perplexing for Nemirovich-Danchenko to witness the strength with which Stanislavsky built his directorial plot, only to see it crumble when the forces of his plot and the author's plot clashed. This is precisely what happened in *The Sunken Bell*, resulting in a production that fell apart. The failure was attributed to a lack of firmness in the internal lines, ambiguity or distortion of the psychological motivations, and ultimately the fragility of the play's core. Nemirovich-Danchenko did not direct this criticism toward Hauptman, however, as Stanislavsky had removed the play's dramaturgical core. Stanislavsky's production values clashed with their self-acting power. Shouldn't they be disciplined by a clearer sense of purpose? Nemirovich-Danchenko considered having a conversation with Stanislavsky about all this, but he was in no hurry to do so. Instead, he began exploring the possibilities of this new concept of "directorial plot-forming," which involved rhythm, sound, light, subjectivity, and the presence of human figures on stage. He sought to understand how these elements could be counterpointed with the traditional literary plot.

Although MAT would later popularize the term "subtext," it is worth noting that the concept covers a broader range than commonly believed. In the realm of new drama, starting with Ibsen, there existed both an external textual plot and an internal "subtextual" plot. These two plots had a complex and tense relationship with each other and contributed to the electric energy of this new form of drama. Literary critic Naum Berkovsky recognized and articulated this observation,[7] and his words will guide our discussion. (It is important to note that these ideas are not limited to the work of a specific playwright.) Berkovsky refers to Hauptmann's play, *Michael Kramer*,[8] noting that the playwright skillfully concealed certain values behind others while maintaining a strict realist approach devoid of symbolism. This play's hidden meanings are directly connected to its more obvious ones, much like a smaller story nested within a larger one. The difference between the hidden and explicit values lies primarily in their scale and how the playwright manipulates them in different situations. The dramatic plot carries a continuous subtext that relentlessly presses against the surface of the text, but without success.

MAT's first challenge was to express the subtextual plot on stage—the clash between the smaller story and the larger overarching narrative, the interaction between the textual and subtextual plots. In *The Seagull*, for example, we witness the collision between a "plot for a short story"—the tale of a young provincial girl seduced out of sheer boredom—and a broader story about Russian life, loneliness, love, and the universal human condition. MAT's initial years and its journey can also be seen as a conflict and interplay between these two plots. The presence of a larger subtextual plot helps us make sense of how they navigated the intricate and fragmented aspects

72 Vladimir Nemirovich-Danchenko and the Moscow Art Theatre

of their material existence. Nemirovich-Danchenko possessed an intuitive understanding of human affairs, and he now felt that the time had come for their arduous efforts to flourish.

Rivalry with the newly established second company of the Maly Theatre was unnecessary, as even MAT's failures were not fatal. He was more concerned about overthinking than the possibility of not achieving his desired outcome. "Of course, the more precise we are in executing our tasks, the more we will accomplish. But to realize our dreams, we must accept the limitations of reality." Nemirovich-Danchenko often used the phrase, "Delve into it, delve deeper into it." Hence, it is important for us to thoroughly explore the meaning behind this phrase. He was not a stubborn perfectionist but both admired and was alarmed by Stanislavsky's uncompromising attitude in seeking the true meaning of something that impressed and delighted him on stage. Taking the necessary time and effort to achieve what is possible from an actor is not unreasonable, but it is also important to accept what an actor cannot do.

Nemirovich-Danchenko brought a sense of calmness to their work, not because he lacked emotion but because he had an intuitive understanding of the mental and physical effort required. He knew what was worth fighting for, what should be put one's soul into, and what was better left alone. He possessed unwavering determination and had a powerful healing effect on others, but he also knew when to let go, even of his own failures. It is pointless to let failures cast doubt on everything else; they should be acknowledged and released. Four years later, after experiencing significant triumphs, he, who was not one for paradoxes, remarked: "The complete failure of one production or another does not diminish the overall impression of a large artistic endeavor." It takes courage to hold onto this belief, and who better than Nemirovich-Danchenko could embody it?

It would be easy to assume that everything aligned with their artistic goals and that everyone would recognize the success of the MAT. However, by 1898, there was ample evidence that the Maly Theatre was not falling behind and that MAT was not so far ahead. The Maly Theatre even anticipated MAT's decision to eliminate bows and applause during the action. Moreover, the Maly Theatre had a diverse repertoire, performing numerous long-running plays alongside novelties. It should not be overlooked that the Maly Theatre's repertoire included works by renowned playwrights such as Ostrovsky, Denis Fonzivin, Alexander Griboyedov, and Nikolai Gogol—all produced during the 1897/1898 season. They also staged plays by Shakespeare, Schiller, and Moliere in the same season.

As for objections to the Maly Theatre's set designs and standardized furniture, the Report of the First Season revealed that MAT used old decorations from the Society of Art and Literature for Goldoni's *Mistress of the Inn*. Additionally, they relied on rented furniture and props for the modern Austrian play *Greta's Happiness*, found at the discretion of a shareholder. They even used scenery from *Greta's Happiness* for Ostrovsky's *The Poor*

Bride, despite the play's setting in old-world Moscow, which conflicted with the fin de siècle Vienna scenery. Similarly, they utilized the first-act scenery from Alexey Pisemsky's *Men Above the Law* for Turgenev's *Breakfast at the Leader's*. This self-contradictory approach was followed by discussions about their search for Turgenev's style and the exploration of the play's color and diction.

Figure 3.1 Vladimir Nemirovich-Danchenko (~1898, the opening year of MXAT). By permission of the Moscow Art Academic Theatre.

74 *Vladimir Nemirovich-Danchenko and the Moscow Art Theatre*

Despite everything, the entire operation was quite successful, and there was some justice in the fact that no one remembered that they had performed Ostrovsky in a Viennese setting. Nobody recalled the poster for the premiere of *The Merchant of Venice* that stated, Before the start of the performance, they performed the national anthem *God Save the Tsar*. At the end of the season, MAT hosted an "artistic, music, and literary evening" as a fundraiser for the epilepsy ward at Moscow's Trinity Hospital. Actress Ekaterina Munt,[9] Meyerhold's first wife, recited *Dreams* by poet Semyon Nadson. The actors also participated in costumed tableaux vivants of Nikolai Nevrev's famous historical paintings. None of this seemed to matter ... After all, they started in a barn at Pushkino.

Personal and National Struggles Amid Historical Discord in *Tsar Fyodor Ivanovich*

Tsar Fyodor Ivanovich—the beginning. At Prince Shuisky's house, there is a wide passageway with tables wrapping around the corner. The feasting and crowding continue outside, creating a spectacle of generous and motley abundance. There are barrels of wine, cooked carcasses, mountains of apples on dishes, and geese and swans. These are not decorative fowls displayed ceremonially over the tables like in historical boyar paintings, but fowls meant for eating. People break off a leg and dip it in salt. The scene is filled with colorful and fanciful costumes, voices buzzing with their own unique tunes—some funny, some serious. The atmosphere is not disorderly or uncontrollable, thanks to the presence of drunkenness, but instead heightens the sense of people enjoying themselves.

Prince Shuisky, leader of one faction of the ruling council, is not characterized by the usual conservative stagnation. Instead, there is an energy of growth and life surrounding him. He believes that the people themselves know what is best for them—a life that grows and expands like a farmhouse, with solid walls that change only to accommodate growth. This perspective highlights the importance of family spirit in this production, as well as the themes of matchmaking, feasting, and a sprawling, tangled garden where nightingales sing until they run out of breath.

The characterization of Boris Godunov, leader of the other faction, also emphasizes the desire for a free nation and the strength of a national dream—a "sacred temple" of enlightened power. Stanislavsky and the designer Viktor Simov created a romantic setting for Godunov's chambers, resembling a dreamy garden with gilded decorations, flowers, and curling vines. The chamber-paradise even had a ceiling held up by realistic iron fastenings, reminiscent of ancient buildings. This setting served as a metaphor for Godunov's residence.

Stanislavsky used the principle of polyrhythm in the production. For example, in the scene of Prince Shuisky's feast, there were multiple rhythms at play. Those focused on a previous victorious war lived in the rhythm of a

Opening 1896–1899 75

domestic holiday, while others focused on eating and drinking and discussed Godunov's oppressive actions. The merchants, on the other hand, lived in a rhythm filled with wariness, fearing that after feasting, they might be pulled into something they should not interfere with. Stanislavsky discovered the polyrhythms of the play by juxtaposing the rhythms of feasting and conspiracy, state ritual and rebellion, and elaborate court etiquette with the fluidity of domestic life. This historical depiction of Russia captured its vibrant and captivating essence, highlighting the mutual bitterness of its extremes, while also emphasizing the importance of blood kinship. In essence, the production effectively reflected the polyrhythms present in the Russian national character.

The central focus of the production was Tsar Fyodor/Moskvin, whose deeply Russian talent and tragic sensibility made him the most suitable actor for the role. The rehearsals took place at the gatekeeper's house in Pushkino. Some believed the decision to rehearse at the gatekeeper's lodgings in Pushkino was due to a lack of alternative spaces. However, it also served as a creative clue for the actor portraying Fyodor. The choice of location emphasized that Fyodor's story was not solely "royal" but could be imagined to take place in any traditional Russian household, such as a provincial bourgeois house with a front garden or a peasant hut. Even the gatekeeper's lodgings, complete with a Russian stove, were representative of a familiar setting where the caretaker himself found resonance in Fyodor's character.

The theme of socio-political discord resonated deeply within Moskvin, reminiscent of a line from a letter written by Nemirovich-Danchenko about Tsar Fyodor: "I do not know of any literary character, including Hamlet, who is so near to my soul." This comparison to Hamlet suggests a connection to the theme of socio-political discord and the dissonance between morality and historical action. Fyodor's simplicity and Hamlet's madness disrupt conventional expectations of their respective situations: a tsar is expected to rule, and an avenger is expected to seek revenge. The introduction of Fortinbras, the true prince who would deploy 1,000 soldiers if necessary, raises questions about what is considered "good."

The production explores the concepts of the state and historical necessity, and how these align with the needs of the soul. All those who wrote about Fyodor's character felt the anguish and absurdity experienced by this mild-mannered individual burdened with royal duties. Moskvin internalized this torment of inadequacy, knowingly transferring his responsibilities onto others, without any illusions about his own capabilities as a tsar. In the end, his despair overwhelms him, prompting him to scream at the top of his lungs, "Executioners!" Finally, wearing his ceremonial robes, Fyodor collapses to the ground, sobbing with his head in his hands. In a state of despair, he utters his final words: "I wanted to do good, Irina … Everything was my fault!"

It didn't matter if some people thought Fyodor was simple-minded; the production wasn't about his "professional unsuitability" for the throne. Moskvin seemed to foresee that the dilemmas facing his character would soon torment Tsar Fyodor's real-life counterparts living in Moscow's shacks,

76 *Vladimir Nemirovich-Danchenko and the Moscow Art Theatre*

attics, and apartments. The twentieth century was barely approaching the doorstep, but some of its problems were already plain in the production created in 1898. The twentieth century would bring a dramatic, catastrophic involvement of "home," where individuals caught in historical events would have to balance their personal beliefs with societal expectations and historical circumstances. It also set the stage for the drama of individuals' creative vigor being paralyzed as their connection with history became polarized or even severed. The course of events directly impacts one's existence, but it is entirely independent of one's actions.

Artistic Innovation Meets Social Resonance in *The Seagull*

The Seagull is scheduled to open in two months.

Life becomes stagnant and fleeting, slipping away unnoticed. The monotony of days at home, which the actors will later refer to as "grinding time"— time that is crushed into powder and scattered into dust—represents the passing of your own life. Each character becomes acutely aware of this sensation, realizing the missed opportunities to truly live and urgently desiring to make up for lost time.

In the third act, the action transitions indoors. The characters navigate their way through a clutter of suitcases, ready to be sent ahead. They stumble around the dining table, peculiarly set for breakfast and amidst a chaotic pre-departure scene. The forthcoming scandals will prove to be embarrassing— the peculiar sound of a domestic dispute, tears shed over insufficient funds, a melodramatic plea from a woman over forty, falling to her knees, begging not to be left behind. However, the story does not commence in this manner.

The characters are not seeking pent-up frustration within closed doors, but rather the languor of the open air. This is why August holds such significance on the stage. As Nemirovich-Danchenko stated, "It is difficult to convey the 'feeling of August.' The weather during this time of year is superb, and the deep lyricism that Russian poets find in their contemplation of nature is at its brightest in August." The silent lightning, the evening rustling of leaves, the shadows, the fog enveloping the lake's banks, the mysterious whiteness of the fluttering curtain at the back of the stage, and the unsettling shimmer of the lake under the moon—the performance will draw inspiration from all these elements. The mood will permeate the people on the shore, intensifying their emotional anticipation. The distant church bells chime the same tune every night; a familiar bird sings its two-note song repeatedly each night, and the reddish low moon consistently rises and transforms into a bright silver glow. In a moment of tranquility, the irrevocable passage of time profoundly strikes you, and the anticipation becomes almost unbearable. This feeling necessitates a tangible expression.

Someone must arrive. Someone must say something. Treplev anxiously inspects the curtain and the stage set behind it, fearing that despite everything being in order, it may still amount to nothing. Without Nina, it will

Opening 1896–1899 77

be a failure—even if she is only slightly late. Treplev is already filled with excitement before the performance of his play, and the kiss Nina bestows upon him amidst the growing darkness under the elm tree merely signifies her reciprocated excitement. Nina arrives, breathless from her hurried sprint, driven by the fear of being late and the uncertainty of the day, unsure if she will make it in time—her time is limited. However, as critic Nikolai Efros recollected, she appears carefree, awkward, already stirred up, lacking harmony within her soul. Her eyes exhibit a tinge of anger rather than affection, naivety, or radiance.

For the first time in Russian theatre production history, a miracle of seamless and melodious development, characterized by a continuous flow of stage action, was achieved. This harmonious progression, in accordance with the principles of music, effectively conveyed a sense of life on the verge of eruption, capturing a pivotal moment of potential breakthrough that was both desirable and dramatic for all. *The Seagull* further captivated audiences with its remarkable portrayal of domestic authenticity, offering a sense of place that felt familiar, as if one resided within its very walls. However, this household lacked the conventional comfort often associated with such environments.

The final act unfolds in the evening, which begins around 4:00 p.m. due to the early onset of darkness. Outside the windows, the garden stands subdued, worn out from its previous uproar, while rain relentlessly pelts against the glass and gusts of wind shake the windows. Upon Nina's entrance, she seeks solace by wrapping herself in a shawl, visibly chilled to the core as she draws near the stove. Treplev, attempting to offer her some warmth, drapes a coverlet over her shoulders, but the once comforting heat has dissipated. As the wind whistles through an open door, slamming shut behind the departing guest, the footsteps fade away. Treplev gazes deeply into the red glow emanating from the stove, pondering for an extended period of time, before deliberately burning every piece of his writings, ensuring that nothing remains.

This extraordinary production owes much of its success to the musical element introduced by Meyerhold's portrayal of Treplev. He continuously conveyed a sense of discomfort, starting his performance with tremendous passion for achieving success, while simultaneously harboring a foreknowledge of failure. Meyerhold injected Treplev's character with personal suspicion, an intensifying resentment, and the torment of an unnatural sensation blended with a mindset of defiance against established norms. Furthermore, he skillfully managed to evoke the authenticity of Treplev's talent, albeit one that remained unspoken. As Nikolai Efros aptly expressed in his review, it can be likened to "a shadow of unconscious talent, a kind of premonition of talent."

In one of Chekov's letters from 1888, he wrote,

The suicide of Russian youth is a phenomenon unknown to Europe. On the one hand, there is physical weakness, nervousness, premature maturation, an intense thirst for life and truth, dreams as vast as the steppe, ceaseless activity, restless introspection, and a lack of knowledge

78 *Vladimir Nemirovich-Danchenko and the Moscow Art Theatre*

juxtaposed with expansive flights of thought. On the other hand, there is the vast steppe, with its harsh climate, bleak and stoic people burdened by a cold and weighty history, the Tartars, bureaucratic machinery, poverty, ignorance, and the dampness of the capital city, among other factors. In Western Europe, people perish due to the suffocating confines and restrictions of life, whereas our country offers boundless space. It is in this vastness that a small individual finds themselves lacking the strength to find their bearings.

Although this statement is from a letter unrelated to *The Seagull*, it provides valuable insight into the underlying themes and context of the play.

For Nemirovich-Danchenko, the home where Treplev eventually takes his own life represents a dwelling within the expansive steppe. In one of his notebooks, while sketching the evening landscape of the first act, he includes "steppe gull" as one of the sounds emitted by the birds.

We are in pursuit of the most subtle sensations, yet we find ourselves reliant on rudimentary stage instruments. In *The Seagull*, we require a rising moon, its reflection shimmering on the water, the ethereal veil of fog adorning the lake, and the glistening of dewdrops. How can we achieve this? What course of action shall we undertake?!

Simov, the masterful scenery designer, expressed his frustration with the outdated technology of the Hermitage stage. The estate and the lake failed to capture the desired effect; nevertheless, the scenery effectively conveyed the predominant theme: an overwhelming yearning aroused by the awe-inspiring vastness of the steppe. This yearning did not stem from destitution but rather from the abundance of life surrounding them and the anguish of our reckless squandering "beneath the snow." For instance, Maria Lilina's portrayal of Masha conveyed a sense of unraveling existence devoid of purpose,[10] receding into the realms "under the snow," enveloped in shame and anguish due to her perceived uselessness.

The premiere of *The Seagull* on December 17, 1898, as recounted by the most trustworthy recollections, finally crystallized the pivotal moment when Masha collapses onto the garden bench, weeping, and utters the words "I love Konstantin." In the final act, they still recall how she mechanically danced a waltz to music emanating from beyond the garden wall, a chance occurrence of Chopin's composition in an incongruous setting. (Masha, as they commented, appeared "unsightly in her coarse attire," "uncomely, gray Masha.") The audience felt incredibly sorry for Masha.

Writer Pyotr Boborykin brought the protagonist of his novel *Classmates* to witness a performance of *The Seagull*.[11] He is an "eternal student" who recently returned from exile. *The Seagull* captivates him, but he refuses to give in to it: "They should all perish, these whiners. But he does not feel sorry for any of them except the 'village girl' Masha, who drinks vodka."

Opening 1896–1899 79

Adhering to the reviewers' inclination to distinguish between "one of us" and "not one of us" in a production, Masha was identified as one of their own. Although they were inclined to single out Medvedenko in his disheveled woolen ensemble, they found nothing exceptional in his performance. It was essential for the characters to represent something universally relatable while also being deeply interconnected with one another. Masha's tears in the closing moments of the first act are "stirred by the allure of the lake, the enchantment of the moon, Treplev's play, and most profoundly, her love for Konstantin." At this juncture, everything resonates: Medvedenko's mundane and heartfelt but futile explanations; the ethereal rendition of Glinka's romance, *Do Not Tempt Me*, sung from across the lake; and Nina's recitation of the monologue about the World Soul in a protracted, melodious manner, surrendering herself not to the meaning but to the ambiance and the melody.

The music, the enchantment of a play exploring solitude performed beneath the luminous full moon, and the cohesive nature of every element cast a spell over the "village girl." Masha/Lilina adores this obscure symbolist play, not only because of her love for Konstantin but also for the play itself. Like in some seven years, everyone in provincial villages will embrace the musical symbolism of Alexander Scriabin and the symbolist poetry of Alexander Blok. The discovery of a home-like sentiment was one of the most genuine and relevant findings of the play, making it one of the most accurate representations in its genre. In less than a year, MAT garnered a deep and profound love from its audience, transcending the usual elitist appreciation for art meant for their consumption; they loved it profoundly and home-like, as the best in their own world.

...

In his letters and interviews, Nemirovich-Danchenko approached *The Seagull* cautiously, acknowledging the necessity of producing it but not expecting it to recoup its costs. He held no promises beyond artistic success. As the premiere drew near, the company should have been brimming with excitement. However, the endeavor was jolted by the censor's prohibition of Gerhart Hauptmann's *The Assumption of Hannele*,[12] which had already been prepared. This setback, coupled with the earlier failure of *Greta's Happiness*, severely shook Nemirovich-Danchenko's confidence as a director, given that his first professional production had been a disaster. Concerned individuals repeatedly voiced their worries, asking if he feared Chekhov falling ill again or not surviving another failure of *The Seagull*. At the eleventh hour, Stanislavsky lost his temper, insisting that nothing was ready and proceeding with the production would be impossible. Nemirovich-Danchenko couldn't help but fret, but his intuition didn't fail him. The play was enthusiastically embraced by audiences.

Consider the idea of "success" in terms of timeliness, maturity, and tailored for the moment. Nemirovich-Danchenko infused MAT with his love for *The Seagull*. He recognized the play's genius and sensed that its time had come, resonating with its intended audience. While there are various

80 *Vladimir Nemirovich-Danchenko and the Moscow Art Theatre*

audiences, the term "audience" does not accurately capture its essence for this particular play; it is the people within the auditorium. Boborykin's novel previously mentioned describes the lobby of the Hermitage Theatre during *The Seagull's* production. The audience's attire at this theatre was more modest compared to other venues. The Report of the First Season contained information on who received the most and least expensive seats, ticket distribution practices, and which performances were in highest demand. MAT provided tickets upon request from factories such as Bromley and Giro Tools, as well as the Jamgarov Bank, the Zoological Gardens staff, and sales clerks from the Faberge store. Although MAT only provided eighteen tickets for employees of the Zindel Weaving Factory, they distributed six hundred and sixty-four tickets for the Gustav Liszt Mechanical Factory. Some argued that in a metropolis like Moscow, these six hundred and sixty-four workers were but a drop in the ocean. Nevertheless, whether a drop or not, audiences expressed a genuine interest in watching *Antigone* and *The Seagull*. You can now envision them—independent and educated young women employed by the Jamgarov Bank in distant Nara or Mozhaysk, and young individuals from the Gustav Liszt Factory. However, their identities are challenging to discern from the photographs housed in the MAT Museum. There is a letter provided by a worker from Marichev's Workshop in Sokolniki, which expresses gratitude for the opportunity to witness the performance. This office worker's writing exhibits clarity and intelligence.

At this juncture, Nemirovich-Danchenko found himself contemplating his additional duty as the Director of the Repertoire, as indicated on MAT's poster. He possessed an entirely novel idea regarding the cultural requirements. He did not perceive these needs as polarized, dividing Russian culture into the so-called elite and the masses. He did not approve of art solely catering to the bourgeoisie and the intermission bar, but instead advocated for what he and his comrades referred to—with a term that may not be entirely accurate but held significant meaning for him and his circle—as "the common people," the democratic cohort. He firmly believed that if Maeterlinck displayed talent and seriousness, then democracy would also require Maeterlinck in due course, though not presently.[13]

Nemirovich-Danchenko recollected with profound distaste the nature of life in the past, ever since 1881 when *The New Times* began striving for an increase in its regular subscribers, specifically targeting purchasers of constipation medicine and respectable cemetery monuments. Like everyone else, he believed that this way of life would persist indefinitely. Where and why would it ever change? It seemed as if there were no alternative existence beyond bourgeois conservatism, with terrorism being its only opposing force. It appeared as if the endless murmurs in the halls of St. Petersburg University, where a young teacher was dismissed following a public lecture opposing the death penalty, did not exist. It seemed as if there were not numerous sites throughout Russia where everyday life thrived with vibrancy, significance, and conscientiousness.

Opening 1896–1899 81

MAT comprehended the essence of this vibrant life and belonged to it. Its stagecraft, dramatic works, and beauty represented its distinctive discovery.

Yearning for Purpose Amid Societal and Personal Challenges in *Three Sisters*

The Seagull did not enjoy the same level of longevity on stage as *Tsar Fyodor Ivanovich*. While its reforms were innovative at the time, they were not without flaws. However, the achievements made during this period laid the foundation for more harmonious and complete productions in the future.

Three Sisters can be seen, however, as the epitome of "Chekhovian theatre" and its enduring artistic formula. Nemirovich-Danchenko wrote to Chekhov prior to the premiere in January 1901, advising that the production should reveal the plot in a manner devoid of "shock effects" commonly found in affectedly dramatic scenes. Instead, the plot should unfold naturally within the ordinary flow of life. The staging of the play aimed to portray familiar elements such as name days, Shrovetide, fire, departures, the presence of a stove, a lamp, piano, tea, pie, drunkenness, twilight, night, living room, dining room, girls' bedroom, winter, fall, spring, and more. The stove on stage will be just as everyone recognizes, remembering the warmth of its big tiles just as if they had leaned against them themselves, just as if they had put their own hands on them and instantly taken them away, stinging from the cold. The large kerosene lamp, with its milky glass shade, would emit a glow reminiscent of the lamps found at home. The production team intentionally selected simple and relatable elements such as provincial wallpaper, the worn appearance of painted floors, and frayed Turkish carpets. A cuckoo clock that chimes tardily and then abruptly rushes to catch up, almost appearing embarrassed. Essentially, everything on stage aimed to mirror real life itself. As Nemirovich-Danchenko stated, "The difference between the stage and life is only in the author's worldview. All the life shown in this play has passed through the author's worldview, feelings, and temperament, and it has received a special coloring called poetry."

From the production of *Three Sisters* onwards, Nemirovich-Danchenko's words served as a guiding principle for Chekhov's productions at MAT. The essence of this approach involved refracting life into stage life-poetry, balancing relatability with a careful study and evaluation of authenticity. The exceptional direction of *Three Sisters* stemmed from the ability to effectively convey this poetic refraction, thereby creating an atmosphere that reflected the ebb and flow of life while maintaining a sense of authenticity. The dialogue in the play was imbued with a poetic quality that evoked associations and imagery beyond the spoken words. This approach incorporated the principles of music, including the introduction and development of voices, orchestration, understated rhythm, and tempo. The production team established an innovative development principle that avoided "shock effects." Instead of relying on established dramaturgical mechanics, they skillfully blended small

82 *Vladimir Nemirovich-Danchenko and the Moscow Art Theatre*

everyday events with a sustained thematic melody. Although the dialogue revolving around mundane activities like eating cake, signing papers, sitting in twilight, and correcting mistakes in high school assignments may initially be perplexing, the sustained thematic melody ensured that nothing stood alone. Instead, everything existed in a state of transition, where preceding events and future expectations cast their reflections on the present moment.

In this remarkably realistic and subtly comprehensible play, one cannot help but notice the presence of unusual leitmotifs that are neither derived from the plot nor fully realized through it. After one of the initial rehearsals, Meyerhold documented the central motifs of the play: the longing for life, the call to work, the juxtaposition of tragedy and comedy, the belief that happiness lies in the future, the importance of work, and the experience of loneliness. These motifs encompass the longing for fulfillment, the perpetual pursuit of happiness that remains ever-elusive, the experience of isolation, as well as the desire to make a difference and contribute to the well-being of others, and are considered by Stanislavsky to represent "the highest sense of truth and justice ... our minds aspiring to the secrets of existence." All of these motifs come together in a harmonious symphony, reaching its crescendo in the final note, "If only we knew..."

Nemirovich-Danchenko later reflected that many elements fell into place effortlessly; the actors possessed such an innate understanding of Chekhov that echoes of his themes were inevitable and organic. However, this did not undermine the immense effort put into the rehearsal process. Challenges escalated when Stanislavsky had to devote time to preparing for the role of Vershinin and composing the score for the final acts, as Chekhov was still in the process of editing them, resulting in their delayed receipt by Nemirovich-Danchenko. Furthermore, Nemirovich-Danchenko had to hastily leave Moscow to attend to his sister, who was critically ill with consumption.

Stanislavsky has a well-known story about when the actors "got stuck" during a rehearsal for *Three Sisters*. They had rehearsed, dispersed, and rehearsed again, tried this way and that, until one evening, they stopped working and fell silent.

Two or three electric bulbs burned dimly, and we sat around in the darkness, hearts beating from the worry and hopelessness of the situation. Finally, someone scratched their fingers nervously on a bench, which made the sound of a mouse scratching. This sound reminded me of a family home; I felt warm at heart; the truth, life, and my imagination worked. I suddenly felt the scene we were rehearsing. Chekhov's people lived. They are not thinking so much about their longing but, on the contrary, looking for fun, laughter, and cheerfulness. They want to live, not suffer. I sensed the truth about Chekhov's attitude towards these characters, it cheered me up, and I intuitively understood what we had to do. Following that breakthrough, our work resumed with renewed vigor.

Opening 1896–1899 83

This event has become one of the foundational stories in *My Life in Art*. However, it is important to note that, on occasion, the biographer must amend such legendary accounts. The incident involving the mouse was not a late life-saving discovery. Stanislavsky not only mentioned this observation in his director's copy, noting "Under the sofa, a mouse scratches," but also included in brackets, "How to create the sound of a mouse? Take a bundle of quills from a feathered pen and scratch with them."

In 1901, the audiences witnessed in *Three Sisters* two overarching themes that were intricately intertwined: the themes of home and departure. Here is a home, characterized by its traditional rooms, a staircase leading from the dining area to a mezzanine, and a small iron stove positioned in the entrance. Although scarcely visible to the audience, the stove held significance for the actors, who would remove their overcoats and bonnets beside it. It was this humble object that infused Victor Simov's scenery with a sense of vitality. After accompanying Irina to the brick factory, Natasha, assuming her role as the new hostess, will undertake the task of felling the maple tree situated in front of the house, along with the trees lining the pathway, as she endeavors to refurbish the home. The previous occupants of this abode were uncertain about the quality of their furniture, pondering whether it was time to replace the worn-out carpet. Have you noticed that the carpet from your childhood has deteriorated, its Turkish patterns fading into oblivion? The absence of a home like the one depicted in *Three Sisters* would undoubtedly diminish the quality of life. It would be far from the enchantment experienced at a joyous birthday party. This home would no longer serve as a refuge for neighbors in times of crisis, like when there was a fire and they sought solace here. Olga had the natural impulse to donate dresses from the sisters' wardrobe, along with the gray skirt, to the neighboring daughters. The home, where the elderly nanny spent her final days as part of the family, and where the amiable Fedotik slept, is destined to fade away. (Nemirovich-Danchenko later commented that Fedotik resembled Leopold Sulerzhitsky, jokingly suggesting he could handle a "fire emergency" with laughter, despite having very little left.) The genuine flow of everyday interactions, and their sincere "sublime way of thinking," will cease. Even if the fervent yearning within these walls was nothing more than lofty aspirations and deep dissatisfaction with oneself, this sentiment remained deeply ingrained within the Russian intelligentsia.

The word "restless" appears in Meyerhold's initial notes for the character of Tuzenbach. This word carried significant weight, capturing the essence of restlessness, rather than nervousness. Tuzenbach's restlessness reflected his personal response to external stimuli, but it was not the only theme in the production. The theme of anxiety and a yearning for a fulfilled existence resonated more strongly in Irina, who repeatedly expresses her desire for a different way of living and working. The craving for a meaningful existence also resonated in Stanislavsky's Vershinin, whose melodic voice painted a captivating picture of life's inherent beauty, even when stripped of personal

84 *Vladimir Nemirovich-Danchenko and the Moscow Art Theatre*

identity. Masha burned with a fervent longing for life. On the other hand, the yearning remains unfulfilled and unanswered in Savitskaya's portrayal of Olga, as she laments, "If only we knew, if only we knew..." Longing for life is contrasted with the harsh reality of living in a small town, filled with mundane "at-home days," gossip about Protopopov's love affairs, and the annoying sound of an accordion playing outside the window. The longing is further confronted by the inconvenience of the train station being twenty versts away from the city due to someone's stupidity and the lack of musical understanding among the townspeople. Protopopov, as the boss, exerts a pervasive influence, leaving no room for escape, and his behavior only worsens over time. Stanislavsky sought to capture the growing sense of this authoritative figure's presence, creating the expectation that he could appear at any moment. However, something more profound is at play; something of immense significance. This longing emerges during one's youth, particularly in the spring, on a crisp and vibrant evening that marks the end of the century. It embodies a yearning for change and an urgency to embrace it. A storm is brewing, and a monumental shift looms on the horizon. Let it come. Excellent. Hurry.

Such longing requires a particular inclination within one's soul. This is why Chekhov insisted on Meyerhold's involvement in *Three Sisters*; he needed the actor's unique "sound," the sound of a personality yearning for transformation. Everything else was ineffective and clashed with the character. Despite attempts to soften his approach, the actor remained stubborn, never truly grasping the joy of simply living. Meyerhold had an unstable and frenzied compulsion to alter the world. "Destroy life and me with it!" In contrast, Vasily Kachalov later interpreted the role differently.[14] His inherent openness to change, although lacking Meyerhold's striking sharpness, was an essential part of his sublime and timid love for life, especially evident in his portrayal of Tuzenbach. His longing manifested as an intensified sensation of being alive. This kind of longing rarely provides answers to questions about desires and what is lacking. Individuals burdened by this yearning are not immune to existential dilemmas.

Following the premiere of *Three Sisters*, *The New Times* took a pragmatic stance instead of indulging in philosophical sophistication. The reviewers criticized the heroines, arguing that these affluent and educated young women were dissatisfied, while others with fewer resources managed to settle down. If they wanted to go to Moscow, they simply went. The reviewers failed to understand what these general's daughters were truly seeking, speculating that Moscow itself would not be any "better" (which incidentally, they found distasteful themselves). Predictably, a parody titled *Nine Brides and No Groom* emerged, with readers of *The New Times* assuming that the play was simply about young women longing to marry, dismissing the rest as nonsensical and decadent. The phenomenon, referred to as the "Tragedy about nothing," was dismissively categorized by newspapers as a manifestation of spiritual anxiety and an "idle lifestyle." There was a provocative

Opening 1896–1899 85

sort of democracy in *The New Times* (inherent with many newspapers): you and I grew up on a shoestring, and we had to keep our noses to the grindstone to work our way out. But these general's daughters and barons experienced no hardship, so nothing is good enough for them anymore. The press provocatively equates spirituality with the bourgeoisie; explains their self-dissatisfaction briefly and rudely: they are "full of themselves" and "spoiled."

Nonetheless, in 1901, the significance of Suvorin's conservative *New Times* had not yet fully captivated the public's attention. The issue at hand was whether the longing experienced by Chekhov's protagonists was ethically grounded and worthy of respect, an inquiry that confronted the MAT at the time. The Prozorov family also held dear their home, a sentiment made evident through the MAT's production. However, the fundamental human need to live in a manner that deviates from the norm and shape one's destiny according to personal desires must be acknowledged. When this desire cannot be fulfilled due to obligations, external influences, everyday circumstances, or the overall disposition of society, suffering and drama naturally ensue. Being compelled to live a life against our will, one filled with shame, tedium, and illness—why should we endure such circumstances? When *Three Sisters* made its debut, this theme seeped into the "most secret corners of the soul." Communicated through the "shadows of feelings" on the stage, as expressed by Stanislavsky, it unexpectedly struck a chord with many members of the audience who shared the same concerns.

What caused this pervasive sense of discontent and yearning to suddenly emerge? Such sentiments do not arise in times that are consistently brutal or even destructive. Instead, they appear when a nation is teetering on the brink of an unbearable and catastrophic collapse, giving rise to desperate rebellions and heresies, much like Russia at the turn of the century. As conditions improved, people stopped regarding hardship as the prevailing norm. After the premiere of *Three Sisters*, the liberal newspaper *Russia* criticized Chekhov, claiming that he had little knowledge of life in the provinces. They argued that life in the provinces was improving with the emergence of various societies and Sunday schools. Despite the article's shortcomings, it highlighted the need for a transformation in public life so that the "ordinary office worker," who wrote an earnest and insightful letter, could truly comprehend the profound meaning embedded within *Three Sisters*. This play was reminiscent of the type of drama that perturbed the audience of *The Seagull* at the Alexandrinsky Theatre approximately five years earlier. People relied on discussion groups and libraries to overcome their constant fear of the authorities and to encourage the local press to do the same. It was through these means that individuals could escape the banality and monotony of everyday life. However, an interesting paradox emerges—one must first cultivate self-respect in order to hold contempt for something, and hatred cannot exist without first establishing a sense of self-worth.

In *Three Sisters*, the directors found great meaning in a line spoken by Tuzenbach as he casually flicked ash from his cigarette. This sentiment was agreed

86 *Vladimir Nemirovich-Danchenko and the Moscow Art Theatre*

upon by Vershinin: "The suffering that we witness now is overwhelming. Yet people still talk about the well-known moral progress that society has already achieved." Tuzenbach's character demanded more than just the natural talent of Kachalov to convey a sense of shame due to the worthlessness and impurity of existence, a belief in the possibility of happiness and the importance of finding joy, and a desire to bring a moral conscience to the overall balance of life. Equally crucial was the aforementioned "well-known moral progress" achieved by society that Tuzenbach alludes to.

In a letter written by a spectator shortly before the production of *Three Sisters*, the importance of the play is underscored:

> I understand why Gorky wept during your rehearsals of *The Snow Maiden*. He wept for the many magical, beautiful, and poetic forces bestowed upon humanity. However, humanity remained unaware of these forces until now—unable to awaken and truly experience joy and happiness.

At the turn of the century in Russian society, there were an astounding number of these "magical" forces present. Also crucial was a sense of conscience, an unwillingness to tolerate any wrongdoing or evil in one's presence. This was exemplified on March 4, 1901, when Cossacks were dispersing demonstrators near St. Petersburg's Kazan Cathedral, brutally beating them at the entranceway and inside the church. Two officers who happened to be there had to draw their sabers in defense of the victims. A rifleman even knocked a gendarme off his horse. Many others willingly took blows themselves to shield women from the horses' hooves and whips. Lieutenant-General Prince Vyazemsky also rushed to their rescue. Moreover, the officer who ordered the beatings faced a request from his comrades-in-arms to leave the regiment. Although this officer was following orders, Russian intellectuals, whether in the military or not, never considered that a valid excuse. (Gorky conveyed all this information to Chekhov, concluding the same correspondence by writing, "And *Three Sisters* is progressing incredibly well!")

Notes

1 Pushkino, a then-favorite summer retreat located about twenty-five miles northeast of Moscow.
2 Lubimovka. Stanislavsky family's summer estate about twenty miles northeast of Moscow.
3 *Tsar Fyodor Ivanovich* (1868) is a historical drama by Alexei Tolstoy about the reign of the last Rurikid tsar of Russia. The play follows Fyodor's struggles to maintain stability in a politically and religiously turbulent Russia. Boris Godunov, his advisor, manipulates tensions and eventually becomes the de facto ruler. However, he is overthrown by a rebellion led by a young prince named Dmitry, leaving Russia with an uncertain future.
4 *John of Damascus* (1858) is a poem by Alexey Tolstoy.
5 Aleksander Fedotov (1864–1909) was an actor and director associated with the Maly Theatre, theatre teacher, and son of the actress Glikeria Fedotova.

Opening 1896–1899 87

6 *Uriel Acosta* (1846) by Karl Gutzkow, a play about the titular Portuguese philosopher who challenged the Christian and Jewish institutions of his time.
7 Naum Berkovsky (1901–1972) was a literary and dramatic critic.
8 *Michael Kramer* (1890) is a social drama by Gerhart Hauptmann.
9 Ekaterina Munt (1875–1954) was an actress associated with MAT and Meyerhold's wife at the time.
10 Maria Lilina (1866–1943) was an actress associated with MAT and the wife of Stanislavsky.
11 Pyotr Boborykin (1836–1931) writer, playwright, and journalist, first to coin the Russian word "intelligentsia."
12 *The Ascension of Hannele* (1893) fantasy play by novelist and playwright Gerhart Hauptmann (1862–1946).
13 Maurice Maeterlinck (1862–1949), Belgian poet and playwright of symbolist tendency. In 1911, he was awarded the Nobel Prize in Literature.
14 Vasily Kachalov (1875–1948) was a leading actor associated with MAT.

4 In the Theatre from Ten to Seven 1899–1904

Theatre Organization and Creative Excellence

Nemirovich-Danchenko was only free for five days and felt happy for only half a day out of twenty-one months. He could have applied the same principle in the years to come.

"In matters of organization, I willingly and readily gave up authority to my new colleagues since Nemirovich-Danchenko's administrative talent was very obvious to me." From Stanislavsky's obliging statement, it followed that if anyone could tenaciously hold on to MAT's "external plot" it was Nemirovich-Danchenko. He never overlooked anything, untangling difficult problems every day, knowing they would be tangled up again tomorrow. He valued the disciplined and organizing role of form and understood that it must be impeccable in order to go unnoticed. He set up an office as if he were visiting a stationery shop:

> Tomorrow, someone must order forms for daily reports, including the box office, assistant director of rehearsals, assistant director of performances, head of crowd scenes, head of student participation (Meyerhold), head of the musical section, and theatre facilities inspector. Each department head must submit a daily report about the previous day so that I can immediately address any small issues.

He knew the importance of being energetic without acting like a boss. He appointed the former Society of Art and Literature actor, Gregory Ryndzyunsky, as his assistant. Nemirovich-Danchenko would soon discover and appreciate charming, skilled, and effortlessly efficient people by his side, but initially, he managed alone.

He explained that people who wanted to see him could always find him at the theatre from ten to seven unless he was unexpectedly called away somewhere. For example, on January 6, 1899, the Moscow Security Office summoned him, and the Chief of Police asked for an explanation. Since MAT did not operate as a national theatre and did not have the repertoire approved for a national theatre, what justified inviting workers to morning performances

DOI: 10.4324/9781003486282-4

In the Theatre from Ten to Seven 1899–1904   89

on holidays? Nemirovich-Danchenko agreed that they had to some extent violated the rules and explained why. In the future, MAT intended to perform for "people of the working class" (not currently, but in the future), as they had clearly stated in a previous report, so this should not be news to the police. MAT wanted to understand the needs and perspectives of the working class, but at the moment, workers did not attend in large numbers.

Even when he leaves Moscow, MAT will not release him from his duties. "It has been exactly three weeks since I have been in the countryside, and almost ten weeks busy with the same theatre." "I will leave Moscow on Sunday, April 2, on the noon train. I will handle the tour situation in Sevastopol on Tuesday afternoon, evening, and Wednesday morning. On Wednesday, I will travel by steamer to Yalta." In the spring of 1900, MAT embarked on a memorable trip to Chekhov in Yalta. *My Life in Art* documents their journey, from leaving their fur coats in Moscow to freezing on the road and singing. They woke up in Bakhchisaray in Crimea surrounded by flowers, sun, and bright surroundings, and then Sevastopol appeared—sparkling blue and white. It was beautiful, but someone had to go ahead and make arrangements. In a letter mentioned earlier, Nemirovich-Danchenko confirmed with Chekhov that everyone and everything would be in place when they arrived at the Yalta Theatre on Wednesday.

Usually, they scheduled rehearsals from ten to seven, with performances starting at eight (sometimes at half-past seven for longer plays) and ending around midnight. Unlike today, Moscow life thrived late into the night, with crowds filling the streets until eleven when conversations became particularly interesting. Evening rehearsals took place at five, six, and seven. They would usually work with two or three evening performers, and the main stage was always bustling with activity. Despite the logistical challenges, the performances appeared incredibly polished. Looking at the archives, you can find large office books with lined paper and the store name Muir and Meriliz printed on sturdy spines. These books served as a reference for future office supply needs. The assistant director diligently recorded the daily rehearsals and comments, revealing that there were problems every day. One entry stated, "Rehearsal ended at 2:45 as K.S. Stanislavsky found the participants lacking spirit today." Another entry read, "V.I. Nemirovich-Danchenko requests the theatre office to officially notify V.A. Simov that the drawings for *The Inspector General* have not arrived as decided on August 12. Consequently, there are delays in ordering props. The required drawings are as follows" (props listed).

These records date back to 1908 when MAT already had an excellent reputation. Nevertheless, every production had moments where it seemed like nothing would work out. In the end, everything worked out. The objective tone of Nemirovich-Danchenko's notes is deceptive: nothing happens by itself. If something is done, someone did it. There are no trivial matters here. By "trifles," they meant that there should be no giving up or doing nothing. Instead, they encouraged taking action and doing

90   Vladimir Nemirovich-Danchenko and the Moscow Art Theatre

something. Everything must be completed. We must ensure that Simov finally submits his drawings of the props for the workshops and that the backs of the flats are properly glued because lights can shine through them from backstage. We must understand why, despite the precautions, there are still cold drafts everywhere. They kept catching colds endlessly. During the rehearsals of *The Lower Depths*, Kachalov had pneumonia, Vladimir Gribunin had a fever, and Nemirovich-Danchenko himself had a cold and had to sit in the auditorium wearing a winter coat. Something needed to be done so that the actress standing in for the third time was compensated for rehearsing a role impromptu while also understanding that she would not play it either for the premiere or after. (The assigned performer was sick, overworked, or absent when necessary. "I am grateful to V. S. Stakhova for supporting the rehearsal with quick preparation of the role. V. Nemirovich-Danchenko-Danchenko").

Everything had to be done, and its measure of importance had to be consistent with the established standard of effort. Chekhov defined grace as investing only as much as necessary in your actions. And his description comes to mind when you think about how Nemirovich-Danchenko carried out the duties of the inelegant position of Managing Director, which was his role in the Partnership Agreement. On the poster, he had a different title: "Chief Director: K. S. Stanislavsky. Head of Repertoire: Vl. I. Nemirovich-Danchenko." The titles would ultimately disappear from the poster, but the duties would remain.

Many troubles went along with being the head of the repertoire. Nemirovich-Danchenko had to know the pulse and thoughts of world drama. He had to read many plays written or translated by well-known, respected people who considered themselves talented writers. A decent theatre should produce their plays.

Here is a note from a business card: "Please accept and listen to Mr. Adolf Hesse regarding Hermann Sudermann's new play *Hymns to Claudian*.[1] Yours as always, Nikolai Mikhailovich." (They did not produce the play since Grand Duke Nikolai Mikhailovich didn't want them to stage it solely on his recommendation.) Here is a presumptuous letter from a certain W. W. Zeghe von Laurenberg, who had sent his drama *The Man Who Laughs* a year earlier. He regrets that the author even allowed himself to bother with MAT, where they had lost the manuscript without reading it. Author, playwright, and critic Pyotr Boborykin sent his play *Ladies* to MAT, and Nemirovich-Danchenko replied, "This letter is difficult for me. Though I am forty, I am a boy before you, a boy as a writer and critic. But I must speak frankly as the head of the repertoire." Theatre also entails numerous relationships, situations, and ongoing issues that arise and require immediate resolution. In Olga Knipper's letter prior to the start of MAT's second season, she observed, "Nemirovich-Danchenko arrived and opened the administrative office (Figure 4.1), where there were many conversations and self-revelations."

Theatre as a Medium for Transformative Truth

"You will inevitably face backstage dirt, no matter how hard you try to avoid it or what actions you take. Theatre is especially plagued by this issue, and I have no idea why." Nemirovich-Danchenko was well acquainted with the shadows lurking backstage, just like Nikolai Efros (historiographer of MAT who wrote these lines in MAT's first year of operation). He described them in their traditional provincial and modern forms, with a touch of decadence. They feature in in his story *The Mist* (1898) when Alexey, the protagonist, visits provincial actress Ancharova's home, with its Japanese fabrics, cockatoo, kangaroo (whom Ancharova refused to dine without), a jar of poison from India, and antique pistols—allegedly her father's, although Alexey didn't believe her. And just as if to confirm his suspicion, he overheard her say: "I want to play Hedda Gabler for my next benefit performance. I'm drawn to that woman with green eyes, and I promise I will have green eyes."

The founders of MAT were concerned about how the *poshlost* (petty wrongdoing and vulgarity) of the theatre infiltrated the soul of those working in it, and how an individual's *poshlost* was reflected in their chosen work. They didn't want this problem to taint the production they were starting, which seemed free of any *poshlost*. It would be dreadful if *poshlost* managed to seep in from the outside. Therefore, they carefully selected participants, looked after themselves, and paid attention to what Chekhov regarded as their essential trait: "intelligence of tone," both on stage and in life.

Nemirovich-Danchenko had an additional perspective on the matter. He didn't view passionate ambition, for example, as a disaster or a shameful characteristic in the theatre. In fact, he believed that intense ambition and the ardent desire to play a role were natural in this field, as long as they didn't manifest as excessive professional hysteria in the director's office. Instead, they should be channeled toward purposeful energy and the unleashing of one's creative potential, along with a deep understanding of the role and oneself. Nemirovich-Danchenko respected the drive to create and knew how to safeguard it from becoming distorted into a relentless pursuit of success and fame. However, he didn't dismiss either of these aspects with self-righteous haste. He recognized the inevitability of enthusiasm in theatre, not as something evil but as something perfectly natural. He didn't suppress these elements; instead, he did everything in his power to prevent them from depleting the dynamic artistic forces in futile conflicts and sinking into the mire. Someone described him as arrogant and incommunicative instead of open and accessible. Nonetheless, the letters from his archive show that many company members would approach him with frantic confessions and did not hesitate to voice their vehement grievances. If someone dared to be impudent, he would immediately shut them down.

There were instances of direct impudence at first as well. It's unclear what Sanin had written to him, but it didn't have any notable consequences, except for some icy remarks in a response: "If you think I'm the one causing

92 *Vladimir Nemirovich-Danchenko and the Moscow Art Theatre*

problems or idling away all day, take a look, think about it for a while, and then write." Many years later, during a tense rehearsal, the elderly actor Yuri Leonidov shouted at Nemirovich-Danchenko,[2] who himself was already elderly, claiming that he had only seen evil from him in the past. Nemirovich-Danchenko shut him down in the same manner: "Think and remember." Despite receiving potentially offensive letters and being engaged in difficult conversations, he wouldn't take offense easily. His ability to understand, his desire to help, and his skill in using opportunities to help others were his most prominent traits, Even more prominent than his private generosity.

During the first few years, there were hardly any letters of this kind. However, as time went on, more and more people were inclined to write to him, including Sophia Khalyutina,[3] a former student and actress at MAT from its early days. Her letter was written in March 1906 when she was in Moscow while everyone else was on a tour abroad, and she was unable to join them due to illness. She waited for them to call her to join them later, but they went ahead without her, which hurt her. However, her letter wasn't about herself at the moment. She wrote,

> The recent [political] events make my personal grievances seem insignificant. It's shameful to only think about myself and my activities, even if they are highly artistic. My heart trembles when I read paradoxes like '10,948 signatures opposing the death penalty,' followed immediately by mockery of this issue with reports of 'the execution of Schmidt and the three sailors.' After four weeks of Lenten fasting, workers' strikes are expected to resume, and there will possibly be a real revolution in May. What can we expect after that? Only God knows!

Six years later, she bitterly questioned her previous dismissal of an actress's "personal experiences," which led her to write another letter. Despite Nemirovich-Danchenko's advice, she had inexplicably performed as Nora Helmer, albeit at Nezlobin's Theatre in Nizhny Novgorod,[4] with kerosene lamps and only four rehearsals. She wrote, "Now I can say as Nora says: You are partly to blame for me. You and Konstantin Sergeyevich are to blame for my lack of progress. If you had given me better roles more often, I could have become a good actress!" Perhaps she truly believed that. In her debut as Annie in *The Power of Darkness*, reviewers noted "a spark of talent." She continues,

> If you don't let me play Masha in Tolstoy's play, I will play outside of MAT. And if you don't let me, I will play in secret. I will play all the roles I want: *The Seagull*, Nora again, Hilda in *The Master Builder*, *Girl Without a Dowry*. I'll even sing the same gypsy songs Masha sang at MAT in that play. And finally, the plays that have been the desires of my life: *The Thunderstorm* and *The Maid of Orleans*. These are my dreams! So, what will you do for me? This is what I want to do!

In the Theatre from Ten to Seven 1899–1904   93

I want to, and I will. But, I have to consider myself since MAT doesn't want to utilize my strengths and abilities. I understand that I'm not at the center of things and I have to put up with it. And I do put up with it. But no one can stop me from growing and dreaming outside of the theatre. I'm forty years old, and my abilities will decline after five to seven years. I won't have a future to think about then.

"If I don't get Masha's role, I won't play Oza in *Peer Gynt*. I refuse. I still have time to play all the Ethels and Ozas, though I would rather not play anything at all. Are you surprised by my audacity? Then be surprised."

No, he wasn't surprised. Khalyutina played Mother Oza in *Peer Gynt* and the older woman Ethel in *Miserere* by Semyon Yushkevich. And she didn't get Masha's role in *The Living Corpse*, even when Olga Gzovskaya, who prepared the part, fell ill two weeks before the premiere. There was an emergency meeting in Nemirovich-Danchenko's office, and the next day, they called in Alisa Koonen instead.[5] "We will try you in the role. Are you nervous?" "No." Sometime later, Nemirovich-Danchenko would write a letter to the Maly Theatre at Khalyutina's insistence; she wanted to leave. Nemirovich-Danchenko had good things to say about her. He knew about her many unfulfilled hopes and that MAT now had quite a few brilliant young actors who inevitably pushed aside the "younger elders," whose hopes and desires were all postponed "for later." He explained to Sumbatov-Yuzhin that, while MAT needed Khalyutina, they couldn't give her what her talent deserved.

Khalyutina didn't leave; Koonen did. They could have complained about her arrogance and ingratitude, but they understood her situation was different. She had signed a contract with the Free Theatre and had already left. She was Stanislavsky's student and didn't dare to offend him, so she notified Nemirovich-Danchenko of her decision instead. (They respected him less; they always respected him less.) Koonen later marveled that despite Nemirovich-Danchenko's understanding of psychology, he didn't see what her decision to leave cost her. Still, she didn't see what their conversation cost him. He told Koonen that it was an insane step, but he didn't assume it was final. However, he wasn't surprised by it and didn't hold it against her. Another letter, dated November 5, 1914, was signed by Chamber Theatre directors Alexander Tairov and Koonen. It said,

> Dear Nemirovich-Danchenko, we are pleased to inform you that the letter you wrote with such kindness had an impact, and she has received permission. We hope to have the official notice signed on Monday. Please accept our sincere gratitude once again. Thank you very much, dear Nemirovich-Danchenko.

It didn't matter what service he provided for the Chamber Theatre, which was set to open in five weeks. What mattered was that he did something for her.

94 *Vladimir Nemirovich-Danchenko and the Moscow Art Theatre*

He urged the actress to stay, mainly because MAT needed her. He also reprimanded her because he knew no other theatre where an actor's life would be as fulfilling, especially in terms of the actor's transformation into their character.

Nemirovich-Danchenko valued this transformation above all else. As Vitali Vilenkin wrote,

> The essence of theatre for him has always been the remarkable ability of actors to infuse the plot and playwright's words with their own feelings, thoughts, intuition, nerves, voice, and charm. They embody a role with their own flesh and blood. They infuse it with their own perspective on life, people, the past and future, and the meaning of existence. They live someone else's life on stage, making it their own and allowing the audience to experience it with them.

No other theatre brought this "marvelous ability" to transform oneself into a character to life more skillfully and wholeheartedly than MAT.

Stanislavsky, a tall man, would silently tread along the corridors on tiptoes, fearful of disrupting someone's creative state. Nothing was more important to the founders than maintaining this creative state:

> To Alexander Akimovich: Because today is a difficult rehearsal for *The Death of Ivan the Terrible* and your complete self-control and peace of mind are essential for it, I demand that you do not talk about the reasons for canceling the *Uncle Vanya* rehearsal at this time. Please suppress it as soon as you feel it's disrupting today's work.

Nemirovich-Danchenko addressed this note to Sanin, the assistant director. It was evident that he was not indifferent to the disruption of the *Uncle Vanya* rehearsal. However, during a time when Stanislavsky was preparing to portray Tsar Ivan—a role he had brilliantly conceived to the point of despair—everything else was out of place. They set aside everything else so that Stanislavsky could fully embody the intense mental anguish of this tyrant, causing the audience to respond with the words, "God will forgive him..." in reaction to his Herod-like repentance.

One time during rehearsal, "it" actually happened.[6] This is the main thing, the thing you dedicate your energy to, the reason the audience is here. It's finally experiencing what theatre is truly about—the ultimate goal. Everything else is just background, only the situation that facilitates this goal. This highly sought-after experience was the reason Nemirovich-Danchenko needed to be at the theatre from ten to seven, and earlier. He would sit in the office until after midnight and write a letter to Stanislavsky specifically about this experience.

Stanislavsky's rehearsals for *The Death of Ivan the Terrible* were painful for him and those around him. Some might have found his struggles

In the Theatre from Ten to Seven 1899–1904   95

whimsical, but to Nemirovich-Danchenko they were anything but whimsical. He wanted to liberate Stanislavsky from all his incidental fears and convince him that if he captured the essence of the role as truly and deeply as he has now, if his ideas developed into a plan, and if he had a sense of proportion that maintained the perspective and harmony of its parts, then his performance might vary in brightness or paleness from time to time, but it would always be beautiful.

The time at the theatre from ten to seven was also a period of constant collaboration and mutual inspiration between the two founders. Nemirovich-Danchenko openly admits to learning from Stanislavsky, and Stanislavsky learned from Nemirovich-Danchenko, especially when it came to a character's psycho-physical state and the given circumstances of the action. Who should be credited with the various dramatic ideas? Stanislavsky and Nemirovich-Danchenko agreed not to worry about who owed what to whom. "We can and should join together."

Nemirovich-Danchenko was delighted when Stanislavsky discovered Gerhart Hauptmann's play *Lonely People*, which he had somehow overlooked despite managing the repertoire. Nemirovich-Danchenko planned to write the play's directorial plan and didn't hesitate to ask Stanislavsky for any imaginative details that came to his mind. Stanislavsky willingly responded, eliminating the need for him to write a full directorial plan for Nemirovich-Danchenko. Nemirovich-Danchenko himself prepared the directorial notes for *The Death of Ivan the Terrible* and *An Enemy of the People*. There are numerous comments in these two notebooks, but they serve mainly as talking points for their upcoming conversation, which would take place in an hour or two. Apart from these writings, which were mostly jotted down in pencil at night, there are no records of Nemirovich-Danchenko's numerous directorial works. Therefore, it's worth taking the time to focus on these "talking points" to understand what lies within and behind them.

Many years after the premiere of *An Enemy of the People*, Nemirovich-Danchenko received a letter questioning if he had forgotten about his invaluable involvement in its rehearsals. "Talking points" from the first act: "Move the street farther away." "The chandelier is too expensive for Stockman." The servant's bell rings: "Isn't that the master?" Mrs. Stockman: "No, it was not him." Director's note: "This means the servant recognizes the ring." "Curiously, Katerina does not recognize the ring" (husband rings from another room). Stockman's line: "Katerina says I earn almost as much as we spend." Nemirovich-Danchenko stresses the word "earns" (not "profits," as it was in the translation). Further entries: "More fun." "Much more fun." "Maybe more affectionately?" One more entry: "Feed the cat." Last one: "K. S. is a little old and should be a redhead."

Let's consider how this would have unfolded and what these notes would have supplied for the "perspective of the role" (as Nemirovich-Danchenko expressed it). First, the locale was moved farther away from the street: a separate and friendlier house, a smaller and brighter domestic circle of light from

96 *Vladimir Nemirovich-Danchenko and the Moscow Art Theatre*

the chandelier above the table. Home: the servants recognize the husband by the ring of the bell; it's comical to ring for your wife when she is always right there. Home: where they do not profit but earn, glad to be making good money. Dr. Stockman

> enjoys his modest profession as a doctor, with a small but reliable income, and the respect of his fellow citizens. He is not a descendant of those "superfluous people" who live alone and unsettled but an honorary citizen of the city, whose prosperity he contributed to, realizing the healing properties of the local waters and baths. A doctor with a good practice was beginning to feel the comforts of affluence increasing with age. He has no internal conflicts. A person created for an active and useful life and intensely appreciative of the happiness it provides.

Nemirovich-Danchenko's comments set all this as the starting point. Therefore, "more fun." Hence, "affectionate." Holding the cat in your hands is a warm, fluffy signifier of coziness: you come home, pour milk in a bowl, and "feed the cat." (If reviewers took this for a naturalistic detail, it did not matter.) Domestic, not old, and with a cat.

And a "redhead." You can imagine how this "redhead" comment stirs the actor's imagination: Stanislavsky always appreciated a carefully pointed word (like, say, Nemirovich-Danchenko's answer to the question of how old Krutitsky is in Ostrovsky's play *Enough Stupidity in Every Wise Man*: a thousand years and he has always lived right here on Sadovaya Street). The "redhead" is a figure of eccentric behavior, the "redness" of enthusiasm, the "redness" of a person's dissimilarity to others, even though he does not feel this difference and evaluates others by himself. Stanislavsky said: "Stockman's terrible guilt lies within himself, and he does not understand other people."

Nemirovich-Danchenko's notes only pertain to Stockman/Stanislavsky's scenes with his business-like friends-citizens in the second act. The changes proposed by Nemirovich-Danchenko were not directed at Stanislavsky himself, but at his partners. If their actions were perceived as long, boring, unclear, or slow-moving, Nemirovich-Danchenko suggested making changes to speed up the pace. For example, the friends-citizens should not allow Stockman to get properly dressed, they should gather early before having their morning coffee, and they should quickly react to the rumor before rushing from their homes. They should know precisely what they want from Stockman and communicate it clearly, without unnecessary wordiness. However, Stockman's lack of comprehension is highlighted. They explain it to him clearly, but he still doesn't understand because he doesn't speak the same language as these businesspeople.

It is evident from the letter questioning whether Nemirovich-Danchenko had forgotten his helpful intervention in the rehearsals of *An Enemy of the People* that initially Stanislavsky's famous fourth act was not successful.

In the Theatre from Ten to Seven 1899–1904   97

However, it eventually became the pinnacle of his acting career. Therefore, it is interesting to understand the reasoning behind Nemirovich-Danchenko's adjustments to this wavering and uncertain performance. He preferred not to interfere with a scene that wasn't working well and instead adopted the approach of stepping back and trying something different. In an interview with a reporter from the *News and Exchange* Reporter in February 1901, one of the earliest sources revealing how rehearsals were conducted at MAT, Nemirovich-Danchenko explained that initial runs are rarely smooth, and mistakes become apparent that were previously overlooked. Fixing a mistake may seem simple but is often challenging. For example, if a scene seems boring, it may be because the preceding scene sets a controlling tone. In such cases, it is necessary to find a balance and adjust the tone.

To enhance the fourth act, they reintroduced the motif of Stockman's misunderstanding of people from the first and second acts. Aristotle believed that the best tragedies involve "recognition," which is the transition from ignorance to knowledge, accompanied by "peripeteia," the reversal of events leading to the downfall of one's fate. In MAT's production, the story of a kind-hearted homebody who poured milk into a cat's bowl illustrates this transition from ignorance to knowledge and the subsequent destruction of his fate. The fourth act primarily consists of a monologue, where new thoughts emerge suddenly. Stockman/Stanislavsky didn't come to the town hall with these thoughts; they arose in the moment. Nemirovich-Danchenko's remarks help establish the connection between Stockman and the people, and how deeply he is affected by them: "The doctor thinks his own thoughts." "After thinking, his entire soul becomes stirred up." "When the crowd's noise diminishes, he composes himself and speaks softly." If Stockman/ Stanislavsky assesses his fellow citizens based on how he sees himself, even though he doesn't really know them, it might be a serious mistake, but it isn't stupidity or naivety. He can evaluate things this way because he doesn't feel like an ignorant outsider.

Stockman has something specific to tell his fellow citizens, not about any falsehoods in the social order, but about the fact that sick people come to our city for treatment and they get infected from contaminated water, which worsens their condition. It's a grave matter. Here are the water tests and a thick notebook of supporting documents. Stockman understands that his message is unpleasant, but he must convey it as it is. He arrives at the hall, appearing nervous and tidy, like someone about to share important information with the public. He feels the stiffness of his collar and the symbolic significance of his "new pair of pants," which he will later regretfully and poetically say: "You should never wear a new pair of pants when you go out to fight for freedom and truth." Many in the town hall live like Dr. Stockman, individuals with modest wealth acquired recently. The town's newfound prosperity hasn't made them wealthy either. Nonetheless, they enjoy roast beef for dinner, dream of buying a new chandelier, and hope to buy even more roast beef and a more expensive chandelier for another room in the future.

98 *Vladimir Nemirovich-Danchenko and the Moscow Art Theatre*

Everything that contributes to Stockman/Stanislavsky's transition from ignorance to knowledge occurs in direct interaction with a crowd of listeners who seems to be united against him. They reject everything that doesn't suit their liking. He presents them with bacteriological analyses, and they accuse him of slander. He shows them more evidence, but they continue to deny it. They reject everything Dr. Stockman says from the podium, eagerly seizing onto words and rejoicing when they find something to respond to indignantly: "Aha! So that's how it is! Only an enemy of the people would speak like that!" The atmosphere becomes almost demonic as they chant: "Enemy of the people!"

Their lives aren't being threatened; only the possibility of not being able to buy a chandelier they saw in a shop window the day before. Of course, it's a wonderful thing—a cheerful new lamp. But who could have anticipated what people are willing to do to acquire it and everything else? Without the passionate intensity of Dostoevsky's "underground man" or his *cri de coeur* but with a full consciousness of their entitlements, these people decided long ago that the world may fail, but they need their tea. They must have their tea. Passion burns not when this question suddenly arises but when it does not get their tea or even when there is a tiny doubt they might not get it. Here is the "united majority" as Stockman/Stanislavsky finds it, deconstructs it, and strongly curses it—precisely "a hero's cry." "The cry is heroic, not impassioned," said Nemirovich-Danchenko.

And here are the last comments on the last act: "The tone is deeper," "stronger," once again, "stronger." "This is the only time he feels sad," when Stockman feels disappointed that no one has blown up his home, has not set fire to it as they threatened, the miserable cowards! "Stronger." "Joyful." "The finale is stronger and uses the same tone as the beginning." The penetrating feeling of loneliness is still present in all of this. The windows are broken; Stockman walks around with a coat thrown over his shoulders. He stands at the window: "How glorious the sun shines today!"

The letter recalling Nemirovich-Danchenko's life-saving participation in rehearsals was large, long, and mostly not about Stockman, and Nemirovich-Danchenko did not answer whether he had forgotten.

Art and Ambition

Nemirovich-Danchenko has been a director at MAT since May 1, 1898. His views on how a play should be approached are clear, whether the director starts from tradition, a new aesthetic understanding of the world, familiar staging, or a fresh, perceptive "feeling of the author" and the life behind him. The director must understand "the atmosphere of the play in which he will involve the performers" and "the emotional coloring of the play and its diction." They must have confidence in setting the tone. The director should come to the first rehearsal with a fully formed and developed picture of the play in their own unique, individual soul. These are the qualifications of the so-called perfect innovator, the strange fusion of Stanislavsky and

Nemirovich-Danchenko that produced *The Seagull* and possessed this power of "a unique, individual soul."

Nemirovich-Danchenko felt better off and freer in this collaboration than when he was the sole director of a production. It is impossible to say what critics thought about the first production he directed by himself, Austrian playwright Emil Mariott's new play *Greta's Happiness*.[7] The reviewers criticized the play amicably, and their reactions were both hypocritical and silly ("Don't take your daughters to this play!" "God knows what they're talking about on stage!"). However, they did not attempt to defend it, as the play was considered old-fashioned. The reviewers were silent about the director's work or briefly mentioned that the production was good. Someone remembered that the author of *The Price of Life* was interested in the drama of a soulless marriage. They praised the "domestic side" and the atmosphere of the citizen's home, from which Greta was quickly married off. "In developing all the scenes, V. I. showed himself again as a sensitive and subtle psychologist." The use of "V. I." instead of the director's full name signified a shared culture and support. Nemirovich-Danchenko had been a critic himself for a long time, and they wanted to support him as one of their own.

Figure 4.1 Vladimir Nemirovich-Danchenko in his Moscow Art Theatre office. By permission of the Moscow Art Academic Theatre.

100   *Vladimir Nemirovich-Danchenko and the Moscow Art Theatre*

Roxanova's performance as Greta, however, outraged reviewers: "Clinical!" "Pathological!" Whether one believes these exclamations or not, a month later, the same reviewers would write that *The Seagull* (not the production, but the play itself) represented a clinic for the mentally ill. Another statement from the review read, "Roxanova lives right on the stage. A whipped up, unhappy, tormented animal who writhes convulsively, defenseless, and miserable. It's disgusting." It would be better to examine this statement more closely and consider whether the performance revealed the raw, painfully truthful power. But this is still only speculation. Nemirovich-Danchenko did not attempt to prove the correctness of his direction in *Greta's Happiness*, nor did he analyze any potential errors. Remarkably, he moved on from his directorial failure, the failure of his literary choice, and the failure of his student Roxanova in the leading role as if none of it had happened. Just two weeks later, he eagerly awaited the premiere of *The Seagull*, experiencing fleeting moments of happiness.

His second independent directing endeavor was a play by his beloved Ibsen, *When We Dead Awaken*. As soon as the play premiered, it sparked articles attempting to interpret its meaning and draw connections to related works. Gabriele D'Annunzio promptly penned *La Gioconda*, a play that explored a similar "life-artist-model" triangle as Ibsen's work.[8] In *La Gioconda*, the sculptor's inspiration vanishes, causing his artistic talent to dry up. Similarly, the model is prepared to destroy the sculpture. D'Annunzio wrote the role of the sculptor's wife, who salvages his creation but is subsequently abandoned by him, specifically for Eleanora Duse.[9] They even intended to produce *La Gioconda* at MAT.

There was no hesitation in translating *When We Dead Awaken* in Russia, with multiple translations being created. Stanislavsky didn't have access to the translation Nemirovich-Danchenko had been working on, but he was still captivated by the play. Unable to resist, he himself wrote almost half of a director's plan. He saw the play as a dissection of petty reality. The setting of the health resort, traditionally envisioned as a place of recovery, was brought to life on stage. These moments, marked by slow and solemn events, included a tall woman in white walking straight ahead without glancing back, followed at a distance by a nun dressed in black. Accompanying this scene was a distant, foreboding sound. It didn't matter to Stanislavsky how the other characters saw Irene or if they even saw her at all. Sculptor Arnold Rubek was the one who saw her, perceiving her as a ghost and feeling joyous.

Like a distant star,
A gentle sound or a breath,
Or a chilling apparition,
It's all right! Come to me!

The other characters in the play acted as if this episode didn't disturb them. Passing cyclists rang their bells with vengeance, Rubek's wife, Maya, uttered

In the Theatre from Ten to Seven 1899–1904   101

sarcastic remarks fueled by petty jealousy, and the hunter Squire Ulfheim was rude and sharp. However, the artistic integrity of their reality had already been shattered. A tense atmosphere prevailed, giving power to the appearance of this "distant star" or "chilling apparition."

> Oh, if this is true, then
> Silent graves will be emptied.

Stanislavsky succeeded in incorporating sound, lighting, and expressive movement into his production notes, but struggled with the sequence of the plot. He didn't delve into his meaning behind the dialogue between Rubek and Irena and paid even less attention to the factual details of their past relationship and its aftermath. Instead, he left them to manage the tension of the rhythm and the disconnection between the figures on stage. What Stanislavsky captured was the "internal plot" of the play, which depicted a man's longing for youth and the life he had abandoned. He perfectly portrayed the "internal story" by giving Rubek an eagerness to meet his former model-lover and overcome his horror, exclaiming, "Come to me, my friend, here! here!"

Stanislavsky sent his notes to Nemirovich-Danchenko, assuring him that he would not be offended if they were not helpful. However, Nemirovich-Danchenko was already rehearsing at full speed and had his own directorial plan in mind. Nemirovich-Danchenko intended to incorporate Stanislavsky's valuable scenic inventions that pertained to the daily life at the health resort. Both directors agreed that the description should be a little naturalistic and grotesque. He chose the title *When We Shall Rise Among the Dead* from another Russian translation. The play depicted resurrection among the half-dead, the non-living, the elegant but skeleton-like young ladies, the apoplectic and relaxed, and the angel-attendants as the resort staff. Death was portrayed as always vulgar, something acknowledged by everyone around the tables based on the resort clients' conversations, attempts at wit, and the ladies' flirtatious chatter. The color scheme was Norwegian, and the architecture had an Art Nouveau style, but these elements only served as time and space coordinates for the universal and impersonal.

Stanislavsky and Nemirovich-Danchenko had differing conceptions of the play in every other aspect. Stanislavsky trusted his own impressions and tried to convey the inexplicable and unsettling poetry he found in Ibsen's dialogue. On the other hand, Nemirovich-Danchenko dismissed this impression and argued that the play was simple, precise, and could be rationally explained. Nemirovich-Danchenko's director's copy included numerous footnotes that referenced his article. This article was a comprehensive analysis of the play published in the September 1900 edition of *Russian Thought*, prior to the premiere. He even saw a copy of it lying on the table beside Tolstoy at Yasnaya Polyana, where he had visited for business and spent the entire day engaging in conversation and playing chess. Regarding Ibsen's play, which

102 *Vladimir Nemirovich-Danchenko and the Moscow Art Theatre*

he disliked, Tolstoy said, "If its contents were the same as what you wrote in your article, then it would be a good play."

Nemirovich-Danchenko's desire to prove that Ibsen's final creation was a pure realist work, with a story that was straightforward and based on facts, forced him to abandon the search for the "internal plot." Instead, he focused on establishing credibility for his logically developed "external plot," which revolved around Rubek's guilt toward his former model, who demanded that the artist acknowledge his guilt and repent. He was confident in his approach, rehearsed enthusiastically, and rejoiced that Irena/Savitskaya found things he did not expect, and Rubek/Kachalov's receptivity also pleased him. However, he struggled with the second act, particularly with the two long dialogues. Unraveling the conversation between Rubek and Maya proved to be challenging. The story was about two people who wanted to be together but could not get along due to mutual guilt and irritation. Despite the pain caused by their separation, there seemed to be no relief in sight. Similarly, he found the dialogue between Rubek and Irena, which seemed mysterious from an outsider's perspective, to be no more mysterious than any conversation between two people who lived in their own world. Although their words may be unclear to others, it made sense in their own reality.

At the end of the play, when the avalanche comes down from the mountains carrying the bodies of Rubek and Irena, the audience was embarrassed by the stuffed dolls and cotton wool used to represent the falling snow. There was another reason for this embarrassment besides the fact that Simov was not skilled at painting landscapes, and the director had not thoroughly considered the stage materials needed to match his imagination. With the changes made to both the external and internal plot of the play, a "transcendent" resolution was no longer necessary. It couldn't simply end with an avalanche or with a theatrical effect. There was no valid reason for Irene to summon Rubek to the snowy peaks, unless she was either insane or a heroine with a dangerous and decadent disposition (as previously observed at the health resort). Hence the cotton wool finale. (The use of cotton wool in the avalanche would later appear in Ibsen's *Brand*, six years later.)

He wanted to incorporate into the production of *When We Dead Awaken* what would have been better suited for a "replica" play, where he could express the theme that initially interested him. Specifically, he wanted to explore the guilt of art before life. Art is seen as a model that one revels in, seduces with its possibilities, and then abandons in disappointment with life and one's own passions and needs. Nemirovich-Danchenko also wrote a similar "counterplay" called *In Dreams* (1902), which delves into the guilt of art before life. However, this play focuses on a life that is embarrassed by dreams of art and resents them.

Although Nemirovich-Danchenko was reluctant to offer his own plays to MAT, he still wanted to contribute something valuable to the new venture. With Chekhov's encouragement, he worked on a dramatization of his novella *The Governor's Inspection* (1896). However, the manuscript remained on

In the Theatre from Ten to Seven 1899–1904   103

his desk until he finished his play *In Dreams* (1901). But then the troupe's cold response to *In Dreams* made him want to forget it ("I would hate to take part in it; it's very unpleasant," one actor said. Knipper was loyal and agreed to replace those who declined). Despite the troupe's coldness, it was a success externally, as were the actresses' costumes designed by a famous fashion designer. Nemirovich-Danchenko sardonically told someone that *In Dreams* perfume was also on sale. Reviewers couldn't help but see it as a motley mix of borrowed elements. The play included everything already seen at MAT: brooding twilight, piano chords heard in old rooms, orchestrated crowds, and decadent, overstrained authoritativeness, which actress Maria Andreyeva learned earlier from her role as Hedda Gabler and used here in the role of Princess Vera.[10]

In a letter to Chekhov, Meyerhold called the play "bad tasting vinaigrette," a model of insincere creativity on demand. Perhaps the saddest thing was that Meyerhold was wrong when speaking of insincerity; his own internal stirrings were the problem here. It's a shame to think about the commotion Meyerhold caused when he was accused (or thought he heard someone accuse him) of encouraging people to hiss at the premiere on December 21, 1901. "I insist that you confirm these insults someone accuses me of behind my back. I do not blame you but those who prompted you to think about me like this" (from a letter to Stanislavsky). Naturally, Nemirovich-Danchenko did not know the whole story. The episode was nasty and disgusting, including Nemirovich-Danchenko excluding Meyerhold from the list of actor-shareholders in the restructuring of the MAT partnership. Things were bad. Knipper understood Nemirovich-Danchenko's situation, tried to talk to him, and asked Chekhov to write to him. [Meyerhold left MAT the following year.]

There was a thaw in the weather at Christmas; mud ran in the streets; Moscow was smelly, then suddenly frozen again. Nemirovich-Danchenko was never himself in wintry weather. "I go around with a frozen brain and frozen energy without any love of life, and I don't want to think, write, or manage anything." He had bronchitis for more than a month. Finally, on December 30, he left for Nice to restore his health.

While recovering in Nice, he said, "I gambled a lot (I won 200 francs), did nothing, relaxed in the sun, read the newspaper, went to the theatre three times (a bad theatre), watched an idiotic carnival, did nothing, thought nothing."

Ambition and Self-Reflection

Failures were rare in Nemirovich-Danchenko's life, but he recognized the importance of taking time for himself—a day, an hour—to step back from everything, clear his mind, and relax in the sun. He understood that these moments of rest were necessary, almost like a remedy for an illness. They were essential because his life was filled with constant activity and public engagements. Sometimes, however, the need for solitude would arise, or he would experience sudden overwhelming fatigue from the continuous and thankless tasks he undertook. Occasionally, his nerves would react negatively to cold and wet weather. Despite these challenges, Nemirovich-Danchenko knew how to handle them. Perhaps few would have noticed these struggles if he hadn't spoken about them, as they would have been invisible to others. Stanislavsky, however, seemed to have a prescient understanding of Nemirovich-Danchenko's inner battles. While everyone admired Nemirovich-Danchenko's active poise and strong will as co-leader of MAT, Stanislavsky recognized another aspect of his personality and its value to the theatre.

True creativity requires moments of self-doubt, periods of self-loathing for not working hard enough, and even contempt for the discipline one has imposed on oneself. In fact, one could argue that these experiences are not limited to creativity but are also a part of life itself. Nemirovich-Danchenko understood that he could overcome these challenges. He belonged to a generation and social circle that took pride in personal growth. He often reminisced about how, as a young boy, he had overcome difficulties. Growing up in Tiflis, he was surrounded by the enticing allure of the streets—playing games with friends and exploring. The shop signs above the wine cellars exuded the scent of sun-burnt metal and peeling paint, while, below, the cool atmosphere carried the aroma of sweaty clay jugs and wine. The black oilcloth tablecloths were stained white from spilled wine long ago. The local Georgian speech was easily understood, especially when sung. Life flowed with its own unique charm, and it was hard to leave it behind. Some Russian officials, like Nemirovich's father, attempted to shield their children from all of this. Sumbatov-Yuzhin recollected that "Volodya" (nickname for Vladimir) was the only Georgian who graduated from high school with him. Returning to the world of formal education was Volodya's own choice; no one forced him to do so. He spent a final summer immersed in his books and made the most of it. In doing so, he severed his ties with the vibrant streets and all that they represented. But he did not consider what he had left behind.

Ultimately, assuming no major external disruptions, everyone chooses their own path in life. Nemirovich-Danchenko couldn't complain that he hadn't lived the way he could have or wanted to. However, when he looked at himself objectively, he couldn't ignore the conflict between his active, consciously chosen principles and what he referred to as "laziness." This internal conflict occupied his thoughts for quite some time. In the spring and summer of 1904, Nemirovich-Danchenko filled half of one of his large notebooks— the same ones he used year after year—with reflections on the temptation of "laziness" when starting an artistic or cultural activity. He desired to write clearly and think consistently, but organizing his ideas was impossible; one topic would lead to another, and so on.

These reflections were prompted by Ibsen's one-act play, *The Warrior's Barrow*. If all the significance he found in the play had been incorporated into it, it would have been a monumental production. Nevertheless, the notebook

In the Theatre from Ten to Seven 1899–1904   105

itself is remarkable. It begins with impressions of Neskuchnoye, an ancient, weathered stone mound in the distance, the steppe, the dusty fleece of the sheep, and the monotonous melody of the shepherd. Nothing has changed; except, things have deteriorated compared to what he saw twenty years ago. However, he doesn't start the play like Ibsen's, with a burial mound and fields of dusty grass in the distance.[11] Instead, his notes attempt to make sense of the political power balance in a country already engaged in an unsuccessful war in the east and on the brink of revolution. As a political analysis, it held little value. Yet, it served as an essential starting point for the play's dialogue.

He had already developed a mature understanding of how to distribute the energies of his artistic organization, MAT. On one side were those who wanted and knew how to work, who aimed to be the best and embraced change, viewing it positively. On the other side were those who did not want or know how to work, obstructing progress—both intentionally and unintentionally, due to their positions of power or simply out of confusion. As a leader, he despised the isolated "fortress MAT" mindset. He particularly loathed staff worker Vasily Spiridonovich, who was always elusive, as well as Kuzma and Sidor, who lacked motivation. Furthermore, he found the Moscow Duma to be frustrating, taking at least a year to reject a request. Nemirovich-Danchenko could not tolerate unwillingness to work, whether it stemmed from profound arrogance or foolishness; it was irritating either way.

Whether a person clung to routine out of fear of losing status or a piece of the state pie, it mattered little to the notebook writer. He observed that the country was as indifferent to Tsar Nicholas II's foolishly conservative affairs as it was to a farmer he had known for years, who approached his own affairs with the same foolish conservatism. This farmer's harvest was diminishing to the point where he might as well give up his land, even though the soil remained fertile. None of this could be ignored, and Nemirovich-Danchenko did not ignore it. The provincial lands were dying, and there had been no progress since he first saw it. Life had not become more affluent, intelligent, or adventurous. Farmers relied on the land for their livelihoods, but they didn't love or protect it. They simply focused on the present without considering the future. "It's good to be healthy today, to have bread, potatoes, and pepper, a woman, and seeds. Next year might also be good, but there is no effort to preserve all of this." All of this was known, but there was more to it. Nemirovich-Danchenko's annoyance with the careless attitude of his peasant neighbor was understandable. But the neighbor showed no urgency to break free and continued to work without direction. Years of slavery had not taught him the value of perseverance. The lesson he had learned was to do less, and less would be taken away from him.

The internal dialogue continued in circles in his notebook. What was once considered historical guilt or misfortune had become the reality of today. He wrote about "Ukrainian laziness," the tendency to lie in the sun and gaze at the sky for hours. However, he also questioned this argument. The peasant was not lazy, and Nemirovich-Danchenko sought to explain their behavior in an economic context. The sun regulated their labor and time. Dependence on nature was not dishonorable. Was it better to depend on the boss's mood or the fluctuations of the stock exchange? He was intrigued by the behavior of the Ukrainian wheat growers and shepherds he knew. They lacked the desire to improve themselves, grow, and expand their property. If the expansion of life was expressed through such actions, then the lives of those observed by the author of the diary seemed weak. "The humor that distinguishes the people of the south may also be a sign of their weak sense of life or a keen sense of transient life." Laziness, too, was seen as a weak sense of life. "Indifference to the death of people from another part of the world is something different; it is indifference to life."

He interrupted himself, feeling that the promotion of this laziness and indifference was terrible. "It's only two steps from this to indifference towards other people and their sorrows." The argument persisted. "There is something noble in this laziness, in the sense of indifference to 'things,' a naïve contempt for 'making a profit,' for the orderliness of well-being." Viewing it this way, a peasant who sarcastically observed a prosperous neighbor was similar to a nearby noble landowner who faced ruin without concern. Acceptance of fate, death, and life's tragedies promotes peace of mind. Nemirovich-Danchenko observed a peasant woman on her deathbed, giving instructions for her funeral and memorial meal. As she listened to those around her preparing food, a candle glowed above her head. This scene adds to the idea of acceptance of life and fate. But what does it truly mean to accept death? Does it imply indifference to life? This new scene with the farewell candle and rising bread is an addition to his thoughts on life and fate, but it does not cancel out his earlier beliefs.

The arrival of new people, who initially admired him and shared similar goals, meant the expansion and conquest of a different spiritual formation. Losing these values resulted in a painful feeling. The newcomers faced their own drama—the withering and destruction of their work, consumed by the local wind and earth. They lived lives that lacked historical significance, with no memory of the past or future; only the "always" and "now."

The notebook contains titles of paintings, such as Ivan Kramskoi's "Christ in the Wilderness" and Nikolai Ge's "Peter I and Alexey — Strong Father, Weak Son." There are also notes about a father figure in the potential play, characterized as energetic and cruel, managing multiple affairs alone. His son is depicted as unfit, withdrawn, and unable to accept his father. This takes place in a country where a new culture needs to replace defeated beliefs, customs, traditions, language, and costumes. Nemirovich-Danchenko used the surname "Alchevsky" for the father (who will either kill himself or be killed in the play), as well as the name Peter the Great. The father and son's draft names are Peter and Alexey, which was likely intentional. However, once modern elements are introduced into the narrative, the themes of right and wrong, historical energy, and achievements diminish and become a caricature of themselves. What kind of achievements? "Business," coal

In the Theatre from Ten to Seven 1899–1904   107

mines, railway or factory construction, imported laborers, stock shares, thieves, and commission agents. Someone gets promoted, only to be promoted over by someone who would rather appease the crowd and the authorities, someone quick to take a bribe—creating an endless and restless spirit of self-interest. Suddenly, the diary writer adds a comical episode: a family of swindlers somehow multiplies in the home of the bewildered business owner's son, robbing him before making a getaway. They appear just after news reports confirm the business owner's downfall. And that was the whole point: the truth always comes out. The passage stops abruptly, but with consequences. It was unnecessary for the play, but necessary for the author of the journal.

Another notable entry emphasizes the importance of long-term reckoning and self-improvement, which was a product of the bourgeoisie. "To maintain social stability and cultural stability, it is necessary to strengthen bourgeois values." The convergence of ideas here is a delicate issue. Culture represents a clash between love and Nemirovich-Danchenko's (and MAT's) ambitions, while bourgeois values are seen as the enemy, a personal threat. However, it is clear that "bourgeois values are necessary for cultural peace of mind." The harmonious existence of culture and the individual relies on freedom of movement within societal stability (as seen in the recurring themes of home and departure in *Three Sisters* at MAT). In Russian reality, the government-imposed constraints on freedom of movement, causing social stability to either grow stagnant and hinder movement or become disturbed by vague underground forces.

The rapid and fruitful development of the cultural sphere, which everyone witnessed in the Russian 1990s, was dramatic. It particularly blocked certain historical pitfalls, while the awareness of the lurking emptiness beneath it continued unabated. Nemirovich-Danchenko's contemporaries could relate to the despair expressed by Godunov in *Tsar Fyodor* ("All in vain! I am building over a failure!").

...

MAT could not exist without a desire for long-term reckoning and self-improvement. Its unique creation consisted of the celebration and joy of Russian life. However, this subject was rarely discussed within MAT itself. How many informed Russians truly reflected on their accomplishments? It was easier to observe from the outside. MAT only became aware of its creation when they embarked on their first tour to St. Petersburg in 1901. The stability they achieved during that time was captivating, and they wanted it to continue. Any sudden change would be seen as dangerous, fearing that something fascinating might collapse. MAT had fallen in love with its own beautiful creations, but there was danger and a lack of freedom in this sentiment. The artist no longer belonged to himself or to something greater, but only to his own artistic development. Furthermore, loving this art came with the fear of losing it.

108 *Vladimir Nemirovich-Danchenko and the Moscow Art Theatre*

So, after its first Petersburg tour, MAT seemingly fell in love with itself. Nemirovich-Danchenko thought that the theatre could love itself this way because it was enclosed within a circle of enduring spiritual themes and lyrical presentations that had received positive responses from audiences. From then on, MAT only sought to create images that matched what it already loved. In the summer of 1902, Nemirovich-Danchenko wrote letters from Neskuchnoye, outlining his thoughts. His letter to the MAT company was sharper, fiercer, and more personal compared to any other addressee. He analyzed the past four seasons to assess the current situation and identify the prospects and dangers. While the analysis focused on small details, it didn't diminish the sense of alarm that Nemirovich-Danchenko needed to convey.

Loving your failures, especially when they involve an unspoken big idea, is important. In this sense, the failure of *The Snow Maiden* in 1900 held more value than the success of performances that echoed what the public already accepted. *Three Sisters* was undeniably better than Chekhov's first production and objectively more beautiful. However, the attitude toward *The Seagull* was unique and went beyond mere excellence. Nemirovich-Danchenko didn't want to create an experimental theatre (it was at this point that his future dispute with Stanislavsky was already on the horizon). He appreciated those moments when art pushed its boundaries willingly, rather than publicly cultivating the continuous development of those boundaries.

Nemirovich-Danchenko never sought to torture or distress himself, but he believed that genuine work in art couldn't exist without a passionate desire to quit everything and walk away. Therefore, he based his thinking on the action of *Three Sisters*—take your hat and go. Experiencing the need to stop and walk away was equally as important as putting your hat down and returning to business.

Tradition, Change, and Resilience in Life and Legacy

Nemirovich-Danchenko was not the oldest member of MAT; much-loved Alexander Artem was older,[12] as were Maria Samarova and Evgenia Raevskaya, who came from Stanislavsky's Society of Art and Literature. Yet, he was older than most. Those who later remembered the early years of MAT would think of them as the years of youth and hope. Nemirovich-Danchenko, too, fondly remembered the summer at Pushkino, the rosy morning light, the balcony overlooking the garden above the river, and everything that happened there. But he would add more: he remembered this time as the last hours of youth.

His life—his everyday life—no longer ran according to the changeableness of youth. Even his address remained a house on the corner of Skaryatinsky and Nikitskaya Streets for many years. In 1938, he and his wife Ekaterina finally moved to Nemirovich-Danchenko Street (formerly Glinischevsky Street) to an apartment building built on a demolished church site, especially for artists of the highest rank. His way to work was unchanged after

In the Theatre from Ten to Seven 1899–1904   109

MAT moved from Carriage Row to Kamergersky Lane. However, what did this mean, unchanged? He lived in a city that had never taken care of itself, haphazardly demolishing house after house. There were still empty lots and holes in the ground, so it was difficult to remember what a building looked like before—the face of unsightly but cordial housing is forgotten.

In time, the theatre in Kamergersky Lane was reconstructed beyond recognition. Nemirovich-Danchenko could not even remember what the auditorium was like before the newly installed curvilinear balconies reaching up to the stage, sconces of pale pink glass, painted side walls with a stylized surf pattern running toward the stage, silver-gray bands around the slightly arched ceiling, dark green leather seats made with dark wood, and walls shaded from olive-green to lilac and silver at the top. The materials and construction were now exposed: lines of footlights, columns supporting the balconies, and angular joints of the rings from which the lighting instruments hung. Earlier, this venue was the Russian Theatre, where they performed the premiere of his play *Bankrupt in France* (1885), after which the building became Savva Mamontov's private opera.[13]

Nemirovich-Danchenko's former home on the corner of Skaryatinsky Street began to look old-fashioned. Kachalov often visited there with his son Vadim, who did not like these visits very much. He was not interested in Nemirovich-Danchenko,—"like at the doctor's,"—with plush upholstered furniture. Misha (his adopted son) played the violin to entertain guests, primarily relatives and female friends of his wife. First young, then middle-aged, then finally older ladies. Their daughters wrote to "Uncle Volodya," thanking him for *The Blue Bird*, then as the girls grew up, for *Woe from Wit*. After that, nothing would remain except their habit of relying on "Uncle Volodya," who could not refuse them anything. What he did for these former young women destroyed by life, the awful hellholes he pulled them out of, was incredible.

In the summers, the family returned to Neskuchnoye. The steward Ludwig was a figure suitable for classic country scenes on stage. Knowing about this man from Nemirovich-Danchenko's stories, Stanislavsky even included him among the guests at the ball in his directorial plan for *The Cherry Orchard*. Later, Nemirovich-Danchenko entrusted the estate's affairs to a teacher from the local school, Evstafy Sidorov, the "eccentric" about whom the peasant Shavkunenko wrote a letter. There were also angry letters from Sidorov himself: why didn't they let him know they were going to the Crimea while he was wasting time and money waiting for them in Neskuchnoye? Madame neglected the farm's needs; he complained and ordered the mowers to release the horses and send them to the train station. How could they blame him for such mismanagement? The old orchard yields nothing and should be cut down, but no one would remove the stumps "for nothing." There was no money to pay for it, so the chopping would have to wait. More resentment: Madame hinted he was living a life of idleness and ease here on the estate, yet he hasn't a moment's rest. He has always had to hedge and dodge: what should he pay for and sell? "Most of the pigs have died over the past two years."

110 *Vladimir Nemirovich-Danchenko and the Moscow Art Theatre*

His writing sounded like the steward, Shamraev, from *The Seagull* or Yepikhodov from *The Cherry Orchard*, but his fate differed. In 1922, just before the new year, a letter arrived in Moscow from Tanya Smorodina, a resident of Neskuchnoye, which was near the rebel Makhnovist region. "Your writings and manuscripts are gone, and someone looted and plundered the entire library. There was no way to defend anything because one would have become a victim just as Evstafy Sidorov was killed three years ago." This news remained ahead until the New Year in 1922; meanwhile, his home library continued growing. Despite the steward's protests, the horses were still used to meet guests at the train station and the mail.

Nemirovich-Danchenko's relations with his neighbors were always excellent and robust. In 1937, a "carefree Russian nobleman" congratulated him on receiving the Order of Lenin:

> I should have done this a long time ago, but I have been a little ailing lately. I'm busy getting my pension back, which I lost in 1929 as a former landowner. As soon as I get it, I will come to Moscow. I love that old place! I might cry a little when I see it. Then, of course, I will visit you, and then, brother, as a tribute to the many smiles of fate you have received, you will give me a half-liter of Soviet vodka. An excellent drink! It is no worse than a wonderful memory of Smirnovka.

One neighbor, Peter Kamensky, was a brave and "unrepentant nobleman" and considered a "man of honor." In 1906, he wrote his usual letter to his neighbor about the chores delegated to him by another neighbor (always unpleasant, opportunistic, and lazy) and about affairs in general. He was untroubled by any subject's dullness or poetry, conveying everything in a calm and clear tone. This year, they were unlikely to see each other at the resort as they were accustomed to:

> It would be a pleasure to escape from our estates, full of threats, fears, gossip, hallucinating inhabitants. I am afraid that I cannot go to Kislovodsk; unfortunately, it is impossible to leave the people nearby. I do not attach importance to the threats I receive from verbal and written announcements at rallies that burn me *ad majorem gloriam* of the revolution. But people would consider my departure cowardly as if I took the rumors seriously. Besides, it's time for next year's agricultural license applications. It's difficult to quit my former soft, sympathetic attitude and become sharply decisive in my explanations; they take my every concession as an escape. Yesterday, I gave first aid to a victim of a gunshot wound.

However, his story was told as comical and not horrific. It was not frightening for Peter Kamensky. At the end of the letter is a transition to inquiries about creative affairs. Kamensky regrets Nemirovich-Danchenko wrote too little: "It's a sin for you to hide your *feu sacré* under wraps." Your sacred fire.

In the Theatre from Ten to Seven 1899–1904   111

Kamensky helped Nemirovich-Danchenko unravel Neskuchnoye's financial affairs; the estate was mortgaged and entangled with debts, but so were they all. This situation did not interfere with the pleasure of visiting, playing chess, and showing guests the ancient burial mound and the nearby river. Whenever they both went to Crimea, the hotel staff there already knew them and would have their rooms ready their rooms in advance.

Nemirovich-Danchenko had one hobby, even a passion—cards. They said he once lost his estate, his wife's diamonds, and even his MAT shares. Idle gossip, most likely. But he was indeed a gambler. There was something in his papers he called "Notes about playing cards," which are essential for understanding his nature.

There is nothing worse than being *afraid of losing* at cards. Either don't put it all in or put in a sum you decide to lose but put it in calmly and bravely. Don't be greedy, but don't cry either.

"Happiness comes in streaks, but these streaks of happiness and failure rarely last."

"Only play with your own money."

"A strong *will* primarily determines the position of the gambler who wants to play successfully."

"Those who are sad and gaze at life unwillingly, and those who drink wine while playing and recklessly surrender themselves to the game are invariably the losers."

"The person who wins is the one who wants to win, is obsessed with it, and believes in it."

He loved cards when he grew older too. As a widower in later years, he played cards with the women who lived in the same building and sometimes came to visit his dacha—they played with tokens, won, or lost eighty kopecks for the evening—one ruble. This settled way of life could vary, of course, but it was essentially the same.

Nemirovich-Danchenko remained in MAT's so-called upper office on the mezzanine level until the end of his days. The mezzanine's balcony door allowed him to enter quietly to watch a performance. When they unlock the office now, it has the odor of being uninhabited. But then, if you let the door stand open, the aromas of the old life will begin to arise—wood, leather, a bit of cologne, unless this is only a fantasy. Nemirovich-Danchenko set up a working office here on November 9, 1905 (Figure 4.1). In a note attached to his diary, he ordered a "cabinet with compartments for director's documents, school, plays read, plays not accepted, plays in preparation, archives, letters, unanswered correspondence, drawings and albums, and trifles." The cabinet stands to the right as you enter.

The room is like a small container, the ceiling is too high, and the window looks out on the building's sidewall next door. There was no building there when Nemirovich-Danchenko moved in; it was built after demolishing an

112 *Vladimir Nemirovich-Danchenko and the Moscow Art Theatre*

outbuilding following World War I. The office was a little dark, so he had to work with electric light even during the day. The chandelier hung from a chain is all twisted in the modernist style. Even the color of the glass is knotty, shimmering mother-of-pearl. When he worked at the desk, he offered visitors a place on the corner sofa upholstered in gray cloth. There was also a small, upholstered chaise on the left of the door where he allowed himself to lie down and rest. On it were pillows he received for memorable dates decorated with silver thread or faded beads. They were fashionable, though not very comfortable; as a keepsake, they were lovely. He was also presented with framed photographs as keepsakes hanging all over the walls.

For a long time, a photo of Maria Germanova stood on his desk[14]—he grew interested in this actress as early as 1904 during rehearsals of Pyotr Yartsev's unsuccessful play *At the Monastery*.[15] Everyone he worked with at the time seemed dull and immovable compared to this young woman, who seemed to fulfill what MAT needed at that time. She captured the sharp impression of novelty, which theatre must have to endure.

Nemirovich-Danchenko did not consider changing his "artistically ordinary" tastes necessary. He lived with them as they were. His "personal interior" was that of the late nineteenth century. It would never be "furnished" anew, either in the sense of furniture or the more profound understanding of his inner self. At the same time, as the head of MAT and a director, he was the first to capture and acknowledge the change in milestones and accept them with extraordinary readiness.

Just as striking is his breakup with Chekhov.

Notes

1 *Hymns to Claudian* (1914) is a play by dramatist and novelist Hermann Sudermann (1857–1928).
2 Leonid Leonidov (1873–1941) was an actor associated with MAT.
3 Sophia Khalyutina (1875–1960) was an actress and teacher associated with MAT. Performed the role of the perpetual teenager in the course of the theatre's first decade; innumerable roles for the next fifty years.
4 Nezlobin's Theatre was founded in 1901 by actor-director Konstantin Nezlobin (1857–1930). Its popularity sometimes rivaled MAT's.
5 Alisa Koonen (1889–1974) was an actress and the wife of Chamber Theatre director Alexander Tairov.
6 Specifically, "the metamorphosis of the actor's self, a living person, into a living person-role," the innovative acting style of MAT.
7 *Greta's Happiness* (1897) is a play by Emil Mariottt (1855–1938) about a young woman ignorant of sex who is given in marriage; on her wedding night, she tries to escape and nearly goes insane.
8 Gabriele D'Annunzio (1863–1938). An Italian poet, playwright, orator, journalist, aristocrat, and officer in the Royal Italian Army during World War I.
9 Eleanora Duse (1818–1954) Italian actress widely regarded as one the greatest of all time.
10 Maria Andreyeva (1868–1953) was an actress associated with MAT.
11 *The Burial Mound* (*The Warrior's Barrow*) (1850) is a play by Henrik Ibsen in which the love of pagan Viking for a Christian woman connotes cultural change.

In the Theatre from Ten to Seven 1899–1904   113

12 Alexander Artem (1841–1919) was an actor, founding member, and lifelong MAT company member.
13 Savva Mamontov (1841–1918) was an industrialist, merchant, entrepreneur, and patron of the arts.
14 Maria Germanova (1884–1940) actress associated with MAT.
15 *At the Monastery* (1904) play by theatre critic, playwright, and director Pyotr Yartsev (1870–1930).

5 First Farewells 1904–1905

Nostalgia Amid Change

Nemirovich-Danchenko paused his writing of *The Burial Mound* to transcribe a telegram word for word: "Anton Pavlovich died of heart failure. Olga Chekhov." Nemirovich-Danchenko believed that his fate was intertwined with Chekhov's and thought that his literary and spiritual life would end when Chekhov's "songs" ended. He could have prepared himself for Chekhov's death from Olga Knipper-Chekhov's many despondent letters from Badenweiler. However, he was not prepared and was shocked and visibly shaken. In this moment of loss, Nemirovich-Danchenko could have said that Chekhov is with us and will live on for many years, never becoming outdated. But he didn't. Seven years ago, Nemirovich-Danchenko wrote that *The Seagull* "throbbed with the pulse of modern Russian life, and that's what makes it so dear to me." However, seven years have passed and Nemirovich-Danchenko only reluctantly agreed to a revival of the play. At best, he believed audiences would accept it as a beloved old song. But as a depiction of and response to life, it no longer worked. The war in the East and the possibility of revolution at home preoccupied the public, so they were no longer responsive to what was beloved or even eternal. Nemirovich-Danchenko wrote, "A quiet life full of the joys of nature, the musical sounds of the world — none of this makes an impression anymore." Chekhov's modest, lyrical characters ceased to exist.

The Seagull was Nemirovich-Danchenko's discovery and pride. He wore a keychain given to him by the author: "You gave my *Seagull* life. Thank you!" But he no longer wanted *The Seagull*. He had given it life, but everything has its time, and he believed that time had passed. If they produced Chekhov now, it would only relegate him to history, as he had already been consigned to the earth. Instead, they will present *Ivanov*. They had considered staging this play multiple times and set it aside multiple times due to doubts about its uncertain structure (Chekhov composed the play for Korsh's Theatre in a matter of days, but already with the core of a different, personal, and unmistakable dramatic system). Chekhov himself objected to its production because he felt that it contained too many elements from the past and out-of-date dramaturgy.

DOI: 10.4324/9781003486282-5

The choice of *Ivanov* can be explained by the director's fondness for the nocturne that formed the first act, which became one of Nemirovich-Danchenko's stage masterpieces. The interplay of the characters' isolated melodies created a unique evening mood. Amidst the rosy glow of the fading sun, the charming old house in the shadows, and the piles of grass clippings in the courtyard, Lvov paces quietly back and forth, listening to the cello's serenade coming from the house. Meanwhile, Ivanov sits behind a newspaper, pressing his hands against his face, showing no interest in reading. The moon casts a whitewash over the poplars, an owl's cry pierces the air, and the melancholy of the cello intertwines with the voices from the servant's quarters and Shabelsky's loud grumbling. Restlessness and guilt-induced boredom hang in the air, in stark contrast to Ivanov's wife Anna's hopeless attempt to dispel the gloom: "Nicholas, let's go and have a tumble in the hay!"

Nemirovich-Danchenko's table work with the actors did not begin by immersing them in the moonlit feeling, the evening melancholy of the manor house, or the torment of an unrequited, empty heart. Instead, table work started with the play's historical background. According to the cast list, Ivanov is described as "A government official concerned with peasant affairs." Nemirovich-Danchenko had to clarify this role because, in the autumn of 1904, it was just as bewildering to the actors of MAT as it is to us now. Ivanov's official position does not hold any special significance for the play; however, the director felt the need to provide an explanation because the position no longer exists. The person himself had also disappeared, necessitating further clarification. The text, first outlined in the diary and then transcribed to the director's copy, was not only meant as an "opening statement before the start of rehearsals." It also marked the actual beginning of rehearsals, immersing the cast in the author's world, the world of the play, and the world as understood by the director.

MAT historians have often referred to Nemirovich-Danchenko's introduction to *Ivanov*, but it's worth revisiting to truly understand its directorial significance and Nemirovich-Danchenko's effort to instill it in the actors' creative subconscious. The most important objective was to repeat the phrase, "Nowadays, you will not meet..." because such individuals no longer exist in modern times. Sasha, with her love of books and passion for self-sacrifice; Lebedev, with his cautious idealism disguised as a gentle alcoholic, ashamed of his present self compared to memories of his happy student years; and Ivanov, with his dying soul that can barely hear his conscience. Departing this life, Ivanov's conscience only becomes a possession of memory and poetry.

"Nowadays, they no longer exist. Completely gone." From the very beginning, Nemirovich-Danchenko recognized the artistic potential of feeling "cut off." As a young critic, he had limited knowledge of the nostalgic tendencies of the World of Art movement in 1879, when he provided a review of a benefit performance of Peter Borborykin's 1860 play *The Smallholders*. Yet, the charm of this old play struck a chord, like a distant song that is no longer sung. Under normal circumstances, a play like this would have faded from

116 *Vladimir Nemirovich-Danchenko and the Moscow Art Theatre*

the stage. The producers attempted to mask its obsolescence by trimming it down, dismissing anything related to the past as irrelevant. However, the poetry of the play resided precisely in these "superfluous" moments, the spaces "between events" that preserved the spirit of the past.

But first came *The Chery Orchard*, whose co-director would certainly be familiar with the sentiments expressed by the young reviewer, Nemirovich-Danchenko. "Let the action of the play be set in our time," he once remarked. "Let everything come from everyday life — the rolled-up travel blankets, willow traveling baskets filled with provisions, jute hat boxes, and bundles of umbrellas." Although everything was contemporary, there was a sense that it would all vanish. In just a moment, they would no longer travel in carriages like this; it would not feel the same. This way of life was already slipping away, fading into the background, only maintained through the existence of the stage.

Creating this impression would have been easy by encasing *The Cherry Orchard* in an elegiac haze of refined grace and farewell playfulness. Alternatively, they could have followed Meyerhold's lead, who sought to emphasize the theme of doom rejected by the actors in *The Cherry Orchard*. However, MAT did not find doom or destiny in Chekhov's work. Instead, they found Reality with a capital "R"—Necessity, History—which they believed could only be conveyed through flawlessly depicted reality: vibrant yet on the brink of extinction, heartwarming yet devoid of a future. The people would disappear and become lost. Everything in the house would also vanish, falling into the hands of resellers. When comparing *The Cherry Orchard* to *Ivanov*, the contrasting personalities of the directors come into view. The co-director of *The Cherry Orchard* differed greatly from the sole director of *Ivanov*. This disparity stemmed from the fundamental differences between the plays and the significant time gap between the productions. More importantly, though, it arose from the distinct individuals who assumed the roles of director. Both "somebody" and Nemirovich-Danchenko, however, understood historical inevitability. When they directed *The Cherry Orchard* together, it felt like a tribute to the inevitability of endings—much like the cycle of life and death. Just as the death of one individual can signify the loss of an entire world, the departure represented in the play symbolize the fading of something profoundly significant within a nation's culture. If something is inevitable, it doesn't mean it's unquestionably and unconditionally good. We don't rejoice in the death of an older person, even if it's natural (natural doesn't mean deserved or fair).

Behind *The Cherry Orchard* was an increasing understanding of the value of the country's moral inheritance, which includes all the Gayevs' sins. Even though the Gayevs themselves were inactive and unproductive, they embodied a unique, refined culture that had developed over many decades. The culture's last, weak, and valueless children conveyed something essential through themselves.

At first, the audience sided with Lopakhin, who continuously expressed anger and despair by throwing up his hands—How can this be? What are

First Farewells 1904–1905   117

they thinking? They must do something! However, eventually, the audience realized that the cherry orchard's bankrupt owners' carelessness was more than just negligence; it was the nobility of accepting an inevitable destiny. In the way seventeen-year-old Anya left her native home without worrying about her future, you could see not only the impractical example of Trofimov but also the ethical examples of a noble house. Ranevskaya and Gayev never asked how they would live without the income from the cherry orchard, but only how they would live without the cherry orchard, which was the meaning, beauty, and poetry of their life, as well as the decline of Russia's poetic heritage.

However, MAT did not want an elegy, so they looked for clear, energetic counterpoints. Therefore, the play needed a sharp, dark note in Lopakhin, as well as that odd, ingratiating, threatening tramp that appeared and disappeared in the soft evening twilight. And the sound of a bucket falling somewhere in a mine shaft far away, prosaic but incomprehensible, unsettling, and prophetic. All of this contributed to the metaphysical music of the production. Nemirovich-Danchenko later concluded that it was the metaphysical music of *The Cherry Orchard* that captivated the audience, not the aristocrats selling their estates. Anya and Trofimov don't notice the empty walls and the old furniture moved out of place and piled together in the last act. They don't see how Ranevskaya and Gayev feel so at home in their old nursery for the last time and try to suppress their sobs so that no one can hear them. Finally, they don't notice that Firs is being left behind in the boarded-up house. In terms of music, we don't accuse the major leitmotif of selfishness and indifference toward the sorrowful, complaining quiet theme. In MAT's production, the "minor key" poetic lyricism subtly counterpoints the "major key" directness of life itself.

"After reading *The Cherry Orchard*," Stanislavsky said, "For an ordinary person, this is a tragedy," and his response provides a significant clue. It may be true that humanity laughs about its discarded past, but you and I would be incapable of this. Therefore, "for an ordinary person, it is a tragedy." These obsolete, idle, frivolous people may not be capable of tragedy, but they can be bitter and hurt. Who knows how Ranevskaya will end up in Paris or where her brother will end up when his incompetence as a "bank clerk" comes to light? Historical inevitability is historically inevitable, but these characters are pitiable. Perhaps because Chekhov and MAT understood the impersonal force of history, they wanted the simplest efforts of humanity—measures of tolerance, care, and pity—to be included in it.

As the theme of history became more noticeable in *The Cherry Orchard*, it was essential for the directors to incorporate historic charm into the mise en scène. This included the warmth of the household stove, carefully heated in the evening for the guests on the road who might be chilly from the frosty nights; the distant sound of a train heard every morning; the commotion of arrival; the fondness of the first minutes, when you wanted to follow on the heels of the newcomers and hold them close; the confusion of unpacking,

118 *Vladimir Nemirovich-Danchenko and the Moscow Art Theatre*

when you got distracted and started talking to your family, being pulled to see how something has changed or not changed in your old rooms; the rush to tell the news, hugging, the smell of coffee, the blue light of an alcohol lamp, and the warmth of the stove bench where Pischik dozed.

None of these elements were independently noticeable, separate, and self-important in the production, but together, they were intended to create an atmosphere of homelike warmth. Against this backdrop, they understood Ranevskaya's affectionate, sociable solitude. They understood the aging, autumn-bright woman torn between her home, homeland, daughter, loved ones, and Paris, "this wild man," whom she knows the true cost of and is not deceived by. But what can you do? She loved him. They understood her desire to forget, envied her knack for forgetting. Knipper knew how bitter and hopeless Ranevskaya's fate could have been if not for her ability to find joy in small pleasures, always grateful and seeking only brief moments of happiness. They understood her laughter, carefree yet ready to abruptly cease. They understood her sense of humor. They pitied her vulnerability, so genuine, feminine, and innate. They also understood how elated Gayev was when his sister arrived. Over time, our early experiences become cherished. This brother and sister may not possess a deep love for each other; Gayev even speaks unfavorably about her. However, they were entwined in each other's lives, just as this house, nursery, and bookcase were vital components of their lives. The bookcase even inspired a ludicrous speech.

The Cherry Orchard swiftly transformed the melodies of Russian life and reflections on Russian life into historical musings. Everything reverberated within the vibrant and intricate soundscape of Russia "off stage," while also foreshadowing what lay ahead from a distance.

Tradition vs. Innovation in Chekhov

The furnishings from *The Cherry Orchard*, which were arranged to be sold at the end, were actually family items that Nemirovich-Danchenko brought from Neskuchnoye. In a similar vein, the melancholy sound of the evening countryside in the director's vision for *Ivanov* was the sound of his own summer evenings there: "The cry of the swamp heron sounds in the distance." Nemirovich-Danchenko placed copies of *The Russian Gazette* from the early 1880s, *The Russian Courier*, and *The Voice* on the desk in Ivanov's office and on the benches in the courtyard—newspapers that contained his own articles. The director's emotions shaped the unique essence of *Ivanov*, which was distinct from that of *The Cherry Orchard*. Even though the production was "his," it was now more important than ever to sever ties with past practices, much like using a knife. The line of "dying-out" (how poetically meaningful the implications of this line are in *The Cherry Orchard*) is crossed out and struck through with the sudden coldness of a statement of fact.

Nemirovich-Danchenko told the actors preparing for *Ivanov* about his own life. He shared memories, but his words had an instructive quality, akin to a

First Farewells 1904–1905   119

history book: "Ivanov exemplifies a landowner's life amidst the remnants of the ideas of the reformist 'sixties. Shabelsky, for instance, is a relic of the 'sixties mentality." The director's notes mention: "costumes and hairstyles from the decade 1878–1888, similar to those in the photographs of uncles, aunts, and friends of the parents of today's youth." These were not direct family connections, but rather figures from the periphery. The 'sixties had come to an end. Out of all the plays by Chekhov, *Ivanov* was the only one that failed to evoke empathy and did not seem to seek it. The dynamic between the stage and the audience was cold toward *Ivanov* in 1904. (Nemirovich-Danchenko wrote, "Ivanov. Unsuccessful.") In 1918, Nemirovich-Danchenko insisted on reviving *Ivanov*, and this time it was a failure in the truest sense of the word. The gap between the stage and the audience was profound, and nothing could bridge it. Nemirovich-Danchenko received desperate letters: "Why? Why? Why are you reviving *Ivanov*? Why are you committing such a sin?" Actor Richard Boleslavsky penned this after a performance on November 6, 1918. The theatre portrayed the past as dead and foreign. "Everyone will say, Bravo, the Bolsheviks swept away all this intelligentsia and good riddance. And they would be right. Does MAT want this, or should they? No, no, Nemirovich-Danchenko!" Chekhov's plays are seen as comic-mockeries, farcical-goodbyes, shouting, "Good riddance!" Others may have produced them in that way, but not Nemirovich-Danchenko. He didn't want the audience laughing, like Boleslavsky did. However, his *Ivanov* made you wonder if Nemirovich-Danchenko could accept the ruthless words of the Gospel, "Let the dead bury their dead," without harming himself as an artist. In his notebook, there appears something like an epitaph, an outline to remember, a short analysis, and a formula for separation and farewell. The entry for February 3, 1905, says,

> What did the immediate past teach us? That the delicate motives of the soul suffered. That delicate souls went into silence. That life taught impudently. People remembered Chekhov as if from an ancient time, like romantic paintings of landlord life in serf times.

And it hadn't even been a year since he died. Nemirovich-Danchenko recognized what they condemned to death as dead and hurried to part with it as dead.

In a moral and aesthetic sense, *Ivanov* ended the Chekhov cycle at MAT instead of just closing it. Previous Chekhov productions had a pulsing, echoing, spontaneous sound; the mise-en-scene had continuous movement, lightness, fragility, and incompleteness. In *Ivanov* 1918, the sound and mise-en-scene were frozen in clarity, the leitmotifs fixed and unchanging. The decision to have a motionless mise-en-scene came from the simplest of motives: "I will intentionally leave Lebedev stationary. What's the point for an old man to change his position?" "I don't want Lvov to walk or sit during his monologue. His lack of resourcefulness, his internal instability, his thoughtlessness fasten him to one spot," although the motionless mise-en-scene also had another meaning in *Ivanov*. Life is always in motion. What no longer exists appears as something else, fragmented into large and small entanglements. The interplay of reactions and reflections that characterizes writing with vitality is nowhere to be found in Ivanov. Consequently, individual moments carried a sharper impact. It was unsettling when Sarah opened the window and stood there, swaying slightly, and groaning with her entire body; then, upon hearing footsteps, she straightened up, folded her handkerchief, and perched on the windowsill. There was also a chilling effect when Ivanov cheerfully interacted with Sarah in their private moments. For instance, when he sat on the edge of a chair, gazing up at her with laughter, while she loomed over him, offering comforting words in her velvety riding ensemble.

Nemirovich-Danchenko did not believe in the power of spontaneously emerging details. He could only mimic this approach, and doing so would be insincere. *Ivanov* marked the first time that Nemirovich-Danchenko's personal and enduring artistic attributes were revealed: meaningful brevity, boundless imagination, and a preference for capturing the structure of life rather than its nuanced textures. Additionally, Nemirovich-Danchenko preserved the familiar, cozy ambiance customary at MAT. Photographs showcased plush armchairs, a sleeper sofa (descriptions included embroidered cushions, their arrangement, and fluffed bolsters; "many guests had slept on it"), and a tiled stove set off with hanging rifles. However, none of the critics thought to depict the house in the same captivating warmth as they did the Prozorovs' home or the Gayevs' estate. The stage imagery was minimal: an empire urn on a pedestal, an empty second pedestal with a rusty spike sticking out from it; gnarled branches crisscrossing the house's exterior; and paint-stripped brick pillars—everything felt decayed. The colors were predominantly dark gray and deep red.

This was a world where people were at odds with themselves and with one another, incongruous with the house, and incompatible with life. "Life is a cheat," as Sara proclaimed, and it had not only deceived her. The production did not aim to settle scores with life, which had been belatedly managed, but only to convey the bottom line: resentment stemming from feeling swindled. Sara/Knipper portrayed the dry, ironic chuckle of a deceived woman. It was unpleasant and not in line with the woman herself, but she couldn't free herself from it. She suffered in the same way that Ivanov couldn't escape, except by choosing a different outcome. Instead of the lyrical quality of the early Chekhov productions, the director aimed for stillness and moments of inner tension. It's remarkable how well the director understood the characters and tapped into their most hidden motives. For example, when Ivanov says goodbye to his wife, Ivanov is about to go to Lebedev's. Everyone is already there when he suddenly reverts to his former self. His affectionate nature returns, instantly shattering Sara's deliberate calmness toward her husband. He kisses her goodbye and touches her so gently, so kindly that she feels ashamed of her jealousy and her habit of constantly blaming his inherent dullness. As a result, it is only natural for her to find a place for him in her heart: "Kolya, my love, stay!" Ivanov/Kachalov spoke with his wife and kissed her hands; it was impossible to express the extent of his guilt and regret. He was speechless because she was waiting for something he couldn't provide. In response to her probing questions of what was wrong with him and how they could help, he responded "dully, nervously, putting on his gloves:" "I don't know, I don't know." His suffering caused her pain. The carriage then drives away. Activity stirs in the house—they prepare for bed, extinguishing the lights. Sarah doesn't break down and rush after her husband to Lebedev's out of jealousy, but out of the same longing that pursues and torments Ivanov. She runs to a place that is noisy and crowded, any kind of life, just not the emptiness of her own existence.

One critic found the key theme of Kachalov's Ivanov to be: "He wants to live up to the last minute; he does everything to live." Even at his second wedding, he carries a revolver, hoping that something will happen which allows him to reconcile with himself and continue living. This demonstrates a deep understanding of the simplest things. This desire to live also drives this "incomprehensible average Russian man" to refer to his melancholy as "merlichlundria" and to crave vodka, gooseberry jam, and the company of a refined woman who cooks delicious mushrooms.[1] He even finds a need for Mikhail Borkin's mischief, as he organizes impressive firework displays.

Reviewers were attracted to the Lebedevs' home environment, with its columned hall and arched ceiling that overlooked the garden. Lights danced and flickered through a large arched window, creating a pleasantly monotonous ambiance. Guests sat symmetrically, leafing through *World Illustrations*, while onlookers gathered around a card game. A hot-tempered whist lover slammed his cards down in anger. Meanwhile, older women sat in a row, eagerly awaiting the maid's arrival with sweets such as pastilles, dates, nuts, pistachios, and raisins. The director referred to them as "eaters." Nemirovich-Danchenko's favorite part of the second act was the sets, customs, and comically familiar characters and groups. He did not see the anachronisms as ironic but as a portrayal of "continuous *poshlost*." Moreover, he believed that all these characters were drawn from authentic Russian life and were timeless.

Reviewers hurried to share their opinions, noting that this play was not set in the 1880s of Chekhov but in the 1840s of Gogol or possibly even earlier. The juxtaposition of disappeared historical and spiritual archetypes with the enduring nature of *poshlost* may not have created a noticeable excitement, but it certainly stimulated reflection. Nemirovich-Danchenko's production shed light on the relationship between individuals and ideals, emphasizing the existence of specific, vanished individuals and their corresponding, vanished ideals. Ivanov finds himself entangled in debts that were not his own, inherited from his spiritual predecessors. He is burdened by unfulfilled obligations and an alarmingly increasing amount of interest. "An inheritance

122 *Vladimir Nemirovich-Danchenko and the Moscow Art Theatre*

entangled in debt (after the 'sixties)," he wrote in his notes for *Ivanov*. Why did the 'sixties fail? "We needed to eradicate many things, but for this, we also needed both an unwavering determination and compassion, and there would be consequences because we were cutting down a forest." "A series of contradictions resulted": the 'sixties revealed "positive aspirations for the common good" and sharpened "a sense of sympathy, acceptance, broad-ranging justice — humanitarianism." Now they regretted the resulting divisions and had doubts about deforesting. Clearly, there is no "unwavering determination" in Ivanov, and this man, who was, after all, "one of the beautiful rebels," as stated in 1904, is not in disgrace. Nemirovich-Danchenko saw Ivanov as a man who personally felt dishonored by the failure of his spiritual rebellion ("Mutiny cannot end in good fortune, otherwise it is called something else." A wryly comic epigraph states.[2]). It humiliated Ivanov in the literal sense of the word—he became smaller and worse.

Ivanov/Kachalov found a graceful, infinitely sweet smile for Ivanov, along with the innate simplicity of aristocratic habits, but he covered everything with a dark cloud of suffering. The time came when "The eyes grow dim, the voice becomes harsh and loud, the movements are sharp, small, and fussy, the face contains an expression of excruciating, almost animal pain."[3] The entire life of someone going through a crisis in their relationship with the ideal; the person becomes different, but the ideal suffers as well. He feels guilty and no longer resembles himself. Nemirovich-Danchenko made this clear when he pitted Ivanov/Kachalov against Lvov/Moskvin, not as adversaries but as foils. The original sees himself reflected in the mediocre copy, while the copy accuses the original. There was a sense of intimacy between them (the director used this word specifically, noting how Ivanov attentively regards Lvov in the text). Within this framework, Lvov was not a dull imitator with rehearsed phrases, but a poetic stammerer who carried each word deep in his heart (even if they were always untimely and commonplace). "If bitterness is present, could it be because he is awkward and unable to play the role of the hero, since that is how he envisions himself in his dreams?" You would also be driven to madness if you suddenly recognized all these parodies of yourself around you: a shabby little Shabelsky, who once pretended to be the young idealist, just like you did; little Borkin, who takes your ideal of rational management to ridiculous and deceitful extremes and stutters with the same passion and courageous citizenship as you. This small man with dreams, as he perceives himself, is you.

By rushing through the final two acts, Nemirovich-Danchenko captured the rapid decline of life. He significantly minimized interruptions, explanations, and domestic delays. The circle contracted, compelling Ivanov to remain stagnant. There were no references to the previous Ivanov and no pretense. Even if the protagonist desired it, he had no opportunity to make any grand gestures. Sasha yelled, "Let's go!" and Ivanov responded, "Where? I'm going to end it all! Stand back!" It is understandable why the director wanted to remove the line, "The old Ivanov has reawakened."[4] It did not align with

First Farewells 1904–1905   123

MAT's aesthetic. However, Nemirovich-Danchenko could have preserved it by having Kachalov sarcastically and hopelessly acknowledge himself as the "old Ivanov" and his own accuser. This would have highlighted the internal conflict between old and new identities. Unfortunately, such considerations were not given much weight at MAT and were merely secondary to the director's vision. In this production, there were few subtle hints or underlying concepts. The meaning was apparent and unambiguous.

The severity of the production became more evident as the run went on. Kachalov's interpretation changed from one evening to another; sometimes he portrayed Ivanov from an external perspective, playing both the character and his own attitude toward him. Creating this distance was a requirement imposed by the director, emphasizing the deliberate detachment of an artist tackling tragedy from an outside perspective.[5]

Chekhov had to be presented as a contemporary figure in order to reestablish him as a classic. Nemirovich-Danchenko personally dedicated weeks and months to achieving this, but MAT took decades to fully embrace it. *Ivanov* was not simply an extension of MAT's Chekhovian interpretations. In the 1901 production of *Three Sisters*, the characters' lives coincided with the current time period of the audience. MAT aimed to synchronize the time-frame of the play with the "audience time." For instance, when societal fashions changed, the characters' costumes changed as well. Germanova replaced Savitskaya as Olga, wearing an English jacket, putting her hands in her pockets, and wearing a tie with her blouse. The same approach was taken with *Woe from Wit*, which maintained its mid-nineteenth-century attire to ensure that the play's psychology, conflicts, atmosphere, and adjustments remained relevant over the decades. However, at some point, these choices became too conspicuous. The audience was no longer fully engaged in the performance. Or perhaps they were, but only in a special sense, similar to the critic Vissarion Belinsky's exclamation about Hamlet: he is me; he is you; he is each of us.[6] But that would be the case later on; for now, the actors continued to perform *Uncle Vanya*, *Three Sisters*, and *The Cherry Orchard*, receiving applause and bringing tears to the eyes of an audience united with them. The 1918 production of *Ivanov*, on the other hand, did not align with MAT's established approach to Chekhov. Paradoxically, however, it marked the beginning of a series of MAT revivals of Russian classics.

Encounters with Gorky

"When it rains, it pours. We have lost two playwrights." The loss brought a series of troubles. Stanislavsky counted thirteen of them and concluded,

> We must let go of personal matters, the battle for superiority, and other trivial passions that demean us, and we must strive to do the impossible to save the season and the theater company. If we fail to do this, it will be our final year.

124 *Vladimir Nemirovich-Danchenko and the Moscow Art Theatre*

It was surprising to encounter such strong words from one of MAT's founders; their colleagues typically admired their unwavering idealism, even if they were skeptical of what they said. But the co-founder knew what he was saying and did not waste words. Without a doubt, they were on the verge of perishing and closing the theatre company in 1905. Historians refer to this as the end of MAT's first period. However, beneath these words lay the complex dynamics and anguish of what unfolded. For them, in their previous capacity, the 1904/1905 season truly was their last year. MAT was the Chekhov Theatre and would soon transform into the Gorky Theatre, in the most immediate sense: a new play, a season, and a season with significance. But not yet; everything or ever-ything hinged on the events yet to unfold, shrouded in uncertainty and peril. Russia was engaged in a war with Japan.[7] The 1905 revolution was about to commence, and its outcome was uncertain. Chekhov was laid to rest in Novodevichy Cemetery, and there was an emerging rift between MAT and the playwright Maxim Gorky, which Nemirovich-Danchenko endeavored to mend. The chapter documenting MAT's relationship with Chekhov has concluded. The chapter chronicling their association with Gorky was just beginning, progressing as if weaving the narrative of a Russian cultural novel.

The relationship with Gorky had begun quite charmingly. Nemirovich-Danchenko had been en route to Yalta to meet Chekhov. In his memoir, he described how he arrived, almost in a dream, and searched for the house he was seeking but could not find it. The coachman was unfamiliar with the route, there was nobody to ask, shadows in the windows seemed to exist in their own mysterious lives, and the steep, winding streets were empty. "But then," he wrote, "a human figure appeared. We waited for him to approach us."

> He gazed at me intently. Gradually, the newcomer became more visible: a broad nose, a thick reddish mustache, a pleasant bass voice, a tall, lean, and solidly built figure. In the initial accounts of this encounter, only a fleeting impression of its significance and peculiarity emerged: he emerged from the fog, showed us the way, and vanished into the mist: tall, cloaked, benevolent, and unknown.

Nemirovich-Danchenko was acquainted with Gorky and was among the first to be influenced by him. With this in mind, it is worth examining Nemirovich-Danchenko's final prose work, the serialized novel *Inferno* (*Odessa News* 1898). In this novel, the author delves into the "Gorky material," capturing the essence of a semi-working, semi-serious life in a southern city, with the nearby sea and adjacent steppe, along with conversations in rented houses where philosophical discussions take place with unexpected passion. Dominating everything here—the barracks, the train station tavern, and the shabby, narrow room with an inconspicuous icon (where people cross themselves and forbid any criminal activity)—is the factory. Inside, the glossy reflection of the fire dances upon petrified soot, creating blistering heat. As people from the previous shift exit, they appear drained, almost worn out. "From a distance, this large, mixed crowd gives the impression of a festive procession." A cacophony of noisy, angry power flows out in a long, narrow stream.

The world of *Inferno* is filled with smokestacks and dust, klaxon horns and alarms, tavern songs about death, and the intense pressure of traditional, seemingly wise perspectives on strength and weakness in life. It also tells a story of pivotal moments and rebellion. Nemirovich-Danchenko admits to leaving *Inferno* unfinished. It was regrettable to deceive the editors, assuring them of completion when it was not to be. (This was not his usual behavior, but it occurred. Autumn 1898 arrived, MAT had started, and he lacked the motivation to complete the novel.) Nevertheless, perusing the pages of the old manuscript is an interesting endeavor. Once again, one can observe the powerful and responsive creativity of Nemirovich-Danchenko. This creativity interfered with his role as a prose writer but became invaluable to him as a director. Gorky's books were just beginning to gain attention, but the connection between these two writers was stronger than commonly believed. Both relied solely on their own abilities and were Russian "self-made men," possessing mental qualities resulting from their drive. This drive included a combination of openness, healthy self-confidence, an all-or-nothing attitude, the capacity for sudden shifts and changes in perspective, a keen awareness of the times, and enormous willpower and belief in it. However, Nemirovich-Danchenko and Gorky were different iterations of the Russian "self-made man." Being ten years older, Nemirovich-Danchenko had a markedly different model of self-realization and self-construction compared to the young Gorky.

MAT embraced Gorky, appreciating his uniqueness as a person while valuing the friendship with this outsider who carried a mysterious new message. This friendship was solidified with an appreciation for the beautiful root of the Russian word "friend," which means someone who is different from oneself.[8] Kachalov and his comrades often mentioned Gorky, who was not only an avid reader but also a singer. Gorky was equally passionate about MAT and would spend all his free time there. The backstage staff happily provided him with food and drinks, knowing that otherwise he would go hungry. Gorky was not accustomed to domestic life and couldn't live in Moscow due to being a suspect under investigation and later being exiled. As a result, he couldn't be at the MAT as often as he needed to be for the work they had started.

As MAT continued its association with Gorky, they began to face negative consequences. Gorky's radical preferences influenced the actors, leading them to express their personal feelings in a more emotional manner than what was customary for their group. MAT attracted a range of personalities like Maxim Gorky, Leopold Sulerzhitsky,[9] and Nikolai Bauman,[10] who shared the same mindset. These individuals were not tied down by the demands of everyday life, were not wealthy, and had no fear of losing money. They were

126   *Vladimir Nemirovich-Danchenko and the Moscow Art Theatre*

brave and selfless, unburdened by the objectionable qualities associated with the bourgeoisie, which MAT wanted to avoid at all costs. The actors were more concerned about being perceived as cowards or Philistines than being reported to the security services. If someone like the leftist sympathizer Bauman needed a safe place, the Kachalovs would willingly offer one without hesitation. The actors were aware that the security services had arrested Sergey Skirmunt, a respected book publisher, because Gorky had been staying with him. They wanted to send Gorky a letter, even if it meant being intercepted and read by the censors. Nemirovich-Danchenko, with heartfelt sympathy, wrote, "Even though I haven't said anything to you, I hope you believe that I sympathize with you through all your recent trials. With all my heart!"

Impressed by how Nemirovich-Danchenko brought his 1901 play *Philistines* to life, Gorky wanted to dedicate it to him. He also gave Nemirovich-Danchenko a collection of stories with a dedication, highlighting his respect and admiration for Nemirovich-Danchenko's efforts in creating a new, truly artistic theatre in Russia. Their bond strengthened, but soon, a few sparks of disagreement began to emerge.

Just as there are those who bring people together, there are also those who drive them apart, and Gorky seemed to be one of them. In 1902, Nemirovich-Danchenko acknowledged that Gorky's arrival had triggered a clash of tastes and desires at MAT. He expressed his concerns, saying, "We toss and turn as if worried about our souls." The extra-artistic interest in Gorky (referred to as "the fame of his arrests" by Nemirovich-Danchenko) posed a problem, as it overshadowed the fame of other supposedly knowledgeable writers. This fame was already evident at MAT when they announced that reform-minded Evgeny Chirikov had written a new play.[11] Nemirovich-Danchenko believed that the general noise surrounding Gorky, though well-intentioned and sympathetic, prevented him from fully exploring his God-given artistic talent. It's a paradox. While one may be fascinated by Gorky, it is important not to overlook the originality of his work.

However, there is no risk. Following Philistines, Gorky's play *The Lower Depths* was a clear testament to his talent. Gorky invited Nemirovich-Danchenko to hear the finished version at Arzamas, where he was living in exile. The conversation continued for a long time, extending past midnight. Soon after, they would read the play at MAT. Journalist Vladimir Gilyarovsky would accompany them to the homeless shelters near Khitrov Market,[12] a den for hundreds of the unemployed and criminals, for background research.[13] The next day, Stanislavsky wrote the director's plan.

The premiere took place on December 18, 1902. "The audience went wild, climbed over the footlights, and cheered. The general impression was unanimously powerful, bright, and unforgettable." It was difficult to calm down and nobody wanted to. After the performance, the actors and the author didn't want to leave the theatre. "There was wonderful dancing and crazy fun. The success of *The Lower Depths* drove everyone to madness." The second performance was similarly enthusiastic: "The audience was roaring with laughter." The responses from reviewers, spectators, actors, and the author were all the same.

Conflicts Interpreting Gorky

Before *The Lower Depths*, MAT produced Gorky's *Philistines*,[14] but Nemirovich-Danchenko was less involved in the production than usual. After the failure of his own play, he went away to rest and recuperate, leaving Stanislavsky to direct it himself. Stanislavsky's director's copy is worth reading carefully to understand the essence of the disagreement that arose during *The Lower Depths*, of which hardly any evidence remains.

It's hard to believe that, according to Stanislavsky's accounts, he was in love with Gorky as a romantic and saw him as a discoverer of "new figures from a little-known world," a messenger of the will, charging into tomorrow's day "with a battle cry." However, the world that emerges in the director's notes is depicted coolly and objectively. It is a world that is both familiar and surprisingly unfamiliar. Why unfamiliar? If the royal chambers in *Tsar Fyodor* were portrayed as cozy dwellings, similar to a present-day home with jars of jam in the cupboard and lithograph prints from *The Field* on the walls, couldn't one recognize it as analogous to one's own life as well?

However, Stanislavsky's director's copy reveals a strangely abnormal world and the inevitable events that take place within it. He interpreted the world of Philistines with an extreme lack of empathy. In contrast, one of MAT's charms was that what was depicted on stage felt lifelike and unique, similar to experiences in one's own life. Yet, the director's copy of Philistines is filled with feelings of monotony, regularity, repetitiveness, and lifelessness. Stanislavsky portrayed the monotonous spiraling of petty-bourgeois quarrels, the nature of their traditional grudges, in painstaking detail. His starting point was their boredom, which they expressed through endless bickering.

At first, the conflicts are minor and unfold in the same manner as the loud, carefully orchestrated scandals in the later acts. As the characters move from place to place, they draw you in like whirlpools in the stagnant exterior of this "abnormal world." Akulina, the wife of the protagonist Bessemenov, moves from the kitchen to the living room, the living room to the bedroom, and back to the living room. She cannot find a place for herself. Bessemenov's daughter Tatyana, a school teacher, grabs a stack of school notebooks, sits at a desk, and shuffles between the desk and her room. She moves with a slow, monotonous pace from her room to the piano, picks a tune, abandons it, and returns to the desk. Provincialism, idleness, loafing, and unsatisfying work—haven't these themes been explored at MAT before? Of course they have, but not in this way. In *Three Sisters*, Stanislavsky discovered that the characters' motivation was their desire to live rather than simply exist. Unlike the melancholic characters in *Three Sisters*, the inhabitants of Bessemenov's home are bored. They not only acknowledge their boredom but also take pride in it. For instance, Peter (Bessemenov's son and a "former student") considers being bored with the newspaper a sign of his superiority over those who find it interesting. Similarly, Tatyana's boredom while checking school notebooks signifies her superiority over those who perform this kind of work. Being bored with a book is also seen as a sign of superiority over both the book's author and the book itself.

128 *Vladimir Nemirovich-Danchenko and the Moscow Art Theatre*

Stanislavsky portrayed the Bessemenovs as representatives of a mundane and repetitive life, which can be found in abundance. Both the father and the son adopt an annoyingly superior tone whenever they give platitudes as advice to others. While they do not resemble each other physically, their traits are simply faded replicas. They are like human clones, just as the scenes between them are stale repetitions that have been played out countless times by many others. The vibrancy, originality, and colorful aspects of life vanish in the monotonous cycle of repetition. The characters use self-affirmation, seeking to be superior to others, as a defense mechanism.

To compensate for the lack of expressive encounters, Stanislavsky deliberately emphasized the unbearable nature of this "theatre," its slow pace, climaxes, traditional effects, and poses while also hinting at the genuine feelings of the fake and corrupted characters. The younger Bessemenov's emotions are weaker, as if trapped within a cliché that has grown increasingly feeble over the years, while the older Bessemenov's emotions overflow.

Upon waking up from a nap and barely opening his eyes and putting on his shoes, Bessemenov Sr. pokes his head out of his room and asks, "You haven't written that petition yet, have you?" Bessemenov wakes up with the belief that the world has come to a halt without his involvement. He allowed himself to doze off for an hour, and during that time, the world ceased to move. Disheveled and barefoot, he rushes to set it in motion again. And the world begins to move again, wound up by the hands of the masters. The cook clangs the dishes (she also slept while he slept). Akulina emerges and brings a lamp (let there be light). The samovar emits steam, and the glow of its embers reflects on the walls. Nothing would happen without him, but nobody appreciates him! None of the characters in Stanislavsky's notebooks possess the same level of pathos as Vasily Bessemenov, the foreman of a paint shop. He embodies a truly Philistine quality: the belief that one is superior to everyone else and yet worse off. According to him, if you suffer, no one has suffered like you. No one has ever experienced such a painful toothache, been so hurt by their children's misunderstanding, or endured such a devastating blow as when someone else is chosen for a position you desire.

The distasteful melodramatization of someone's suffering also involves the spectacle of others "consuming" that suffering. In the director's notebook, the scene unfolds after Tatyana attempts to poison herself, dramatically "acting out" her suicide. (Chekhov advised Gorky to include suicide in the cycle of local recurrences to clarify that Tatyana had previously attempted to take her own life.) However, what is equally appalling is that those who rush in to witness the scene are more interested in the drama surrounding the victim than the victim herself. Even Tatyana's genuinely pathetic suffering fails to elicit sympathy from anyone. In the aftermath of the turmoil, Gorky presents a dialogue between Yelena, a young widow and boarder, and Grouse, a popular singer and freeloader, while the unfortunate suicide victim lies groaning in her room. Yelena observes, "Here we are talking away, while in that room, a woman may be dying." Grouse casually replies, "And we're not sorry for

First Farewells 1904–1905 129

her." Yelena agrees, showing no pity but also not perceiving anything wrong with her lack of compassion.

In the director's plan, Yelena is depicted as agreeable, sweet, and lively, providing a refreshing contrast to the other characters who appear faded and artificial. The director particularly appreciates Yelena's vibrant attire, adorned with rings, beads, and a bright pink blouse. He enjoys her ability to maintain a sense of life, unlike the young person who had visited the hospital ward. In the third act, Stanislavsky suggests that Yelena and Grouse assume the roles of caregivers, anticipating a call for help. This mood is relatable to anyone who has experienced the initial frantic rush for a doctor and medication, followed by a frustratingly slow period. Yelena drinks tea and is embarrassed when her liveliness emerges, considering it inappropriate given the gravity of the situation. The director does not condemn her for this, realizing that her exuberance is a necessary part of her nature that must be allowed to flourish, even though it clashes with the seriousness in the room. However, the director and the actress face a creative impasse. The author portrays a person who is unhappy and eventually dies. Does the author's intention merely involve allowing her to die without eliciting pity? To begin with, Stanislavsky did not want to detach from the real, factual content of the event. He writes, "Everyone has abandoned the patient, and she is alone, helpless, in an empty room. We can hear Yelena's quiet laughter continuing upstairs." However, that approach is not satisfactory.

It is one thing in Ostovsky's play *The Snow Maiden*, for instance, when "the bright rays of the sun" melt the Snow Maiden, transforming her into a heavenly stream. It is a completely different situation when Tatyana burns her stomach with concentrated vinegar in *Philistines* vomits blood, and nobody even brings a basin for her. However, for Stanislavsky, this distinct situation remains at the forefront. Furthermore, he shows no hidden sympathy when Yelena proudly declares that she feels no remorse for Tatyana's suffering or when Grouse asserts a fully capable person's right to push aside someone struggling to get up after a fall. He says, "It's nothing. Go ahead, walk. You're good and strong and should be able to walk." This discourse contradicts Stanislavsky's belief system. His personal morality upheld the inherent kindness, empathy, and plain compassion that characterized Russian democratic morality. The cruel treatment of the unfortunate appalled Stanislavsky, not only because he saw Nietzschean nihilism in it but also because he understood the real causes and consequences of such thinking.

The director admired Neil's strength (a locomotive engineer and Bessemenov's protégé) because he believed it to be a benevolent, indulgent, and even diplomatic power. Neil is a young worker who is knowledgeable, well-read, with a zest for life, and, simply, enjoys food. He eats with the pleasure of a hardworking man. Stanislavsky liked his liveliness and the fact that he avoided the tedium and hardships of the Philistines. During the reading of the play at MAT, the actors debated about Neil. Some predicted that he would become an even more identical Philistine in the future than his

130 *Vladimir Nemirovich-Danchenko and the Moscow Art Theatre*

foster-father, Bessemenov. They argued that he was "a good worker, striving for freedom, but only in the limited, personal sense." However, both Stanislavsky and Chekhov favored Neil and disagreed with those who saw him differently. They wanted to adhere to the concrete reality of the play itself. Neil says he will physically confront someone, and Stanislavsky adds, "You have to believe it." Does this mean it happens everyday? Would it become reality? During an argument, Neil says, "The person who does the work is the true owner." But in such disagreements, aren't there always rude echoes of similar phrases? It's easy to imagine Neil taking the abacus that Stanislavsky had given to Bessemenov and using it to calculate the amount of money he had provided for the family over the past ten years. He would deduct the cost of food and housing and determine how much he still owed his foster-father. The fear of deviating from everyday authenticity weighed heavily on Stanislavsky's mind when directing Gorky compared to Chekhov. His intuition and sensitivity allowed him to perceive the embellished, non-textual nuances in Chekhov's poetic language. The abstract and oratorical dialogues in Gorky's plays alarmed him, as well as the play's tendency to advocate for a specific viewpoint. He saw these as obstacles between the author and the creative expression he sought to achieve. In notes he made ten years later (1912), he wrote, "Schiller wanted and was capable of providing beauty and truth, but politics interfered with his art. Gorky is the same. Andreyev's career also hindered his art. Ostrovsky prioritized theatrical biases over art."

The public eagerly followed the battle between the artists and the censors, curious as to whether the play would be allowed or not. They paid close attention to the attacks and appeals in the press. These emotions were palpable behind the scenes and in the auditorium during the play's tryout in St. Petersburg in 1902. However, when the production premiered in Moscow, it didn't elicit much of a reaction at all. It simply didn't bother anyone. The audience wondered, where is Gorky? Where is the activist associated with this name? The truth is, in *Philistines*, Stanislavsky didn't find the outward expression of the author's presence that he had so skillfully achieved with Chekhov. But when directing *The Lower Depths*, Nemirovich-Danchenko managed to find (and insist upon) the appropriate embodiment of the author's presence.

Stanislavsky quickly shared this revelation with Chekhov. He acknowledged it beforehand and was the first to express what Nemirovich-Danchenko had to explain to Nikolai Efros for his monograph on *The Lower Depths*. Yes, Nemirovich-Danchenko had indeed found the right tone and form for Gorky. "As I recall," said Stanislavsky, "he found it in Moskvin's monologues in Act Three and Satin's monologues in Act Four."

The astonishing success of *The Lower Depths* was only surpassed by Stanislavsky's refusal to take credit for it. "It's not mine. It's not me." Initially, he even argued against the decision to produce *The Lower Depths* as if it were someone else's decision. Eventually, he came to accept it, though he still saw it as someone else's decision, not a convincing one. It is challenging to

First Farewells 1904–1905 131

grasp the essence of this dispute because they kept their disagreements secretive. The correctness of one side over the other or the survival of sufficient evidence was not of utmost importance to them. What mattered most was that the significance of their disagreement did not lead to gossip or discord within the troupe. According to Sofia Giatsintova, the young people involved were unaware of the complex relationship between their teachers. There was no vague or stressful atmosphere among themselves or in their surroundings. However, it is worth considering whether Giatsintova is idealizing the past with her memory. Some information did leak out, but it is fortunate that Giatsintova remembered exactly what those two individuals wanted to leave behind: the philosophical, moral, and aesthetic value of their dispute.

The actual content of their argument was observable to anyone from the moment when Stanislavsky and Nemirovich-Danchenko disagreed about their impressions of the excursion to Khitrov Market.

Existential Tragedy in Russian Theatre

The preparation for *The Lower Depths* barely made an impression on Nemirovich-Danchenko in terms of life experiences. He found the visit to the Khitrov Market flophouses unremarkable, describing them as ordinary, uncomplicated, and not typical in their atmosphere. However, for Stanislavsky, the excursion had a significant impact. At the time, Gorky's name was associated with romanticism for everyone, including Stanislavsky. "The religion of the wanderer ... is freedom. We were seeking an atmosphere of romance and a unique untamed beauty," Stanislavsky recalled. To find this, they went to an alley near the Solyanka district where lodgings were located. Stanislavsky reminisced about the romance of the "expedition" and provided a description of that night. The secret police had declared martial law at Khitrov Market, and they believed they heard hidden signals. They had to know secret words to gain entry and had to proceed cautiously in certain places to avoid being overheard. Eventually, they arrived at the flophouses. Stanislavsky noted that they were large dormitories with numerous wooden beds occupied by exhausted and tired-looking people, both men and women. Sadly, there was nothing more to see than what one would find in a hospital, military barracks, or prison. The smell of bleach overpowered the scent of tired and frail bodies.

The ceiling lamp hung too high for anyone to reach, and the lighting remained the same regardless of the situation. The distinct enlarged shadows, which would later play a role in the production, were absent here. This lack of variety in lighting is what Stanislavsky decides to include in his director's copy. He doesn't emphasize or magnify any of the figures. Instead, he wants to capture the crowdedness of the dormitory from a distance, all at once. The sense of crowding was essential, so Stanislavsky imagined a multitude of people who were equally tired and marked by a weary pallor. People often say of those who resemble them, "the land shows through." In the midst of the crowded scene, everyone is absorbed in their own affairs, oblivious to those around them. There's a young copyist writing intently, without engaging with others. An organ grinder inspects his instrument, a puppeteer with consumption examines his dolls and folding screens, a mother dries linens while rocking a baby, a prostitute slumbers off the effects of her occupation, and a melancholic individual, who spent his last bit of money on alcohol, gazes into the distance, lost in thought. Each person operates at their own pace, disrupting the actions of others. The baby's crying disturbs everyone, the faulty street organ's sound irritates everyone, as does the scraping of locksmith Kleshch's file, and dying Anna's persistent cough.

Here, indifference is not just about self-preservation but also seen as the only way to live. One must disconnect not only from the suffering of others but also from the unpleasant sounds, smells, and sensations, such as the locksmith's screeching metal or the freezing cold. Sadly, some individuals find it difficult to naturally disconnect themselves, as seen in the characters of Kleshch and the Actor in the director's copy. In a passing exchange, the laid-back food vendor Kvashnya says something to the locksmith. Kleshch could have ignored it, but instead replied, revealing his nervousness and vulnerability. If these sensitive areas are repeatedly touched without forming calluses, they can develop into dangerous ulcers. Stanislavsky envisioned a world where every touch was irritating, and no movement could be made without encountering a neighbor. Whether accidentally stepping on the person below when getting out of bed or opening a door for fresh air, only to be met with complaints about the draft—it is both a moral and psychological burden. The director, who saw "communication" as a key element, captured the essence of communication within a confined and unpleasant compound of people. It is comparable to the crowded conditions of a hospital ward or a concentration camp, where personal space is nonexistent. People sleep, pray, and even die among one another. Vaska Pepel, who holds some money and power, is considered a local deity because he possesses his own partitioned "personal space," even if it is flimsy.

Reflecting on his experience with slum dwellers, Leo Tolstoy observed their calmness and good nature. During a conversation with Gorky, Tolstoy advised that these traits should be emphasized in his new drama. Tolstoy believed that homeless individuals did not fear falsely, and there was no profound abyss beneath them. If they wished to stand on their own, they could effortlessly do so because they had solid ground beneath their feet. Tolstoy concluded that it is easier to transition from poverty into manual labor, such as farming, logging, or weaving, as compared to the idleness of the nobility, government officials, or intellectuals. MAT always respected Tolstoy's judgments. However, if Stanislavsky had read the conversation published in *The New Times*, he would likely dispute its content. According to the article, Kleshch struggles to get up despite exerting great effort because it is beyond his control. There is an oppressive force that keeps him trapped in the basement, preventing his ability to rise. There is no solid ground for him to stand on; instead, the terrain is unstable, muddy, and treacherous at the bottom. A person does not come here of their own free will, nor do they change of their own free will. However, changes still occur, true and permanent, nonetheless. Even if there are illusions of naturalness and freedom in the lower depths, these are merely illusions. The spiritual essence of freedom is "Freedom — at any cost!" as stated by Stanislavsky. He also added, "That freedom for the sake of which people sink to the bottom of life is belying the fact that there they have become slaves."

In *The Lower Depths*, people become slaves in both familiar and direct ways. The director's plan captures the entire system of these explicit and base dependencies. The Baron clumsily kowtows to the criminal, and the Actor, who is usually bragging and disrespectful, begins to sweep the floor at the owner's command. Even though it's not his turn to clean the floor, the owner has ordered it, and the Actor has not paid for his bunk this week. Additionally, the elderly pilgrim, Luka, constantly remembers that he has no identity document. Hence, the good-natured police officer Medvedev or someone else could always take him to the police station, where he would have to make excuses and provide evidence. However, people at the bottom also become slaves in another sense—they become unable to act for themselves. The director's copy contains striking examples of deep drilling under the crust of society's "cultural layers." Stanislavsky saw Gorky as a researcher of the accumulating explosiveness of the fading bourgeois world. He considered him a researcher of the likelihood of fascism, historical conditions that foreshadow the emergence of fascist Brown Shirts. However, what Gorky was for the audience at the beginning of the century, and what he wanted for this audience himself, did not align with the director's plan.

Nemirovich-Danchenko also understood the depths beneath the play, but in a different way.

> There were many years of outward tranquility, complete well-being, even prosperity, meanwhile currents of heavy breathing, deaf, anxious, were sweeping up from the depths of the 170-million-person sea. [...] From deep invisible waves came the odor of sweat and smoke exhaling the freezing wind of ruthlessness. Public Russia, the crown of which was St. Petersburg, appeared immovable, but invisible waves were undermining it.

The feeling of two hostile worlds became increasingly palpable. It is crucial not to suppress this feeling; Stanislavsky's excessive psychological detail would only drown it out. Nemirovich-Danchenko repeated to Stanislavsky that it couldn't be slowed down, broken up, or lingered ponderously. He emphasized "Spirited lightness" repeatedly.

Stanislavsky was initially unconvinced and had difficulty yielding. "Vishnevsky and Kachalov will confirm the efforts it took me to lead Stanislavsky to 'Gorky' or 'street-tough romanticism,' as I called it then." Both Stanislavsky

134 *Vladimir Nemirovich-Danchenko and the Moscow Art Theatre*

and Nemirovich-Danchenko recognized that a performance captures the audience when it is "a harmonious whole, the creation of a single soul." However, in working on *The Lower Depths*, they were unable to create this united soul. The "main idea" had to be determined and carried out by someone alone, and in this case it was Nemirovich-Danchenko who took charge. Stanislavsky's lack of conviction and skeptical acceptance of the performance was a source of offense and pain for Nemirovich-Danchenko. It was hurtful that Stanislavsky did not say a kind word, and thousands of others' kind words could not compensate for this loss. It was also unfair for Stanislavsky to think that the play harkened back to the aesthetics of the Maly Theater when, in fact, it was a completely new phenomenon to play a tragedy in this tone.

The beginning of the production made use of the fanciful mise-en-scene that Stanislavsky had created for *The Sunken Bell* and *The Snow Maiden*. In these productions, the forest and mountains would suddenly move, and various elements of nature such as trees, stones, snowdrifts, and thickets would transform into magical creatures. In *The Lower Depths*, when the flophouse appeared, it seemed deserted at first, but then gradually came to life with the emergence of the characters. The rags that initially seemed to conceal people were actually the people themselves. The characters separated themselves from the corners of the flophouse, resembling toxic fumes emerging from poison-soaked walls. The setting of the play is a cellar with a sagging stone ceiling, moldy walls, crumbling plaster, and dark bricks exposed through the decay. The arches disappear into the darkness at the back of the stage. In the third act, the outdoor action takes place against a massive wall, with a deep window at the bottom. Stanislavsky interpreted the play based on what the broken and faded characters could truly be as they melted away into drains and frayed into the mud.

Nemirovich-Danchenko, on the other hand, had a different vision. The superfluous aspects of the "accursed questions" of the modern intelligentsia have alchemized in Gorky's characters.[15] Nemirovich-Danchenko was initially fascinated by the free and bold resolution of these "accursed questions," as well as the mocking disdain for "clean habits" and physical strength. However, when it came to questions of the spirit, the "naked man" of his performance was too preoccupied with the pressures of necessity. Nemirovich-Danchenko understood *The Lower Depths* as a world of existential tragedy. In Stanislavsky's notes, Nemirovich-Danchenko found a remark next to Satin's Act Four monologue: "barroom orator." However, in this production, the characters did not speak like barroom orators, eloquent for a bottle of vodka. Their phrases did not come from somewhere above, worn-out and mangled. Instead, their speech was primal, addressing the themes of tragedy and the concepts of existence and justice, both on a societal and universal level. Later, Nemirovich-Danchenko wanted to stage Gorky's *Yegor Bulychov and Others* (1932) because of its tragic firebrand nature. The opening lines of the play delve into the purpose and meaning of life: "because I was born for a reason, right?" Primal speech contemplates

First Farewells 1904–1905 135

"the law of the soul," as the Tartar says in *The Lower Depths*. However, it turns out that the "law of the soul" can be broken or lost, leaving only the "The Penal Code is a strong law too, it will not soon wear it out."

The Lower Depths identifies Russian tragedy as a tragedy of existence, where conscience motivates action and rebellion and harmonizes the relationship between human beings and the limits of reality. Existential tragedy is the most general and inclusive of all types, with tragedies of fate, power, duty, and emotion being more selective. It is also the most "experienceable," as it passes through the flesh and nature, which is particularly important for MAT. Through Luka/Moskvin, the tragedy of existence achieved a specifically national context, emphasizing its roots in Russian culture, similar to the tragedy of fate in the ancient world. Gorky, Dostoevsky, and Leo Tolstoy all focus on existential questions and the national culture of philosophical thinking.

Artistic Struggle Amid Political and Societal Turmoil

"I owe much of the success of this play to your intellect and passion, comrade," Gorky wrote on a copy of *The Lower Depths* that he gifted to Nemirovich-Danchenko. During a new chapter in their relationship, Nemirovich-Danchenko chose not to remind Gorky of his previous praise. However, this significant development weighed heavily on his mind during the challenging summer of 1904. Given his responsibilities, he should have given this relationship more consideration.

The fate of Gorky's new play, *Summerfolk*, still remained uncertain. Gorky had read it to Nemirovich-Danchenko in the spring, and a few weeks later, he read it to the entire troupe when they arrived in St. Petersburg for their annual tour. The actors were unsure about performing in this play. Gorky himself was uncertain about whether to give it to them. *Summerfolk* left them perplexed.[16] Stanislavsky believed he may have misunderstood the play, as it wasn't ready for them if his interpretation was accurate. He hoped his perspective would change when he read the play again alone, but he still had the same impression afterward. Many actors waited for Moskvin to explain the play's meaning after he read it at home. He described it as unpleasant and disappointing. He hadn't liked it before either, as it seemed like empty and cruel dialogue without any action. Gorky's aversion to people surprised him. It felt cold, harsh, and disappointing. Knipper was also taken aback. She found it incomprehensible and believed staging it in its current form was impossible.

Nemirovich-Danchenko's evaluation was more ambiguous. He found it exhilarating and talented, but ultimately, he was the one who had to deliver the company's negative opinion to the author. His letter outlined what everyone was saying. The play was surprising. Why was there such tendentiousness and a malicious refusal to empathize with the characters from the beginning? Why was there an obsession with conclusions that didn't

136 *Vladimir Nemirovich-Danchenko and the Moscow Art Theatre*

follow from the action but rather stemmed from preconceived biases? Then Nemirovich-Danchenko wrote again. The conversation could have been more diplomatic, but he believed honesty was always best. Though he had a reputation as a diplomat, this time it was ineffective. His letters clumsily attempted to avoid ambiguities and ensure that he conveyed things as they were. It was crucial for Gorky to understand "for himself" what was happening and why. The problems didn't start with *Summerfolk*. Since *The Lower Depths*, things had been strained between them. Their relationship was terrible. They judged and misunderstood each other. They eventually stopped corresponding due to mutual suspicion. Nemirovich-Danchenko's response to their earlier dispute about *Summerfolk* was to not engage further. It was clear where he stood—Gorky saw the issue one way, while Nemirovich-Danchenko, or someone else in MAT, saw it differently. However, this was not the main point. Regardless of its success or failure, and regardless of their personal connection to it, Gorky's play was Gorky's play. "It will have brilliant scenes, images, and thoughts. The theatre that stages this play will have a glorious, lively work. But you cannot give it to us!" "I believe that it could happen. And I could handle the blow if it was deserved. But this is exactly what I cannot assure myself of."

After receiving the first letter—the review letter—Gorky wrote, "I sensed in your attitude a fundamental disagreement with issues that I have resolved for myself once and for all. Unfortunately, this issue is irreversible, and therefore I cannot entrust the play to a theatre under your leadership." However, he did not send this letter. Instead, he responded with destructive and demonstrative contempt. Not toward the unfavorable review but toward Nemirovich-Danchenko's assurance that he would be happy to stage the play regardless:

> Vladimir Ivanovich: Firstly, I will publish the play, and then, if it proves suitable, anyone is free to stage it. And in regards to your claim that your attitude towards me 'remains unchanged,' let me say that my attitude towards other people is always more significant and intriguing than their attitude towards me. A. Peshkov.[17]

"I could hardly bear this insult," Nemirovich-Danchenko wrote to Olga Knipper, quoting Gorky's letter almost word for word. The essence of the letter was: I detest this so-called readiness of yours! You can practice it on someone else, but not on me. Gorky demanded a definitive choice: whose side are you on? He rejected any letters that began with "I am not with you, but..." Not with you, but we appreciate you; not with you, but we acknowledge your talent; not with you, but our attitude toward you is the same as when it seemed we were on your side. Understand this, wrote Gorky: "My attitude towards people is always more important and fascinating to me than their attitude towards me." "We lost two playwrights," Stanislavsky summarized the unfortunate events of 1904. They lost Chekhov, who had passed away, and they lost Gorky by deciding not to accept what they saw as a withering of life, not to take a biased point of view that taints and colors everything with itself.

Ibsen, Shakspeare, and

Fear of tendentiousness from their acquaintance with Gorky echoed throughout MAT. This was evident, for example, when they worked on Ibsen's *Pillars of Society* in 1903. Nemirovich-Danchenko, who chose the play and had the primary task of directing it, suddenly cooled toward it, developing a dislike for its "authorial firmness" (as if it wasn't already noticeable from the start!). Despite forcing himself to become fond of it, he interpreted the play more boldly than usual. Instead of focusing on ideological unmasking, he unexpectedly delved into psychology. He painted a brilliant picture on his favorite theme of the "lucky man" or fortune's favorite, portraying Consul Bernick as a happy, spoiled child. ("Bernick is, above all, a lively, fortunate man." "Such people are dictatorial." A paradox? Perhaps not.) Under his direction, the entire plot became more interesting. Suddenly, it became important—and the director boldly imagined it—whether it was a circus or a menagerie that paraded under Bernick's window after arriving at the local harbor. It suddenly became important how greedily Bernick snatched a colorful magazine from the mail, with Nemirovich-Danchenko imagining it contained the next installment of a popular adventure story.

However, the play responded to such directorial fantasies reluctantly, and as a result, the production was unsuccessful. Audiences only remembered how Bernick/Stanislavsky ate a soft-boiled egg at breakfast. He did nothing more than eat, but at that moment, audiences understood everything about the character. Other than that, they only remembered how the reviewers criticized MAT for using non-Russian speech melodies. (However, a few months later, they admired the use of Latinate diction in the production of *Julius Caesar*.) Nemirovich-Danchenko interpreted not only Consul Bernick's narcissism and love of life as a comedy of manners and a historical tragedy but also Mark Anthony in *Julius Caesar*. However, unnecessary comparisons can be avoided here. Besides, he conceived *Julius Caesar* for the sake of change, for the refreshing novelty of its challenges, and it achieved exactly what it was supposed to.

The immense effort and speed with which MAT prepared *Julius Caesar* proved to be crucial. Nemirovich-Danchenko understood the benefits of such work from the very first minutes, an atmosphere that was both impossible and confident. The atmosphere of creating the production and the actual production itself were interdependent. The power of *Julius Caesar* primarily stemmed from the vibrant life that permeated everything: the congestion of the steep, winding streets, the bustling crowds, and the dynamic characterization. The thoroughness of this portrayal is evident in the published director's copy. While the production wasn't intended for scrutinizing subtle details (which, in truth, were not actually subtle), the mise-en-scene was rapid and monumental, progressing by deploying dense crowds until they

138   Vladimir Nemirovich-Danchenko and the Moscow Art Theatre

spilled out of Rome's suffocating heat and bustling diversity onto an endless, rugged, empty plain. The Battle of Philippi took place in this barren, frozen, yellow-earthen setting, with a high rocky horizon and scarce sky. What had initially been congested, noisy, and lively in the city took on a leaner meaning in this environment.

On the table near Nemirovich-Danchenko and his assistants were stacks of books used for inspiration, sourced from the museums of Rome and Pompey. However, the true essence was not found in the museums but in the steep descent of the ancient stone streets, carved out over millennia like stone gutters; in the heat of the earth among the ruins where lizards hid; in the red clay from which Rome was built, instead of marble. *Julius Caesar* emerged as an intoxicating portrayal of the spectacle of life, which differed greatly from Nemirovich-Danchenko himself but was just as palpable and undeniable. The unexpectedness of this performance and its rugged charm stemmed from societal contrasts: a diverse population, a different pace of life, a distinct passion in its people, and a unique history. The color of the earth underfoot was not Russia's ashen-gray soil, but the vibrant red and yellow soil of a fertile, war-torn southern land. The production focused on the unique aspects of Roman life and its grand scale. Nemirovich-Danchenko's portrayal of Brutus's fearless determination captivated audiences, as did Antony's absolute power and his connection with the common people. Antony's character was portrayed as ordinary, driven by self-interest and opportunism. An example of this is the scene at the forum, where Antony's "ingenious boldness" leads him to shed tears over Caesar's body and deliver a moving speech, presenting himself as submissive to the masses. The production depicted life realistically instead of idealizing it. Reviewers debated whether MAT portrayed the Roman dictator in a positive or negative light, endorsing or discrediting the principle of autocracy. However, these viewpoints were not considered when evaluating the performance. Caesar simply existed, following the director's vision and portrayed exceptionally by Kachalov. Kachalov portrayed a man burdened by the weight of his position, carrying the symbolic golden laurels on his aging temples. His face was stern and gaunt, his skin saggy, and the downturned corners of his mouth conveyed a mix of energy and disgust. He had the right to play the role of a demigod, but he was tired of it. On his own tragic stage, he was nervously cautious yet defiantly careless. He was aloof, lonely, troubled, amused, and plagued by suspicions, with a repressed fear that evoked the terror he felt. In contrast, Brutus failed to comprehend the bitter cynicism that shaped Caesar's perspective on the worth of the people.

Nemirovich-Danchenko claimed that he made Kachalov famous. In addition to his performances as *Julius Caesar* and Ivanov in Chekhov's play, Kachalov played the scientist Protasov in Gorky's *Children of the Sun*, which was produced in 1905. Despite their previous quarrels, he and the director briefly reconciled in an unsatisfying manner. Interestingly, Kachalov's talents became crucial for MAT's overall balance and Nemirovich-Danchenko's artistic pursuits. Alongside his other skills, Kachalov's love for the stage was so vibrant that he almost felt ashamed of it. This contrasted with the self-sacrifice of his fellow actors, giving rise to a longing to please and a love of success. However, this sense of guilt and shame was appropriate, as it was a reflection of Kachalov's creative joy. He did not seek applause or a higher salary out of vanity, but rather for the selfish pleasure of understanding and discovery—the very essence of creativity.

In the summer of 1905, Gorky's play *Children of the Sun* was indispensable to the actors.[18] Kachalov's portrayal of Protasov, though overshadowed by current events, stayed with him for life. He remembered the role for its exploration of creative egoism and guilt, themes that resonated strongly in Russia due to the societal problems of increasing culture and rising social deprivation. Stanislavsky's director's copy, used by Nemirovich-Danchenko to work with the actors, left no doubt about the protagonist's talent and the societal value of his work, which reflected Russian life at the beginning of the century. It was a time of remarkable productivity in intellectual pursuits, with notable figures emerging in science and art, as well as many independent, intelligent individuals working in agriculture, construction, and medicine. Cultural values were accumulating daily. However, it was also a time when the Russian intelligentsia found itself caught in a two-way conflict that intensified as Russian culture flourished. Intellectuals clashed with crude capitalists, the "buyers" of their labor. Moreover, they clashed with the all-powerful authorities that had engulfed the country, even if they didn't directly threaten their labor. While the prohibitions didn't extend to architecture or agronomy, their thoughtless actions paved the way for the most severe and fundamental conflict. Russia remained a poor and uneducated country. Starving individuals, surviving on meager bread, could vomit blood uncontrollably. Centuries of deprivation could trigger a massive inability to digest. Material and spiritual poverty bred a hatred for the fruits of science and art, as they were seen as the property of the elite. This created a fierce rejection of the daily sustenance of culture.

This raises the question: can the "high comedy" of the play, as suggested by Stanislavsky in the director's copy and rehearsed by Nemirovich-Danchenko, resolve this conflict? After all, Stanislavsky interpreted *Children of the Sun* as a comical "drama about business." The key to this interpretation lay in the scenes between Professor Protasov and industrialist Nazar Vygruzov, who had bought Protasov's house and now wanted him to apply his talent to the production of toilet soap in his factory. On the other hand, Stanislavsky was also inclined to comically depict the people's misunderstanding of the intellectual's work. However, for Stanislavsky, Liza's role, which he considered essential and "beautiful," did not fit into the general plan due to its unsettling tone. As Liza naively prophesies to the "children of the sun," "Hatred is blind, but you are brilliant. They will see you!" Gorky's play revealed an ominous, tangible, symbolic alarm that emphasized how far the cultural elite had detached themselves from the millions who were deprived of everything, including the ability to think. The vanity and guilt of creativity enjoying itself

140   Vladimir Nemirovich-Danchenko and the Moscow Art Theatre

in such problematic circumstances disturbed Gorky. There is no evidence of Gorky's alarm in Stanislavsky's director's copy. The tone convincingly portrays a light, determined naive outlook, and an indestructible calm somehow prevails. In the early twentieth century, the problem of "culture vs. poverty" was particularly severe and persisted throughout the century. However, Stanislavsky did not intend his interpretation to elicit sarcastic laughter. Somewhere deep within his confidence, there was a sympathetic rightness of a genius.

Nemirovich-Danchenko limited his contributions to *Children of the Sun*. He knew that Gorky did not want him involved with the play, but Stanislavsky refused to work without him. However, during rehearsals conducted by Stanislavsky, Gorky frequently questioned the staging, stating that he "cannot be said to feel important" about it. For Nemirovich-Danchenko, the sound of the play's deep alarm would have been organic and robust. He once said, "Hungry and unhappy people do not go to the theatre; well-fed people go to the theatre." These were Nemirovich-Danchenko's words, and he worried about it.

Gorky had not participated in MAT rehearsals since October 1905. After the dress rehearsal, he didn't care how they grappled with his troubled play, saying, "It was disgusting. Their acting is nasty." (Hadn't Gorky said the same actors performed like angels not long before this?) But even if they acted like angels, he could hardly have been less interested.

Actress Maria Andreyeva approached the director's table where Stanislavsky and Nemirovich-Danchenko were sitting and asked directly if now was the time to do theatre at all.

It was December 1905, and they were rehearsing Griboyedov's *Woe from Wit*. They did not interrupt the rehearsal, even though they heard shots fired in the courtyard outside.[19] It was not a question of courage; Stanislavsky was afraid of his own shadow and didn't even want shots fired on stage, something Bulgakov joked about in his novel *Black Snow*.[20] When *Woe from Wit* was being rehearsed, no one showed any special courage or displayed any defiant response as to whether this was the right time to be concerned with theatre. They carried on because they were passionate about creative work and naturally could not halt it midway.

They revived *The Seagull* on September 30, 1905, and the result was just as Nemirovich-Danchenko predicted: "Reception very dry." *Children of the Sun* premiered on October 24, 1905. There were no reviews, and only a few reviewers mentioned anything about the performance. The actors only remembered feeling perplexed during the premiere when the audience believed that rioters had stormed onto the stage. However, inside MAT, the audience's reaction was incomprehensible to the performers. Since they had interpreted the play comically themselves, there was laughter even during dress rehearsals. After the opening, though, newspapers wrote that the audience had protested the spine-chilling replication of the stage action happening outside the theatre. Moscow theatres closed during the December 1905 Moscow Uprising (the government knew about it in advance) but reopened once the military quashed the revolt at the end of the month.[21] Audiences rapidly refilled the theatres. Meanwhile, there was a fall and rise in ticket costs that paralleled the conditions in the streets.

Nemirovich-Danchenko's notebook has columns of calculations illustrating the dire financial situation of MAT at the time. Its primary benefactor, Savva Morozov, had retired from such matters long before committing suicide in Nice the previous spring.[22] The question was whether they should resume production. Their financial calculations included determining how much the management owed to the actors and other employees, how much they would have to return to season ticket holders and other estimates. At MAT's main entrance, they put up a notice that looked like a funeral announcement rather than a theatrical poster because the wording retained the oily blackness of printer's ink: "MAT has discontinued performances for the season. Refunds are available at the box office of MAT every day from 10:00 am to 4:00 pm."

Nobody knew what would happen next.

Notes

1 Merlichlundria is a term invented by Chekhov, variously meaning a sad mood, melancholy with a touch of self-irony, spleen, something confusing or unnecessary with a touch of contempt. Chekhov's letter to Alexey Suvorin, August 24, 1893, says "One undoubted misfortune is that your nerves have gone and over-powered you with mental semi-illness, which the seminarians call merlechlundia." He goes on to say that Suvorin has brought it upon himself.
2 Mutiny cannot end in good fortune... From *A Simple Truth* (1946) by Samuel Marshak based on an epigram by the poet John Harington (1561–1612). Printed according to the Works, Vol. 3.
3 Possibly from *Voice and Eye* by Alexander Green (given-name Grinevsky) (1880–1932), a Russian writer of neoromantic prose and poetry. The Soviet government banned his works in the last years of his life.
4 "The former Ivanov has reawakened." As translated by Ronald Hingley: "I feel like a young man again, it is my old self that's speaking."
5 Cf. Brecht's concept of actorly alienation.
6 Vissarion Belinsky (1811–1848), influential literary critic of westernizing tendency, supporter of the MAT's artistic and educational aims, and pioneer of Russia's radical intelligentsia.
7 The Russo-Japanese War was fought between the Empire of Japan and the Russian Empire during 1904 and 1905 over rival imperial ambitions in Manchuria and the Korean Empire.
8 The Russian words for *friend* (droog/друг) and *other* (droogoi/другой) share the same root.
9 Leopold Sulerzhitsky (1872–1916) was a theatre director, painter, and pedagogue of Polish descent closely associated with Stanislavsky, MAT, and the society of Leo Tolstoy.
10 Nikolai Bauman (1873–1905) was a professional revolutionary of the Bolshevik Party.
11 Evgeny Chirikov (1864–1932) was a populist novelist, short story writer, dramatist, essayist, and publicist.
12 Vladimir Gilyarovsky (1853–1935) was a writer and journalist, best known for his reminiscences of life in pre-Revolutionary Moscow.

142 *Vladimir Nemirovich-Danchenko and the Moscow Art Theatre*

13 Khitrovka (Khitrov Market) was crowded job market for unskilled laborers, attracting many unemployed peasants. This led to a rise in poverty and crime and the area becoming notorious for its dosshouses and as a refuge for escaped convicts.

14 *Philistines* (1901) is a play by Maxim Gorky about the Voinitsky family, who struggle to maintain their intellectual freedom in a conservative Russian town. The play explores the conflict between traditional values and modernity, and the struggle to uphold personal ideals in the face of societal pressure. The play ends tragically.

15 "Accursed questions" are issues about the meaning of life and death, justification of sufferings, belief and disbelief, and the search of social harmony and justice. When all the comforting promises of faith are answered absolutely negatively by man, and at the same time he finds no other point of reference for himself, eternal questions become accursed.

16 *Summerfolk* (1904) is a play by Maxim Gorky about wealthy vacationers who discuss art, politics, and morality, but whose personal lives are full of affairs and betrayals. The play satirizes the bourgeois lifestyle and ends with a tragic accident that exposes the fragility of their lives.

17 Aleksey Peshkov was Maxim Gorky's given name.

18 *Children of the Sun* (1905) is a play by Maxim Gorky about a group of intellectuals who are disconnected from the working class. The play ends tragically, as the intellectuals are forced to confront the consequences of their actions.

19 The shooting of protesting factory workers in St Petersburg in January 1905 sparked what became known as the 1905 Revolution, the twentieth century's first major challenge to tsarist autocracy.

20 *Black Snow: A Theatrical Novel* (1930–1936). satirical novel MAT by Mikhail Bulgakov (1891–1940) about the backstage life of MAT.

21 The Moscow Uprising of December 1905 was the climactic scene of the disillusioning 1905 Revolution, which started in St. Petersburg.

22 Savva Morozov committed suicide in 1905 under puzzling circumstances.

6 Returning to a New Place 1905–1906

Resilience Amid Societal and Financial Upheaval

On September 26, 1906, MAT opened its season as usual with the play *Woe from Wit*, which had been prepared well in advance. Over the following three months, MAT performed its regular repertoire, which included Chekhov's three plays: *The Cherry Orchard, Uncle Vanya, and Three Sisters*, as well as *The Lower Depths* and *Children of the Sun* (although *Children of the Sun* had low attendance, they still performed it). Lastly, they performed *Tsar Fyodor Ivanovich*, which drew packed houses not seen in a long time.

The author apologizes to the reader for abruptly ending the previous chapter without addressing the disruption mentioned. So, let's discuss what happened after MAT senior actor-administrative assistant Alexander Vishnevsky departed early for Berlin, and MAT's main company left Moscow.[1] We will start by talking about the sudden appearance of a traveling admirer, Nikolai Tarasov, a millionaire who provided MAT with the funding they needed to complete their successful, yet financially devastating, foreign trip.[2] Nemirovich-Danchenko also describes this episode in his book *From the Past*. He was known for having strokes of luck and enjoying these sudden turns of events, which he even called "coup de théâtre."

Instead of using a well-known document, we will look at a lesser-known one from the MAT archives. This document consists of a draft letter from spring 1906, as well as a carefully handwritten copy on fine paper. It's interesting to compare both versions. Nemirovich-Danchenko appeals to Count Sergei Witte, who was the Head of the Cabinet of Ministers.[3] In the first draft, he respectfully requests the count to report to the Emperor. However, in the final version, Nemirovich-Danchenko removes all the "respectful requests" and writes:

> Your Excellency Count Sergey Yulievich: The Art Theatre finds it impossible to continue its performances in Moscow under the circumstances it has found itself in after the [violent political] events of December. Hence, the theatre has undertaken a tour abroad with its entire ensemble and all its equipment, including 87 personnel and five train cars of theatrical equipment.

DOI: 10.4324/9781003486282-6

He also explains how MAT's performances were greatly appreciated in Berlin, Dresden, Leipzig, Prague, and Vienna. He states, "I would never dare to report this to Your Excellency if it were merely a theatrical success and not a momentous phenomenon in Russian life."

MAT has more entitlement than most to adopt this dignified and independent tone. However, the mention of five train cars is questionable. The problem with the art of theatre (and cinema, too) is that it cannot thrive in poverty and solitude like poetry, painting, or music. Theatre is the most financially dependent art form. Aware of this reliance, Nemirovich-Danchenko would often say,

> Let's imagine that you have a magnificent building with an orchestra, designers, stagehands, and an office. Everything is in place, but it is not yet a theatre. If an actor arrived and rolled out a carpet, then there may be a theatre. However, building a theatre on a rug is not the intended goal.

They had left behind the stench of Moscow's fires as their spirits commanded. However, their art required more than a backpack or a motley truck—they brought five cargo train cars, with all the consequences that entailed.

> I must inform Your Excellency that since the death of S.T. Morozov and other financial backers, MAT has received no financial support and exists solely on the contributions of fellow artists. A trip abroad proved so costly that all those funds have dried up. MAT may have to seek government assistance.

In the papers related to Nemirovich-Danchenko's memoir preparations, there is an entry that states, "The main [MAT] shareholders were Savva Morozov, Alexey Stakhovich, and Nikolai Tarasov; they all committed suicide." Nemirovich-Danchenko described Tarasov in *From the Past*. Legendary actress Alisa Koonen and Vadim Shrerubovich, the future head of MAT productions, both mentioned him in their memoirs.

The term "mental breakdown" was commonly used at the beginning of the century, and in this case, it referred to Tarasov and the rumors surrounding him. A breakdown in material life or psychology can be incredibly intricate, although at its core, there are likely to be cataclysmic societal transformations as well. It would be worth incorporating Tarasov into the story, but since there is no space, we can at least remember the day when MAT canceled a performance as a sign of mourning for him. They rarely did this; that same year, they had canceled another performance only once, when Leo Tolstoy died. The above-mentioned suicides were stories that reflected the spirit of the times, mannered but still stained with real blood. Tarasov's entire persona embodied the spirit of the times, something impossible in the city where MAT began but characteristic of the city they had now returned to.

Returning to a New Place 1905–1906   145

However, the point is not what occurred during their absence. Things around us rarely change instantly, but sometimes we suddenly become aware of those changes. It hits your consciousness that you have been living in a different place, a place that is no longer the city you once knew. Thirty years ago, *The Alarm Clock*, where the boy from Tiflis would joke with fellow "Nicks and Kicks" columnist Pyotr Kicheev, was still being published.[4] The professors of Moscow University, who in their early years were familiar with the newspaper where young Nemirovich-Danchenko collaborated, were still lecturing to students and held in high regard. In his trilogy *The Beginning of the Century*, poet Andrei Bely wrote about the many changes in the material and societal landscape of newly modern Moscow.[5] Tensions and Perseverance in MAT's Evolution

The author does not want to unnecessarily create suspense about MAT's fluctuating tensions. Everyone knows that MAT has not closed to this day, but readers should understand that it could have closed. "We are in our last year," which Stanislavsky wrote in the summer of 1904, was not just empty nervousness. Something was indeed coming to an end. It was unclear if it would be the end of everything they had worked for, although that was also a possibility. Was it because their time had passed (as everything has its time)? Was it because they had exhausted the artistic idea that brought them together (as Ibsen suggested, ideas are often recognized only when they are already half-dead)? Or was it because they had exhausted the meaning of their relationship?

They were all tired of each other. During a rehearsal of Chirikov's play *Ivan Mironych*,[6] replacing Gorky's *Summerfolk*, Stanislavsky grew annoyed with everyone and declared that there was only one true actor in the troupe, Anton Los.[7] It was easy to smile at Stanislavsky's eccentricities. But why such extremes? Why Los? Shortly before this, Nemirovich-Danchenko, not known for being eccentric, also grew annoyed during a rehearsal of Yartsev's play *At the Monastery*. The actors were difficult to motivate, and each was only thinking of themselves. They did not inspire Nemirovich-Danchenko, and he did not inspire them.

It was even more troubling that the individuals who started the enterprise did not inspire each other. Nemirovich-Danchenko criticized his colleague. Was it not shameful for Stanislavsky to consider Meyerhold's voice, which had recently returned to the theatre, as good news when he had previously disregarded that same voice? Did not Nemirovich-Danchenko propose the symbolist dramas of D'Annunzio and Hamsun?[8] Did he not initiate the conversation about finding a new tone for new plays? When Stanislavsky struggled with the actors' lack of expressiveness and weak spiritual energy during the rehearsal of Maeterlinck's *Blue Bird*, Nemirovich-Danchenko experienced similar frustration with the ill-fated *Monastery*. (The play itself was not of much value, but the director was searching for something he needed for an entire cycle of plays, which did not work out.)

They did not assist each other; they only hindered each other. One annoyed the other with cautious experimentation, and the other irritated the former

146 *Vladimir Nemirovich-Danchenko and the Moscow Art Theatre*

with their recklessness in discarding the jointly acquired artistic legacy. Even Nemirovich-Danchenko himself suspected that they might be too quick to dismiss ideas. He warned them not to assume that everything was exhausted and perhaps they should search deeper in familiar places. Nemirovich-Danchenko's soothing tone usually prevailed, but not this time. It sounded too artificial, too deliberate. This tone must have even angered Nemirovich-Danchenko himself for a few minutes. Why did he always have to be the one to calm everyone down when he was trembling inside? Why couldn't Stanislavsky see this? And why couldn't he, Nemirovich-Danchenko, allow himself the captivating, come-what-may attitude that had newly emerged at MAT? Meyerhold at MAT again? However, it was a rhetorical question. He couldn't allow himself to be irresponsible; it was not in his nature. He couldn't experience the exhilaration of breaking and exploding. However, he could recognize that it was necessary and the only way to find salvation. If not breaking and exploding, then simply ending it all at once. He could leave. He had enough reasons to do so.

The archives contained a letter written in pencil, though not all the words were legible. Normally, Nemirovich-Danchenko had noticeably clear handwriting, but it differed when he was worried and nervous. In the letter, he sorted through his grievances, cataloging the many that had accumulated since the first season. Sometimes, for example, he didn't even go out for the curtain call to discourage gossip about whether he had the right to applause. (He couldn't imagine this now, but his note to Chekhov was intact: "Maybe I offended you when I didn't go out on stage with you in response to the audience's calls…") He recorded how they didn't allow him to work on *The Snow Maiden*. He wrote about how Stanislavsky and the late Savva Morozov tried to reassure him by saying, "'We need you for this and that.' 'This is very unkind of you.' 'We need you,' which I fell for.'" He recounted how he toiled on the trip out of the country in 1906:

> I had no time to see any galleries except in Dresden, not a single attraction. And yet, the trip only took place through my efforts. If I didn't have friends from the Literary and Artistic Circle, we wouldn't have gone abroad.

(The truth was that Sumbatov-Yuzhin, who ruled over this wealthy and influential circle mentioned, demonstrated his friendship at the right time by obtaining a loan for MAT's trip.)

Around this time, Alexey Stakhovich also appeared at MAT.[9] "This man sees me as a draft horse and you as an inspired genius […] I swallowed that, too, even though it virtually choked me." They attempted to clarify themselves on numerous occasions. Even the late Morozov implored him not to write any further letters, and he was correct. They tried to explain and reconcile; however, "I realize nothing will change. You will continue to believe everyone else before me—Stakhovich, Vishnevsky, Meyerhold, Sulerzhitsky.

Anyone you favor who visits your home. My artistic preferences still irritate you, which hinders our collaboration." He pressed his pencil down firmly for a long time, filling the page with his customary doodles—flowers, underlines, and strikethroughs. Then he proceeded with the letter, stating, "I cannot depart from the Art Theatre." "It is not that I am clueless regarding where to go if I were to leave the Art Theatre. I could simply utter a single word, send a brief telegram, and become the leading figure at the imperial theatre." He did not even need to send a telegram: soon enough, they would formally invite him to assume artistic direction at the Maly Theatre. "I cannot leave the Art Theatre, yet my dissatisfaction with my work here grows, and I am indifferent to its numerous flaws." It is a conversation with himself, a process of blaming and disregarding grievances.

His unspoken interlocutor is Stanislavsky, the perpetual companion of his soul. As it appears they will part ways, their pursuit "outside" MAT begins to take form. It is worth noting that they were searching for innovative concepts that closely resembled what they once had and lost with each other. Stanislavsky establishes a studio with Meyerhold, whose relationship with Stanislavsky filled Nemirovich-Danchenko with envy. Stanislavsky endeavors to recreate everything—the summer, Pushkino, rehearsals in the barn, the settling-in of students. However, Stanislavsky persistently confuses it all: "At Pushkino before, we..." Unconsciously, he attempts to summon the past.

The poster for the unrealized performance at the Studio on Povarskaya Street (1905) remains intact. It is peculiar to see it printed on an ordinary piece of paper:

Studio Theatre (Arbat Gate, Povarskaya Corner)
Friday, October 00
will be presented for the first time
Schluck und Jau[10]
By Gerhart Hauptmann

But it would never come to pass. It is over. All that remains is the wound, the pain. Nemirovich-Danchenko did not want to recollect Stanislavsky's experience:

> I do not even wish to delve into the details, for you would not believe me regardless. If you had shown me what I witnessed yesterday earlier, before seeking my advice on what to do — I would have said, the sooner you put an end to this grave error in your life, the better it will be for the Art Theatre and for you, even for your artistic prestige.

A diary entry from 1905 reads: "November 11, Friday. My discussion with K. S. about the future of the theatre." Their farewell at that meeting felt like a test of closure.

148　Vladimir Nemirovich-Danchenko and the Moscow Art Theatre

Upon returning from the tour and working in Moscow for a year, additional plans emerged in a letter to his wife in August 1907. He didn't complain about censorship or being prohibited from working. He wasn't like Evgeny Chirikov, who preemptively listed the faults the censors would inevitably find in his plays, the symbols that would outrage them. Nemirovich-Danchenko was not part of the noisy breed who merely complained about censorship; if he said censorship got in the way, we could believe it indeed did. An example of this is when the censor's ban fell on Byron's *Cain*. At the time, Nemirovich-Danchenko was already preparing the production. He was re-reading Milton's *Paradise Lost* and considering Yuri Leonidov for the title role and Kachalov as "the fire-throwing Lucifer." But unfortunately, they couldn't produce it.

However, Nemirovich-Danchenko had another idea: produce it in Vyborg, Finland,[11] where they could stage everything allowed in print. The plan was to establish an accessible Russian theatre there. The public response to this step was also important to him. He believed that by doing this, they would play a brilliant and honorable role in the history of Russia's liberation. Simultaneously, other plans arose. Nemirovich-Danchenko had not yet given a definitive response to the proposal to lead the Maly Theatre. He warned them that he couldn't accept the position at that very moment because he was committed to next season's work at MAT. Leaving would severely let them down. However, in principle, he did not refuse and said he needed to consider the possibility of reforms. He immediately told Stanislavsky about this and explained how tempting it was for him "to create a state academy."

In the end, Nemirovich-Danchenko did not go to the Maly Theatre or leave for uncensored Vyborg. But his dual readiness was curious and reflected his leadership style at MAT—indirect and robust. The story is concluded by Kachalov's letter to actor Nikolai Podgorny on March 10, 1908.[12] According to the letter,

> Nemirovich-Danchenko officially declared that he was leaving for the Maly Theatre, only if he was sure the Art Theatre could carry on with Stanislavsky alone. Hearing this, Stanislavsky took out his watch and announced: 'It's 5 o'clock. I can't leave now but will be home at quarter past six.' After that, they talked for a long time and settled the matter. Nemirovich-Danchenko stayed.

Adaptation and Tension in Theatre's Evolution

All the problems remained unresolved. Theatre is an addiction that consumes your entire life and essence. It is an addiction that heavily relies on the past—the experiences and forms you have already developed. It is an addiction that only comes with maturity, something that a person, artist, or business lacks in their youth when they do not yet fully know themselves.

Returning to a New Place 1905–1906 149

Shortly after the tenth anniversary of MAT, Nemirovich-Danchenko wrote a letter in response to Stanislavsky's appeal to the troupe. Stanislavsky titled the appeal "Be on Guard!" and Nemirovich-Danchenko agreed that the title was appropriate. Specifically, Stanislavsky requested that his letter be read first during the Board of Directors meeting. Despite not needing anyone's permission to address the troupe, Stanislavsky wanted the board to acknowledge the undeniable facts in his letter or challenge them and seek clarification. Nemirovich-Danchenko explained all this to the board, expressing a different viewpoint. He remained silent during the meeting. Stanislavsky believed that his urgent call to "Be on Guard!" originated from negligence and ill intentions within the troupe. If only this were the truth.

Nemirovich-Danchenko, on the other hand, believed that the underlying cause of the situation lay in MAT's maturity.

The Art Theatre itself is the source of the complex breakdown, as it attempts to balance various elements. It exists as a theatre with a strong tradition, a theatre of artistic exploration, a theatre with experienced and inexperienced members, and a theatre that operates daily, compensates actors, distributes dividends to shareholders, relies on income, and, therefore, heavily relies on the support of the audience. It is also a theatre school with a set of ethical and pedagogical requirements. As soon as you delve into the various needs of MAT as an organism, you can see that these desires often clash with one another. There seems to be no resolution, and there won't be any!

Nemirovich-Danchenko saw his theatre in a broad sense, similar to how one perceives the opposing forces in life—spirit versus flesh, dreams versus practicality, pursuit of ideals versus stability, and so on. Let's avoid resorting to the cliché comparison of MAT's founders—attributing the spirit and intent to Stanislavsky and the practicality to Nemirovich-Danchenko. Instead, for many years, Nemirovich-Danchenko acted as the driving force that harmonized these opposites within MAT without attempting to eliminate them. Nemirovich-Danchenko did not expect a complete resolution and did not propose accepting things as they were through compromise. His constant effort was to harmonize. He saw the life of the theatre as a movement through insolvability, with the belief in an extrinsic purpose and in harmony with the moral law. Conscious effort, even if only for a single second, creates agreement, moderation, and the balance between "spirit and flesh." Everything may break apart in the next moment, but a new opportunity for harmonization will also arise.[13] All it takes is goodwill.

Nemirovich-Danchenko's concern is to prioritize certain demands over time, temporarily setting aside others, and allowing new demands to take precedence over earlier ones, as long as the elimination of certain demands does not seriously impact the entire enterprise because others will support it. His task is to carry in his heart a constant dissatisfaction with many things

150 *Vladimir Nemirovich-Danchenko and the Moscow Art Theatre*

and bear the constant dissatisfaction of others. His problem is not choosing between an ideal and a compromise but finding an agreement between the ideal and life. Nemirovich-Danchenko accepted the intricacies of a mature theatre, just as he accepted the complexities of the state. He was ready for it, interested in it, and capable of realizing it while calmly and radically changing ideas and approaches.

The organic change of ideas and means was a "structural" mystery of Nemirovich-Danchenko's life. These changes did not involve dramatic displays or public breakups with himself. He did not change his appearance like Meyerhold did, with a pale profile and sad eyes, or a cold, hard look of a man in a crumpled uniform jacket. However, Nemirovich-Danchenko underwent more remarkable historical and artistic transformations. Nemirovich-Danchenko understood his reliance on time without discussing it, and the impermanence of the theatre prevented such discussions. Books can wait to see if their turn will come, but one should not trust too much in the enticing words of Bulgakov's devil in his *Master and Magarita*, who claimed that manuscripts do not burn. While manuscripts may not ignite, they can smolder when locked away and gradually lose relevance. Audiences can forget the words and their meanings from earlier times; only what was esteemed in its own time is remembered and understood forever. You do not need to explain the significance of "Veuve Clicquot or Moet's blessed wine," but those who see the champagne bubbles surrounding these names wouldn't call it anything else. What is not openly esteemed in its own time will inevitably vanish and never return with such clarity. In contrast, there is no possibility of receiving recognition after death in the theatre; it exists solely in its own time.

Writer and memoirist Alexander Gladkov met with Nemirovich-Danchenko in his final years.[14] They questioned why the acclaimed director placed so much importance on what succeeded or failed, what could or could not succeed. It seemed beneath his status as a genius. We have previously discussed "success" and "succeeding"—being on time. The benefits and drawbacks of being on time. It is sheer joy to arrive at a time without actively considering it, at a lively and captivating moment. MAT experienced this kind of happiness initially. But only initially; later on, the relationship with time became problematic. Art that communicates the essence of a specific era—if it has not exhausted itself together with its own time, the time that came to replace it—can engage in a meaningful societal dialogue. Rather than simply embodying a new era, it can interview it, listen to it, and constructively challenge it with insight and depth.

It is worth noting that Stanislavsky never played another contemporary role after *The Drama of Life*.[15] It is also worth noting that he did not direct any contemporary further plays until 1926. So, you can imagine the significance of his meeting with author Mikhail Bulgakov. The play *Days of the Turbins* (1926) would draw from the opening pages of Bulgakov's novel *The White Guard* (1925),[16] incorporating the warmth of a tiled stove, the customs of hospitality, the recent memory of a funeral, the scent of old books, and the circle of light from a shaded lamp. But this is not our theme at the moment.

Nemirovich-Danchenko would never have encountered the kind of disruptions and "rejections" involved in preparing for this play. Firstly, he could never understand a theatre that did not stage modern plays, including "classical plays that captured the noblest modern ideas." Whether subconsciously or intentionally, Nemirovich-Danchenko always juxtaposed them with minor plays that conveyed similar ideas, presented in a realistic manner. Therefore, Ibsen's *Brand* found itself in the intellectual context of Sergey Naidanov's 1907 play *The Walls*.[17] The theme of an uncompromising lofty calling and the torment of breaking free from the constraints of humanity, which tormented the radical idealist, also unfolded in *Walls*. However, it was transformed from Ibsen's collapsing mountains into a Moscow garden with a wicket-gate, neatly trimmed shrubbery, and smoky yellow houses blocking each other's light.

There is another reason. Nemirovich-Danchenko never used those cliché phrases that everyone says: "Do whatever you want, but I won't understand." "It's too late for me to change." "My time has passed." Instead, he always remained open to understanding. If he needed to change his point of view to better comprehend something, he did so willingly, believing it to be essential for a creative life. He did not feel time as his own or not his own: he felt it as an extrinsic object; time is like this now. Just as he approached a new play, he would also approach a new sense of time, appreciating its unique "color and diction" in order to give it the best possible representation. He intentionally avoided evaluating the play using anything other than its own logic and the concepts of the author. This approach differed from Stanislavsky's, who constantly evaluated plays based on his own worldview. Stanislavsky's approach sometimes resulted in interpretations of relationships and events that were not in harmony with the author's intentions, creating a struggle that he couldn't overcome.

Nemirovich-Danchenko possessed the gift of understanding what the theatre needed at that moment, and he always had the desire to fulfill that need. He had the ability to mold his inner artist so that it became natural to fulfill the demands of the theatre. What was truly remarkable and unique about Nemirovich-Danchenko was that he exercised this gift with dignity and authority. He was generally strict when it came to flattery and the desire to please, which is not necessarily a negative trait. In his interactions with the audience, he was more firm than flexible, especially when dealing with a changed audience upon MAT's return.

Evolving Audience Dynamics and Theatre's Creative Tension

MAT's audience was not a problem in the early days, but it has now become one due to the increasing diversity and ambiguity of society. They cannot overlook the audience that was cultivated by an earlier Moscow society. As a result, the repertoire of MAT has become a mixed bag. The pressure from the audience can uplift the actors. Was that not the case in 1898? The pressure was invisible then because it harmonized with the actors' self-expression. However, this situation did not last long.

In the summer of 1906, while resting in a remote Finnish resort, Stanislavsky was shocked to discover a truth that he had long known. The unnatural and impossible duty of the actor to create in front of a public that may not even care about the actor's creativity horrified him. There is a dialectical relationship between self-sufficient creativity and its communicable expression for the public. Theatrical creativity is a public act in this sense. Discord between the artist and the audience can occur when they have little connection to each other, which is common to all arts. The art of representation aligns the actor's solitude to some extent with that of other artists.[18] Like experts in other arts, actors in representational acting present what they have already created and are now showing publicly. Stanislavsky and Nemirovich-Danchenko distinguished this from the "art of the living person," the art of experience, which is effective because it is accomplished publicly. A living feeling is born right before the audience, acquiring value and charm in that very moment. This creative method is captivating but defenseless. The audience can destroy everything without even noticing it, just as the actor can unknowingly destroy everything. It is humbling to realize how much one's art depends on audience feedback. When the audience stirs in their seats, rustles their programs, or exudes boredom or disapproval, the performance changes in tempo and meaning, disengages from conversation, and begins to force itself. Audience approval is equally demanding. Thus, a successful scene must be "re-presented" in response.

Stanislavsky was afraid of the dark and crowded auditorium where creativity could shut down. That's why the first term of his "system" is the "circle of attention." It helps to have a way to isolate oneself, where you are invulnerable and focused, creating for the sake of the audience but not at its request or will: self-expression and public service. In happy and harmonious times, this happens naturally. However, when the harmony of self-expression and public service is disrupted, the theatre can degrade itself by primarily appealing to the consumer. It may also rebel, withdraw, or engage in scandalous, provocative, and mocking communication with the patron. Ironically, the twentieth-century public quickly turned the theatre's isolation from the social order—its overwhelming isolation of form and spirit and its "slaps in the face" to public taste—into objects of prestigious consumption. Finally, when MAT had developed an excellent ensemble with *The Drama of Life* (subject to a long dispute between Stanislavsky and Nemirovich-Danchenko), author Valery Bryusov hurried to congratulate them. But at its premiere, amidst the applause, he heard both cheers and catcalls. Strangely, in the minds of Russian actors, defiant and self-indulgent playing with the offended public revived an old rule: "The sounds of approval are not heard in the sweet roar of praise but the wild shouts of anger." The abstract staging of *The Drama of Life*

Returning to a New Place 1905–1906   153

and the uniquely aggressive communication that Nemirovich-Danchenko put forward in the production of *Brand* stemmed from a crisis in audience relations, which were no longer as harmonious as they once were.

Radicalism, Theatrical Innovation, and Audience Engagement

Nemirovich-Danchenko contrasted Stanislavsky's dark, isolated direction in *The Drama of Life* with his own open, declamatory approach in *Brand*. He established a strong connection with the audience, challenging them directly with thought-provoking questions, grand spectacle, powerful choral sounds, and exciting rhythms. He "seized" the audience with passionate evangelistic speeches in a recurring four-beat verse pattern. He also "seized" them with endless, thrilling, and difficult-to-pronounce monologues that combined passion and method. Coarse humor was employed against Brand's enemies, providing a contrasting perspective. Within the play's main story, Nemirovich-Danchenko introduced mocking factions, notable minor characters, and visually poetic images of Brand's face.

Kachalov, portraying Brand, embodied a man whose internal tension reflected the pressure felt by the hungry peasant crowd. Meanwhile, a high-ranking bureaucrat distributed useless aid packages to address the suffering of the townspeople. "Their need is so great that they sit, see, and hear nothing. They somehow froze while sitting in a dreamy, philosophical, concentrated position." It would be unexpected when they eventually erupted and stampeded. Brand's radicalism responded to the radical realities depicted in the play, including mountains, winter storms, famine, pestilence, and despair. Brand's words on the frozen shore denounced indifference to misfortune, cruelty, and greed, shocking all but the indifferent.

Externally, Brand/Kachalov resembled one of those young heretics that the hungry crowd unexpectedly relies on for sustenance. He possessed the mannerisms, habits, and appearance of an explorer, effortlessly carrying his backpack, wearing tall boots, and a long coat. When he leaped onto a boat in the midst of a stormy sea, no one grabbed his sleeve, but they clung to him with desperate seriousness, much like the wives of fishermen who cling to their husbands ready to follow Brand. There was also a sense of lightness about him, unburdened by baggage or constraints. Some say that Kachalov Russified the character of Brand. In the end, maximalism permeated the entire performance. Brand/Kachalov completely captivated and electrified the audience with his intense portrayal. "Lead us!" cried Alisa Koonen, one voice among the crowd, expressing her desire to be led. She couldn't even recall saying it. In fact, no one remembered what was said; they simply yearned to be guided.

You would be amazed at how freely the director treated the play he called "the most brilliant work of the century." Even if it was the most brilliant work of the century, he freely omitted anything that wouldn't work today. Nemirovich-Danchenko drew from the play's text; indeed, his ability to read closely was the foundation of his directing career. At first, he sought mountains, storms, and crowds, but then stopped: Brand had to live in a wretched parish, where, however, there was no plague or famine. There was a church, a structure that could be considered an architectural monument, or perhaps just an old dilapidated house. The town had a school, local dignitaries, a madwoman, and a house where the priest had to endure the dampness at the bottom of the valley, alongside the gooseberry bushes.

Kachalov played Brand as someone in love with an idea, devoted to it fanatically, and eagerly seeking to embody it. However, he also portrayed something else. The actor later admitted his desire to separate the person from the idea but lacked the courage to do so. "I should have liked to separate the person from the idea—but I couldn't do it," he confessed. This separation, a face-to-face confrontation between the person and the idea, would have been remarkable.

In *Peer Gynt*, the Great Boyg [compromise] seduces and ridicules Peer; in MAT's *Brand*, the protagonist could have engaged in a similar conversation with the "Great Straight Path" [radicalism], which had its own allure and mockery. In Act IV, Brand urges Agnes to give the blanket that covered their recently buried baby to a poor Roma girl. The child in the arms of its homeless mother is pitiful, so Agnes reluctantly agrees to share. However, Brand insists that she give everything, and through sheer willpower, she gives away her remaining possessions. Once the girl departs, Agnes confesses that she did not give everything—she had hidden their infant's cap in her blouse. Words fail to express how difficult yet necessary it is to give the blanket of a deceased infant to a stranger's child, even if that child is cold and crying. However, who else but the mother of the deceased infant would need the poor, useless cap? Yet, when they say you must give it away, the pressure itself raises the question: Who needs it? Why?

The Great Straight Path of radicalism is seductive, guiding, and teaches you to scorn the most obvious questions: where it leads, why, and whether it is definitely better to continue on this path rather than turn back. Nemirovich-Danchenko was concerned that Brand's posture, which emphasized the haughty, educational tone of the play, would repel audiences. "If Brand were to stand with his hands behind his back and present Agnes with his harsh demands in this posture, it would be repulsive." He proposed a different staging, with Brand speaking with his arm around his wife, crouching in front of the lower drawers of the dresser. Nemirovich-Danchenko was not concerned about whether the demands themselves would be disgusting or if there would be any arguments against them.

Audiences debated *Brand* on multiple levels. The Trinity Monastery released a brochure written by a theologian who placed *Brand* in the context of the revolutionary events of 1905. The theologian appreciated the revolutionary and political goals of the revolution and discussed how it ignited public interest in spiritual matters. He mentioned conservative publications that protested the spiritual hunger of the semi-literate population in Russia and advocated for Church reform. *Brand* had achieved an

> extraordinary success … MAT enjoys the well-established and well-deserved reputation of an advanced, ideological theatre … But it wouldn't be an exaggeration to say that *Brand's* success surpassed everything that came before it. Despite running every other day for six months, it consistently advertised 'tickets are all sold out for another week. So, Go see *Brand*.'

"Go see *Brand*" became a cultural expectation for every intelligent Muscovite, and they strove to fulfill it despite obstacles and sacrifices. "People in society constantly discussed *Brand*; they delivered lectures, wrote essays and articles about it. In short, the evidence suggests that *Brand* deeply and strongly captivated our intellectual society."

Now, let's return to the previous questions. These debates covered various topics, but none addressed why anyone would willingly give away a worn-out cap that still smelled of damp infant hair. Who would want it, and for what reason? Like the rest of Brand's demands, his requests were not evaluated based on reality or genuine emotions. People refused to face this reality check; they were prepared to criticize the actor for evaluating things based on heartfelt sentiments. Brand's claims should remain unchallenged by the demands of reality, and he should be seen as "a man of fire and steel." This phrase is from an angry article titled "About Idols, about the Crowd, about *Brand*, the Art Theatre, and Monastery Theologians" by the renowned author Eugene Maurin. Imagine this adventure writer who insisted that Brand must be a man of fire and steel.[19] The appeal of radicalism is strongest when it pertains to someone else's morals and life. Evgeny Maurin unintentionally revealed that dissatisfaction with one's own life also plays a role. Nemirovich-Danchenko, like others in his generation and social circle, felt a sense of shame in light of the norms of the time and a mistrust of accepted standards. He was ashamed of what he called "everyday conservatism." People with such conservatism rarely broke away from the norms of life but only desired to do so. Chekhov used to talk about how nice it would be to live without settling down, to wander around, stay wherever he wanted, and then leave. Nemirovich-Danchenko's letters touched on the same sentiment—how he would like to change his lifestyle "to make it somehow newer, or perhaps more spartan." The news of Tolstoy's suicidal escape from home was actually a relief to ordinary Russian society, as it confirmed their belief that older people often go off somewhere before the end, as if someone were waiting for them. People silently agreed to consider his departure a generous, tragic gift—a great man who did what everyone would like to do for us. They were too self-satisfied to view their own lives as "contemptible, philistine lives," and too self-satisfied to assess the actions and spiritual laws that captivated the protagonist of *Brand*.

156   *Vladimir Nemirovich-Danchenko and the Moscow Art Theatre*

Other moments in *Brand* could touch your heart. Looking at the elderly Brand, with his prematurely gray hair, his cold house, his weeping wife wrapped in a shawl, and his agonizing anger at her grief, the critic Ilya Ignatov unexpectedly revealed something about his own pain: "In every strong Russian ideological crusader, there is the melancholy, dissatisfaction, and corrosive self-reflection of a 'superfluous person.'" At other moments, a completely different meaning emerged: Brand seemed like a mysterious man. Audiences recognized in him a disturbing flame that passed before their eyes, just beyond the edges of their existence.

Ibsen constructed Brand through monologues. The intervening dialogue only hinted at, created, and set up these monologues, constantly spinning around them like whirlwinds. The voices of ordinary common sense and ordinary protest did not participate in the dialogue. Nor did MAT's production restore this absence As a result, the play appeared as a monologue and sermon about radicalism, in which the moments of dialogue counterpointed the same radicalism. Brand had the impact of a monologue but with the lasting effects of a long and complicated dialogue.

Although Nemirovich-Danchenko spoke modestly about it, the production possessed a strong internal structure, allowing it to deviate from its obvious thoughts and associations. It spilled over into objects and issues far removed from Brand's personality and the play's core ideas. Andrei Bely recalled being at MAT with Leonid Andreev and how "we remained silent beside Ibsen, who spoke so powerfully to him and me." During intermission, they tried to discuss what they had been silent about, "and the conversation effortlessly shifted into *The Drama of Life.*" Brand sparked discussions about heresies, the proletariat, and the radical interpretation of Christ in Matthew's Gospel. In theology departments, students debated Brand, citing the theologian's pamphlet as evidence that their arguments aligned with holy scripture. They also drew from Nietzsche's works and the aesthetic concepts of human behavior explored by D'Annunzio and Hamsun.

Audiences pondered how the spectacle of power, wholeness, and self-actualization, detached from conventional morality, resonated with them. They grappled with the risks involved in embracing the beauty of these triumphs of human will. These reflections could be explored in conjunction with *Brand*, even though the play itself did not explicitly contain these ideas. This allowed critics like Ilya Ignatov to incorporate lines from poet Nikolai Nekrasov into their reviews. Ignatov, quoting Nekrasov,[20] described Brand as the epitome of the "superfluous person" who came to thrive during challenging times and performed miracles. Nemirovich-Danchenko, the playwright, connected the radical themes in *Brand* to himself and the people he associated with. He believed in the necessity of such individuals, without whom direct action would be impossible. He did not regret leaving behind the young agitators he once knew, as he believed he could better serve his homeland and bring about more good in the world through his chosen path.

Returning to a New Place 1905–1906 157

When Stanislavsky introduced him to Gerhardt Hauptmann's play *Lonely People*, Nemirovich-Danchenko was grateful.[21] He wondered how he hadn't noticed the character of Anna Mahr earlier, a young, weary woman with an unnamed and unknowable life purpose. In a modest household, she found temporary shelter without revealing much about herself. Her presence, however, disrupted the Fokerat family and left a lasting impact. Her rootlessness, iron sensibility, and willingness to embody heroism touched the souls of those who encountered her. She personified the notion that being such an individual was difficult but necessary, leaving a charismatic impression on the audience.

Brand's production stood out from anything similar in terms of its scope and scale. Nemirovich-Danchenko, proud of his direction, was thrilled with the victory and wanted to build upon this success. He wrote to Kachalov about it, considering that the holiday season was approaching. In this context, Nemirovich-Danchenko sent Kachalov a New Year's wish: "Do not let mundane tasks dampen your spirits."

Notes

1 Alexander Vishnevsky (1861–1943) was a founding actor of MAT often entrusted with the organizational and financial concerns of the theatre.
2 Nikolai Tarasov (1882–1910). An oil-industrialist and devotee of the theatre.
3 Sergei Yulyevich Witte (1849–1915) was a Russian statesman who served as the first prime minister of the Russian Empire, replacing the tsar as head of the government.
4 Pyotr Kicheev (1845–1902) was a journalist and poet.
5 Andrey Bely (1880–1934) was a symbolist novelist, poet, theorist, communist, and literary critic. Omitted at this point in the text is a lengthy excerpt from *The Beginning of the Century*, whose distinctive style is virtually untranslatable. Bely humorously writes that quirky, old-school Moscow continues to live on amid huge, if not immediately noticeable, changes taking place and that nobody knows what will happen next in this emerging twentieth-century metropolis.
6 *Ivan Mironych* (1904) is a drama about the banality of Russian provincial life, ala Chekhov. It was the first MAT play Stanislavsky directed solo, without Luzhsky, his regular assistant.
7 Anton Los (?–1914) was an actor with Suvorin's Theatre in St. Petersburg and later with MAT 1904–1906.
8 Knut Hamsun (1859–1952) was an author, playwright, and recipient of the 1920 Nobel Prize in Literature.
9 Alexey Stakhovich (1856–1919) was an Imperial Russian Chevalier Guard Regiment officer who in the early 1900s became a popular stage actor associated with MAT. Horrified by Bolshevik atrocities, he committed suicide in 1919.
10 *Schluck and Jau* 1900 is a play by Gerhart Hauptmann loosely based on *The Taming of the Shrew*.
11 Vyborg is district located northwest of St. Petersburg near the Finnish border on the Gulf of Finland. At the time referred to in the text, it was a transit point for revolutionary literature, arms, and agitators going into Russia. It remained Finnish until WWII, after which it was ceded to the Soviet Union.
12 Nikolai Podgorny (1879–1947) was an actor and dramatic reader associated with MAT.
13 Hegel's dialectics seem to have inadvertently shaped Nemirovich's perspective.

158 Vladimir Nemirovich-Danchenko and the Moscow Art Theatre

14 Alexander Gladkov (1912–1976) was a playwright and screenwriter.
15 *The Drama of Life* is a play by Knut Hamsun about a young man named Ove who becomes involved in a love triangle and must confront his desires and psychological struggles.
16 *The Days of the Turbins* (from the novel *The White Guard*, 1924) is a play by Mikhail Bulgakov about the Turbin family and their White Army friends trying to survive the aftermath of the Russian Revolution. See *Stanislavsky Directs* (Minerva Press, 1954), 351–391.
17 *The Walls* (1907) is a symbolist play by Sergei Naidanov about those who suffer from tsarism. People who feel the injustice of power are considered lepers, the hungry are not heard, and the wall is stained with the blood from fallen heroes.
18 The art of representation... See "The Stage as Art and Stock-in-trade" in *An Actor's Work* (Routledge, 2008), 16–36.
19 Evgeny Maurin (?–1925) was an author of historical and adventure prose.
20 Nikolay Nekrasov (1821–1878) was a poet, writer, critic, and publisher, whose poems about peasant Russia made him the hero of the politicized, social-oriented circles of Russian intelligentsia. The passage referred to is from his 1862 poem, "A Knight for an Hour."
21 *Lonely People* (1891) is a play by Gerhardt Hauptmann about the disillusioned poet Paul and the lonely seamstress Anna, who form a bond as they struggle to find meaning in their mundane existence in a run-down apartment complex in Berlin.

7 At Home 1906–1909

Balancing Classics and Contemporary Relevance

Before the establishment of MAT, Nemirovich-Danchenko wrote, "We must stage the classics. If the contemporary repertoire were as diverse and vibrant as the classical one, the theatre would solely produce contemporary plays. Its mission would be broader and more impactful with a mixed repertoire." The classics are used as a support, selecting only what aligns with "the noblest modern ideas." The "first MAT" poster listed Chekhov, Gorky, Tolstoy, Hauptmann, and Ibsen—all living authors.

Nemirovich-Danchenko writes potential plays for a "Second Art Theatre" in his notebook—written sharply, in dark pencil, diagonally across the page: *Brand*, *To the Stars* by Andreyev,[1] *Woe from Wit*, *Pelleas and Melisande* by Maeterlinck, *La Gioconda* and *Glory* by D'Annunzio, *The Eternal Fairy Tale* and *The Mother* by Przybyszewski,[2] *Rosmersholm*, and *The Drama of Life* by Hamsun. Other names were also mentioned nearby: Strindberg, Hofmannsthal,[3] Wedekind, and, from the Russians, Leonid Andreev. This collection is comprehensive. Among the disagreements surrounding *The Drama of Life* was Stanislavsky's belief that Nemirovich-Danchenko had prevented him from borrowing ideas from Meyerhold, Bryusov, Voloshin, and the symbolist poet Jurgis Baltrusaitis. However, it is incorrect to imagine that Nemirovich-Danchenko ever tried to isolate his colleague from "new art." Depending on your taste, you can find either merit or fault in Nemirovich-Danchenko's alleged restriction; however, the point is that there was no such restriction.

Was it possible for a theatre to have such a hastily written and time-pressured repertoire? It is quite possible if the goal is solely to attract an audience in Moscow. The mentioned authors were no longer exclusively published by progressive publishers. In 1895, *Suvorin's Cheap Library* included the first Russian translation of Maeterlinck's *Interior* with a preface. In 1915, *The Field* released Maeterlinck's four-volume collection as a supplement, including complete collections of the works of Ibsen and Wilde. Even Knut Hamsun's plays were published in mass editions, similar to Jack London's novels. MAT would stage some plays from the list, while others would be experimented with by students. It's not about the suitability of specific

DOI: 10.4324/9781003486282-7

160 *Vladimir Nemirovich-Danchenko and the Moscow Art Theatre*

plays, but rather that MAT did not consider itself an avant-garde theatre. Since its second decade, MAT has built its repertoire based on Nemirovich-Danchenko's harmonizing principle. His approach involved actualizing some demands while setting others aside temporarily, allowing new demands to take precedence.

In a previously read letter, Nemirovich-Danchenko shared his thoughts on this development. Furthermore, he recalls a decision that guided the composition of their repertoire. It consisted of five categories: restoring the Russian repertoire, producing a spectacle, showcasing plays in the vein of *Lonely People* (authors like Hauptmann, Przybyszewski, Hamsun, Ibsen, Herman Heijermans,[4] Hofmannsthal, Dreyer, and Schnitzler), presenting a new Russian play, and exploring new forms. Interestingly, Nemirovich-Danchenko excluded *The Life of Man* from the category of "new Russian plays," despite it being a new work by a Russian author. Evidently, by "new Russian," he referred to plays depicting contemporary characters and customs, thus categorizing them as part of the "domestic repertoire." However, this aspect of MAT seems to be lacking authenticity—a degeneration of sorts. While their performances reflect the spirit of the time, its pulse, and currents, it is questionable how long the stage can survive without capturing the essence of the era, its texture, and ultimately, its politics.

For a while, Nemirovich-Danchenko expressed deep concern about this decline. It was during this time that he became hesitant to let anything slip through his fingers. After reading *Princess Nastya*, he exclaimed, "It has such a spicy, piping hot brew, everything that interests people now, and we don't have it." In his letter to Stanislavsky, Nemirovich-Danchenko didn't recount the plot of *Princess Nastya* in detail. However, he emphasized its abundance of intrigue involving aristocratic embezzlers, automobiles, trotting horses, terrorists, and sisterly rivalries, which also included a cold and lecherous seducer who also happened to be a prominent entrepreneur. Yet, what truly drove the play was its rapid conversations about the pressing issues of its time. Reflecting on Amfiteatrov's play and the idea of elevating its ideological importance, Nemirovich-Danchenko muses, "I'll find something in it..." But what could they do? After the third season, there were no premieres that depicted contemporary Russian life.

Before the establishment of MAT, Nemirovich-Danchenko wrote, "We must stage the classics. If the contemporary repertoire were as diverse and vibrant as the classical one, the theatre would solely produce contemporary plays. Its mission would be broader and more impactful with a mixed repertoire." The classics are used as a support, selecting only what aligns with "the noblest modern ideas." The "first MAT" poster listed Chekhov, Gorky, Tolstoy, Hauptmann, and Ibsen—all living authors.

Nemirovich-Danchenko writes potential plays for a "Second Art Theatre" in his notebook—written sharply, in dark pencil, diagonally across the page: *Brand*, *To the Stars* by Andreyev, *Woe from Wit*, *Pelleas and Melisande* by Maeterlinck, *La Gioconda* and *Glory* by D'Annunzio, *The Eternal Fairy*

At Home 1906–1909 161

Tale and *The Mother* by Przybyszewski, *Rosmersholm*, and *The Drama of Life* by Hamsun. Other names were also mentioned nearby: Strindberg, Hofmannsthal, Wedekind, and, from the Russians, Leonid Andreev. This collection is comprehensive. Among the disagreements surrounding *The Drama of Life* was Stanislavsky's belief that Nemirovich-Danchenko had prevented him from borrowing ideas from Meyerhold, Bryusov, Voloshin, and the symbolist poet Jurgis Baltrusaitis. However, it is incorrect to imagine that Nemirovich-Danchenko ever tried to isolate his colleague from "new art." Depending on your taste, you can find either merit or fault in Nemirovich-Danchenko's alleged restriction; however, the point is that there was no such restriction.

Was it possible for a theatre to have such a hastily written and time-pressured repertoire? It is quite possible if the goal is solely to attract an audience in Moscow. The mentioned authors were no longer exclusively published by progressive publishers. In 1895, Suvorin's *Cheap Library* included the first Russian translation of Maeterlinck's *Interior* with a preface. In 1915, *Field* released Maeterlinck's four-volume collection as a supplement, including complete collections of the works of Ibsen and Wilde. Even Knut Hamsun's plays were published in mass editions, similar to Jack London's novels. MAT would stage some plays from the list, while others would be experimented with by students. It's not about the suitability of specific plays, but rather that MAT did not consider itself an avant-garde theatre. Since its second decade, MAT has built its repertoire based on Nemirovich-Danchenko's harmonizing principle. His approach involved actualizing some demands while setting others aside temporarily, allowing new demands to take precedence.

In a previously read letter, Nemirovich-Danchenko shared his thoughts on this development. Furthermore, he recalls a decision that guided the composition of their repertoire. It consisted of five categories: restoring the Russian repertoire, producing a spectacle, showcasing plays in the vein of *Lonely People* (authors like Hauptmann, Przybyszewski, Hamsun, Ibsen, Herman Heijermans, Hofmannsthal, Dreyer, and Schnitzler), presenting a new Russian play, and exploring new forms. Interestingly, Nemirovich-Danchenko excluded *The Life of Man* from the category of "new Russian plays," despite it being a new work by a Russian author. Evidently, by "new Russian," he referred to plays depicting contemporary characters and customs, thus categorizing them as part of the "domestic repertoire." However, this aspect of MAT seems to be lacking actuality—a degeneration of sorts. While their performances reflect the spirit of the time, its pulse, and currents, it is questionable how long the stage can survive without capturing the customs of the era, its texture, and ultimately, its politics.

For a while, Nemirovich-Danchenko expressed deep concern about this decline. It was during this time that he became hesitant to let anything slip through his fingers. After reading Alexander Amfiteatrov's *Princess Nastya*, he exclaimed, "It has such a spicy, piping hot brew, everything that interests people now, and we don't have it." In his letter to Stanislavsky, Nemirovich-Danchenko didn't recount the plot of *Princess Nastya* in detail. However,

162 *Vladimir Nemirovich-Danchenko and the Moscow Art Theatre*

he emphasized its abundance of intrigue involving aristocratic embezzlers, automobiles, trotting horses, terrorists, and sisterly rivalries, as well as a cold and lecherous seducer who also happened to be a prominent entrepreneur. Yet, what truly drove the play was its rapid conversations about the pressing issues of its day. Reflecting on Amfiteatrov's play and the idea of elevating its ideological importance, Nemirovich-Danchenko muses, "I'll find something in it..." But what could they do? After the third season, there were no premieres that depicted contemporary Russian life.

Shifts in Realism and Experimentation

The Walls had a lack of success, as journalists quickly recognized its flaws. There was significant confusion surrounding the protagonist's departure from home for revolutionary activities, and critics correctly pointed out the author's literary borrowings. Nevertheless, the play had its merits. It highlighted the poetry found in its courtyard and trash heap, along with scandalous yet subtle social exchanges and the unique way the enclosed world within the play handled outside influences. Predicting how the public would react to all of this proved difficult. Stanislavsky, who spoke of the "poetry of the trash heap," admired the play. Nemirovich-Danchenko also incorporated his understanding of the "given circumstances" into it, portraying a broken home in pain.

Even before the public, however, MAT became dismissive of such domestic realism. This attitude infuriated Luzhky, who insisted that *The Walls* was outdated and that no one had any use for such plays anymore. He expressed his frustration to Nemirovich-Danchenko in a desperate letter, stating, "I can hardly control myself. Sorry, but I have to say it aloud. I can't take it anymore. My patience has run out. I have none left!"

While Nemirovich-Danchenko shared the same opinion, he approached it with more philosophy. The lives of the characters fascinated him. At one point, he even considered writing about a similar subject. During his time in Nice, he outlined a play called *A Nice Drama* appreciating the ambiguity of the word "Nice" in the characters' lives. "The play is set in Moscow and centers around modern characters and their problems. The husband is a poor noble bureaucrat, while the wife resembles a semi-Carmen." The playwright wondered what would happen to the characters' self-centered and passionate lives on "Bourgeois Street" when they were confronted with random and exciting ideas. However, Nemirovich-Danchenko never finished the play.

On January 1, 1910, *The Voice of Moscow* conducted a poll of celebrities in which they asked MAT actor Alexander Vishnevsky, "What does the upcoming year have in store for us?" He replied, "What am I waiting for? A new play by Nemirovich-Danchenko." The author's notebooks were filled with new ideas, and the list of characters included a diverse range of individuals from all walks of Russian life, such as tramps, cabinet ministers, men, women, social revolutionaries, and industrialists. For one of his new plays, he wrote, "Modern Moscow, Moscow's Minister of War Alexander Guchkov, industrialist Pavel Ryabushinsky, opera star Fyodor Chaliapin,[5] artists Konstantin Simov and Alexander Benoit, Stanislavsky, the Archbishop, Paquin, and Sergei Rachmaninov. The range is wide." For the character of Paquin, he described her as "a model from Jeanne Paquin's French fashion house." Other characters mentioned in the play include Maxim Gorky (who used the pseudonym Goloshchekov) and the late Savva Morozov. Nemirovich-Danchenko was inspired by Morozov's solid and intelligent persona, which fueled his creative imagination. Although Nemirovich-Danchenko displayed great writing discipline and had sufficient time, nothing significant came out of these notebooks.

In addition to being a director, Nemirovich-Danchenko also took on the roles of writer and head of the repertoire. He maintained his preference for everyday characters and accurately depicted dramatic situations. Later on, he would express his disbelief in how someone couldn't love life in the theatre and everyday life. However, there comes a time when artists suddenly find representations of everyday life to be extremely dull. At that point, everyday life becomes a blur, and what remains are fleeting images of light, the swish of a dress, and the faint scent of perfume. Artists then mockingly and cynically pounce on everyday life, shaking it up and turning it into the subject of a brutal game. In Nemirovich-Danchenko's notebooks, the titles *Earth Spirit, Pandora's Box*, and *The Dance of Death* were present. These expressionist plays by Frank Wedekind depicted a bold, eccentric world set in drawing rooms, business offices, train stations, hotels, and restaurants. Fashionable life had fallen victim to the grotesque. The plots meandered and dangerously mocked the principles of the "Great Books," incorporating them into secular adventures with murdered bankers, countesses, brothels, and tailcoated robbers. Everything unfolded with cynical arrogance, with the rhythm and lighting reminiscent of a basement cabaret number, like "The Apache Dance" or "The Snake Woman." Nemirovich-Danchenko tackled Russian versions of expressionism, such as the dance of beggars traversing the spattered and trampled steppe in Andreyev's *Anathema* (1909)[6] or the older women with stony, satisfied eyes observing the hopeless wedding in Yushkevich's *Miserere* (1910).[7]

Nemirovich-Danchenko explained that he had a goal, an ideal, and an approach to his work. He believed that contemporary life, when filtered through the artist's feelings and temperament, takes on a poetic quality and is preserved as life, treasured as a pearl of creation. However, he admitted that it was currently impossible to work with new Russian plays in this manner (Alexander Blok's symbolist plays had thoroughly perplexed MAT). For now, he had to set aside these requirements and allow others to explore them with fresh energy.

The first priority was to focus on a cycle of Russian classics—the "restoration of the Russian repertoire."

Revisiting Russian Classics with New Artistic Lenses

Titles were selected from classic works featured in anthologies. Nemirovich-Danchenko did not burden himself with a philological education. He wasn't

164 *Vladimir Nemirovich-Danchenko and the Moscow Art Theatre*

fascinated by masterpieces from forgotten geniuses or theatrical mischief-makers, nor did he have a particular passion for any historical period. Others would discover and revel in the world of the baroque stage, Venetian masks, courtesans, or courtly games of the Middle Ages. One could never imagine Nemirovich-Danchenko resurrecting, for example, the expressiveness of Elizabethan theatre and becoming captivated by John Webster's *White Devil*.

Nemirovich-Danchenko was even skeptical about classics that had already been rediscovered by others. In a sincere but joking manner, he wrote that Lope de Vega's *The Star of Seville* was an inferior work. He never changed his mind about the great Spanish authors and considered Shakespeare's comedies as nothing more than artistically executed jokes. He also distrusted historical chronicles. At one point, MAT raved about *Richard II*, describing it as a captivating character and a stunning collision of guilty weakness and right-wing force that loses integrity and nobility in its victory. Nemirovich-Danchenko did not challenge this enthusiasm, but ultimately, he was glad they didn't produce the play. He couldn't explain it and wasn't curious enough to do so. Rediscovering something forgotten for three or four hundred years was not appealing to him. Once forgotten, it was worth forgetting. That's why they didn't produce *Richard II*, but instead chose to stage *The Merchant of Venice* (a touring production had recently passed through Moscow), *Twelfth Night*, *Julius Caesar* (memorable ever since the Meiningen tour), and *Hamlet*. These Shakespearean titles were the first to come to everyone's mind.

Nemirovich-Danchenko didn't have a personal collection of Russian literature that he wanted to be the first to present on stage. However, there was an exception with Alexei Tolstoy's *Tsar Fyodor Ivanovich* (1868). While other historical titles disappeared, the anthology titles consistently remained. In 1906, each succeeding season opened with *Woe from Wit, Boris Godunov,*[8] *The Inspector General, Enough Stupidity in Every Wise Man,*[9] and *A Month in the Country*. Nemirovich-Danchenko directed or co-directed all these productions, except for the last one. *A Month in the Country* was supposed to be the first in this sequence, and it was Nemirovich-Danchenko who desired to stage it in the first season.

> My dream is to stage Turgenev's play in a manner that captures his soft, fragrant talent and delicate analysis, while also expressing the style of the era. We need to bring Natalya Petrovna, Rakitin, and the other characters to life by fully embodying the external and spiritual aspects of their time. This new approach to staging would be quite innovative.

The sudden surge in popularity of plays that were traditionally not considered "historical," along with the fascination for non-historical objects, is an intriguing phenomenon. It is not the authentic sword of Prince Dmitry Donskoy or Napoleon's cocked hat that captures attention, but rather everyday items like a jotting pen, a porcelain inkwell, a small sandbox for blotting, a

At Home 1906–1909   165

snuffbox, and even framed silhouettes made from black paper or embroidered sofa cushions. It seems that the mundane becomes historical when it is suddenly stripped of life, infused with a sense of catastrophe, and claimed as inevitable by history.

This shift in artistic perspective is also evident in painting. In the 1880s, a painter might portray a dilapidated house with columns, a lapdog, and an elderly woman with ringlets as a representation of the past. However, by the early twentieth century, this theme took on a different meaning and mood. Natural aging and decay were replaced by a sense of historical necessity, revived through poetic effort. It emerged from the past as if by magic. The imagery of young women bending over a water's edge, misty green vistas floating in fog, and a white ghostly manor house in the dark of the park—all seen as if from the other side, brought to life only through poetic effort. It emerges from the past as if under a spell. Spells always require something tangible that still carries the essence of what is lost or distant—a strand of hair, a ring, a handkerchief, something touched by the spell-caster. This tangible connection is crucial to the magic. Collecting, which became a popular trend in the early twentieth century, also held this significance.

The peculiarity and vulnerability of the "country estate theme," a traditional element in Russian art emerging at the turn of the century, was unmistakable. Even long after serfdom, accepting this perspective was challenging. Russian country estates were still active places; people still resided there. They still sought help from soldiers in the city, fearing the fate of neighbors who had been "burned out." They continued to mortgage and remortgage their estates in an attempt to establish a rational economy. What remains preserved is what is known as the landed estates. What can be done with them? Plans multiplied, ranging from modest to radical. (By the way, Nemirovich-Danchenko corresponded with Prince Pavel Dolgorukov, leader of the left wing of the Kadets [Constitutional Democratic Party] and future MAT shareholder, on this very subject—about the peasants, their sentiments, the land, and whom the peasants would or would not support.) What kind of melancholy, what kind of invocation of historical shadows? For heaven's sake, this is not the time for shadows; it would be better to address the living matters here. However, the paradox of the situation was that landlord tenure and the remnants of serfdom remained a harsh, living reality, a vestige of old Russia. Russian estate culture completed the circle. It receded in its material beauty, spiritual uniqueness, and awareness of its immorality and guilt, which nonetheless continued to deeply influence it. As it died out, it accepted its punishment, and in accepting punishment, its beauty and value were rediscovered. Thus, there was a renewed perception of estate culture at the turn of the century. Stylized admiration and mourning were not the only emerging ways in which people sought to understand and master the world that they recognized as the past at some crucial point. Finally, people re-engaged with this world with a profound appreciation

166 *Vladimir Nemirovich-Danchenko and the Moscow Art Theatre*

for its poetry. Poetry like that of Afanasy Fet,[10] which had long been seen as foreign or "manorial," became less so over the years: "Nightingales, a sigh, a whisper / In a shady nook / And the lullaby in silver / Of a lazy brook." This line of poetry, often parodied, once again captured attention with its clear and evocative sound.

This illusion was the distinctive world that MAT's production of *A Month in the Country* aimed to recreate. It was understandable why, in the summer of 1899, Nemirovich-Danchenko was truly "overwhelmed by the desire" to stage Turgenev's play. He was one of the first to grasp the growing interest in the era, and it was also evident why he later cooled to the idea. Projects that remain in the planning stage for too long rarely come to fruition, and when they do, they seldom do so successfully. Something fades away, leading to the director's once-cherished relationship with the play coming to an end. Subsequently, it was Stanislavsky who felt the "gnawing" desire to produce Turgenev, not Nemirovich-Danchenko. He wrote, "I would place *A Month in the Country* as our top priority." Nemirovich-Danchenko responded coolly,

I don't see Maeterlinck's *Pelleas and Melisande* and *A Month in the Country* fitting into our repertoire. I'm still considering the repertoire from my perspective. I'm seeking plays with a confrontational tone that resonate in our modern life. To me, *Pelleas and Melisande* and *A Month in the Country* belong to more peaceful social movements, and contemporary society will remain deaf to their treasures. But don't take my current position too seriously. I'm not objective enough yet.

He wrote the letter in early 1907, following the ongoing and unfortunate 1905 revolution, which deeply resonated with him due to its tragic timing. It was the feeling of shame that Russian artists were all too familiar with, especially those who claimed to have been influenced by writers and critics from the 1860s. Shame upon shame, as poet Nekrasov wrote—"And an even greater disgrace / Is to sing of skies, seas, and valleys, / Or your lover's gentle touch / In a time of distress."[11] This perspective may not be objective, but it was not the right time for *A Month in the Country*.

Nemirovich-Danchenko believed that even *Woe from Wit* needed a different perspective now.[12] There was an excess of comfort in its gentle appearance, the cozy atmosphere of the home, and the solid, comfortable Empire style. Too much sweetness was present in the domestic comedy of Famusov, the patriarch, with his hair curlers, the quiet anger of an older man who was always irritable in the mornings, the chimes of an old porcelain clock, and the dainty figures dancing around the fact that it had either struck eight or nine o'clock. The antique clocks were beautiful, and their discovery was a pleasant surprise. When Nemirovich-Danchenko wrote to Kachalov about the danger of "small elegance, porcelain figurines," he was not referring to these figurines. But still....

In the end, Nemirovich-Danchenko agrees to let Stanislavsky prepare *A Month in the Country*, thus making room in next season's repertoire for Pushkin's dramatic poem *Boris Godunov*, "a story of many revolts."

Struggle to Synthesize History, Poetry, and Realism

Nemirovich-Danchenko never revisited his unsuccessful productions, and his memoirs are nothing like the captivating story about the unsuccessful Snow Maiden in *My Life in Art*. However, his artistic thoughts about Pushkin's *Boris Godunov*, a sequel to *Tsar Fyodor Ivanovich*, will be worthwhile regardless of their failed realization.

Nemirovich-Danchenko collaborated with Luzhsky on the play, with Luzhsky writing the first two drafts of the director's copy. The first draft resembled typical MAT manuscripts: an inexpensive edition of the play's text with numbered references and commentary on separate sheets. However, in this case, each numbered reference corresponded to a fragment of historical research. Pushkin's verses and actions served as the "soundtrack" of a documentary film with abundant, raw material that was difficult to organize. The manuscript included descriptions of kinship, localities, social rules, and state rituals. It also depicted episodes from the past and future lives of historical characters. Some details, like the Austrian emperor Rudolph sending six parrots as a gift to Tsar Boris, were comical. Additionally, Nemirovich-Danchenko included gruesome details from the murder of Tsarevich Fyodor, such as his testicles being pressed while he frantically cried out. The juxtaposition of Pushkin's verse as the "soundtrack" and history as the "film" made reading this director's manuscript a powerful experience. The challenge, however, was to determine how much of this historical knowledge could be conveyed on stage.

Nemirovich-Danchenko suggested focusing on depicting Boris as a boyar from the late sixteenth century. He wanted to explore the difficult and burdensome conditions of Boris's life, as well as the magnitude of statehood. However, this type of directorial speculation was akin to Hamlet's advice to "throw away the worse part of it." In other words, it was not recommended. While MAT was capable of handling historical knowledge, the challenge was finding harmony between the light, poetic language, and beautiful verse of the play and its historical imagery. The real task was not to harmonize Pushkin's poetry with bloody and weighty subjects, but rather to juxtapose them. The question remained: how could this be achieved?

Luzhsky also contributed to the second directorial copy, which followed the typical format of MAT. It included the characters' psychology, their relationship to the main event of the play and its scenes, the psycho-physical circumstances of the roles, and notes about blocking. Nemirovich-Danchenko perceptively captured everything in the directorial interpretation, whether it was Tsar Boris's role or the people's involvement. However, it is impossible to tell what the actual performance would have been like—how it would have blended history, psychology, and everyday life, how it would have conveyed the tensions and resolutions emerging from history, how it would have balanced blood and dirt with Pushkin's poems, and how it would have embodied moral authority and historical necessity.

> The production should first capture our characteristic manner of 'experiencing' — vibrant, temperamental — assisted by light, sonorous verse and a feverish pace. The intention is to dissolve the boundaries of history, life, psychology, and lively romanticism, merging them into one dynamic, excited, resonant, harmonious symphony. From the very beginning of the production, history, psychology, and everyday life take the forefront. Even if only one scene can successfully achieve its intended purpose, it would allow us to understand what we need to strive for after such a challenging work.

Unfortunately, the threefold action—seeking historical truth, depicting ev-er-y-day life, and embodying the author's poetry and style—only served to confuse the tasks at hand. Rationalism stifled creativity right from the start. The concept's artistry, or the ability to speak of an idea's artistic quality, did not translate into an artistically pleasing production. As a result, the performance ended up being muddled and lackluster.

The director's goal of achieving synthesis for Pushkin's play was an aspiration he had pursued throughout his entire life. This synthesis revolved around "three elements" or "three truths"—the truth of everyday life and plausibility, the truth of history and social reality, and the truth of poetry and theatre. Working on Chekhov's plays brought happiness because it allowed for the synthesis of these three truths. However, achieving the same synthesis in the overly determined environment of *Boris Godunov's* production proved to be an impossible task. Nemirovich-Danchenko will be cautious about rationalistic formulations for a long time, if not forever.

Balancing Tradition and Relevance in Theatre

In the letter "Be on Guard" that we have already mentioned, Stanislavsky was concerned. They were preparing *The Inspector General*, but the troupe did not feel the responsibility and anxiety he felt were necessary to tackle a national masterpiece. Nemirovich-Danchenko objected:

> Maybe this is how it should be? Is it good to worry too much about external motives rather than those arising from the composition, the work itself? Wouldn't it interfere with the work if one were constantly mindful of the production's importance?

An independent approach is priceless.

In the directorial copy of Alexander Griboedov's comedy *Woe from Wit*, Nemirovich-Danchenko writes,

> First, we need to free ourselves from the constraints the glorious past of *Woe from Wit* imposes on the performers. Read the text as if you were doing it for the first time. Figure out what is happening, with whom, where, what kind of people, and what kind of home.

"Perform the play in the simplest sense of these terms." Nemirovich-Danchenko prepared the director's plan for *Woe from Wit* using the 1870 edition, which was problematic because the verse was typeset as prose. Nevertheless, it provided a distinct advantage. The eye did not have to go through the usual columns of the regular theatrical edition, and the text could be seen differently—literally, differently. Involuntarily, you read it in and of itself. Even so, the director will still carefully follow the versification to track the lines and maintain the rhyme.

The staging could draw from the system used in Griboyedov's time, recreating the graceful Russian comedy performances of the 1820s. However, Nemirovich-Danchenko never liked the idea of recreating "historic theatre" (Stanislavsky was absolutely intolerant of it). MAT's production of *Woe from Wit* did not represent the theatre of Griboyedov's time, but rather the way people lived in that time, and from an emerging sense of its continuity and heritage. The directors compiled the script from manuscript versions and consulted with expert philologists. The public was proud of MAT and the level of culture in its work. Still, with all due respect to literary critics, stage interests prevail over philology. The production placed a high value on the original text, which was the most natural. They also attached significant importance to the comforts and curiosities of life embodied in the play's many everyday references.

Nemirovich-Danchenko believed that although the social controversies and the lofty ideals of protagonist Alexander Chatsky's monologues were outdated, the way of life was as interesting as the recognizable morality. The gentleness and amiability of Russian comedy, which the author of the director's plan considers a national characteristic, has always balanced its gentleness and melancholy with a cry: "How boring this world is."

Satire and Self-Reflection in Theatre

Melancholy has no place in satire, where the attitude toward the subject should be in clear opposition. The satirist should stand outside of what is depicted. None of the three Russian comedies produced at MAT—*Woe from Wit*, *The Inspector General*, and *Enough Stupidity in Every Wise Man*—are actually satires. Nemirovich-Danchenko, who was strongly influenced by the Russian enlightenment of the 1860s, may have blamed himself because satire was revered as the highest genre and most important goal by the "men of the

170   *Vladimir Nemirovich-Danchenko and the Moscow Art Theatre*

'sixties." However, researchers have identified another important tradition in Russian national culture: self-mockery or mockery of one's environment was quite normal. Medieval and ancient Russian authors often made their readers laugh directly at themselves. The mayor's words in *The Inspector General*, "What are you laughing at? You're laughing at yourself!", were sharper than usual, and it would be unwise to dismiss Gogol's remarks about the "nasty city" in the play as simply an unfortunate slip of the tongue. Thus, this great Russian comedy always falls short when it is staged as a satire about "them," someone else, instead of themselves. Gogol had reason to be upset when people primarily interpreted his work as satire.

MAT's 1908–1909 season featured *The Inspector General* to commemorate the anniversary of Gogol's birth. Nemirovich-Danchenko knew he had to participate in the production but felt terrible about it. In a letter to Stanislavsky, he wrote,

> I am a poor interpreter of *Inspector*! I cannot find the inner impulse that inspires my imagination. I read the play, think about it, and try to perform it, but all I find are theatrical stereotypes. I attempt to find something to internally laugh at, but even that feels forced.

It is important to emphasize the phrase "internally laugh at" because it suggests the possibility of interpretive progress (as opposed to simply finding something external to laugh at, which leads to little progress). There is not enough information to determine whether he made any progress in this regard. *The Inspector General* provided an opportunity to explore homegrown fantasy. As clarified by Stanislavsky,

> I told you about the mayor's daughter from a provincial city, who went out in a low-cut dress and a pink satin gown in the summer heat, supposedly to meet the King of Nigeria who was arriving on a ship. All of this happened in the 20th century.

The absurd reality, born from fantasy.

For the finale of *The Inspector General*, Nemirovich-Danchenko wanted the military officer who arrived "by personal order of the Tsar" to have fantastic, jangling footsteps. He requested, "Give Znamensky the spurs worn by Dmitry the Impostor in *Boris Godunov*, or if they are not jangling enough, then two pairs of the loudest." In addition to this, there were "muslin curtains covering the top half of the windows, pulled up by a frilling that draws them apart in two halves." There were flowers in the windows: fuchsia, cacti, agave, geranium. Flowerpots stood on small white stands … The furniture covers were white, with little ribbons, and the seats had a border … On the wall, in a blue frame, hung a portrait of Nicholas I on a horse; on the other side was a portrait of Napoleon embroidered in worsted. These were extracts from the August rehearsal journal when Nemirovich-Danchenko led the work.

At Home 1906–1909   171

MAT's Literary Director, Pavel Markov, remembered this production of *The Inspector General* as problematic and oppressive. Their original idea had assumed a different color scheme: they seemed to be searching for everything all at once, but most of all a happy idyll.

The production started "in medias res;" the curtain had barely risen when the Mayor spoke his first lines, "I have invited you, gentlemen...." The makeup followed Pyotr Boklevsky's famous illustrations of pumpkin-shaped figures and swollen, wrinkled faces. The Judge's thick black eyebrows, raised in thought, complemented his quiet bass voice—a thoughtful skeptic and a drunkard. The Postmaster was portrayed as languid, foppish, and preoccupied with extracting the life he was missing from other people's letters, even living it. There was a gracefulness in Artemy Zemlyanika's incompetence as he suddenly and beautifully kissed Khlestakov's hand, not as a sycophant, but as if he were kissing the hand of a noble lady. Officials presented themselves to Khlestakov in a military-style march. Merchants bowed at Khlestakov's feet, as in Alexey Tolstoy's play, *The Death of Ivan the Terrible*. The townspeople didn't bring the usual paper bags with sugar loaves and fish jerky, but actual gifts. It's impossible to know how many of them; in the end, servants gathered them into piles on Khlestakov's carriage. It bursts apart: they bring gifts and more gifts, more requests. The townspeople break into tears at his departure.

The Inspector General, proved to be challenging during rehearsals, as indicated by one of the letters which stated, "We are suffering." As the production progressed, it took on a darker, harsher tone, veering away from any amusing details that could elicit a smile. Much of the original decor had disappeared, such as the embroidered picture of Napoleon, the dried mushrooms strung over the bishop's portrait, or the risqué pictures beneath the staircase leading to Khlestakov's room, featuring a brave general with a twisted mustache and a "nude" woman seductively posing next to him. During rehearsals, Stanislavsky urged for everything to be scaled back and narrowed down as much as possible. One of his sketches even demonstrated how to flatten the doorway's arch. He instructed the scenery designer to portray the backdrop outside the windows as a city on a dusty plain in the distance, devoid of gardens or mountains, rather than a city nestled in a mountain valley with gardens. The jail also needed to appear smaller, accommodating only 20–30 prisoners, without the typical architectural features associated with a jail. The intended atmosphere was that of a dirty, small town situated by a dirty river on flat terrain. Pavel Markov referred to *The Inspector General* as "naturalistic hyperbole," wherein standard realistic elements were elevated to a heightened level. Gogol's epigraph, "Do not blame the mirror if your face is crooked," was included in the program.

The co-directors, Stanislavsky and Nemirovich-Danchenko, seemed to be engaged in a heated argument between themselves. Stanislavsky's notebook expressed his frustration with Nemirovich-Danchenko cutting him short and restraining his imagination. It would have been helpful to have specific details regarding their dispute, but alas, there was no one to ask. Taking

172   *Vladimir Nemirovich-Danchenko and the Moscow Art Theatre*

into account *Woe from Wit* and interpreting Ostrovsky's *Enough Stupidity in Every Wise Man*, one could speculate that Nemirovich-Danchenko should focus less on the imperfections of others and instead pay attention to the other parts of the epigraph: "don't complain" and "mirror." Complaining is futile; it is best to recognize one's own reflection in the mirror. Yet, speculation can only take us so far.

Curiously, Nemirovich-Danchenko's name was absent from the poster for *The Inspector General*, leaving only Stanislavsky and Moskvin as signatories, despite the rehearsal journal clearly indicating Nemirovich-Danchenko's significant contributions to the production.

Among the plays produced at MAT, Ostrovsky's *Enough Stupidity in Every Wise Man* stands out as the most peaceful and well-balanced. Simov's scenery is light, symmetrical, and authentic without being overly meticulous. The characters gracefully live their lives, creating a sense of continuous flow. An article in *News of the Season* noted that MAT's production captured Ostrovsky's authentic moods. The underlying intrigue and other patterns in the dialogue were clearly accentuated while still maintaining a poetic quality. Ostrovsky's theme of "our own people" can sometimes have a mocking or accusatory tone. However, the underlying feeling is that we truly are connected to our own people and have a strong bond with them. Our own people, our own life. You cannot change that. "All's well that ends well here." At least because nothing truly ends here. By clarifying the structure and trimming the plot, the continuous flow of life, from which everything arises and ultimately returns, is effectively expressed.

Self-Aware Humor in Russian Theatre

Markov noted that *The Inspector General* lacked humor. The humor at MAT, and among MAT's people, was a type of self-observation similar to native Russian humor. Russians don't often tell jokes or puns—there's always a critical smile. You pay attention to what feels ridiculous in yourself and what doesn't, which makes it funny all over again. You won't find witticisms or stage jokes in Nemirovich-Danchenko's copies of *Woe from Wit* and *Enough Stupidity in Every Wise Man* (he didn't like them in others' productions). The humor is precisely of the "native" kind. At MAT, classic Russian comedies are comedies of the Russian household, which come in two forms: what is found in any house, and what is "within your own household," that is, among your own. In MAT's productions, there was no raucous laughter, no sarcastic or spicy gaiety, and no ironic distancing. Nevertheless, audiences laughed frequently, especially during *Three Sisters*—the soft, light laughter of recognition.

The Bat cabaret opened in the basement of the Pertsov House apartments near the Moskva River on St. John Cassian's Day in 1908.[13] After starting as a club for MAT actors, Nikita Baliev soon transformed it into a public "variety theatre." One of the first performances was a puppet show. Puppet versions of Stanislavsky and Nemirovich-Danchenko, playing the characters Tiltil and

Mitil, embarked on a quest for *The Blue Bird*. Then the scenery changed, and a comedic interpretation of Maeterlinck's play followed, along with comedic renditions of the year's theatrical debates. Famous actors, writers, and critics were portrayed as puppets—and everyone received a good scolding, especially MAT. They parodied *Anathema* as well as a scene from *The Brothers Karamazov*—Nemirovich-Danchenko and Yuzhin appearing in the "Over Brandy" episode discussing theatre projects.[14] In The Bat's lobby, patrons were required to sign a form stating that they wouldn't take offense if a joke was directed at them. However, there was no mockery of performances or cast members; this was a different kind of humor. The aim was simply to "represent" someone, and the humor came from the accuracy of the portrayal. If you didn't understand what made the "presentation" funny, it wouldn't be amusing. These shows at MAT were true works of artistry, with some performers brilliantly embodying figures like Stanislavsky, Nemirovich-Danchenko, and Kachalov. Critic Nikolay Efros recounted, "At one of the Cabbage Parties,[15] they first showed the actual Stanislavsky, Nemirovich-Danchenko, and Sumbatov-Yuzhin, and then their imitations, and the audience groaned with delight. These imitations were delightful and subtle, capturing something essential about the originals." One skit featured Stanislavsky as a circus trainer with Vishnevsky playing the role of a trained horse. Stanislavsky commanded the horse to jump over obstacles labeled with the names of plays from MAT's repertoire, but the horse balked at an obstacle named *Rosmersholm*, hinting at its failure. Then, Nemirovich-Danchenko appeared as a provincial bandmaster conducting a tune, transforming the church from *Brand* into the temple of Venus. Nemirovich-Danchenko had a fearless and endearing willingness to laugh at himself without any embarrassment. He portrayed an exuberant and determined circus trainer with a stubborn horse or a conductor trying to maintain dignity while leading a lively operetta.

Let's not forget the cabaret skits and the overall tone of Nemirovich-Danchenko's everyday life. Vadim Kachalov, the son of Kachalov, described their humor of self-observation by saying, "They didn't like anything that they couldn't find amusement in." For instance, Nemirovich-Danchenko recounted a story about how he and his wife dealt with revolutionary news in the spa city of Kislovodsk during the tumultuous summer of 1906.[16] He described a resort that was popular among politically liberal vacationers, where guests at the Art Nouveau Grand Hotel had to serve themselves snacks on the balcony due to a staff strike. The strike was announced during a rally at the park's outdoor stage, where summer music played every night. The restaurants closed, and Vishnevsky humorously invited friends to join them for dinner, predicting a great revolution. Interestingly, his prediction came true. Something real would unfold amidst all the speeches at the amusement park and the support for the restaurant strike.

It wasn't necessarily the funny situation itself that was humorous (in fact, the situation wasn't funny), but rather one's place within it. This is what Nemirovich-Danchenko amusingly emphasized.

174 *Vladimir Nemirovich-Danchenko and the Moscow Art Theatre*

On MAT's stage, the best comedic characters displayed a genuine seriousness about themselves. Stanislavsky portrayed General Krutitsky as an egotistical member of the State Council in *Enough Stupidity in Every Wise Man*. He remained unsentimental when receiving shameless flattery about his ambitions. Instead, he nodded to show agreement with the speaker's understanding and hummed a tune while drumming his fingers. Nemirovich-Danchenko enthusiastically and effortlessly prepared *Enough Stupidity in Every Wise Man*. Stanislavsky remembered a remark from Nemirovich-Danchenko that set the tone: "Ostrovsky's epic serenity." The characters in *Enough Stupidity in Every Wise Man* exude an epic calm, living their well-fed and contented lives as if they have done so for thousands of years and will continue to do so for thousands more. Their rhythm is unhurried, not sluggish or heavy, but rather reflects the fact that they have all the time in the world at their disposal, arranging it according to their preferences and nature. Despite this personal epic calm, their world is disrupted by an lively, restless, and adventurous energy that lies just beneath the surface. Over time, Gloumov/Kachalov will come to interpret his role differently, feeling angry with his life and considering himself a hero. However, for now, the director suggests that Gloumov and the others should all be played as if Ostrovsky's wise, epic smile has touched them. Realistically, sincerely, and cheerfully. No hint of anguish, introspection, or longing should be portrayed. Everything will end well here. The actors need to put themselves in a positive mood and not hurry. They shouldn't drag out or force anything, but they should also avoid being lethargic.

Among the plays produced at MAT, *Enough Stupidity in Every Wise Man* stands out as the most peaceful and well-balanced. Simov's scenery is light, symmetrical, and authentic without being overly meticulous. The characters gracefully live their lives, creating a sense of continuous flow. An article in *News of the Season* noted that MAT's production captured Ostrovsky's authentic moods. The underlying intrigue and other patterns in the dialogue were clearly accentuated while still maintaining a poetic quality. By clarifying the structure and trimming the plot, the continuous flow of life, from which everything arises and ultimately returns, is effectively expressed.

Self-Reflective Humor and the Continuity of Life in MAT's Productions

Today, it's hard to imagine how much people loved this theatre. One evening in 1910, at the home of Baron von Driesen,[17] someone confronted Stanislavsky. Nemirovich-Danchenko was busy and arrived late; he sat at the door and didn't say a word all evening. The question posed to Stanislavsky was whether MAT was content with itself. Did it believe that it united spectators in the same way the ancient theatre united them in a sacred act, thereby "creating a meaningful event"? Hearing these questions, one might wonder how such an outcome could be achieved in Russia, specifically how a play production could

At Home 1906–1909   175

be transformed into a meaningful event. However, Stanislavsky answered without irony, saying that judging MAT's self-satisfaction was difficult; more often than not, it was self-dissatisfaction. The creation of a meaningful event, he continued, depends on one's understanding of it. During the German tour, the exhausted audience, who had been sitting on hard seats and with dinner waiting for them at home, did not rush to leave immediately after the performance. Instead, they sat silently for a minute or two before departing. "What held them back?" one might question, "the effect of the ancient theatre on the soul?" "I don't know, and I don't know how to disagree."

Consider also the letters received by MAT's Board of Directors, which are currently in storage and may one day be published. These letters tell stories of individuals who sacrificed necessities and saved money for an entire year to attend a performance in Moscow, such as *Uncle Vanya* or *Three Sisters*, only to find that all the tickets were sold out upon their arrival. "Do they have to go home without seeing the plays?" they ask, expressing their disappointment. Stanislavsky, moved by these letters, shared,

> I have read many of these letters and could hardly hold back my tears. Or sometimes you drive up to the theatre in the winter and see a crowd waiting in a single file. They came here in the evening, stood outside all night, and in the morning, sleepy and exhausted, either got tickets or not. It's impossible to forget all this!

Emotionally, he added,

> I ask you, isn't this an event? These people wait for a year to see Chekhov's plays on stage. Obviously, they are waiting for the production as a meaningful event; they feel the production as a meaningful event; they remember it as a meaningful event. To them, it is a meaningful event. In their anticipation, in their psyche.

He paused. "That's all we can give them." And he smiled.

If you peruse any memoirs, whether related to the theatre or not, whether published or in personal notebooks, you will encounter numerous examples. For example, a young man traveling to the capital by train happens to be on the same train as the actress Maria Samarova (not yet famous). Samarova asks him to send a telegram for her in Moscow. Describing the experience, the young man says, "I did it willingly, as if I had been instructed to save the world." Upon arriving in Moscow, he goes with his friends to find MAT in order to deliver the letter.

In the summer of 1904, a visitor attends a memorial at Novodevichy Cemetery forty days after Chekhov's death. The first production he sees is Maeterlinck's one-act plays. By chance, the spectator leaves during the intermission, frustrated with the "decadents" and gives his ticket to a visitor, who had been waiting hopefully at the door. This event is recounted in

176   Vladimir Nemirovich-Danchenko and the Moscow Art Theatre

the unpublished memoirs of Vakhtang Mchedelov, a man dedicated to MAT until his dying day.[18]

People with vastly different personalities and fates have the same lasting memory of MAT. Actor Vladimir Yakhontov recalls *The Cherry Orchard* for the rest of his life because Madame Ranevskaya bears a striking resemblance to his mother. It is 1914.

It is important to understand the significance of MAT, not only for critics or historians who experience new premieres every year but also for the people who lived in Moscow in 1908 or 1914. It is also significant for those who occasionally come from their hometowns after securing tickets through friends, or for those who plan a holiday every few years and spend an entire week in Moscow, exploring everything they can during that time.

Fleeting Plays and Enduring Themes

How did the repertoire evolve? After 1905, new productions of new plays rarely lasted more than two seasons. *The Walls*, staged in 1907, had only two performances the following season. *The Drama of Life* had eight performances in the next season. *The Life of Man*, only one in the second season. *Anathema* closed in its first year (not at the behest of MAT). *Miserere*, one season. *Ekaterina Ivanovna* and *Thought* by Leonid Andreev, one season. *Rosmersholm*, one season. *Peer Gynt*, one season. *The Brothers Karamazov* remained in the repertoire for just two years; *The Living Corpse*, only two years; *Nikolai Stavrogin*, one year. *Brand*, with its exceptional success, lasted three years. I apologize for these figures but they have only recently become available. They provide insight into the inner life of MAT during its early years and Russia's spiritual life during that period.

What did "all of Russia" witness? Everyone viewed Chekhov's plays: *Uncle Vanya*, *Three Sisters*, and *The Cherry Orchard* were each part of the repertoire for one year, with audiences eagerly awaiting a repeat performance of *The Seagull*. It holds a special place in the hearts of the audience. Everyone also saw *Tsar Fyodor* and *The Lower Depths*. Some witnessed *An Enemy of the People* during its revival in 1908. The play remained in their minds the following season when they witnessed a new and long-running work, Knut Hamsun's *At the Gate of the Kingdom*, which audiences enjoyed. (Ibsen's theme of an intellectual's loyalty to himself and his beliefs, combined with the theme of "home.") And still, everyone sees *The Blue Bird* as a symbol of MAT, along with its cricket and seagull.[19] To commemorate MAT's tenth anniversary, a newspaper cleverly combined these symbols:

Cricket and bluebird. Two extremes.
With a white-breasted seagull in between.
The cricket represents home.
The seagull represents the sea.
And the bluebird represents a dream kingdom from a fairy tale.

At Home 1906–1909   177

It's worth noting that while the bluebird of happiness may seem unattainable, it resides in the same place as the cricket: at home. The newspaper's catchy phrase fails to fully grasp the significance of "home" for MAT. Chekhov bestowed this motif, in all its complexity, to MAT. In May 1908, Blok also presented it in his play *The Song of Fate*, writing in his diary about "The enthusiasm of Stanislavsky and Nemirovich-Danchenko." However, MAT never staged Blok's play.

MAT, for everyone, brought newly adapted classics to the stage every day: *Woe from Wit, The Inspector General, Enough Stupidity for Every Wise Man, A Month in the Country*, an Turgenev's one-act comedies, *The Death of Pazukhin*,[20] *The Mistress of the Inn. Hamlet* ran for three seasons; Mikhail Bulgakov's play *Moliere, or, The Cabal of Hypocrites*, had two seasons.

Tolstoy and Dostoevsky hold a special place in Russian life, regardless of the number of performances.

Notes

1 Leonid Andreyev (1871–1919) was a novelist, playwright, and short-story writer, and senior figure of Russian expressionistic writing.

2 Stanislaw Przybyszewski (1868–1927) was a Polish writer, poet, dramatist, and essayist. A key figure in the Młoda Polska (Young Poland) modernist movement.

3 Hugo von Hofmannsthal (1873–1929) was a novelist, librettist, poet, dramatist, and essayist.

4 Herman Heijermans (1864–1924) was a prominent Dutch author, playwright, and social critic known for his naturalistic and didactic works that attacked bourgeois hypocrisy.

5 Feodor Chaliapin (1873–1938) was an operatic basso profundo admired for his vocal expressiveness and actorly truthfulness.

6 *Anathema* (1909) is an expressionist play by Leonid Andreyev (1871–1919), senior figure of Russian expressionism, speculative fiction, and horror writing. The play tells the story of David Leizer who inherits a fortune and sets out to reduce all the world's misery. He is manipulated throughout by "Anathema," who represents the spirit of reasoning, of revolt, and sometimes Satan. Anathema wishes to have something to strengthen his case against God the Creator.

7 *Miserere* (1910) is a play by Semyon Yushkevich (1868–1927). Set in Paris, December 2006, the play tells the story of Wilhelm Goetz, a choir director from Chile, who is murdered in an Armenian church. Lionel Kasdan, a retired police officer and member of the church, takes it upon himself to find the killer instead of relying on the official investigation. Cedric Volokin, a troubled juvenile police officer with a history of drug addiction, also gets involved, suspecting the involvement of children. They collaborate to uncover the killer's secret and understand their motives in a case centered around the power of the human voice.

8 *Boris Godunov* (1831, perf. 1866) is a play by Alexander Pushkin telling the story of Boris Godunov, who becomes the tsar of Russia after the death of Ivan the Terrible. Boris is a ruthless leader who orders the murder of the young heir Dmitry to secure his power. However, a pretender claiming to be Dmitry appears and gains the support of the people, leading to Boris's downfall and death.

9 *Enough Stupidity in Every Wise Man* (1868) is a comedic play by Alexander Ostrovsky that satirizes the greed and superficiality of the merchant class in late nineteenth-century Russia, through the story of Glumov's attempts to sell his estate to a naive young woman named Liza.

178 *Vladimir Nemirovich-Danchenko and the Moscow Art Theatre*

10 Afanasy Fet (1820–1892) was a poet regarded as a master of lyric verse in Russian literature.

11 From the poem *Poet and Citizen* (n.d.) by Nikolai Nekrasov.

12 *Woe from Wit* (1823) is a comedic verse play by Alexander Griboyedov (1795–1829) that critiques the superficiality and hypocrisy of nineteenth-century Russian society through the story of Chatsky, a disillusioned young man who clashes with various characters.

13 The Bat was a cabaret founded by Nikita Balief (1873–1936), vaudevillian, stage performer, writer, impresario, and director. In a basement near MAT, he created a theatre group that he named La Chauve-Souris after a bat flew up out of the basement door and landed on his hat.

14 Cf. *The Brothers Karamazov*, I, 3, 4.

15 Cabbage Parties (Kapustniki) are in-house theatrical gatherings known for their humorous performances.

16 Kislovodsk is a spa city in the North Caucasus region of Russia.

17 Anatoly von Osten-Driesen (1872–1932) was a chamberlain, court counselor, employee of the Ministry of Justice and honorary member of the Central Committee for the collection of donations to orphanages.

18 Vakhtang Mchedelov (1884–1924) was a theatre director and teacher associated with MAT school.

19 *The Cricket on the Hearth* (adapted from the story by Charles Dickens) was produced at the First Studio in 1914 and considered a landmark in the development of Stanislavsky's system.

20 *The Death of Pazukhin* (1857) is a play by Mikhail Saltykov-Shchedrin (1826–1889). The story revolves around the characters' relentless pursuit of elderly Pazukhin's wealth. As the story unfolds, it becomes evident that their motives are solely driven by greed, and their actions reflect their moral decline. In their quest for inheritance, they are willing to sacrifice their principles, reputation, and conscience.

8 Russian Tragedy 1908–1910

Dedication and Sacrifice in Artistic Legacy

Year after year, MAT becomes increasingly cherished in Russia. During times of internal strain, Stanislavsky, Nemirovich-Danchenko, and the other founders worried about the potential demise of their work, not just for themselves but for everyone involved. Nevertheless, MAT stands as a reassuring example of a lasting and magnificent enterprise for all those involved. It is not a fleeting success, like a shooting star that burns out upon entering the earth's atmosphere. It is not a conspiracy of dreamers who disregard the "needs of real life," nor are they "high priests of beauty" who do not concern themselves with money, homes, the environment, and social conditions. Everyone knows that these realities exist for actors, just as they do for everyone else. It is widely known that actors have small incomes, their theatre building is rented, and censorship constantly threatens them. Failure is not something they desire. Many important undertakings in Russia have already succumbed to the self-fulfilling prophecy of "Oh, how gloriously we shall die!"

Stanislavsky and Nemirovich-Danchenko declared from the beginning that it would be a disgrace if they and their cause were to perish. Their objective is for their concept to take root and become a thriving reality in their lives and in Russia as a whole. If they cannot achieve this and their initial efforts quickly perish, then they are merely skilled at making grand plans and attracting attention. Stanislavsky lamented a peculiar trait of the Russian people: "We love to make great sacrifices for our favorite cause with one hand and destroy it with the other." This is perhaps why there are so few well-organized and reliable enterprises. Such enterprises often become consumed by self-interest, lose sight of their mission, or are overwhelmed by tensions and conflicts arising from a lack of harmony with ideals. As a result, the enterprise feels ashamed of its mundane purpose and seems cheap to itself. It is already difficult for an individual to reconcile with their own soul, let alone with those of others. However, the actors at MAT were able to accomplish this. As the theatre progressed, it became increasingly recognized by its audiences and the nation as an exemplar of implementing an idea without compromising its integrity. MAT reassured Russians that they too could achieve this.

DOI: 10.4324/9781003486282-8

180 *Vladimir Nemirovich-Danchenko and the Moscow Art Theatre*

It was also cherished because it stood in stark contrast not only to the folly of genius but also to the prevalent attitudes of uncertainty and indecisiveness. MAT's cult of responsibility, of seeing projects through to completion, and of patient artistry served as an example beyond the realm of the theatre as well.

Nemirovich-Danchenko was determined to become a director at MAT to ensure that everyone involved in the project was fully committed. However, things didn't go as planned with the production of *Rosmersholm*. He could have decided not to show it to anyone, given his dissatisfaction. However, he felt obligated to the season ticket holders and promised to release it for this season. Nemirovich-Danchenko understood that an unsuccessful production at MAT wouldn't upset anyone, but the sight of nervous irresponsibility would worry people. Despite this, MAT was a meticulously run organization with a welcoming atmosphere. The general impression was personified by Stanislavsky's warmth and good looks, as well as Nemirovich-Danchenko's impeccable appearance, even after sleepless nights or long hours of uninterrupted work.

During MAT's tenth anniversary on October 24, 1908, everyone discussed *The Blue Bird's* search for happiness, the pursuit of the ideal, and the paths of a free spirit. These sentiments were expressed sincerely and justly, just like the words about MAT's crucial role in national culture. This time, however, the celebration was toned down due to the death of Alexander Lensky, Chief Director of the Maly Theatre. Yermolova telegraphed, expressing her grief and inability to join the festivities. MAT had scheduled its anniversary celebration for two o'clock, but at one o'clock, the entire company moved to a nearby church to hold a memorial service for Chekhov, Savva Morozov, and Lensky. Afterwards, went to Bryansk Station to send off Lensky's casket. Lensky had never liked Moscow, and even in his dying moments, he expressed the desire to leave. Lensky's death deeply affected Nemirovich-Danchenko as his sister-in-law was Lensky's widow and even outlived him and her own sisters. While Lensky was about ten years older than his brothers-in-law Sumbatov-Yuzhin and Nemirovich-Danchenko, he passed away suddenly in 1908 at the age of sixty-one. Shortly before his death, he wrote about feeling exhausted and in pain, unable to endure it any longer. He had decided to leave the theatre, to which he had dedicated half his life and all his soul.

Some time ago, Vladimir Nelidov, the Director of Imperial Theatres, had offered Nemirovich-Danchenko the position of Chief Director of the Maly Theatre. This same position was what troubled Lensky's soul and led to his death. Nemirovich-Danchenko's response to Nelidov at that time was, "I won't say no." However, in the end, he did decline the offer. So, starting from April 1907, Lensky took over as the Chief Director of the Maly Theatre, not Nemirovich-Danchenko. This situation quickly became overwhelming for Lensky. No matter how much he pushed or encouraged, nobody wanted to

Russian Tragedy 1908–1910   181

make any changes. There is always a certain level of drama associated with responsibilities like this one. Even when your contributions to the cause are successful, personal sacrifices are unavoidable.

In a report from MAT's first year, Nemirovich-Danchenko wrote, "It is difficult to distinguish where our personal life ends and our professional duties begin. What really is a personal life?" Nemirovich-Danchenko rarely had the chance to travel. On one vacation, he had to go to Carlsbad to address his liver problems and planned to meet up with his brother, Vasily.[1] After that, he underwent "post-treatment" in Kislovodsk and Yalta. Alexandre Benois vainly invited him to travel to Italy, but Nemirovich-Danchenko couldn't find the time. Someone else promised to show him the romantic palaces of Ravenna, the northern region of Italy, the abbey in Normandy's moorlands, or the North Sea, but it simply wasn't feasible. He usually returned to Moscow in early August when aspiring employees of MAT and students of its school came for examinations. However, he did have free evenings during this time. In letters to his wife, he described the joy of walking to Strastnaya Square and then taking a tram to Sokolniki or Petrovsky Park,[2] where it felt like being at their country house.

But once the season began, Nemirovich-Danchenko had very few free evenings. According to the newspapers, when his play *Gold* (1895) was staged at the Nezlobin Theatre,[3] he couldn't even find the time to attend a dress rehearsal. MAT consumed all his time. In 1907, he said something troubling: "I did not create at MAT, but primarily established an institution where others create." He was satisfied knowing that he had built a place, pleased with the knowledge that MAT would not exist without his contribution. But where was Nemirovich-Danchenko himself? When he was much older, he realized that life was expansive and there would be time for everything. In his thirties, forties, and fifties, however, he had a sense that these were the final years, the last opportunities. It was high time for him to nurture his own creativity—if not through writing, because he was no longer accustomed to writing by hand and was burdened with administrative work, then through directing. He convinced Stakhovich (and later Alexander Benois) to take on some of his managerial duties. He dismissed Stakhovich's doubts about his sincerity in refusing to remain in a leadership role. What did it matter?

> I don't view my leadership as a formal position, but rather as the strength of my influence on the actors and on K.S. If my influence diminishes with those who obeyed me simply because I was the main director, they can go to hell. And those who believed in me would continue to do so even if I assumed Mchedelov's teaching role in the school.

These lines could serve as motivation for Lear's abdication from the throne: it's not about the crown or the visible symbols of power, but about how true of a king I am within myself. He needs to test this.

182 Vladimir Nemirovich-Danchenko and the Moscow Art Theatre

Leadership Through Collaboration and Resilience

In *the Russian Word* of May 8, 1910, a journalist wrote about an evening at Driesen's Restaurant, where he encountered Stanislavsky and Nemirovich-Danchenko in person for the first time. Stanislavsky made a strong impression on him, despite not having conventional good looks. He was tall, charming, and artistic. The journalist initially assumed there must be some negative aspect about him, but was surprised to discover that he was also extremely intelligent. Stanislavsky's thoughts were bright and unexpected, further highlighting his graciousness. Nemirovich-Danchenko, on the other hand, sat near the doorway and remained quiet. He was unknown to most people present. The journalist observed that someone important had arrived, but externally, Nemirovich-Danchenko appeared well-mannered, a quality he possessed in abundance. As the journalist followed him and stood near the door, he contemplated that this seemingly reserved person must have a rich internal world of thoughts and emotions. It was the first time the journalist had ever seen these "gods" in real life. Indeed, on that particular evening, Nemirovich-Danchenko did seem immersed in his own thoughts.

Did he know about the popular opinions regarding his partnership with Stanislavsky? Stakhovich, who believed in materialistic thinking, wrote, "It would be useful and desirable if the talent, ability, and artistic creativity of one merged with the knowledge, experience, and intellect of the other." However, Nemirovich-Danchenko was too ambitious and self-involved to settle for being just Stanislavsky's employee. He had no intention of merely helping Stanislavsky and contributing to his fame. This theory seemed logical and reasonable, but perhaps it could be argued otherwise. For one thing, Stanislavsky was no less knowledgeable than Nemirovich-Danchenko. He was a better speaker and writer as well. It was time to disregard the nonsensical ideas spread by tabloids about Nemirovich-Danchenko being the writer while Stanislavsky was merely an amateur merchant. If someone traveled to Europe, disappeared in museums, and collected art objects and books on its history, it was not Nemirovich-Danchenko, the writer. As a young person, he had no opportunity to do so, and his circumstances did not change much in terms of time or money. In contrast, Stanislavsky could gain knowledge and insights from his conversations with scholarly individuals like Bryusov and Benoit,[4] things he may not have necessarily gained through his relationship with Nemirovich-Danchenko.

They needed each other in different ways. As poet Nikolai Yazykov put it,[5] it meant something for the soul of a "genius in flight" to touch the movement of air stirred by another genius's wing. Stanislavsky and Nemirovich-Danchenko referred to their partnership as a marriage, a great mystery. They believed marriages were made in heaven. Stanislavsky once compared himself to the frivolous spouse in a public setting, while likening Nemirovich-Danchenko to the responsible wife who managed the household and children. Although the responsibility for managing the household fell on Nemirovich-Danchenko, it is

Russian Tragedy 1908–1910 183

important to note that his work was truly appreciated. In fact, when the salaries were adjusted, Nemirovich-Danchenko received twice as much compensation as Kachalov and twenty-five percent of the dividends. However, Stakhovich, known for his straightforward manner, expressed his opinion, saying, "With that salary, my friend, you should be more energetic!" Reading Stakhovich's accompanying letter is heartbreaking. Stakhovich [a member of MAT's Board of Directors] accuses Nemirovich-Danchenko of being lazy and points out that he has been living in a passive dream lately. Feeling the need to defend himself, Nemirovich-Danchenko explains, "You think I'm lazy. If you notice that I get tired more often and quickly than before, I won't argue with you. But it's not the same thing." Nemirovich-Danchenko continues to explain that he cannot be blamed for receiving a raise that he did not ask for. Stakhovich granted him the raise without any objections from Nemirovich-Danchenko. Two years prior, after independent evaluation, Stakhovich helped to decide on Nemirovich-Danchenko's salary. If that decision was made to alleviate his financial troubles and provide him with a gift, it's unfair to bring it up now. If Stakhovich believes he made a mistake or overestimated Nemirovich-Danchenko's worth, then they should reassess his value together.

Unfortunately, Nemirovich-Danchenko's financial situation was deteriorating. He faced even worse circumstances than before. Attempting to convince the aristocratic actor Stakhovich, who had the typical habits of military officers, owned a villa near Rome, and had an estate in Russia with a chef de cuisine, eighteen riding horses, and an English butler always ready to entertain guests from MAT, was an arduous task. It was challenging to make a case for Nemirovich-Danchenko's salary being well-deserved, even though he had been promised a comparable salary at the Maly Theatre, a position that led to Lensky's demise. How could future generations appreciate the evidence of Nemirovich-Danchenko's creative contributions if those around him didn't make an effort to understand? Until the end, only Stanislavsky truly understood and continuously emphasized this. Unfortunately, his words were often dismissed as mere generosity on his part. Despite facing financial challenges, Nemirovich-Danchenko's high salary remained intact. However, the financial difficulties persisted until the revolution arrived. These troubles were compounded by lingering debts that were impossible to forget, regardless of the tact used by creditors. (Nemirovich-Danchenko had borrowed a thousand rubles from Stanislavsky for a week, but had yet to repay it despite his intentions). Additionally, there was a circulating absurd story about a bill signed by Yuzhin that was mistakenly given to a scoundrel due to Nemirovich-Danchenko's error. There were constant explanations about banks, mortgages, and other problems at the provincial level in Russia, all compounded by empty pockets and embarrassment.

In a book about Nemirovich-Danchenko, it is worth mentioning his calmness as a Russian nobleman and his deep-rooted belief that everything will work out in the end. If it doesn't, he will consider alternative solutions. Does this temperament align with Nemirovich-Danchenko's personality? He is

184 *Vladimir Nemirovich-Danchenko and the Moscow Art Theatre*

reserved, efficient, firm, and intelligent in his plans. Although it contradicts certain aspects, it does align with others and helps to clarify certain things. If it weren't for this serenity and underlying lightness within him, he wouldn't have been able to tolerate his situation. His meticulously drawn-up plans for the upcoming season (which always delighted Stanislavsky) are preserved in the archives. These plans can be compared to the realities of the theatrical year. There was never a consistent policy or rational approach to economizing. The persistence with which Nemirovich-Danchenko would sit down every summer to outline future affairs according to the clock is both touching and comical.

He also grapples with his own life. He becomes angry at the shameless self-scrutiny of his feelings, even though he gives everyone a reason to talk about them. For example, the letters he writes to Stanislavsky, asking for help to combat the "priggish morality" that limits his repertoire choices and opinions. He suspects that someone's unknown mistress is behind it all, and that he is being persecuted. He acknowledges his own sins but believes that a higher power will judge him for all his faults and mistakes.

He is in love with actress Maria Germanova. He writes to Stanislavsky, explaining that he comes to watch her perform as Agnes in the Christmas Eve scene of *Brand* every evening. He mentions that he would like to direct Ibsen's *The Lady from the Sea* with her. He provides a simple, concise outline of the plot, describing it as a "high comedy" and "pure comedic impetuosity." He presents it as a simple, intimate family story with a touch of fantasy, featuring a husband who drinks a little, wonderful daughters, and the friendly ambiance of a modest country doctor with fond memories of his deceased wife. Nemirovich-Danchenko convincingly portrays Germanova as an exceptional actress (he is correct) and as a person of utmost purity and devotion (he is hardly correct). It is tragic when Stanislavsky, whom she values more than anyone else in the theatre, turns his back her.

His life would have been impossible without a certain inherent lightness. This lightness can be glimpsed amidst his moments of pride, his inclination to "sort things out," and his apparent superiority. In reality, everything always seemed to go smoothly for him. Nemirovich-Danchenko once wrote a letter that is essential for understanding his mindset. In it, he describes his wife Ekaterina as a rare person who always supported him and willingly endured material hardships to defend his integrity and independence. The same letter also reveals his reasons for his feelings towards MAT. When he notices people's flaws, he expresses his disapproval passionately, much like in a marriage. Sometimes he even considers a divorce. However, he quickly recalls why he appreciates the person and what exceptional qualities he sees in them. Then it becomes clear—this person is his whole life, "he loves them very much."

Some may envy his certainty that everything will turn out all right and not become nonsense. But this confidence was an intrinsic characteristic of Nemirovich-Danchenko and a gift from his generation and circle. He believed that everything could and should turn out for the better. At a young age, he depicted himself in a story called *Karasyuk*.[6] The protagonist possesses his tutorial classes, youthful pride, independence since high school, and the authoritative tone he developed early on, which sometimes resulted in lower grades. He also has his punctuality and meticulous self-expression, as well as the self-assurance and propriety that accompany countless comic misadventures—"he could never get off the droshky without falling or tripping over the carriage shafts."

This was his fate. Misfortunes were abundant in his life, although he managed them well. He nearly drowned in a small river near the house in Neskuchnoye. The river becomes shallow, almost dry in the summer, and he fell into a small water hole despite not knowing how to swim. Fortunately, his son's teacher pulled him out, and the simple outcome was that "he swallowed some water." After reading about this incident, Stanislavsky was sympathetic but horrified. Furthermore, even before Nemirovich-Danchenko almost drowned, he narrowly escaped being shot when someone robbed the train he was on. At MAT, they enjoyed discussing Nemirovich-Danchenko's comical mishaps. In a tense pause following the director's sharp remark about an actress, he abruptly jumped up and flung himself away from the director's table into the aisle, exclaiming, "Ouch, ouch, ouch!" He spun around, hitting himself on the hips and chest before removing his jacket and stomping on it. As it turned out, the matches in his pocket had caught fire, resulting in large holes in his trousers and jacket. On another occasion, he elegantly sat on the edge of the director's table, causing it to overturn and sending the carafe, ink, and lamp crashing down onto him. Once, he accidentally knocked over a glass of hot tea onto his lap. He promptly turned to Kachalov and asked, "Why do things like this always happen to me, and always in your presence? I know you collect anecdotes like these." (Kachalov indeed collected them all, and we took these stories verbatim from his son's memoirs). Was it wrong to remember these amusing anecdotes? Should we also remember Germanova, debts, being a man of strong passions, and a slight resemblance to Semyonov-Pischik and Yepikhodov?[7]

"When he rehearsed in the dimly lit auditorium, his solid shoulders were silhouetted by a small table lamp, and above them was the beautiful head of a wise man. He appeared to be an athlete of will and intellect." This passage was written by Seraphima Birman, who joined MAT in 1911.[8] Nemirovich-Danchenko was concluding the season that began with the premiere of *The Brothers Karamazov*. His newly hired collaborator first saw him at the director's table during rehearsals for *The Living Corpse*.[9] Great masters have their magnificent and joyful moments. After completing his play *Boris Godunov*, Pushkin exclaimed, "Well done, Pushkin, you son of a bitch." Blok finished his long and controversial poem *The Twelve* and wrote, "Today I am a genius." Nemirovich-Danchenko could have said the same on the evenings of *The Brothers Karamazov* and *The Living Corpse*.

Achieving Unity in Complex Adaptations

Why do people believe they remember or know something, even if they haven't seen or read it? However, they do remember what *The Brothers Karamazov* was like. One person wrote that it was a Russian mystery. Another person wrote, "Rejoice, rejoice for Russian art!" However, the Black Hundred's conservative newspaper *Russian Land* wrote,[10] "The audience ... pretended to be interested in what was happening on stage, but secretly it bored them." (It's a common attitude: since I'm not interested in this, how could anyone else be interested in it?) "I marveled at Nemirovich-Danchenko's courage," the sympathetic person continued,

> when I learned of his determination to stage *The Brothers Karamazov*; I marveled and was horrified, but now I am amazed and delighted. He has knowingly gone ahead despite the production's imperfections and the obvious partial failures in his plan's embodiment. Still, great things happen only to those who strive for perfection and can act without hope of achieving that perfection.

Nemirovich-Danchenko initially wanted to restructure the play and produce it in one evening under the title Dmitry Karamazov. However, he soon abandoned this idea because it was precisely in the inexhaustible themes, the unity of the background, and the integrity of the organic fantasy life of the production that this play revealed its nature and power. From Alexey Dikiy's memoirs:[11]

> I came to MAT when work on Karamazov entered a decisive phase. Before me, in the previous season, were fascinating table rehearsals, where Nemirovich-Danchenko deeply and vividly analyzed Dostoevsky's novel. The parsing of the internal line of all the various passages of the subtext was finished. Now it was time to move onto the stage and bring the performance to life in time and space.

Here is how the dates and events unfolded, based on Nemirovich-Danchenko's notebook:

"August 6, Friday—Board meeting (in the evening), where they decided the choice of the play is my responsibility."
"August 7, Saturday—I decided to direct Karamazov."
"August 8, Sunday—The first meeting about Karamazov."

In *The Brothers Karamazov*, the author explores the theme of "displaced persons" and dramas "in the passageways," which deeply resonate. This includes the misalignment of a person with their position and the misalignment between a person and the idea they live by, which once troubled the author. These themes also resonate with the feeling of being "on the road," searching, and drifting that the author experienced when traveling to Moscow after completing a frantic, premature novel. The feeling of the shaking carriage and social upheaval reverberate, as does the haunting presence of the "aphids" in the old house, a childhood fear. Even the perennial question of the author's youth, "Is there a god in the world I am rushing toward?" continues to resonate.

While the author claims in his memoirs to have been captivated by Dostoevsky since his youth, his letters tell a different story. In these letters, he casually, yet confidently, evaluates Dostoevsky's works, stating that "*Demons* is a very weak work.[12] *The Adolescent* is also weak." It is worth noting that these remarks were made in 1908, not during the author's self-assured journalistic phase. However, the author speaks more favorably of *The Brothers Karamazov*.

Each summer, the author diligently records his thoughts in a notebook. He outlines the novel's scenes, providing details such as

In front of the monastery. At Zosima's. The gallery. Again, at Zosima's. Another room at Zosima's. In the forest near the monastery. At the Father Superior's. Reading about the village madwoman Lizaveta. Reading in front of the pavilion. In the pavilion. At his father's, in the hall.

It is unclear whether this is a plan for staging the novel or simply an outline created with a director's eye. The author divides the sections, numbering them—twenty-six in the first part and twenty-four in the second. A year later, he takes more notes in another notebook, this time listing the characters that appear in each scene. The theatrical principle is evident: only excerpts from the novel are included, with no additional words or reshaping. The author emphasizes the role of the reader-narrator and dialogues. On the fourth day of rehearsals, the author writes the sequence of scenes. The novel requires minimal adaptation with only a few cuts in the chosen text; it fits the stage perfectly.

The Brothers Karamazov premiered on October 12 and 13, 1910. The following day, the newspapers published reviews of the production. The production's inner unity and strength stemmed from the fragmented events of a single tragic game. Rather than relying on a conventional plot structure, the production achieved its cohesion through the magnitude of its scale and the unity of its spiritual world. Nemirovich-Danchenko had previously made many unexpected discoveries by determining the time of day and weather based on how and where a character entered the stage. However, he did not concern himself with those details here. Whether Dmitry hurriedly ran in rain, heat, or snow, whether Ivan was hungry or full, whether Alexey slept without a mattress at night, whether the "soup-maker" Smerdyakov entered from the kitchen or the drawing-room. It didn't matter. It wasn't significant.

188 *Vladimir Nemirovich-Danchenko and the Moscow Art Theatre*

One critic remarked that it would be impossible to produce Dostoevsky without the damp smell and the rustle of cockroaches. Perhaps! But there were no cockroaches in the play, no newspaper story about a man skinned alive, and no advertisement for malt extract, as in the novel. There was no ribbon tying up the envelope containing three thousand rubles for Grushenka, along with the inscription "For my little chicken." There was also no torn mistress's cap or rag that held the "dishonor" of Mitino, which represented half of the bride's money. All of these items were mentioned in the reading and actors' preparation, but they were not physically present.

The performance space was visible from all directions. The corners of the stage, referred to as "Petersburg corners" in the conventions of the novel, were without walls. The director incorporated visual ideas that he had previously tried and failed with in his production of *Rosmersholm*. This meant that there were no walls at all. The indoor scenes had a gray-green neutral background that matched the general color of MAT's auditorium, while a white background replaced it in outdoor scenes.[13]

Nemirovich-Danchenko allowed himself two months to prepare for *The Brothers Karamazov*. However, an additional week had to be spent due to actor Apollon Gorev dropping out of rehearsals because of illness, which meant a replacement had to be found for the role of Smerdyakov. If it weren't for this setback, the deadline would have been met. Nemirovich-Danchenko had confidence that his ability to succeed in extreme situations would come through for him. He always felt artistically freer in those moments when everything was in danger of falling apart and something had to be done. This was the moment he had been truly prepared for.

Isolation, Anguish, and Theatrical Innovation

Nemirovich-Danchenko first encountered Ibsen in 1907 following disagreements with Stanislavsky. At that time, Nemirovich-Danchenko felt compelled to explore the connection between objects, lighting, and sounds on stage and their influence on the subtle movements of the soul and the poetry of everyday life, as exemplified in *Tsar Fyodor* and Chekhov's plays. Here, like Stanislavsky, he believed in relying solely on the actor's internal technique, including their will, imagination, feelings, and thought processes.

When it came to directing *Rosmersholm*, Nemirovich-Danchenko rejected both a realistic approach (depicting a typical Scandinavian house) and a metaphorical approach (creating a space reminiscent of the inside of a cathedral, with windows, doors, and portraits). Instead, he opted for a simpler version—a back wall with a deep bay window, dark olive-green draperies, and benches aligned parallel to the footlights. There were no ceilings, walls, or doors, and very few props. He brought everything forward and reduced the depth of the stage. Nemirovich-Danchenko believed that the play's inner life would shine through against this minimalist backdrop. He expected the

Russian Tragedy 1908–1910   189

actors to enrich the stage experience and convey the play's mood and ideas entirely through their performance and energy.

Unfortunately, *Rosmersholm* was not successful. "Expressing passion in a simple and raw manner, without relying on theatrical conventions, proved to be an extremely challenging task." Nemirovich-Danchenko could have echoed the same sentiments as Stanislavsky did after his own similar experience with *The Drama of Life*. He could have expressed his embarrassment over the mechanical acting and clichés that the masters of MAT suddenly employed. The tasteless tone haunted him. After the disappointment of *Rosmersholm*, it is understandable why he was willing to experiment with *Princess Nastya*, where tastelessness had a place at least.[14] The actors in *Rosmersholm* did not experience the passions that arose from the spiritual problems the director spoke about, except for Knipper, who partially embraced them. She felt an oppressive and joyless love for Rosmer, and her genuine pride made her stand with perfect posture and stare directly into everyone's eyes. She fully lived what she understood: that she was dead. It wasn't that she lacked the will to rebel or that her pagan life force was weakened by the harsh spirituality of *Rosmersholm*. Both her will and life force remained strong. She was ready to accept the loss of thought as an error of excessive indulgence, rather than a sin or mistake.

At this point, we were entering the realm of Dostoyevsky's problems, or about to enter it. Sometimes, it's interesting to create simple lists to see the sequence of events. After directing Rosmersholm, Nemirovich-Danchenko went on to direct *The Inspector General* with Stanislavsky and Moskvin, followed by Knut Hamsun's *At the Gates of the Kingdom* with Luzhsky, *Anathema* by Leonid Andreyev, Enough Stupidity for Every Wise Man, *The Brothers Karamazov, Miserere* by Yushkevich, Hamsun's *In the Grip of Life* with Mardzhanov, and finally Tolstoy's *The Living Corpse*. Isn't this list intriguing? The role of the director is to unravel the author, capturing their "tone and language." However, the director's worldview, character, and state of mind should also influence the interpretation, shouldn't they?

At that time, the art of directing was still emerging. It had not yet fully comprehended its own laws, or perhaps initially defining them too rigidly; they may have been more diverse and flexible. In any case, for Nemirovich-Danchenko, directing was not a means of revealing himself or embarking on a journey of self-discovery. His goal was to objectively illuminate the play, if not permanently, then at least for a significant duration (this matter was specifically discussed when he returned to *Woe from Wit* in the 1930s: should they present a textbook version or delve deeper into an insightful interpretation?).

Stanislavsky shared the same principle, but his subjective presence in his productions was much more pronounced. It was possible to glimpse Stanislavsky's inner world through his productions. Trying to discern Nemirovich-Danchenko's mindset from his productions would be risky and likely unsuccessful. If you were to say that Nemirovich-Danchenko was more aligned with Ostrovsky's calm epic than Leonid Andreyev's ecstatic and rationalistic despair, closer to the desire to publicly confront the locked gates of world

190 Vladimir Nemirovich-Danchenko and the Moscow Art Theatre

problems, you would be partially correct and partially incorrect. It was his nature to be equally interested in both, constantly adjusting based on an inner, deeply experienced, and organic understanding of what was appropriate for the present.

We know that in the decade before 1917, Nemirovich-Danchenko had an affinity for Leonid Andreyev's works. He even argued for the opportunity to direct *Anathema*, deliberately taking it away from Yuzhin, who was originally slated to direct it. In one of Nemirovich-Danchenko's letters, he mentioned, "I love you, Leonid Andreyev." It was an unusually expressive phrase for him. Leonid Andreev was a complex person to love. He was spoiled, prone to despair, and a hypochondriac. He fostered jealousy among the theatre community. He claimed that he was a godsend, bringing happiness to the "artistes," and that his plays were transformative, like a new *Seagull*. He believed they held the key to a new mystery and the possibility of a new kind of theatre. However, he could also joke and suggest that among the plays he produced, one should be saved while the rest drowned like unwanted puppies. Nemirovich-Danchenko found it puzzling that his private conversations with the playwright would end up in the press, as it went against his sense of privacy. Andreyev's life, on the other hand, was completely opposite to Nemirovich-Danchenko's life and social circle. Every aspect of Andreyev's life was public and easily accessible to anyone interested. His income, relationships, passions, illnesses, travels, quirks, and connections with current thoughts were all part of a narrative that newspaper readers followed. Even Andreyev's attempts to resist these intrusions and hide in the mountains eventually became part of the plot. He became our first "celebrity" with his own myth and the expected adventures that came with it, similar to film stars.

Theatre critics either believed that Nemirovich-Danchenko failed to recognize *Anathema's* pretentiousness or somehow managed to overcome it, although neither seems likely. The play didn't succeed in justifying its excessive eloquence internally, resulting in a jumble of overlapping sounds. Nemirovich-Danchenko used Ilya Sat's music in both *Anathema* and *Miserere*,[15] presenting a musical plot rather than a plot with clear meaning. It was also important for the language to sound foreign, as the foreignness of a language always carries a poetic quality. Andreyev, along with Yushkevich, the author of *Miserere*, fascinated audiences because they rejected the fragmented sound of naturalistic writing. They aimed to build upon the insights and breakthroughs made by Chekhov.

Chekhov brought about a revolution in dramatic form and revealed that traditional human relationships were worn out. He portrayed these relationships as weakened, stretched, and interrupted. Similarly, Nemirovich-Danchenko discovered a unique style of communication among the characters in Chekhov's plays: "the object is outside the partner." In conversations, only a part of the soul engages with the other person, while the other part turns inward, leading to a continuous internal process. However, such diminished human relations also bring about a dangerous sense of pressure and isolation.

Individuals feel lost in solitude, just as they feel lost in the overwhelming crowd. In Leonid Andreev's plays, a dark and destitute multitude is a constant and menacing image. The individual is consumed by the groaning, shifting mass, briefly emerging before being engulfed again without hope of escape. Furthermore, there is no conflict in *Anathema* between this groaning mass and the man it will ultimately destroy. The multitude simply seeks light, justice, and a mere piece of bread, just as the man desires these things for himself and others. Andreev intended to initiate a broad discussion of various issues. He envisioned *The Life of Man* as the central theme of a cycle that would include titles like *King Hunger, War, Revolution,* and *God, Devil, and Man* (which eventually became *Anathema*). Nemirovich-Danchenko-Danchenko was particularly fond of *Anathema*. His work on the play involved confronting numerous challenges: on one hand, addressing the "cry of world poverty," and on the other, expressing anguish and anger in the face of a silent God. There is no answer to be found. The play features Nullius/Kachalov's dog-faced, bald, lifeless head, howling with mocking eyes for extended periods, symbolizing the need for sentiment, and begging for mercy and expecting nothing. Audiences were reminded of Nemirovich-Danchenko's productions of *Anathema* and *Miserere* when Vakhtangov directed *The Dybbuk* two years later.[16] In *The Dybbuk*, poverty is vividly portrayed through fantastical elements, reflecting the grand scope of existence, and the spirit of music permeates every aspect, transforming naturalistic grotesque into tragedy.

Artistic Vision Versus Ideological Conflict

The Lower Depths was Nemirovich-Danchenko's first encounter with Russian existential tragedy. When considering his earlier works and the ideas that prepared him for *The Brothers Karamazov*, Gorky's tragedy stands out, with its exploration of life's meaning from both an individual and universal standpoint. Questions such as "Why do people live?" and "Wasn't I born for some purpose?" are raised.[17] Additionally, there are questions about social and universal justice. "A man can believe or not believe. That's his own business! Man is free ... he pays for everything himself: for faith, for unbelief, for love, for intelligence."

In *The Lower Depths*, Nemirovich-Danchenko captured both the national speech and the national gesture of Russian tragedy for the first time. However, later on, Gorky objected to the successful continuation of his own explorations in Dostoevsky's productions.

Many of Gorky's criticisms in his articles on Dostoevsky stemmed from the traditional challenges of Russian literature, where an outsider insults an opponent on their own turf. Gorky's hostility toward Dostoevsky also came from an attempt to overcome a natural affinity. If, besides Dostoyevsky, there was a second writer who deeply understood and wrote about suffering, whether it is a bloody pogrom or a child enduring the rod of a torturer, wouldn't that writer be Gorky? Gorky's dispute with Dostoevsky about human suffering was also a dispute on the highest level. He paid a high price for the right to hold his own convictions. Their disagreement about the national character was also profound. On this issue, Gorky confronted both Gogol and Tolstoy as adversaries. In addition to these weighty matters, Gorky's pamphlet attacking "Karamazovism" also contained sharp personal attacks against Nemirovich-Danchenko, who could not understand why he deserved such treatment and ruthless public criticism. After all, what was he guilty of? On the other hand, Gorky, like Dostoevsky, believed in the power of "evil geniuses," individuals who embody demonic ideas. Both authors condemned those who set such ideas loose, allowing them to take human form.

Another aspect of the story is how an idea becomes distorted when it enters a dark and frightening environment. Some time ago, Nemirovich-Danchenko considered the fate of an idea that had taken root in a remote village, wondering if it might manifest itself in a Tolstoyan, Nietzschean, or anarchist form. The destiny of an idea, how it could divide a village and how an idea that originated in Moscow could disrupt the stagnant local life there, preoccupied Nemirovich-Danchenko's thoughts. In this regard, Nemirovich-Danchenko and Gorky could have found common ground. However, Gorky was not seeking points of connection, only points of repulsion. He deliberately stated that "the highest demands of the spirit" only distract from the work of living. In a brief answer composed by Alexandre Benois, MAT expressed bewilderment at Gorky's disdain for the highest demands of the spirit. For MAT, abandoning the desire to serve those demands would mean abandoning their art and all of Russian literature.

From the beginning, Nemirovich-Danchenko knew that Gorky would protest the staging of Dostoyevsky's novel *Demons* (also known as *Nikolai Stavrogin*, 1913). He regretted not communicating with Gorky during the previous summer, but many points were difficult to express in writing. His eventual letter was polite but brief. He did not attempt to persuade Gorky to refrain from a public protest, nor did he assure him that it was a mere misunderstanding between them. He simply asked if Gorky would just listen to him, look at their work together on the stage, and reconsider his judgment. Nemirovich-Danchenko became infuriated whenever he perceived an insult. He wrote to his wife, describing Gorky's article as a tasteless stunt and a narrow, unartistic view of Dostoevsky, literature, and theatre. "The question that troubled me was whether I was wrong," he wrote. "That's why I eagerly read all the newspapers that morning. I had a few worrying days, which coincided with a strike by tram workers, street demonstrations, and news of railway accidents." The tram workers had their own reasons for striking, of course, but the timing of these events only fueled his anger.

Ultimately, Nemirovich-Danchenko conceived of *Demons* brilliantly but not convincingly. The novel's title and background embarrassed him, although he was confident that he could isolate some of its "demonic" motives and themes. He considered creating a play titled *Nikolai Stavrogin*, or perhaps one centered around Shatov and Kirillov. A third option

Russian Tragedy 1908–1910 193

involved focusing on the revolutionary aspect of *Demons*: the first episode would involve a gathering of revolutionaries, with the events culminating in the murder of Shatov. The atmosphere would be one of "confusion," with the provocations of Peter Verkhovensky taking center stage. Verkhovensky would be the main character.

Before Gorky's controversial articles, and especially after them, Nemirovich-Danchenko settled on *Nikolai Stavrogin*, ensuring that there would be no trace of the "demonic" in the production. Dostoevsky's productions at MAT were impressively cohesive and stood as remarkable lived experiences (without any gloominess, breakdowns, or sentimentality).

Strangely, despite his complete conviction in his artistic vision, Nemirovich-Danchenko did not share Dostoevsky's views. He had different ideas and a different perspective. In fact, his viewpoint aligned more closely with the way Chekhov approached such questions. Nemirovich-Danchenko could relate to what the professor in Chekhov's *A Boring Story* called being a citizen of a Christian state, but not a Christian himself. He completely lacked religious faith. The absence of God was not a tragedy for him; it was simply an accepted reality he lived with. While there may not be a general idea of creation, it does not mean that everything is permissible. The absence of such an idea actually motivates people to try even harder to behave as if there were such a dream—it's an unreasonable and unsteady hope that the labor of their efforts would produce or reveal it. For Chekhov, this was not just a thought but a kind of motif or melody.

During this time, Nemirovich-Danchenko often thought about Chekhov. He made notes about *The Seagull*, stating that "we must do it all over again." In another entry, he refers to *The Seagull* in noting how unhappy everyone is and contemplating refinement and brooding.

During his Christmas vacation, Nemirovich-Danchenko took a volume of Chekhov's recent letters with him. In his notebook, he reevaluated himself, stating, "I'm not a liberal, not a conservative, not a gradualist, not a monk, not indifferent. I want to be a free artist, that's all."

However, he couldn't express this to Gorky, as he already knew the reply he would receive: "What do you want to free yourself from? Isn't it from all the duties of man and citizen?" Nemirovich-Danchenko never wanted to be exempt from these duties. Nevertheless, it is important to consider whether he shared Dostoevsky's beliefs. In this regard, he did not believe it was necessary to separate the director's thoughts from those of the author or to only produce works by authors whose thoughts he agreed with or whose interpretation of the world aligned completely with his own.

Nemirovich-Danchenko explained all of these considerations to a certain author to clarify why MAT could not stage his plays. He emphasized that they do not argue whether the author's thoughts are true or false. Even if they are seen as mistaken, they would accept them if they infected you with a force that reflected the author's organic truth and if they attract them artistically. For example, Dostoevsky infected us with such a force. Of course,

194   *Vladimir Nemirovich-Danchenko and the Moscow Art Theatre*

Nemirovich-Danchenko could have criticized Gorky instead of attacking him. He could have questioned the appropriateness of Gorky's rude comments and publicly writing in such a way. "Who knows? Did the production of *The Brothers Karamazov* lead to an increase in suicides in Moscow?" And how should we interpret Gorky's statement, "Russian reality is full of suffering; it has more than enough genuine grief and real torment. And now MAT wants to show suffering that's unreal, artificially imposed"? As our own proverb says, "There is no defense against misfortune." Drought will inevitably occur, and one will inevitably have to hold a tin cup, and people in uniforms will inevitably take one to jail. So, what does "unreal" mean in this context?

You can imagine how this conversation between Nemirovich-Danchenko and Gorky would escalate. It is also possible to imagine a conciliatory tone, where they acknowledge that staging *Nikolai Stavrogin* this season was an accident, and admit that they may have overreacted. However, it is impossible to argue with a person who is convinced of the infallibility of their position. "We were obsessed with art," Nemirovich-Danchenko said about himself and MAT. However, it is unlikely that someone who genuinely worships something would refer to themselves as an idolater, nor would they refer to their god as an idol.

Justifying Theatre Through Truth, Ethics, and Human Genius

It's a paradox. The great explorations of the two masters of theatre, Stanislavsky and Nemirovich-Danchenko, reveal a hidden source of energy in that they both viewed theatre as something shameful and questionable. They felt the need to justify it. According to Pavel Markov, Stanislavsky's system stemmed from

> an ethical justification of 'acting,' from the desire to discover and emphasize the inner truth and ethical rightness of the actor; to overcome the suspicion that acting was inherently false. Therefore, the 'Stanislavsky system' represented the integration of techniques with their ethical justification, combining the actor's creative personality and their creative act.

In 1910, Nemirovich-Danchenko wrote to Stanislavsky about his work with *The Brothers Karamazov*. Finally, they had found what they had been searching for all these years. They had "broken through the wall." Stanislavsky said, "Let the actors sit still, feel, speak, and captivate thousands of spectators with their experiences." Both Stanislavsky and Nemirovich-Danchenko had already faced this problem in works such as *The Drama of Life* and *Rosmersholm*. They wondered how to expose the souls of the actors on stage so that the audience could see and understand their inner emotions. It was a challenging task! It couldn't be done through gestures, hand and foot movements, or the actor's technical skills alone. There needed to be an invisible radiation of creative will and feeling. Everything that hinders the audience from perceiving the actor's true emotions and thoughts must be eliminated. However, at the same time, the actor must possess thoughts and passions that are worthy of the attention of thousands of people. It requires both original artistic power and artistic "amplifiers" or "translators" of spiritual radiations. Additionally, the actor needs to have a series of enthralling artistic tasks that bring the role to life and give it structure, logic, and internal action.

The new principles of internal technique were successfully tested in *A month in the Country*. By employing a carefully refined, almost motionless mise-en-scene, the actors achieved the most subtle mental changes in their characters. Next, the actors' internal technique would be tested in pushing large blocks of action all the way in one direction and then all the way in another. In other words, they would need to push harder and display more intensity.

The Brothers Karamazov would be the ultimate embodiment of the "Stanislavsky system" in the realm of tragedy. Moskvin referred to his work in *The Brothers Karamazov* when he said,

> The greatest and most precious thing is when you dare to be yourself in front of the audience, discarding your character's uniform. Suddenly, everything else fades away—objectives, adaptations, and 'acting'—and I am filled internally. In those moments, it feels like I can do anything, and I am on the verge of tears ... What's truly wonderful is that I don't have to do anything during these moments. I have discovered that it's not me, Moskvin, but the fusion of the author's character and the actor's nature. So, I am not idle. For my most powerful moment as Mochalka, just before the main "crackup," when Alyosha offers me money, all I need to do is look at his hands—how he reaches into his pocket, rummages, pulls out the money, and holds it out—only look....

This is exactly what Nemirovich-Danchenko desired in *The Brothers Karamazov*. Sometimes, it seemed hopeless to him.

> No matter how much I pleaded with Ivan Karamazov/Kachalov to listen carefully and not show anything with his hands, mouth, or eyes, he wouldn't listen. It seemed too uninteresting to him; he believed his job was to act everything out. And this was the great Kachalov! I even had to convince Mochalka/Moskvin not to play tears.

Eventually, I managed to persuade them.

Then, one must wonder, what kind of soul does an actor need to possess in order to "stop acting" in this way? What level of understanding and empathy for the soul must they possess? What initial connection to these circumstances must exist in Ivan Moskvin, Vasily Kachalov, and Leonid Leonidov? At the same time, it is crucial to recognize that "capable, gifted, talented, genius" are not degrees of comparison for a single adjective like "good, better, best, very

196 Vladimir Nemirovich-Danchenko and the Moscow Art Theatre

best." Each of these terms represents unique qualities. Talented refers to ease of training, reliability in a particular area, and potential for future growth. Gifted suggests possessing an inherent talent that is independent of the individual; a significant gift is often referred to as talent. The word "genius" retains a double meaning, as it is derived from the Latin words for "genus" (birth, living growth) and "spirit" (as in the spirit of a place, "genius loci"). Ultimately, humanity is genius; its nature is genius. Nemirovich-Danchenko's explanations help clarify why *The Brothers Karamazov* became known as an "authentically Russian" work for the actors. Stanislavsky's system is based on the concept of the genius of human nature, which must be allowed the freedom and support to be creative. While some may see this as idealistic, it is motivated by a lofty understanding of the human being.

Not long after, Stanislavsky wrote another section of his forthcoming book entitled *"How to Use the System."* In this section, he provided an example featuring Vishnevsky, who portrayed Uncle Vanya using the system. Unfortunately, Uncle Vanya's character came across as unpleasant—old and grumpy toward everyone. In other words, Vishnevsky depicted Professor Serebryakov instead of Uncle Vanya. Despite this, his acting was lively and uncomplicated because he adhered to the system. As a result, he could proudly claim to live a genuine life. However, this genuine life was shaped by his own perspective, influenced by his current situation. Over time, Vishnevsky himself changed significantly, growing older and adopting the habits of an elderly man. Every aspect of life carries a certain level of risk and holds multiple meanings. Even the belief in humanity's inherent genius is both dangerous and ambiguous. After all, human nature can exist without any sign of talent. Furthermore, the power of time holds sway without exception, as it continually guides us into old age.

Notes

1 Carlsbad is a European spa resort in Bohemia (now the Czech Republic) that is still famous for its therapeutic springs.
2 Strastnaya Square is two miles northeast of Red Square, Sokolniki is eight miles northeast, and Petrovsky Park is five miles northeast.
3 *Gold* is a play about a wealthy and corrupt businessman, his daughter's engagement to an artist, and the consequences of his unethical business practices.
4 Alexander Benois (1870–1960) was an artist, critic, and art historian, one of the ideologues and organizers of the "World of Art" association, and member of MAT's directorate for several years.
5 From *Genius* (1825), a poem by Nikolai Yazykov (1803–1846).
6 Karasyuk is a Ukrainian surname.
7 In *The Cherry Orchard*, Boris Semyonov-Pischik is a landowner and elderly aristocrat, and Yepikhodov is an unfortunate and clumsy accountant.
8 Serafima Birman (1890–1976) was a theatre and film actress associated with MAT, as well as a director, teacher, memoirist, and theorist.
9 *The Living Corpse* (1900) is a play by Leo Tolstoy. It tells the story of Fedor Protasov, who fakes his death to free his wife, Liza, to marry another man, but his actions lead to tragic consequences.

Russian Tragedy 1908–1910   197

10 The Black Hundred were reactionary, monarchist, and ultra-nationalist movement in Russia in the early twentieth century.

11 Alexey Dikiy (1889–1955) was an actor associated with MAT and later the Habima Theatre in Tel Aviv.

12 *Demons* (1871–1872) was adapted from the novel of the same name by Dostoyevsky. It is set in the fictional small town of Skvoreshniki and follows a group of intellectuals involved in a political conspiracy that leads to murder and chaos.

13 Here is MAT's scene arrangement the *The Brothers Karamazov*: First Evening: Scenes 1 and 2. The Controversy. Over the Brandy. The Sensualists (III, 7–8–9). Scene 3. Both Together (III, 10). Scene 4. Another Reputation Ruined (III, 11). Scene 5. At His Father's (IV, 2). Scene 6. At the Khokhlakov's (IV, 4). Scene 7. A Laceration in the Drawing Room (IV, 5). Scene 8. A Laceration in the Cottage (IV, 6). Scene 9. And in the Open Air (IV, 7). Scene 10. For a While a Very Obscure One (V, 6). Scene 11. An Onion (VII, 3). Scenes 12 and 13. Sudden Decision (VIII, 5). Second Evening: Scene 14. The First and Rightful Love. Delirium. The Sufferings of the Soul through Ordeals. The Prosecutor Catches Mitya. They Carry Mitya Away (VIII, 7–8; IX, 2–3–4–5). Scene 15. A Little Demon (XI, 3). Scenes 16 and 17. Not You, Not You (XI, 5). Scene 18. Last Interview with Smerdyakov (XI, 8). Scene 19. The Devil. Ivan's Nightmare (XI, 2). Scene 20. Judicial Error. Sudden Disaster (XII, 5).

14 *Princess Nastya* (1908) was adapted from the novel of author, playwright, and historian Alexander Amfiteatrov (1862–1938). is an ironic reference. The book centers on Prince Radunsky, a powerful aristocrat, and his scandalous tricks and wild amusements. Each province seemingly has a dominant landowner who ruled autocratically with no intervention from higher authorities or neighbors. The second part of the book focuses on escaping this slavery and subsequent wanderings.

15 Ilya Sats (1875–1912) was a composer and music director of MAT.

16 Evgeny Vakhtangov (1883–1922) was an actor and director, co-director of MAT's First Studio with Leopold Sulerzhitsky and Boris Sushkevich, and director of the Third Studio (after 1926, the Vakhtangov Theatre). He directed the Solomon Anski's 1913–1916 play *The Dybbuk* (1922) at the Habima Theater (performed in Hebrew, 1922). His direction of Carlo Gozzi's 1762 play *Princess Turandot* (1922) introduced his signature style of "fantastic realism."

17 Cf. Satin, *The Lower Depths*, Act IV.

9 Options for an Ending 1910–1914

Authenticity and Self-Fulfillment in Tolstoy's *The Living Corpse*

MAT obtained the same play for which the head of the MAT repertoire once went to Yasnaya Polyana—Leo Tolstoy had died. They couldn't cancel performances upon Tolstoy's death due to religious mourning being considered as anti-government. Instead, they had to act as if Moskvin were sick and organize a civil memorial service for Tolstoy at the theatre. Many people gathered in the street hoping to attend, but police officers stopped them at the main entrance.

Nemirovich-Danchenko talked about his encounters with the late author. Literature professor Yakov Grot took him to Khamovniki the first time.[1] The Tolstoy family was at the table, with Tolstoy's wife Sofia sewing and one of his daughters reading passages from Alexander Herzen's autobiography *My Past and Thoughts* aloud. Tolstoy then asked the guest to read and praised his reading. On another occasion, Tolstoy visited him on Chudovsky Lane to return a borrowed copy of *An Enemy of the People.* "He liked our small apartment, especially the garden outside with the chickens and pigeons." Regarding the play, he said, "No, it's not good. Dr. Stockman is very arrogant." Nemirovich-Danchenko concluded by describing his visit to Yasnaya Polyana to request *The Living Corpse.* Now they were set to produce it.

There was much discussion about why MAT rather than the Maly Theatre acquired the advantage. *The Living Corpse* and the other unreleased plays were now at MAT's disposal. The far-right newspaper *Zemshchina* adopted the same smirking tone for *The Living Corpse* as the newspaper *Russian Land* did for *The Brothers Karamazov.* They said the play bored them and that people only pretended to be interested in it. They even added a chuckle: Nemirovich-Danchenko and Sumbatov-Yuzhin had nearly come to blows over the rights to *The Living Corpse,* and now it appeared the Maly Theatre would also stage the play—"boring as autumn rain." Indeed, the Maly Theatre did produce the play, although their manuscript differed from MAT's. The newspapers questioned whether the manuscript they had was

DOI: 10.4324/9781003486282-9

the definitive version. In fact, they didn't have the author's manuscript; but only a rewritten copy. Accordingly, they offered their copy for comparison, but the differences were minor. Literary historian Nestor Kotlyarevsky,[2] in response to persistent questions from reporters, declared he couldn't decide since MAT's manuscript was only a draft. Nemirovich-Danchenko did not dispute these findings. However, while others considered the draft to have annoying faults, this director had a different perspective. In *The Brothers Karamazov*, he had recently discovered the artistic possibilities of arranging scenes in a non-plot-oriented manner. The acts were not equally proportioned, and some episodes lasted over an hour while others were under three minutes. Thus, the rhythm of the action exists not only "within the scene" but also in the changes of their durations, in the effect of montage. Although designer Viktor Simov was skilled in creating scenery for a rotating stage, this specific arrangement was not utilized here. There is no somber empty space or abstract backdrop, but sections, corners of rooms, walls, and ceilings unfolded before the audience.

Meanwhile, other matters also needed attention. Previously, Nemirovich-Danchenko had been involved in every aspect of MAT. However, now he was interrupted by a rare business trip to Paris. The building on Kamergersky Street had been in disrepair for some time, and they were tired of constantly making repairs and paying rent for a property that did not belong to them. With that in mind, they considered using the MAT Partnership's funds to construct their own new premises. In the meantime, their plan was to embark on a two-year tour as performing artists. But first, they needed to assess the situation in Paris and determine if they could rent the Chatelet Theatre there.

When Nemirovich-Danchenko arrived in Paris on a Sunday, the city was practically deserted as everyone was either at the races or out of town. He found the quiet evenings, when the streets were sparsely populated, quite enjoyable. Daylight persisted for an extended period, allowing him ample time to wander around and observe his surroundings. He jotted down various business-related notes in his notebook, including measurements of the theatre boxes, details about the local stages, payment practices of the staff, and the names of important contacts. He had preliminary meetings with Anatole France and attended a French reading of Dostoyevsky by the actor Louis Jouvet. When he visited the Chatelet Theatre, he felt a sense of affection for its aging architecture, particularly its expansive stage and balconies that ensured every word on stage could be heard clearly.

During his time in Paris, the Russian season of Sergei Diaghilev's *Ballets Russes* commenced at the Chatelet.[3] Paris was adorned with posters advertising the ballets, which prominently featured the silhouettes of Tamara Karsavina and the profile of Vaslav Nijinsky,[4] designed by Jean Cocteau.[5] Since Nemirovich-Danchenko had not yet experienced these ballets, he watched *Scheherazade* and Stravinsky-Benois-Fokine's *Petrushka* with great

200 Vladimir Nemirovich-Danchenko and the Moscow Art Theatre

fascination. All this captivated Nemirovich-Danchenko more than expected. It's not what he wrote about after *Petrushka* ("I have fallen behind. We have fallen behind"), although this phrase was unusual for him. The fear of falling behind, of others moving ahead further and better, was not his fear. Instead, his strong feeling was that if MAT was imperfect, it only concerned his own standards, not those of others. MAT actors needed to remember Nemirovich-Danchenko's words if and when another groundbreaking play like *The Seagull* ever appeared, and a different theatre had discovered it. Someday, the actors might find themselves in the same position they were once put in by the ranking Alexandrinsky and Maly theatres. Such a lofty ambition required continuous watchfulness and teaching. Nemirovich-Danchenko would never say that some artist had discovered "new, deeply captivating secrets," nor would he rush after such artists "like someone mistaken and gone off in another direction." But he would say that it was not Pushkin's Mozart who talked about such "new secrets," it was Salieri; Salieri was talented and could learn secrets, but geniuses like Mozart were inscrutable. It was not a matter of whether MAT was falling behind. Nemirovich-Danchenko watched the great ballets and wrote, "It upsets me" whenever some lovely word or intonation appeared out of harmony with the charm of the whole. In something so beautiful, so full of life, it breaks your heart and brings you close to tears. He felt sad in such moments.

The director who was about to interpret Tolstoy's posthumous manuscript would not need impressions of Paris but rather how to work out what the production in Moscow would need. For Nemirovich-Danchenko, Tolstoy meant an artistic love of the subject, a natural deification of it. A warm, flooding light that preserves the lively aura of the subject—this is the impression that becomes the guiding light for the director. For Nemirovich-Danchenko, everything begins with the writer's nature and proceeds from that.

They had already prepared the scenery when rehearsals of *The Living Corpse* began. He approved it and offered comments in early August— "It needs some kind of flaw: a samovar, a decorated thing on the wall, or something like that." He had to find someone who could clarify the timing of the action, and he wanted to know how to pronounce the word "English" in the play. It's interesting to consider how the play would have been produced if Nemirovich-Danchenko had obtained the manuscript in 1900 when he went to Yasnaya Polyana for it. However, this thought would be misleading. In this production, MAT kept the physicality of everyday objects but without inherent eloquence, as if the objects merely identified themselves on stage and then faded away. They only showed the general outlines of the given circumstances, as the meaning would have been incomplete without them and the production would have become ambiguous. On stage, they concisely and correctly showed the given circumstances; the actors began with them but did not fully experience or live by them throughout.

Options for an Ending 1910–1914 201

As part of the director's work on *The Living Corpse*, an extract from Tolstoy's manuscript was included. It is unlikely that they rewrote one page out of mere interest in the play's stage history. It is more likely that they wanted to capture the play's fundamental spirit, the emotions that existed within and between the characters. Another rewritten page reads:

Fedya says: What a strange thing life is! Why is all this so? Why am I married to her? Why Masha? Why is there a crack in the plaster? All this could have been different—completely different. This is the sun, and this is my body. Why is it so? How different it all could be! It's strange. All gone to waste. I know it was not a waste. But I know even more that something was completely wrong.

The phrasing is Tolstoy's, although the protagonist Fedya Protasov did not say these words in the production. Textual specialists may recognize the source passage, but it wouldn't be surprising if the page records Protasov/Moskvin's internal monologue.

When the public heard about the play and the distribution of roles before the premiere, it surprised them. Why is Moskvin assigned the part of Protasov, a socialite and a public figure? However, Protasov/Moskvin lived the boredom and shame of a life that wasn't authentic to himself, constantly forced to conform to the stereotypes of a social role. Why does everyone think they know in advance what a socialite should be? They do because it's all predetermined.

What a telling expression: a person is 'ill at ease.' Ill at ease, and it makes you feel sick and sad. How precious those moments are when you are alone with yourself and your soul. When you truly listen, like Protasov does—lying on a sofa, changing your position, sitting down, leaning forward a bit, gazing at the Roma singers. The women leading the song with their hands by their sides, sitting down, serious, wine on the table, and flowers.

Moskvin discovered his Protasov through the influence of the Roma people. It is crucial to understand why people believed this to be the case. The Roma community in Moscow lived in a patriarchal manner, practicing devout faith, having numerous children, and settling down only to the extent they desired. The inclusion of the Roma element in Protasov/Moskvin's life offered an opportunity to deviate from the predictable and tiresome path, a call for possibility and necessity. Under its spell, you could shed tears over their own existence.

The dramatic works of the late nineteenth and early twentieth centuries fervently debated the concept of self-fulfillment, the right and duty to be true to oneself. For instance, upon seeing *Uncle Vanya*, Leo Tolstoy was outraged and felt compelled to write a play titled *The Corpse*. He even sketched a summary. Uncle Vanya vociferously declares that he has squandered his life. He could have achieved great things but did not. He became nothing, and this was the tragedy. Tolstoy envisioned a different play—one where it was far worse for someone to attain greatness and be confined to it indefinitely. It mattered little whether one became a noble leader, a bank director, or even a philosopher. The most mundane aspects of life, such as marriage or choosing a career, trouble us not because we are indecisive or weak, but because we fear the finality they represent. If you became a manager, you were trapped in an office. If you got married, your life was effectively over. Toward the end of the play, Protasov/Moskvin is confronted by the Investigator, who is naturally inclined to classify and define people. Where else would the Investigator fit? Falling into that role was comfortable for him.

To claim that *The Living Corpse* derived its energy solely from the incompatibility with one's own life, the wavering and trembling of Protasov/Moskvin in contrast to a confident, steady, and growing "non-life" would be an exaggeration. The meaning emerged in a different way, through the uncertainty of existence, the struggle within Protasov/Moskvin's soul, and the blending of happiness and grief in the Roma singing. This was quietly present in the scene where state councilor Protasov is in the tavern with the artist Petushkov, where the encounter between bureaucratic machinery and a person organized by entirely different laws is starkly juxtaposed. Critic Serge Volkonsky characterized the world on stage embodied in the character of Lisa, Protasov's wife.

> What a familiar image of Russian life: this fashionable lady, both shallow and profound, with established 'principles' but unpredictable behavior; extreme in her sympathies, intense in her anger, and unsteady in her loyalty. Everything, from head to toe, was perfectly in place. The folds of her dresses, the short sable jacket, the lace around her delicate, aristocratic hands — all enchanting and incredibly natural, commonplace. The same routine of French phrases interspersed throughout the role.

In the play, Victor Karenin kisses his mother's hand, pleading, "Please, don't change." Volkonsky's entire argument, of which this passage is a part, revolves around the audience's sentiments mirroring those words: "Please, don't change."

Renewal and Doubt Amid Cultural and Generational Change

"I manage the theatre without enthusiasm, without great love, as if anticipating some catastrophe to finally reveal the truth."—Nemirovich-Danchenko wrote this in January 1915. Five years earlier, he wrote (but did not send) a letter to Stanislavsky where he expressed his bewilderment and admiration for Stanislavsky's ability to maintain good relationships with people, including himself. He wondered what else one could possibly need when they were already experiencing such success and prosperity. MAT had gained world-wide fame, their revenues were excellent, performances went smoothly, and Stanislavsky was at the peak of his fame as an actor. Nemirovich-Danchenko believed that MAT was following Stanislavsky's ideal path and couldn't imagine anything more to wish for. Now, in hindsight, Nemirovich-Danchenko pondered whether he should revisit this previous praise as a reminder to himself. If everything seemed so good, why did everything feel so wrong? He could find an answer in an old letter that accurately described the current situation. While the performances were still running smoothly and revenues were impressive, there was something missing. Nemirovich-Danchenko couldn't help wondering if MAT was truly on the path to its ideal goal at present.

After the success of *The Brothers Karamazov*, Nemirovich-Danchenko believed they had made a breakthrough and that new opportunities had opened up. However, it turned out that these opportunities either quickly diminished or simply disappeared. Over the past five years, Nemirovich-Danchenko has devoted a significant amount of his time and energy to various projects. He collaborated with Konstantin Mardzhanov on directing *Peer Gynt* (1912) and Hamsun's *In the Grip of Life* (1911), although these productions were primarily the work of Mardzhanov. He also assisted Alexandre Benois who had limited experience working with actors, on Moliere's *The Forced Marriage* (1913). In addition, he directed Turgenev's *The Parasite* (1912) as a one-act play, which focused on Turgenev's production style but was not Nemirovich-Danchenko's strong suit as a director. Furthermore, He staged *Miserere* (1910) by Yushkevich and two expansionist plays by Leonid Andreyev: *Ekaterina Ivanovna* (1912)[6] and *Thought* (1914).[7] Moreover, Andreyev submitted these two plays at MAT's request. Nemirovich-Danchenko wrote, "Why didn't the great novelists write their outstanding works for the theatre?" He answered: First, "because the theatre required action and movement. Chekhov destroyed that requirement, but how many more remained?"

Leonid Andreyev picked up where Chekhov left off.

Does the theatre need action in the conventional form of activity and movement on stage? I can posit an answer to this heretical question: No. External action is unnecessary because life, in its most dramatic conflicts, is increasingly moving away from external action, going increasingly into the depths of the soul and the silence and external stillness of intellectual experiences. With all the luxury and variety of his surroundings, the smartly dressed artist-adventurer gives way to the black frock coat, the stillness of deaf and dreary rooms, and the silence and gloom of the bedroom and the office. Nowadays, only the traveling salesperson wanders energetically around the world, while Leo Tolstoy, with his inherently universal drama, sits at home motionless for a quarter-century.

Andreyev laughed at the fear of monologues in modern theatre: "Unnatural, not like life! Was it like life to do things without stopping, to chat

204 *Vladimir Nemirovich-Danchenko and the Moscow Art Theatre*

continuously like a cheerful parrot, and never once think deeply for over twenty seconds?" Leonid Andreyev seems to have been inconsistent; in fact, his plays have traditional action scenes at their core. *Katerina Ivanovna* begins with the husband shooting his wife, whom he suspects of infidelity. In *Thought*, Dr. Kerzhentsev kills his friend Savelov, who has married the woman Kerzhentsev loved and who rejected him. However, after the premiere, Andreyev regretted including the murder scene; a Reader should have come out and read: Dr. Kerzhentsev killed Savelov. The protagonists of these two Andreyev plays had a proud faith in themselves and put it to the test. Katerina Ivanovna's depraved husband tested her spiritual purity through debauchery. Dr. Kerzhentsev tested the impregnability of his mind by feigning the madness of a murderer. These tormenting experiments ruined them both, revealing their hidden natures to them as a black hole, swallowing them up. Kerzhentsev could not find the answer in himself, whether he was playing madness or genuinely mad; no one could say whether Katerina Ivanovna was playing a profligate or genuinely so. Repression changed the thought, suppression changed the body, and black uncertainty was everywhere.

The thing is, attitudes toward everyday life come and go. The savoring of life, the novelty of its nuances, and the strategies of their presentations repelled rather than attracted Nemirovich-Danchenko. He read play after play, saw this talent, and did not like it. The alignment of art with life, which sometimes provided tremendous aesthetic energy (as it did in MAT's first productions), relied on "everyday externals" and their aesthetic and moral potential. For instance, the productions offered at Nezlobin's Theatre closely mirrored the fashionable world of St. Petersburg's Kamenostrovsky Prospect or Moscow's Arbat district, capturing and expressing life there. The repertoire of Alexander Tairov's Chamber Theatre displayed the aesthetic tastes of its specific audience. Specifically, the inherent reality of artistic creativity, closed and sublime, contrasted with the uniformity and polemics of vulgar reality. Its first production, Kalidasa's Sanskrit play, *Sakuntala*, was characterized by a sharp, emotionally charged external form, as well as the energy and refinement of expression. The Chamber Theatre sought to isolate a simple, exciting, and novel action that had no relevance to us and did not represent us as such. It was the simplicity and lyrical monumentality of another world.

From the beginning of the 1914 season, Nemirovich-Danchenko was inundated with compliments from spectators and journalists. After a long hiatus, someone revisited *Three Sisters* at MAT and wrote an article about it. "More than half the cast has changed [...] But the older performers were just as wonderful as before, and the newcomers were even more wonderful." MAT revived *Tsar Fyodor*, and "Shuisky/Luzhsky was as good as before." However, they did not like Vladimir Gribunin's new characterization of Bogdan Kryukov, as it differed too much from the late Alexander Artem's. Critics enjoyed the revival of *Woe From Wit* in 1914, with admiration for the "art of restoring gestures and even intonations." Everything seemed exactly as the audiences remembered from the 1906 premiere though it was not a precise restoration. For example, Stanislavsky portrayed Famusov, the patriarch, in a completely new manner, and Chatsky/Kachalov was more than just the offended young lover from the previous production. Molchalin/Podgorny no longer behaved like a clerical angel but rather like a young man with a Napoleon complex, eagerly waiting for his moment of glory in a tavern or bedroom. However, it is noteworthy how the reviewer formed their opinion: they wanted to believe that they were witnessing the same thing they and others had already seen. Going through the press clippings for that year, one can find comments such as "As good as before." Certain roles were considered "still magnificent."

"Please don't change!"

MAT had developed an extensive repertoire. By refreshing what they had already done every few years, they could continue to exist. A new audience would come in, and a new audience would grow up. All the plays formed an inventory. The scenery could be stored, always ready for a refresh. Program notes could always be provided for a new generation of audiences. This was the first option for the future of MAT. In 1916, Nemirovich-Danchenko attended plays at the Alexandrinsky Theatre in St. Petersburg and developed a strong appreciation for its unique art. He admired its refined and harmonious maturity, simplicity, straightforwardness, clarity, refinement, and sentimentality. He stated, "My tastes align with the Alexandrinsky." The statement "Veteran actor Vladimir Davydov was still Davydov, and the public liked it that way" suggests that actors at the MAT should be able to age gracefully in their roles, as Davydov did. There is no shame in this, as both the actor and his artistry were not getting any younger. The joy of the "Davydov style" or the "Sumbatov-Yuzhin style," along with the love for the theatre and the familiar scent backstage, were all still present at the Alexandrinsky and Maly theatres.

As a result, MAT posters always maintained simplicity and spoke softly with a small font, rather than shouting to grab attention from a distance. The experience of entering the theatre remained consistent, with the heavy brass ring on the main door and the gradual dimming of the sconces between the spectators' boxes before the magical parting of the olive curtain. However, to captivate audiences in this manner, one must live a different life with a different beginning and different biorhythms. It is unrealistic to expect a quiet retirement after the energetic and sectarian years of youth. Elderly revolutionaries cannot maintain their kindness, and intolerance becomes pitiable when creative energy no longer exists. The end of this journey is pride, a confident belief that everything is going well. If certain authors fail to resonate with the audience, it is seen as a testament to the high and truthful art that exposes the weaknesses of these individuals. At times, there may be a sudden fear that things are going terribly wrong and new ideas are needed. In such moments, people may eagerly grasp onto the first concepts they come across.

206   *Vladimir Nemirovich-Danchenko and the Moscow Art Theatre*

The end result is the transformation of the theatre into a tourist attraction. MAT, like the Tsar's Cannon, the Tsar's Bell, or even "Moscow artisanal bread," is celebrated as a landmark of Moscow. Whether the assigned status is low or high, such as the Tretyakov Gallery or the Cathedral of Vasily the Blessed, the difference ultimately seems insignificant. Time passes, and the story of MAT is not particularly long. Nemirovich-Danchenko recognizes that dying is not a noble experience. "Dying is always decaying, and there is nothing noble about decaying!" While a prolonged death is not beautiful, it may be possible to die gracefully.

Stanislavsky's fascination with the Studio sometimes appeared suicidal to Nemirovich-Danchenko, though he also shared an interest in nurturing young artists. He was acquainted with them. One example was when the daughter of the renowned Professor Vladimir Giatsintov came to visit him.[8] She waited outside his office on the mezzanine, while he advised her to take the examination and test her abilities. Another individual, Seraphima Birman, a tall and serious stage performer but painfully shy in real life, received an acceptance note from him. To ensure it wasn't mistaken for an April Fool's joke, he dated it as April 2nd instead of April 1st. Aside from these two, there were many unfamiliar faces at the MAT. Among them was a young man named Mikhail Chekhov, who had a surname cherished at the MAT. Unfortunately, Nemirovich-Danchenko had limited opportunities to interact with them. In a letter to Sumbatov-Yuzhin, someone he felt comfortable being honest with, he expressed his disappointment that his obligations to the collective and senior actors hindered his desire to foster young talent.

One of the new interviewees was of mixed Russian and Armenian heritage, with dark skin, striking eyes, and tired eyelids. He, like Nemirovich-Danchenko, came from the Caucasus. Nemirovich-Danchenko had already heard about him and recognized the surname—Vakhtangov. "Please have a seat. What do you hope to gain from us and contribute to us?" A fresh face, a different approach, and perhaps new ideas. This was exactly what Nemirovich-Danchenko believed in. He believed that ideas did not last forever but instead rejuvenated every seventeen to eighteen years. It had been a long time since he taught at the Philharmonic School. Eugene Vakhtangov, his interviewee, responded, "I would like to gain everything I can; I haven't thought about what I can give." His response was modest, as he felt others had recognized something in him. However, there was more to his reply. MAT would offer something to them, but it was unclear what they would offer in return.

While everyone assumed that the MAT Studios would eventually bring prosperity to MAT and that their students would join the troupe, Nemirovich-Danchenko had a different perspective. He believed MAT needed to plan for the future. Eventually, the emergence of the First Studio and other entities would lead to their pursuit of independence and fulfillment, possibly as the Second MAT. This should not be seen as a betrayal, but rather as a natural progression of development. Did Stanislavsky's indifference towards

Options for an Ending 1910–1914 207

mainstage MAT indicate a desire for the same outcome? It wouldn't be the worst outcome. Just like separate branches taking root in new soil, the old trunk may continue to exist, but it would undergo a complete transformation. Perhaps it would become an entire grove. However, it was crucial not to deceive oneself by believing that the old trunk was thriving. Some things simply would not happen. Was it worth sacrificing oneself for such a cause?

A conversation with Stanislavsky convinced Nemirovich-Danchenko of this—remember your own experience. Who knows if a new theatre would emerge from the current student auditions, with similar tasks and prospects for renewal that had enthralled everyone during the launch of MAT?— and why not celebrate if a new theatre grows up? There is a letter from Nemirovich-Danchenko that reads like a continuation of this conversation. The point is, how can you compare? To begin with, the repertory idea that was once so important to us no longer exists. There are no unread Chekhov plays or stage routines to challenge. There are no new ethical and organizational ideas. There is no talent anywhere near the scale of what we once had. There are no new directors....

Nemirovich-Danchenko did not send this letter, and he did the right thing. How can you compare? His arguments were baseless, sentimental, and worked against him. He wrote that it was absurd to compare the capabilities of newcomer Eugene Vakhtangov and veteran Alexander Sanin— absurd, of course, but not from the other perspective. And the great writer who remained unread was now Alexander Blok. And the ethical ideas of the emerging First Studio, where Sulerzhitsky once worked, were undoubtedly new. He could have said something different; that there was a fertile ground beneath them when they started, something to take root and from which a national theatre could emerge. Therefore, it would have been reasonable to argue that something was emerging in the First Studio, surging and pulling from a deep crevasse. It was not the time for a serious and enduring new theatre to emerge. Perhaps it was the time for a theatre of cutting-edge "trends" (Mikhail Chekhov, whom Nemirovich-Danchenko singled out in his letter, was born to be the first actor of such a theatre—with his introspective nature, subtle undercurrent, natural and primal emotions, irony, pain, and lyrical pessimism). Maybe it was time for MAT to share some of its extensive collection of stage culture, both old and new, so that the ancient passion that flows through Racine could be expressed through constructivist scenery. Perhaps it was time for the theatre to be fashionable and follow current trends. However, the theatre's time was never long; true tragic depth and style are always brief. There will be no happy, welcoming fate for those in whom Stanislavsky believed in so strongly.

Another possibility for an ending was to give oneself away, to propagate oneself. But choosing this self-inflicted end should not involve a vague interest in expecting a revival of one's original seed. Various new ideas will grow in those minds for whom you have now laid the groundwork. The fear was whether they would flourish. Was the soil suitable? Would there be

208 *Vladimir Nemirovich-Danchenko and the Moscow Art Theatre*

hailstorms? And the uncertainty: perhaps you should cherish your current life more (even if you were dissatisfied with it) than the potential one? Maybe you need to reinvent yourself and not give up? It was not the theatrical idea that was coming to an end, as Nemirovich-Danchenko feared. The monarchy and the era were coming to an end. And as always, the conscientious artist sought blame within himself. *Tsar Fyodor* resumed in the fall of 1914. Once again, *Tsar Fyodor* stood at the end huddled with his wife on an empty town square. Messengers had already delivered the news: the enemy had crossed the Oka River and were advancing toward Moscow. Moskvin's voice pierced his soul: "It was my fault; everything that happened was my fault!"

There was a world war going on.

Notes

1 Tolstoy had bought a house in Khamovniki in 1882, which was on the outskirts of Moscow at that time.
2 Nestor Kotlyarevsky (1863–1925) was an author, publicist, literary critic, and historian.
3 Sergei Diaghilev (1872–1929) was an art critic, famous ballet impresario, and founder of the Ballets Russes.
4 Tamara Karsavina (1885–1978) was the principal dancer of the Imperial Russian Ballet and later the Ballets Russes.
5 Vaslav Nijinsky (1889–1950) was a dancer and choreographer; considered by many to be the greatest male dancer of the twentieth century.
6 *Ekaterina Ivanovna* (1915) is a play by Leonid Andreyev and the first Russian play about women's emancipation. It revolves around the lonely, unfulfilled life of a middle-aged woman living in a small Russian town. Her chance encounter with a young man whom she falls deeply in love with becomes the turning point of her life. However, her hopes are shattered when she discovers that the man is already engaged to someone else.
7 *Thought* (1914) by Leonid Andreyev is a play that delves into the inner thoughts of a man contemplating suicide. As he reflects on the meaninglessness of life, he concludes that death is the only way out of his misery.
8 Vladimir Giatsintov (1858–1933) was an art historian, playwright, and professor of art history at the University of Moscow, father of Sophia Giatsintova (1895–1955) who was an actress associated with the First Studio and later MAT.

10 Fifth and Sixth Life 1914–1919

Artistic Reinvention and Adaptability

Nemirovich-Danchenko's productions, particularly those from the 1930s, exemplified the focused, self-aware, and unwavering integrity that had always drawn him. They all seemed to merge into one perfectly condensed and expertly directed work, which fortunately came about in our own time. We recognized his earlier work as stepping stones to his current reputation. However, he did not share the same perspective. The productions in MAT's early years were flawless creations of a specific time and creative disposition. Then came another era and disposition. It is not necessary to compare whether *Three Sisters* of 1901 was superior or inferior to *Three Sisters* of 1940. What matters is the inclination of the soul toward one or the other. How can you determine whether a soul leans more toward the Russian icon of *The Miracle of St. George and the Dragon* or Raphael's painting of *St. George Fighting the Dragon*? The same dragon recoils under the spear, the white horse and young warrior are present, and the same world exists in the distance, but from vastly different artistic perspectives.

The mystery and intrigue of Nemirovich-Danchenko's story lie in how the same person could naturally immerse themselves in two different periods and create two masterpieces with distinct artistic perspectives using the same literary material. And that is exactly what Nemirovich-Danchenko did. His new production of *Three Sisters* was merely the conclusion. Prior to that, he directed a masterful production of Gorky's *Enemies* (1935), juxtaposed against his masterful production of *The Lower Depths* (1902). A remarkable stage adaptation of *Resurrection* (1930) versus a mesmerizing *Living Corpse* (1911).[1] Different interpretations of Chekhov, Gorky, and Tolstoy on the stage, even though these three names had once defined the three pillars of MAT. In Bulgakov's novel, *The Master and Margarita*, the Master writes his book about Yeshua [Jesus], knowing it will ultimately end with a line spoken by Pontius Pilate, the fifth procurator of Judea. To the public, again, especially in the 1930s, it might have seemed that Nemirovich always knew what conclusion he would lead them to. There were individuals who lived such lives, possessing a clear plan from the start and an unwavering commitment

DOI: 10.4324/9781003486282-10

210 Vladimir Nemirovich-Danchenko and the Moscow Art Theatre

to it, who understood their singular purpose and its ultimate conclusion. But Nemirovich-Danchenko did not live like that. "At times, I feel like I have lived a fifth or sixth life," he wrote in one of his letters. He rarely contemplated himself in a reflective manner, but on certain occasions, he did discuss essential matters. So, let us attempt to comprehend him.

He did not dwell on the duration of his existence, how everything around him had changed, how much time had passed, or how many new things had materialized. Although he could have, at the age of sixty-five when he wrote the letter to Olga Knipper in 1924 (the reference to the fifth or sixth life is from that letter). In that same year, Stanislavsky's *My Life in Art* was published in English in America. The opening states:

> I was born in Moscow in 1863, a time that marked the transition between two significant eras. I have vivid memories of the landmarks of the age of serfdom: the flickering oil lamps, the lard candles, the pony express, and the peculiar Russian conveyance known as a tarantass. There were flintlock rifles and tiny cannons that resembled playthings.
>
> In my lifetime, I have witnessed the introduction of railways to Russia, along with express trains and steamboats. The searchlight, the automobile, the airplane, the battleship, the submarine, the telephone (with or without wires), the telegraph, and the twelve-inch gun were all invented.
>
> Thus, I have experienced a transformational journey from tallow candles to searchlights, from rickety carts to airplanes, from sailing boats to submarines, from couriers to radiotelegraphy, from flintlocks to Big Bertha, and from serfdom to Bolshevism and Communism. My life has been a diverse and multifaceted tapestry that has undergone numerous seismic shifts.[2]

However, this is just one narrative; Nemirovich-Danchenko's own story is different. He spoke about the constant changes and multiple life cycles he had lived through, where one life did not begin until another had concluded. Up until 1924, Nemirovich-Danchenko had lived five or six distinct lives, with several more awaiting him. Among these lives were both successful and unsuccessful ones, filled with love and heartbreak. He did not mark their endings on his calendar, as he disliked ceremonies, mournful farewells, and displays of detachment from what he had outgrown within himself (as we have discussed previously). In a letter to Luzhsky in 1919, he wrote, *Le Roi Est Mort, Vive Le Roi!* The theatre may be crumbling, but long live the theatre! During moments of crisis, he usually avoided such exclamations, but he could not entirely do without such moments.

This is where the biographer faces a challenging task. Firstly, it is not easy to define Nemirovich-Danchenko's talent for starting anew and its underlying psychological mechanics. He had one fundamental requirement: to start from scratch every time. However, this principle applied not only

Fifth and Sixth Life 1914–1919 211

to life but primarily to new work circumstances. In accordance with the laws of the "theatre of the living person," an artist raised with this principle should not simply represent but truly be. Discover the basic elements within yourself, the potential for emotions that drive you to perform on stage based on the actions of Hamlet or Fortinbras. "Myself in the given circumstances." The "Magic If." Such concepts must be assessed and acted upon, first by wholeheartedly believing in them. Nemirovich-Danchenko's upbringing, position, and experience placed him in the same whirlwind of circumstances as others. While he may have initially ignored or misjudged these circumstances, he eventually accepted them as reality. Invariably, he discovered the potential within himself—the capacity to feel, which made him energetic, genuine, and able to adapt to his new circumstances by stepping outside of himself.

That being said, it is also possible to understand Nemirovich-Danchenko's nature through other parallels and similarities. When he was dying, he uttered the unexpected words: "My feet have walked enough…"[3] This statement was surprising because it contradicted the persona that everyone knew. How could the Director of MAT resort to a humble proverb? After all, he held prestigious titles such as the head of the Committee of the Stalin Prize and had even passed away in the exclusive Kremlin Hospital. Nemirovich-Danchenko was struck down by illness shortly after returning from a performance of *Swan Lake*. His death came swiftly, while he was out on business. There was no one to take care of Nemirovich-Danchenko. He did not have a high social position, wealth, extraordinary talent, or extensive education. From the age of thirteen, he relied solely on himself and took great pride in this independence. He never allowed himself to be subservient to others, materialistic desires, rumors, trends, political maneuvering, or street protests. He was confident not only in his autonomy but also in his ability to navigate the various shifts and changes within society. His genius lay in his intuition to distinguish between the fleeting disturbances caused by those around him (to which he was proudly indifferent) and the underlying revolutionary potential hidden beneath the layers of life. These shifts revealed inherent qualities that had not previously been recognized in public and personal life. Consequently, people would often wonder, "Where did this come from?" The tone in which they asked this question—whether out of joy, fear, or resentment—was inconsequential. While some artists draw strength from opposing the social order and make it the purpose of their creativity, this was not the case for Nemirovich-Danchenko. When he found himself at odds with something, evoking deep emotions and thoughts that were not in harmony with him, these times were not fruitful for him as an artist.

One life that he despised began during the First World War and was out of sync. It was a life where intellectual pursuits remained potent but allowed little room for artistic expression. It was a perplexing, headache-inducing, and poignant existence, which was tragically cut short.

World War I and the Role of Art Amid Social Crisis

Austrian and Czech film archives show patients walking around the Carlsbad Medical Health Spa grounds during the summer of 1914, and Nemirovich-Danchenko was likely among them. He arrived in Carlsbad a little earlier than usual, and his host apologized because his permanent rooms would not be ready for two days. However, the rooms temporarily provided for him were just as good, and cheaper. The staff gave him his shoes, which were neatly wrapped and placed exactly where he had left them the year before. The weather was fine, and he praised it every day. In a letter to his wife, he included a sketch of a new dress style (she was a fashionista). He also reported on what he ate, mentioning that today's meal consisted of beef bouillon and strawberries with cream. The porter was unusually eager to tell him something, but the guest only understood fragments of German. Half an hour later, his host was watering the flowers on the patio beneath his window and explained what had happened. A Serbian student had assassinated the heir to the Austrian throne. Nemirovich-Danchenko sent his wife the details: "A murder took place in Sarajevo, a town in Bosnia." That single shot marked the beginning of the First World War. We know this now, but they didn't. The owners canceled the music in the garden as a sign of mourning but resumed it the following day.

On July 21, a thunderstorm broke out—though not the figurative storm of war, just heavy rain. He wrote a letter while listening to the sound of the rain: "A soggy dog howls to be let inside." They let him in, and he no longer cries. The rain eventually stopped. "Should I go to Marienbad or not? I think I'll go."

The train to Marienbad was almost empty, and a large window at the rear allowed him to admire the views. He spent the entire day in Marienbad, accompanied by the whole of Moscow's Carriage Road—Stanislavsky and his family, the Kachalovs, the Leonidovs, and their "favorite" critics: Nikolai Efros and Lyubov Gurevich. They strolled around, had lunch, and then Nemirovich-Danchenko read a new play by Alexei Tolstoy to everyone (though they didn't like it), and they had drinks. They escorted him back to the train with joking solemnity—Stanislavsky's idea was to show the Germans how Russian artists honor their director. The train was empty on the way back, and the smell of mowed grass and fog permeated everything. In his last letter to his wife from Carlsbad, he mentioned that he was on his way home, saying "soon now." You could consider expanding the significance of these words by transferring their meaning to upcoming events. "Soon now." The unexpected hostility on the faces of the Germans frightened the actors the most while they were on vacation in Germany. They wondered when the Germans had become so aggressive. The first sound related to the war the actors heard was not gunshots, but the terrible, soft sound of blows on a lifeless body—someone was being beaten outside the walls.

The scene then shifts to Moscow, where the First Studio performs the "war premiere" of *The Cricket on the Hearth*. Studio members recalled that Nemirovich-Danchenko attended but did not take part in the post-show discussion, which lasted until well past midnight. The production was more intricate than usual, with a copper kettle singing on the hearth, an infant's cradle, and a fairy wearing a cap, who urges John Peerybingle to restore the gift of tenderness and kindness to the people. The challenge lay in translating the dual themes of home and departure, which are constant themes for MAT, into a fairy-tale theme. Indeed, it is even more complex than that. Leopold Sulerzhitsky's animated lyrical interpretation of the play did not captivate Nemirovich-Danchenko. In comparison to what MAT had already accomplished, the production would not endure, even if some individuals would cherish the play's handwritten program as a keepsake and a pledge of loyalty during the turbulent years to come.

The tasks that Nemirovich-Danchenko deems feasible for MAT from the beginning of the war may contradict one another, but they are all demanding, as demanding as his personal experiences. Stanislavsky wrote about his experiences during the first days of the war because they were uncommon, while Nemirovich-Danchenko did not write about his experiences because they were the same for everyone. The war caught up with him in Neskuchnoye, with mobilization, departures, and the first sound of locomotive whistles piercing through the darkness. The steppe surrounding the train station, the heat, and the night were filled with "the roar of young soldiers." To reach Moscow, he had to obtain a certificate stating that a certain individual was traveling from his estate in a specific village and heading to Moscow. The war expanded the responsibilities and significance of officials at every level; it was impossible to go anywhere without proper documentation and official stamps.

There is no basis for believing that life grows stronger from war. Even though newspapers published articles asking: Are we the same as those once seen by Chekhov? Isn't Vershinin's regiment currently at the front; aren't the three sisters caring for the wounded at an infirmary? The time when calls for "work, work!" relied on the Germans (symbolized by Tuzenbach) has passed. Now, we will rid ourselves of this dependency. Tuzenbach, the journalist noted, probably worked for German intelligence and went into hiding somewhere about a year ago. "The old cry 'to Moscow' has given way to a cheerful and courageous outcry 'to Berlin!' Or does this still have to be proven?"

Nemirovich-Danchenko, like everyone else, has patriotic feelings and feels horror at the Germans for brutally shelling historic Belgian cities. However, there is something in his initial emotional response that allowed the newspapers to twist the war into something shallow and trivial (*poshlost*). The newspapers reported that Moscow women were collecting jewelry for Belgian women victims and described the collection as "original, beautiful, and touching." They also wrote about visits to the Belgian consulate with donations, recounting an incident where a gray, bearded man emptied his old

214 Vladimir Nemirovich-Danchenko and the Moscow Art Theatre

wallet on the table, revealing only a ruble and some loose change. In the same style, the newspapers reported that Nemirovich-Danchenko donated the proceeds from the first performance of *The Blue Bird* to Belgian citizen Maurice Maeterlinck for his compatriots and asked the audience to welcome the Belgian Consul, who was also present.

At The Bat, now a variety theatre that replaced the original actor's club, they sang *The Song of the Belgian Lace-Makers*. One newspaper commented that when the song was sung, the usually lively basement became solemnly quiet, and many shed tears. Yermolova also sang the same song at a daytime concert for the war-wounded. The mention of Yermolova in this context is jarring. Why is everything so distorted and false? In the winter, the actors began collecting tobacco for the soldiers. Luzhsky, Kachalov, and Moskvin were particularly enthusiastic among the actors. It was reminiscent of Christmas caroling as they rode around in wagons with an orchestra, visiting the homes of the wealthy who were both honored and generous. They also conducted collections at restaurants, with Martinique's patrons being the most generous. Many business people frequented the place, as the food there was excellent.

Around the end of 1915, a word that was previously uncommon reemerged in daily speech: "razrukha" [Разрух], which means destruction, devastation, falling apart, and the event itself. It signifies rupture, the end of the world, harmony, friendship, strife, dissent, hostility, war.

Nemirovich-Danchenko buried his mother on September 5 at the beginning of the war. It is a commonplace that as dreadful events approach, older people delicately begin to depart, knowing that time will not be on their side. The church priest at the Armenian cemetery takes advantage of propinquity to request tickets to MAT, which are becoming increasingly hard to obtain. Nemirovich-Danchenko worried in vain about whether stage productions would be in demand. However, it wasn't the box office that concerned him. Who could have imagined that he had a guilt complex and an inferiority complex about his art? Who could have imagined that he wanted to leave his job at MAT to do something more directly helpful? He had figured out exactly where he could have the most impact. His office at MAT had a window that now faced the side of the office building for Lianozov Sons' Oil Company, which had an infirmary and an administrative center for the wounded. Nemirovich-Danchenko believed he would excel as an organizer in any field and even considered managing the hospital trains. Lives depended on efficiency and organization, not on theatrical productions at MAT. He wrote a concise and deliberate phrase in his notebook: "No one needs art." He went on to explain that no one needs the development, movement, or the "personal life" of art, although there may still be demand for its final products. A vague notion of an "other" took shape in his mind. *They* were doing what *they* were supposed to do, and he respected that. "We," on the other hand, were not. Our only justification was providing people with "legitimate, necessary artistic rest" to "boost morale on the home front." In times of war,

Fifth and Sixth Life 1914–1919   215

we should let go of the self-centeredness of creativity and artistic exploration and give the people something familiar and dear to them if we were lucky enough to possess it.

Another idea that troubled Nemirovich-Danchenko was his growing aversion to the audience. He believed that the audience was deceiving him, that they were not the individuals for whom he sacrificed his creative desires—they were strangers who came from nowhere. He also used the term "refugees." There was a genuine surge of refugees coming to Moscow. By the summer of 1915, Russian troops returning from Spain, Poland, and the Baltics were arriving in Moscow. However, for Nemirovich-Danchenko, "refugees" was a blanket term for all foreigners coming to Moscow. Again, he sees some of *them*, only now it is a disgusting, mean-spirited *them*. *They* were engaging in shameful behaviors, and the theatre was being corrupted because of them— these "refugees" were aggressors.

In those days, no one conducted sociological studies, so it is difficult to say if the composition of the MAT audience dramatically changed. Perhaps it wasn't just the rambunctious and disrespectful newcomers in the audience, who were growing in number and spoke loudly, but rather an unfavorable shift in his own life and social circle. It was like an ugly, trembling wall inside of which people's lives have been going on for quite a long time—a year or two, and it can't go on like that. Eventually, all this must end. Life deteriorates and becomes barbarous; people feel it as disgustingly foreign—our life behind the wall.

Bold Artistic Expression Amid Social Upheaval

Nemirovich-Danchenko will soon say the words people would frequently cite later: "We remember and are fully aware that before the Great October Socialist Revolution, we were in extreme confusion. Our art had stagnated. It was not as passionate as when we started MAT and was lukewarm at best. We began to lose faith in ourselves and our art. Now all of us will remember and realize that our art would have died out if there had been no Great October Socialist Revolution."

Nemirovich-Danchenko was strikingly unfit to deal with confusion. He did not know how to handle it. (One must learn to tolerate confusion, like any misfortune of the soul!) He was confused by the firmness with which he asserted one thing and did another. He put on three productions in the season, before the beginning of which he wrote: "It's a given that no one needs art." He did not put on a single performance in any season when his main, favorite thought was: "Beauty will save the world." (He repeated these words in his notes of 1916 and 1917—again and again.)

When he directed Ilya Surguchev's play, *Autumn Violins*,[4] someone in the newspapers remarked: "Some joker made a bet that MAT would stage a parody of itself and won the bet." Surguchev's play had been around for a long time. Initially, it went to Savina's Theatre, when Nemirovich-Danchenko

216 *Vladimir Nemirovich-Danchenko and the Moscow Art Theatre*

described it as "harmless ... water with lemon and sugar. There's no harm done." It was neither the first nor the last work made "for the theater." Now it was "for MAT." If Nemirovich-Danchenko took for granted that "nobody needs anything new," if he only cared about giving people a break from the labors of war, if he imposed this duty on MAT as they impose obedience in a monastery, then he should have been happy with *Autumn Violins*, especially since the play comes out "nice and literary." But his letter said, "I screamed that if we put on *Autumn Violins* ahead of Pushkin's trilogy of one-acts, I would defiantly leave Moscow, but 'circumstances' will probably crush me, and 'something stagnant' will prevail."

Pushkin's *Little Tragedies* goes on ahead of *Autumn Violins*. Both Nemirovich-Danchenko and Stanislavsky worked on them under Benoit's directorial byline. The co-direction and design by Alexander Benoit—with his love for colors and unusual materials, the stylization of everyday life and history—was darker and more elaborate than necessary for Pushkin's lean "spirit dialogues." The critics were probably correct about *Mozart and Salieri*; the detailed scene of a street, a fireplace, and a glass bottle of poison served no purpose. Similarly, *Feast in a Time of Plague* did not benefit from a city with alleys, a cathedral with flying buttresses, or a cluttered banquet table. Without a clear focal point on the stage, viewers' gazes were free to wander.

Lermontov's play *Masquerade* also appeared in Nemirovich-Danchenko's notebooks.[5] Meyerhold's staging of the play at the Alexandrinsky Theatre, planned for production as early as 1911 but delayed until just before the Revolution, featured a glossy and demon-like ambiance. The setting in St. Petersburg at midnight included a mourning-lace bed canopy and black-curtained mirrors. Nemirovich-Danchenko only made a few notes about *Masquerade*.

Instead of staging Lermontov's tragedy, Nemirovich-Danchenko chose to produce a satire, *The Death of Pazukhin* by Saltykov-Shchedrin. Shchedrin's style clashed with MAT's Customary authors. Reconciling MAT's affection for the images it created with Shchedrin's biting satire is challenging. The play's heavy rhythm carried a fiery passion, as the fight over Pazukhin's inheritance in the garish city of Krutogorsk exposed universal anxiety over fate. The director appreciated this feature of the play: a satire "in the presence of and in participation with death." Shchedrin's play was a little surprising. Critic Yakov Lvov wrote, "What a huge evolution, what an unexpected leap. The theatre of half-tones turns into a theatre of burning colors, rich life, and intense action." In previous productions, there had always been a flickering effect; everything was perceived in flashes—some saw one thing, while others saw another. However, there would be no more flickering in his productions; their illumination would be bold and unwavering, regardless of what it revealed.

Ideals and Realities Amid Creative and Personal Crises

"It is a given that no one needs art. [...] For the kind of art that MAT serves, the best thing would be to disappear, retire into the background, and relapse into silence until its time comes again." But above this entry, Nemirovich-Danchenko-Danchenko writes: "Is that so? Or maybe art should never stop ringing—that's its beauty!" Nemirovich-Danchenko's life during the war looked like this page of his notebook: a definite statement crossed out and followed by a question with no answer.

It was unimaginably cold in his office, and MAT did not receive firewood according to the norms for private theatres but for universities—it was flattering but still cold. At one meeting, Kachalov said: "If all of Russia has grown dim, why shouldn't the Art Theatre do so as well?" Nemirovich-Danchenko noted what needed to be said at a meeting with the younger actors: the uselessness of "passionate sermons" about corruption and the weakening of the Good. "All the best dies away and is forgotten[6]... In our age, 'virtue must from vice pardon beg.'[7]" The first season's energy was rapidly dwindling. New productions were less frequent—one premiere in 1915–1916, nothing in 1916–1917. MAT was entirely in debt to season ticket holders. They waited patiently enough, however, and refused the offer to get their money back.

In early 1916, MAT finally began two new works. Written on the first page of the rehearsal diary for *The Village of Stepanchikovo*:

Lord, good luck!!!
January 11, 1916.
　　　　　A. Vishnevsky, K. Stanislavsky

Nemirovich-Danchenko wrote to Alexander Blok in Petrograd [formerly St. Petersburg] because MAT wanted to produce his play, *The Rose and the Cross*.[8] Vishnevsky and Moskvin helped Stanislavsky direct *The Village of Stepanchikovo* ("through-action: the longing for and pursuit of utopia, a pure love of life. Hatred for the destroyers of utopia"). Luzhsky helped Nemirovich-Danchenko direct *The Rose and the Cross*. The designer for both productions would be Mstislav Dobuzhinsky.

In the summer of 1917, Nemirovich-Danchenko reflected on some options for MAT's future:

First: Open the season with *The Rose and the Cross*—a new aesthetic standard.
Second: Open the season with a new but second-hand (his term) standard: *The Village of Stepanchikovo*.
Third: Do not open since there is no recognizable aesthetic standard.
Fourth: Postpone the new standard again and open the season according to the standard of the last two years, namely, for the attraction of refugees from neighboring allied countries caught up in the war.

218 *Vladimir Nemirovich-Danchenko and the Moscow Art Theatre*

The season will open with *The Village of Stepanchikovo*, but Stanislavsky will not play his beloved Yegor Rostanev. And Nemirovich-Danchenko will not direct *The Rose and the Cross* either. Stanislavsky did not "give birth" to Rostanev, and this became a sore spot in MAT's collective memory. It was distressing to witness Stanislavsky weeping backstage in his makeup, tears streaming down his cheeks, with the stage already lit and everyone waiting for his signal to open the curtain for the dress rehearsal. Eventually, it was decided that another actor should play the role. Initially, it appeared to be an unfortunate mistake. There was not enough time for an unprepared actor to step into the role. Could they postpone the show for another year for the season ticket holders? In the end, they had to wait because it took longer than anticipated to introduce another actor into the play. Actress Serafima Birman regretted it for a lifetime: "It was just too early for Rostanev to shine in the spotlight." Which was the right decision, we can't say for sure. What do we really know?

We do know that those present had been worried about Stanislavsky's well-being since the beginning of 1917 (Dobuzhinsky and Dikiy believed he was unnecessarily nervous and couldn't have asked for a better Rostanev). Stanislavsky's notes mentioned: "You can delve so deeply into a role, expand your plan, overanalyze, dwell on clichés until you lose all motivation to perform it." We are aware that Nemirovich-Danchenko joined the team as early as February 1917 and, as expected, was supposed to rectify the apparent "disarray," restore order, and bring a comprehensive understanding of the work and its significance. It's almost inevitable for a play's comprehension to falter at some point; sometimes, there's a crushing feeling of leading oneself and the entire production into a dead end. A similar breakdown happened during the rehearsals of the successful production of *An Enemy of the People* and even *Three Sisters*.

Was it a mistake by Nemirovich-Danchenko or was he wrong to accept Stanislavsky's distressed refusal of the role? Did he embarrass him by contrasting his interpretation of the character of Rostanev (which hinted at mockery) with Stanislavsky's developed and cherished portrayal that had now become muddied? We can only speculate. Stanislavsky couldn't bring his work on Rostanev's character to completion, just like Nemirovich-Danchenko couldn't complete his work on *The Rose and the Cross*.

This situation represented a profound clash of two "irreconcilables," the decline of two artistic models, old (*The Village of Stepanchikovo*) and new (*The Rose and the Cross*), neither of which could be sustained any longer. One of Stanislavsky's biographers described his vision of Rostanev as follows: "He envisioned portraying a benevolent manor-house uncle, full of love for and protectiveness of the Good, of a kind not done before at MAT. He aimed to embody the force of good capable of bringing harmony to a war-torn land." Nemirovich-Danchenko had the same impossibly chief hope for *The Rose and Cross* as he expressed in a draft of his letter to Rachmaninoff, the play's composer. He set himself the same task for the production as well. "No wonder someone said that whoever composed the music for Gaetan's song would create a new national anthem."

Fifth and Sixth Life 1914–1919   219

Some artistic works have dedications, and accordingly, Stanislavsky could have dedicated his creation of Rostanev to the memory of Leopold Sulerzhitsky. The death of Sulerzhitsky in 1916 instigated the crisis at hand, a consequence of impossible goals the actor did not want to give up. At Sulerzhitsky's fortieth-day memorial service, Stanislavsky delivered a reading of his memoirs, ending with the poignant words: "Lord, take to yourself the soul of the deceased, our darling, unforgettable, dear Suler because he knew how to love; because in his life, amidst temptation, vulgarity, and bestial self-destruction, he preserved in himself an abiding sense of mercy." Stanislavsky's interpretation of Rostanev sought a "rebirth" born from the feeling of guilt gnawing at a good person when bad things were happening around him, and someone was suffering. Nemirovich-Danchenko also spoke about Sulerzhitsky at the memorial. His notes revealed a beautiful, clear, and elegant line of reasoning. No tears, no affectionate details, just a desire to understand the refined and necessary meaning of a departed life. "A conscience set before truth" is what Sulerzhitsky was all about. "Art reveals ideal truth, showing beauty and life's truth through poets. Life lags behind art, just as truth, adorned in beauty, moves the soul more deeply than a prophet's words." Nemirovich-Danchenko chose his words carefully here and said just what he wanted.

"Never in my long involvement in theatre," said Nemirovich-Danchenko. "have I felt such a pressing need for art to be 'above,' not 'on' or 'under,' but above life." It's not the well-known warmth of humanity (like *The Cricket on the Hearth* or *The Green Ring* in the Second Studio),[9] but the poet's spirituality that should be communicated through the works conceived or endorsed by Nemirovich-Danchenko—like Blok's *The Rose and the Cross* and Rabindranath Tagore's *The King of the Dark Chamber* (planned but not produced).[10] The dogma "beauty will save the world," which Nemirovich-Danchenko now professes, contradicts the incantatory and fortune-telling assurances that the world will be saved by its "simple truths," the warmth of the hearth, and the warmth of the heart. Stanislavsky suffered a defeat of his maximalist utopia, and Nemirovich sustained a loss of his maximalist heaven.

Stanislavsky would never recover from his misfortune; he would never perform a new role again. Nemirovich-Danchenko did not talk about his misfortune but would overcome it in an extraordinary, complicated, and unique next life—fifth or sixth? It was also easier for Nemirovich-Danchenko to recover because the utopia of beauty and its doctrine of salvation were only a temporary, yet reasonable, distraction for him. Such rational diversions poorly nourished the artist in him. There were clear traces of genius in *The Village of Stepanchikovo* and none in *The Rose and the Cross*, merely information from books about the customs of French knights, local moral ideas, housing, and clothing. How this could come to life on stage was uncertain. The rehearsal participants did not discuss it much afterward.

220 *Vladimir Nemirovich-Danchenko and the Moscow Art Theatre*

The utopias of hymn-salvation, beauty-salvation, and the utopia of moral salvation are disconnected from reality. These contradictions frequently culminate in revolution and the subsequent quest for resolutions.

Leadership and Theatre's Role Amid Revolutionary Upheaval

It was the summer of 1917. Nemirovich-Danchenko didn't so much ask questions as list them:

> How will the war unfold? How will our domestic policy unfold? What power will the Kadet Party unite behind?[11] Will there be a Constituent Assembly, and what will it be like?[12] Will the assault against the tsarist dictatorship expand, and to what kind of state?

Everyone knew Nemirovich-Danchenko was a gifted leader and believed he would head a government department someday. Now he was offered the directorship of the former imperial theatres (it was assumed MAT would also become a national theatre). He was summoned to negotiations in Petrograd (formerly St. Petersburg). Besides having leadership talent, he also had a talent for diplomacy, which he considered an essential part of the talent for power. That and a calm acceptance of "people envy power most of all." But he was called upon to manage and lead a revolution at the former imperial theatres. He argued that revolutions only occur when there is an accumulation of latent forces and ideas and an entrenched routine that does not accommodate them. And although it hurt his artistic pride to admit it, there was no gunpowder for a revolutionary explosion in the former imperial theatres. The accumulation of such forces and ideas was negligible there at best. He agreed to accept the offer but eventually turned it down.

In his notebook of this year, he continued to ask himself,

> What role do theatres play in public life? What do we think we are? Soon they will ask us. What will we answer? That we are troubadours, proud of our rags? Where are the feelings needed for such an answer? Or shall we frankly say we are simply artisans of expensive trinkets; our workshop, sad as it may be for our artistic greatness, is the same as that of Faberge and Khlebnikov [jewelers], Abrikosov [pastry chef], Skuryatnikov [retailer of stylish shoes], and Dellos [fashionable tailer]. We work for those who pay us more. Who are we?

In the summer, the tasks of active, focused self-determination, the commitment to "managing, anticipating," and energetically choosing a solution— none of this characterized his inner life. He wrote to Luzhsky: "The only thing clear for us now is that everything is unclear and not worth guessing about. But there's no need to guess; we must be prepared." This

Fifth and Sixth Life 1914–1919   221

principle is the starting point from which he began his new life. He felt calm inside, a kind of high-level curiosity illuminated by readiness for whatever serious situation might occur. He had never been as skillful as he was in those moments when everything was rapidly deteriorating. Now, he was avoiding any unnecessary or meaningless actions. Confusion plagued him during the war, especially when they attempted to remove portraits of German writers from MAT's foyer and when he burdened himself with unnecessary tasks. He mentioned finding solace in the light-hearted and delightful works of vaudeville writer Eugene Labiche and Merezhkovsky's *Joy Will Come* in his writing.[13] Merezhkovsky's play displays philosophical concepts to the audience, prompting them to reflect on their responses and needs. Leonid Andreyev briefly mentioned the play in his letters to Nemirovich-Danchenko, dismissing it with a simple response to a sneeze: "God bless you!"

In Nemirovich-Danchenko's 1917 notebook, a passage from Dostoevsky described a dream where Petrograd's fog lifts, unveiling a decaying city fading away. This dream motif recurs in other works such as Blok's *Retribution* and Alexei Tolstoy's *The Road to Calvary*. Twelve years later, Nemirovich-Danchenko's production *Blockade* depicted a city striving to emerge from the fog.[14] *Blockade* portrays the failed Kronstadt Mutiny of 1921, symbolizing a rebellion against the strictness of the revolution. In this production, fog engulfs ruined houses as a battalion marches diagonally in line non-stop across the stage. After *Blockade*, Nemirovich-Danchenko frequently directed plays explicitly or implicitly linked to the events of 1917. These included *Our Youth* by Vitya Kartashov, based on the novel by Viktor Kean; Gorky's *Yegor Bulychov*; Konstantin Trenyev's *Lyubov Yarovaya*; Nikolai Pogodin's *Earth* and *The Kremlin Chimes*;[15] the operas *North Wind* by Vladimir Kirshon, *Quiet Flows the Don* by Mikhail Sholokhov, and *In the Storm* by Tikhon Khrennikov. He repeatedly says that works like these dealt with "the sincerity of the Revolution," a distinctive phrase. Other artists also found common ground with the October Revolution: its spontaneous rage, justice, power, romance, and optimistic outlooks of the revolution—"There is a sunny land beyond the mountains of grief."[16] Nemirovich-Danchenko connected with the revolution through its seriousness.

In the diaries of the MAT Partnership (dates in o.s.): "1:15 a.m. I was alive on November 3, I. Moskvin." "I was alive on November 3. O. Knipper." "Midnight. The corner of Bolshaya Nikitskaya and Skaryatinsky streets is the heaviest. Shooting on Bolshaya Nikitskaya, Malaya Nikitskaya, and Skaryatinsky Streets. Shooting from heavy guns on Kudrinskaya square. All are healthy and uninjured. Vladimir Ivanovich Nemirovich-Danchenko." On the night of October 26–27, Arkady Gennert passed away. Though not widely beloved, in early 1898, he was among those who donated money "at the disposal of K. S. Alekseev and VL. I. Nemirovich-Danchenko" to

222 *Vladimir Nemirovich-Danchenko and the Moscow Art Theatre*

help them fulfill their task. Gennert was not young and passed away on October 26. Unfortunately, "It's still impossible to bury him! All the roads are under gun fire."

Living in the gap between how others see you "as a sign" and how you see yourself is challenging. For many who were soon to be considered "former persons,"[17] MAT stood as a symbol of what needed to be restored. Young officers Alexander Kolchak and Anton Denikin fell in love with the character of Finochka (Alla Tarasova) from *The Green Ring* and went to the front in the spring of 1917 with that feeling.[18] Memories of Moscow provided warmth in the trenches —the gray-blue corridors, the pink glow of the auditorium's sconces, the kettle on the fire, and Finochka/Tarasova in a checkered dress.

The anti-Bolshevik General Anton Denikin held MAT in high regard. Following their performance in Kharkiv, where an attack by the White Army stranded a group of actors on tour, he spoke with Kachalov, Bersenev,[19] and Knipper. The general was confident that his army would soon reach Moscow, though without a guarantee. Actor Nikolai Podgorny returned to Moscow from the front lines, bringing more news. In a letter to Luzhsky, Nemirovich-Danchenko retold the entire story in excruciating detail and expressed skepticism about the troupe reuniting anytime soon. In his view, it remained uncertain when they might meet again. As a result, he didn't wait for them but proceeded to discuss the Central Theatre Committee and a state subsidy for MAT with Lunacharsky.[20]

Following Mamontov's Raid,[21] where the White Army's cavalry breached the Bolshevik lines on August 30, 1919, the Bolsheviks detained Stanislavsky, Moskvin, Luzhsky's son (also a MAT actor), and others at Nemirovich-Danchenko's apartment while he was away. His own arrest was imminent. By evening, thanks to some connections, Stanislavsky was released. The young Bolshevik stage director, Valentin Smyshlyaev, remarked that it would have been easier if Lunacharsky had been in Moscow at the time. He managed to avoid arrest that day through certain channels and assisted in the negotiations for the release of the others.

For some individuals, MAT symbolized what was lost, evoking a desire to return. For others, it represented the values and aesthetics of the former regime and, therefore, should be discarded along with it. They believed the state should prevent such values and aesthetics from influencing the younger generation. Notably, there were articles in the White Guard press condemning MAT after the Civil War, accusing them of leading to defeat and deception during perilous times. You doomed us to defeat, the press said; you disarmed us in the face of danger. Everything to do with bourgeois life was wrong for you; everyone drowned their disgust for kvass, old-fashioned goose and cabbage, and the world of ordinary life. Little did we anticipate that we would have to defend it one day. Well, you are getting what you requested—horse meat instead of beef on holidays.

Indeed, Stanislavsky had horse meat for dinner on New Year's Day, 1919.

Fifth and Sixth Life 1914–1919 223

Can we say that MAT bravely withstood the challenges of their daily existence? The actors adapted to their circumstances with such humility that it would be a disservice to draw attention to it. Must we discuss nails that wouldn't grow, hair loss, and memory lapses due to malnutrition? These were realities, but the topic was avoided. You won't see any complaints in Nemirovich-Danchenko's documents. MAT actors didn't lose their appetite for goose and cabbage or afternoon naps. However, they grappled with unfavorable conditions, the chaos and limitations of their lives, their adjustment, and subjugation to those challenging circumstances. How often did Nemirovich-Danchenko insist they had to live more simply, in a Spartan manner?

Understanding their appreciation for what the revolution stripped away is challenging yet crucial. When young actors questioned why MAT wasn't producing tragedies, Stanislavsky had a clear response. He didn't just mention their impatience or lack of technique. He explained they were lacking the profound and intense emotions necessary for tragedy, and they had not yet experienced life to the fullest extent. Their gratitude toward the revolution stemmed from the increased intensity of life it brought. While Nemirovich-Danchenko's life was challenging in its everyday aspects, it also had a vibrant and expansive quality. He made a note in his notebook twice: "He who is a little late waits a long time."

It's easy to let circumstances unfold naturally when conditions are favorable and people are enthusiastic. However, lingering thoughts of reform had drained MAT, as the necessary forces and ideas had not yet coalesced. In contemplating the resistance to change in the former imperial theatres and the superficial nature of attempted reforms there, Nemirovich-Danchenko also considered MAT. Although the prevailing atmosphere was not entirely positive, life at MAT's studios was dynamic and filled with talent. Nonetheless, obstacles emerged, such as demanding mutual affection and a selfless dedication to their collective goals. During company meetings, it became increasingly apparent that many at MAT were struggling. The harsh self-assessments and critiques exhausted them.

Newspapers periodically reported that MAT might close voluntarily, leading to mixed reactions until a denial was issued: the theatre was not closing. The uncertainty stemmed from whether Nemirovich-Danchenko desired to save it. He had previously written, "Let them bury us. If we are alive, we will rise again, and if we are dead, good riddance!" The wording seems puzzling, as why mention resurrection if alive? Before the funeral, one needed to ascertain if there was any trace of immortality left.

Notes

1 *Resurrection* (1899) is the last novel written by Leo Tolstoy and was adapted for the stage and produced at MAT in 1930. It is the story of a wealthy aristocrat who serves as a juror and recognizes the defendant as a woman he wronged years ago. He seeks to redeem himself by helping her and working for social justice.

224 *Vladimir Nemirovich-Danchenko and the Moscow Art Theatre*

2 Stanislavsky, Konstantin, and Jean Benedetti. *My Life in Art*. (Routledge, 2008), 3. The translation has been slightly altered.
3 Possible reference to "My steps have held to your paths; my feet have not stumbled." Psalms 17:5.
4 *Autumn Violins* (1915) is a play by Ilya Surguchev (1881–1956) that tells the story of a husband who receives an anonymous letter accusing his wife of having an affair with his business partner. His wife reveals that the partner is in love with their step-daughter, which initially relieves the husband. However, he later discovers that the letter was correct and his wife had lied to him.
5 *Masquerade* (1835) is a play about a young man who suspects his wife of infidelity and becomes increasingly obsessed with discovering the truth. His sanity begins to unravel as he delves deeper into the mystery, and he ends up murdering his wife.
6 Attributed to Marcus Aurelius, *Meditations*. 7.6.
7 *Hamlet*, III.4.2557.
8 *The Rose and the Cross* (1906) is a symbolist play by Alexander Blok about a young man who becomes involved with a secret society and learns about the dualistic nature of the world, but ultimately becomes caught up in a web of intrigue and deception.
9 *The Green Ring* (1914) is a play by Zinaida Gippius (1869–1945), poet, playwright, novelist, editor, and religious thinker, one of the prominent figures in Russian symbolism. Finochka, a troubled teenager caught in familial turmoil, finds solace in an idealistic youth group, The Green Ring, whose pragmatic solution to her struggles—a marriage of convenience with her father's disillusioned flat mate—forces them all to confront the tension between idealism and practicality.
10 *The King of the Dark Chamber* (1910) is a symbolist play by Rabindranath Tagore (1861–1941), poet, writer, composer, philosopher, and painter. The story revolves around a mysterious, unseen king who rules his kingdom from a dark chamber.
11 Kadet Party (Konstitutsionno-Demokraticheskaya Partiya) was a Russian political party advocating a radical change in Russian government toward a constitutional monarchy.
12 Constituent Assembly. Deliberating body established as a result of October Revolution of 1917 to form a new constitution after the overthrow of the Russian Provisional Government.
13 Dmitry Merezhkovsky (1866–1941) was a novelist, poet, political thinker, literary critic, and co-founder of the Symbolist movement. In *Joy Will Come* (1916) the protagonist grapples with profound suffering and existential dilemmas, embarking on a spiritual journey that underscores the transformative power of faith, hope, and divine grace in the quest for ultimate joy and redemption.
14 *Blockade* (1929) is a play by symbolist poet Vyacheslav Ivanov (1866–1949). The play is set in a besieged city, symbolizing humanity's existential struggle against isolating and overwhelming forces. Archetypal characters reflect facets of the human spirit, intellect, and emotion, exploring profound philosophical themes through their interactions and conflicts.
15 *The Kremlin Chimes* (1941) is the second of a trilogy by playwright Nikolai Pogodin (1900–1960) about Lenin's role in the early stages and founding of the Russian state. Stalin's role was written out after 1955.
16 From *Left March* (1919), a poem by Vladimir Mayakovsky.
17 "Former persons" were those who lost their social status after the revolution, including members of the aristocracy, imperial military, bureaucracy, clergy, etc.
18 Anton Denikin was a Lieutenant General in the Imperial Russian Army and later served as the second Supreme Leader of Russia during the Russian Civil War of 1917–1922.

Fifth and Sixth Life 1914–1919   225

19 Ivan Bersenev (1889–1951) actor and director associated with MAT, MAT II, and later head of the Lenin Komsomol Theatre.
20 Central Theatre Committee. Group responsible for subordinating the theatres to the Bolshevik ideology and for giving them "indications of a repertory character to link them with the popular masses and their socialistic ideal."
21 A surprise attack by the White Army's cavalry, commanded by General Konstantin Mamontov, which seriously weakened the rear of the Soviet southern front.

11 Chapter from another Book 1919–1943 (The Soviet Years)

Prologue

The following letters, papers, and miscellaneous notes spanning the final decades of Nemirovich-Danchenko's productions are not all in his specific archives. I compiled them from other MAT archives for "convenient presentation." Although perhaps that wasn't the sole reason....[1]

Initially, I intended to write a book different from what you are reading now. My initial approach is quite well known. The author, myself, would present herself as the editor of a manuscript found in Nemirovich-Danchenko's archives. The story would go like this: within Nemirovich-Danchenko's collection, I discovered a series of letters, holiday cards, notes, condolences, and greetings signed by someone with the last name "Lapshin." According to the letters, this fictional "Lapshin" had been part of the MAT troupe for a while. Thus, I would have expected to find information about him in the museum's card files. "Peter Lapshin," naturally, does not exist. He was an unnecessary literary device that I eventually abandoned. I realized that Nemirovich-Danchenko's character was not suitable for experimenting with subjective narrative techniques, even minor ones. This was particularly evident considering the abundance of actual materials already present in the museum, from which I gathered most of the information for this biography as presented in the style of earlier chapters.

Inna Solovyova

Musical Theatre Innovations

Peter Lapshin's First Letter (1919–1924)
Dear Vladimir Ivanovich,[2]
Isn't it remarkable to be sending letters to Carlsbad again after all this time? It's interesting that the town is now part of the Republic of Czechoslovakia instead of Austria-Hungary, and you're showing up there with a USSR passport, not from the Russian Empire.[3]

I still remember your work at what others call your Comic Opera or Music Studio.[4] (I like to call it the Nemirovich-Danchenko Musical Art Theatre — long title, I know!)

DOI: 10.4324/9781003486282-11

Chapter from another Book 1919–1943 (The Soviet Years) 227

I wasn't jealous of your shows with the Bolshoi Theatre, your rehearsals of *The Snow Maiden,* or your plans to team up with their choreographer on staging Nikolai Tcherepnin's ballet *The Mask of the Red Death.* Personally, I thought the Bolshoi Theatre's stage was way too big. Elena Konstantinovna seemed a bit too pushy and self-centered while trying to mesh your ideas with hers (talking about the Bolshoi stage, not her as the former director of the Imperial Theatres! Oops, that was clumsy). What more could you have achieved at the Bolshoi Theatre apart from a slight refresh from the usual stuff? I bet you're keeping busy with other wonderful projects. I was planning to write to you after your production of Lecoq's comic opera, *Madame Angot's Daughter,*[5] but I finally gathered the courage to send my congrats.

Even though I'm not that far from Moscow out here in Borisoglebsk, I tend to lag behind sometimes, flipping through theatre magazines now and then. Recently, I was told to check out the April 1921 issue of *Theatre Herald,* and I was shocked that I'd missed it, feeling bad about being behind a few years.[6] I've heard about Meyerhold's current opinions and his not-so-great feelings towards you, his theatre "father" (sounds like fodder for Freud's theories!), but I don't think it's a good idea for a director-artist to disrespect a colleague in public, no matter what. I wonder if Meyerhold thought you were challenging the authorities and doing counterrevolutionary stuff or if he just wanted to disrespect the "trailblazers." He sure picked the perfect time to share his thoughts. With everything happening in April 1921, any accusation of a "counterrevolution on the Soviet stage" would have been a big deal. It all looks like a giant conspiracy: the Kronstadt mutiny, Alexander Antonov's rebellion,[7] and *Madame Angot's Daughter's* show in Moscow (funny that Meyerhold didn't label you with "unfettered market forces" too!). Fortunately, as far as I know, you weren't condemned by the authorities, and the commotion didn't harm the MAT. Right, dear Vladimir Ivanovich?

After I saw *Lysistrata,* I meant to write to you but never got around to it.[8] Pavel Markov put it beautifully, saying,

> It's been ages since we saw such a lively and monumental performance at the theatre. It was bold, captivating, sharp, and uninhibited, sometimes cynical, sometimes calm. The real star was the crowd itself, stripped of unnecessary details and decorations. Nemirovich-Danchenko's handling of the crowd stole the show.[9]

Absolutely! But, I agree with the reviewer's point about the translation and the clichéd writing in the libretto. The only good thing was that they didn't overshadow your work too much.

Out of all your musical theatre pieces, I hold *Carmencita and the Soldier* closest to my heart.[10] Maybe it's because of my unwavering admiration for you, who I once called "the tragic poet" in a respectful way. Even though you weren't a fan of that title, the sentiment still holds true.

Why are they accusing you of "distorting" Bizet? You didn't mess with the lyrics or the music! The heart of the opera, as the audience knows it, remains intact, perfectly stageable just like before—"in its original form." One can see where they're coming from, but after seeing your version, how can they accept anything less?

I don't know much about opera history; has anyone experimented like this before you? Has any production ever separated the chorus so distinctly from the main action? How did you portray "passion without communication" as the chorus watches the drama below? Your chorus doesn't have that ancient sage feeling; instead, it feels primal, echoing back to ancient Iberian roots or sometimes more current. Your idea about "The narrative unfolding in a space where bystanders witness the turmoil but stay inactive," is clever. They're totally absorbed, leaning in with curiosity, aware but clueless about what's to come. Everything's set, but nothing's certain. In one of our chats, you brought up Adele Borghi's performance, saying she's the best *Carmen* you've ever seen. You pointed out how well she captured a woman's power over a man. But, after watching *Carmencita and the Soldier*, it seemed like the director disapproved of the soldier's stubborn honor, his refusal to give in, and his efforts to win over Carmencita. Do you think José's actions are off-track? The quiet Michaela is ignored, and maybe that's fair. Still, is the idea of home, country, family, and loyalty—opposing Carmencita (whom the show seems to pit against these values)—actually fragile and unworthy of respect? I'm finding it hard to understand your perspective.

I might not fully get it, but I won't argue with it. I appreciate how José openly declares his love for Carmencita when he's upset.

Regarding my upcoming trip to Moscow, only time will tell.

Artistic Vision Versus Cultural and Political Changes, Alongside Experiences in Hollywood[11]

Nemirovich-Danchenko's ideological nature emerged during the Revolution, surprising many. Among Russian artists on this path, Nemirovich-Danchenko was perhaps the least inclined to "justify the Revolution," viewing it through the complex moral and ethical perspectives of the intelligentsia. He did not perceive the Revolution as an inevitable fate that warranted acceptance, setting new demands, or presenting tragic dilemmas. He did not view himself as burdened or needing validation within the Revolution, nor did he refer to the October Revolution as "My Revolution." While it was not his Revolution, he was aligned with its objectives.

Some individuals identified with the Revolution based on facts or emotions, while others needed a tangible encounter to internalize the Revolution's stark reality, symbolized by brief yet impactful interactions. For instance, Evgeny Vakhtangov witnessed a cheerful worker repairing wires damaged by shelling outside his window in November. Similarly, Seraphima Birman was guided by a soldier under gunfire to the First Studio's entrance over snow-covered

Chapter from another Book 1919–1943 (The Soviet Years)   229

cobblestones, instilling courage. While it's natural to perceive such instances symbolically, the interpretation's significance can be subjective. For some, the aftermath of shelling on St. Basil's Cathedral embodied the Revolution, while others found symbolism in mundane objects like dirty toilets, refining everything into symbols.

Nemirovich-Danchenko did not emphasize symbolic events or armed guides' kindness but approached the Revolution with solemnity, acknowledging personal growth and ideological alignment. Reflecting on the past five years, Nemirovich-Danchenko noted a newfound confidence and resilience facilitated by the Revolution, allowing him to overcome everyday conservatism and align with his true self.

In a letter to Sumbatov-Yuzhin in 1926, Nemirovich-Danchenko carefully articulated that the Revolution did not shape his ideological beliefs but rather reinforced his innate ideological inclination, returning him to his core values. His ideological character fostered a genuine connection with individuals from the Communist Party, shaping him into an artist dedicated to the Party's ideals. There seemed to be no obstacles in this rapprochement at first. Over the years, however, Nemirovich-Danchenko was often irritated by the blunt cautiousness of subordinate officials who were "more left-oriented" and vigilant than even Anatoly Lunacharsky, the People's Commissar of Enlightenment. It's important to note "over the years" because the severity of the General Repertory Committee in the 1920s did not directly correspond to the rigidity of the senior officials' positions. MAT did not face the hasty and inept interventions they had to fend off during the Civil War (1917–1923). Nevertheless, on New Year's Day 1924, when asked whether they would allow the Second Studio to complete its work on *The Rose and the Cross*, he was told, "Expect the worst." At that point, Vladimir Ivanovich wrote that the General Repertory Committee disapproved when they found a play counterrevolutionary, not sufficiently Soviet, contained kings (like in Ostrovsky's *The Snow Maiden*) or power (like in Ostrovsky's *Dream on the Volga*), a beautiful past, a church (as in Turgenev's *The Home of the Gentry*), or anything else they deemed unsuitable. The committee also disapproved with the same severity of any "bureaucratic complications," which the Soviet government had created and already condemned. This mindset stems from distrust. "I have always been a determined enemy of policymaking like this. Either a person is suitable, or they are not. If suitable, they should be allowed to make mistakes rather than be restricted at every turn."

But this was not about him. He did not feel bound hand and foot. "Communist Party people" genuinely trusted him. For example, he was permitted to undertake bold plans to bring back part of MAT's troupe, which had toured Europe and the United States for two years (1922–1924).

Nemirovich-Danchenko stuck to the term "part of the troupe." If we assume the entire MAT was on tour, what role did he play in Moscow during those two years? Was he a company clerk? Did he manage their Moscow apartments while they were away? At various European theatre festivals he

230 *Vladimir Nemirovich-Danchenko and the Moscow Art Theatre*

attended, he received greetings "from MAT in America." The first time this happened, he was taken aback: "I wanted to leave the festival right then, in my tailcoat and white tie. I was preparing a speech 'from MAT' myself, from those who left, those who stayed in Moscow, and the Studios as a whole."

As the MAT was returning, what did that signify? Would everything go back to how it was before? The previous repertoire? The old problems? The "old-timers" accused Nemirovich-Danchenko, the oldest among them, of being too Revolutionary in his attitude toward their celebrated past. They claimed he had a sense of Revolutionary snobbism. While Nemirovich-Danchenko denied this accusation, he expressed in a letter to Kachalov that the Revolution had crucially propelled them out of a creative impasse they were all stuck in. He believed he had a clearer view of these deadlocks compared to the others. Confident in his abilities to guide MAT out of its stalemate, Nemirovich-Danchenko was adamant about not burdening the theatre with outdated productions. He revamped the repertoire by adding *The Death of Pazukhin* and *The Inspector General* (1921 staging featuring Michael Chekhov as Khlestakov) as they aligned more with his vision. He considered *Tsar Fyodor* and *Enemy of the People* worth exploring with contemporary updates. He was enthusiastic about this task, as he felt more invigorated and dynamic now.

Nemirovich-Danchenko reflected on the posters of MAT and The Society of Art and Literature, embracing the idea of evolving past the previous artistic standards. He aimed to lead the theatre toward newer and grander horizons rather than dwelling on past achievements. He emphasized the importance of gaining trust and commitment for the long term, akin to Lenin's ideals.

His ambitious goal was to revolutionize the production of Russian tragedy and possibly delegate the task to the Musical Studio for Mussorgsky's opera *Boris Godunov*. He envisioned a similar modernization for Ostrovsky's works and Russian comedies, particularly *The Ardent Heart*.[12] Although faced with setbacks in productions like *Pugachev's Rebellion*,[13] he acknowledged the need for internal coherence and unity of spirit in his work.

Nemirovich-Danchenko was unfazed by the challenges, emphasizing the importance of maintaining a cohesive artistic vision. He recognized that perfection was a continuous pursuit that required focusing on foundational aspects. He urged for consistency and unity in spirit in upcoming productions such as *Prometheus* and *The Ardent Heart*.

With a critical eye toward the traditions of the past, Nemirovich-Danchenko distanced himself from the outdated theatrical practices from his previous experiences. He reminisced about a recent evening at the jubilee of a renowned actress from the Maly Theatre, where he found the performances lacking innovation, akin to aimless wandering in a dark cemetery. *The Ladies' Battle* by Scribe is also instructive when observing how convinced the actors from the Maly Theatre were that their art was timeless. A cemetery is cool in the evening with jasmine and nightingales, making it a lovely place for a stroll.

Chapter from another Book 1919–1943 (The Soviet Years) 231

During his time in Hollywood (1926–1928), they wrote to him, stating that the old repertoire perfectly justified itself. They mentioned that famous guests admired *Uncle Vanya* and *Woe from Wit*. In response, he scornfully rebuked them, questioning when MAT started considering the opinions of famous guests. He suggested that if there was a need to justify the presence of these so-called "rags" in the repertoire, it was better to act them out simply. He noted that famous guests typically praised what the general audience already loves, contrasting it with what the leaders of MAT no longer appreciated.

Why was he even in Hollywood? What was the allure of this sky where the moon appears upside down and the Big Dipper stands upright and spins?

A newspaper reported that Nemirovich-Danchenko, as an emigre, was ineligible for the state title of People's Artist. An accurate report would have noted that the government officially sanctioned his leave of absence and contract with an American film company. If there must be gossip, then it should be about the possibility of Nemirovich-Danchenko not returning to MAT after Hollywood, but rather going to Goskino [the State Cinema]. At least that has some truth to it.

In addition to the letter to Lunacharsky discussing the upside-down moon, there was also a reflection on the Americans' first rule, "Keep smiling." It appears to be the only thing he could do in Hollywood, a principle he seemed to embrace: "Keep smiling."

His letters reflect the life of a man about town: "We are leaving Carlsbad on the 15th and heading directly to Paris, then to the Mediterranean." In August, he'll be on the border with Switzerland in Divonne-les-Bains, followed by a visit to Paris as the guest of Nikita Baliev from the 1st to the 8th. Then, on to the Majestic, where it seems they will be in New York, briefly. He asks to subscribe to *Izvestia* for him.

In September, they find themselves in New York at the Hotel Ansonia, then travel by train to Los Angeles for four days on the famous cross-continental journey.

As of September 25th, they reached Hollywood, where the mayor presented him with the key to the city. Ekaterina, his wife, was well and served as a beautiful translator. The place was delightful, with

no New York skyscrapers, traffic noise, subways, or elevators—a lovely villa awaited him, complete with cypresses, palm trees, terraces, and a garage. We've been here for six weeks, enjoying a sparkling summer full of foliage and warmth, with just one night of rain. Though we are 20 miles away from the ocean (imagine, right by the Pacific Ocean!), our group recently visited the foggy, cold, and windy shores. While they were out, I stayed back at home on the terrace, listening to a California nightingale singing nearby.

The silence at night felt reminiscent of a Russian village.

Keep Smiling!

232 *Vladimir Nemirovich-Danchenko and the Moscow Art Theatre*

He did not need lessons; he had carried this principle with him from Tiflis fifty years ago. Yet, he also strongly believed that failure was shameful, and for that reason, life under the serene California Nightingale turned out to be worse than failure; it felt meaningless. Despite his efforts to remain constantly cheerful and correct, one day, he exploded. His secretary, Olga Bokshanskaya, complained that he seldom wrote about himself. He erupted, questioning whether she, with her years of acquaintance, did not realize that his silence spoke volumes about his unbearable life.

American film historians could delve into the archives of Douglas Fairbanks, Mary Pickford, Lillian Gish, John Barrymore, Charles Chaplin, Greta Garbo, Conrad Veidt, and the businesspeople of the company (with whom Nemirovich-Danchenko interacted). Perhaps yet-to-be-discovered documents could shed light on why they had rented a house with verandas for him, where, day after day, a theatre genius who had signed a contract with "UA" (United Artists) penned scripts for films that never came to fruition.

From an external viewpoint, it was hard to decipher Hollywood's perceptions of him. Was he seen as a director, a screenwriter, or as an intellectual import from Europe, akin to castles transported stone by stone—a source of fascination for the millionaires of that era?

Amidst a multitude of projects and manuscripts, there was a list of Chekhov's stories ripe for film adaptations, scenarios for plays by Ostrovsky, *Eugene Onegin*, *Carmen*, and Dostoevsky's *The Gambler*, as well as scripts for unique film concepts. Additionally, there were script outlines tailored for Chaplin and Mary Pickford, and screenplay adaptations for literary works by Byron, Jacob Wasserman, and Fyodor Sologub, along with works inspired by historical figures like Pugachev and Cleopatra. There were also scripts crafted to feature legendary stars like Lillian Gish and a scenario designed for twin sisters. And the list went on. When the staff member assigned to help Nemirovich-Danchenko asked his superiors what to do until they settled the shooting schedule, they replied, "Clean Mr. Danchenko's boots." This reply was perhaps intended as flattering; otherwise, they might have said something like, "Sweep away the dust from Mr. Danchenko."

Nemirovich-Danchenko found himself intrigued by the shifting, mysterious secrets of an unfamiliar art; the style and myth of Conrad Veidt captivated him,[14] as did the legends of Chaplin and Lillian Gish. However, he ultimately wasn't interested in theorizing about which laws of commerce or mythology were necessary for Catherine the Great to love Pugachev in prison or for Anna Karenina to marry Vronsky. He presumed that behind such requests lay merely the audacity of the uneducated.

If Olga Bokshanskaya wanted to know, here it is. He lay awake at night, sifting through "fragments, broken pieces of something precious in which were invested last energies and, maybe, fnal dreams." His days dragged on without meaning. The friends of his life didn't even realize what they had done. He felt compelled to explain: "You have killed my plans in mid-flight. You have slaughtered my dreams."

Chapter from another Book 1919–1943 (The Soviet Years)   233

His letters seemed to offend his friends in Moscow. "A man is beaten, he screams, and those doing the beating are offended—'why is he screaming?' 'You want me to write more about myself.'" "Maybe a meeting to put 'everything on the table' would help to remove the pain from my heart... I don't know."

Counting on time to smooth everything out was futile. "Something must be done; something effective would also help to eliminate or replace these terrible memories."

Abstaining from further dramatic explanations, Nemirovich-Danchenko praised Valentin Kataev's novel, *The Embezzlers*,[15] as "one of the most remarkable works in recent times." He wondered what was happening at the Second MAT.[16] "How is *Eugene the Adventurer*? Alexey Faiko's first play, *Lake Liul*, at Meyerhold's Theatre of the Revolution?" "What about Ivan Bersenev?[17] "I imagine he is jealous of the young Second Moscow Art Theatre's success. I should probably write a letter to them (MAT's younger actors)." "Sakhnovsky is directing at MAT now.[18] That's quite an event!" "Smyshlyaev should have listened to me and taken Rabinovich as the designer for *Prometheus*. He has an amazing feeling for the new tragedy." "Did *The Death of Ivan the Terrible* go to the Second MAT?"

The failure of *Prometheus* wasn't even its most offensive outcome, though Nemirovich-Danchenko acknowledged it was a colossal failure. Still, its consequence was a distrust of further new steps. "And again, they will avoid all the roads that might lead to a way out."

How was *The Marriage of Figaro*?

Don't let Beaumarchais—the harbinger of the French Revolution, etc.—frighten the performers or make them too serious. The meaning and genre are only important for the directors. As for the performers, 'the words must become their own, and tempo, tempo, tempo!'

The Days of the Turbins has withstood all the persecution that you [Stanislavsky] are describing. There is something valuable and something malevolent in it. This whole story is a win for Lunacharsky and those who supported the play, defending a freer approach to the repertoire.

Nemirovich could say that he foresaw this turn of events: "I feel you [Stanislavsky] have a bias to the right, crossing the line all the time. Not just you and all of us at MAT, but also Moscow. We'll pay for it later, and it will hurt."

Olga Bokshanskaya wrote about his "gift of forgiveness." Did they admit guilt and ask for his forgiveness for their unkind remarks?

"The work here is very dull, and I miss MAT, its people, and even the Russian audience greatly, often unbearably."

...

On September 17, 1927, a telegram arrived from Nice. Alexander Sumbatov-Yuzhin had died unexpectedly. Vladimir Ivanovich's letters to him must be somewhere; both belonged to a generation that valued letters.

234   *Vladimir Nemirovich-Danchenko and the Moscow Art Theatre*

It was to Sumbatov-Yuzhin that Nemirovich wrote: "Fame depends on a thousand details." Luck plays a part. Both of them were lucky more than anything else. They discussed an actor they both knew who was talented, yet forgotten.

Around this time, he also sent a telegram to Stanislavsky: "I extend my hand to you for complete reconciliation and the full resolution of all our grievances." Stanislavsky replied: "You have made me infinitely happy. I firmly shake your offered hand for complete reconciliation, the resolution of all our grievances, and a full reunification as before. Live together, die together. I look forward to seeing you very much."

The "old-timers" at MAT also cabled him in America: "We are waiting for you, dear Vladimir Ivanovich." At the Moscow train station welcome on January 22, 1928, Nemirovich said: "I feel like I did in 1898!"

Influence, Theatre Ideology, and Adaptation to Public and Political Demands

Destiny allowed him to begin another one of his multiple lives. Once again, there was a lengthy introductory period and many difficulties, delays, and explorations of capabilities and possibilities. Teaching occurred once more. As usual, Nemirovich-Danchenko spent long hours at the theatre, from ten to seven, driven by his desire to delve into the details, understand every aspect thoroughly, and oversee the "monarchical peace" his colleagues sought to maintain around Stanislavsky. Once more, he contributed to other people's work without receiving credit, sometimes to projects that would remain unproduced. Once more, he possessed knowledge of stage blocking, character relationships, and stage business. He could write a letter to Boris Pasternak discussing his interpretation of Shakespeare just as easily as he could draft a business letter or remind the receptionist by phone to watch for important guests in the audience,[19] whom the viewers should acknowledge with applause. The structure of life remained constant, yet life itself felt new and entirely different once more. However, we have already covered everything that can be said on this subject (Figure 11.1).

In a literary portrait painted by Pavel Markov, Nemirovich-Danchenko and his "algorithm," a term commonly used today, are described, along with his internal formula and the set of his internal laws, as unveiled in the performances of the new [Soviet] era.[20] There is a concise portrayal of these performances. Only one element is required to finalize the portrait: Vitaly Vilenkin's account of Nemirovich-Danchenko's creative evolution and how these internal laws yielded results.[21]

Nemirovich-Danchenko's creativity in this new phase lacked the internal resonances that had previously allowed him to perceive his productions and make subtle subjective adjustments. His shows now crash into us rather than penetrating the soul to change its composition. They were not designed for free

Chapter from another Book 1919–1943 (The Soviet Years) 235

Figure 11.1 Vladimir Nemirovich-Danchenko on vacation with Art Theatre personnel. By permission of the Moscow Art Academic Theatre.

exploration, let alone free interpretation. His messages were resolute, exuding self-assurance. Nemirovich-Danchenko even critiqued the director collaborating with him on Konstantin Trenyev's *Lyubov Yarovaya*,[22] who had outlined his concept in the newspaper, suggesting that viewers would soon compare it with others and form their opinions on MAT's approach. Nemirovich-Danchenko disagreed: "We must view our approach as the only correct one. That's why the notion of 'time will tell if we were right' is unacceptable. Any doubts must be resolved from the outset." His firm belief in "the only correct approach" gave his productions an air of authority. They were carefully crafted in this way and presented to everyone in this exclusive manner. Anyone who remembers the MAT stage adaptation of Tolstoy's *Resurrection* would point out the clarity of its scenic divisions: the court, the prison, the village, St. Petersburg, and the "stage." The clarity of each division is highlighted, emphasizing the power of an observing gaze that sees with both clarity and detachment. MAT embraced and upheld this perspective, giving it integrity and applying it to Tolstoy's profound ideas, examining spiritual pursuits with the same detachment as everyday routines like brushing one's teeth.

The intentional disconnect in the performance served a specific purpose. MAT examines and evaluates everything happening "there" from its vantage point "here." In Gorky's *Enemies*, for example,[23] Nemirovich-Danchenko expresses even more strongly that the workers' animosity was justified, and

236 *Vladimir Nemirovich-Danchenko and the Moscow Art Theatre*

settling scores was unavoidable. MAT conducted this assessment by placing itself "here" above what was taking place "there." "There," the factory owner's niece, Mariette, enjoys *petits fours* in the living room. "There," on the terrace furnished with wicker furniture reminiscent of an aristocrat's estate.

"There," with lilacs displayed in a crystal vase and fresh milk poured from a pitcher every morning. Nemirovich-Danchenko wasn't hesitant to utilize this contrasting technique again: the privileged sympathize with the hungry while indulging in sweets. Khmelev later reminded Nemirovich-Danchenko about a rehearsal with Knipper-Chekhova: "It's just like being here, rehearsing in this very foyer, when you showed her the scene at the table with a knife and fork in *Enemies*, and she promptly developed a characterization from that."

Those who recall the production of *Enemies* will remember the dull red and green scenery, the impenetrable fence dividing a soot-covered factory and a two-story art nouveau house glaring at each other. The designer cleverly connected the interior lines of MAT as if the same architect constructed factory-owner Bardin's residence. The director only proceeded with the set design after establishing this fence that divided everything in two. Nemirovich-Danchenko verbalized the central point of *Enemies*: "On one side, the working class; on the other, landowners, manufacturers, exploiters." The most bitter among them stood on the right: Mikhail Skrobotov, his business partner Bardin with his wife, the captain, the officer, and more. On the left were the workers, including Sintsov. The palpable hostilities between the two factions had to captivate all those involved in the performance.

"Each actor seeks a characterization, a psycho-physical representation of their role. While their creativity can be unrestricted, when choosing adaptations, stage movements, and establishing connections with others, the fundamental source should be the hostility between the two classes." When the main focus was on 'enemies as such,' the approach had to align accordingly. The play's unique structure emerged as the director addressed the theme of the title-subject by channeling everything through the psychophysiology of the actor. *Enemies* was a flawless embodiment of the "theatre of the living person."

Nemirovich-Danchenko occasionally conveyed his ideas through drawings. It's possible to visualize how he crafted his exceptional performances in the 1930s. A radiant beam of light emanated from a single point (the play's subject), passing through the psycho-physical essence of the actors—dwelling within them with all their emotional and artistic richness, drawing out delight from this abundance — before converging into another luminous beam that targeted one and only one point.

Surprisingly, the director's unwavering commitment to ideological clarity on stage contrasted with the numerous elderly ladies who tearfully expressed gratitude to Nemirovich-Danchenko, believing they would have been utterly lost without him. For instance, he often sent financial assistance to a woman

Chapter from another Book 1919–1943 (The Soviet Years) 237

in a remote village in Kazakhstan, a kind soul who wrote, "Dearest Vladimir Ivanovich, forgive my helplessness!" Facing harsh weather conditions and relying on the school janitor for meals, she deeply appreciated Nemirovich-Danchenko's caring gestures.

Zinaida Grigorievna, the widow of MAT benefactor Savva Morozov, received her pension from a specific MAT fund. When the fund was dissolved by the state, Stanislavsky and Nemirovich-Danchenko personally supported her financially while maintaining the facade of the fund's existence. Regular monetary assistance came through his secretary, Olga Bokshanskaya. These women were not solely noted for their social status. Among Nemirovich-Danchenko's beneficiaries was an elderly peasant woman whom he accommodated in a home for the disabled, which she fondly referred to as "shelter for the weak." In a poignant letter, she wrote,

> My dear and esteemed Vladimir Ivanovich! Congratulations on your recent recognition; meanwhile, I am nearing the end of my days. My health is failing. I extend my heartfelt wishes for your well-being and health. Please pardon your former servant Agrafina. Accept my blessings in your old age. May you find joy in all your charitable acts.

While such narratives are often overlooked, a fitting title could be inspired by a book published posthumously about Stanislavsky's father: *S.V. Alekseev and His Acts of Kindness*. Throughout his life, Nemirovich-Danchenko performed numerous acts of kindness, with increased opportunities to do so during the 1930s. People often sought his generosity. For example, an aspiring writer named Ivan Klimentyevich once lamented, "I am facing yet another setback in my life," prompting Nemirovich-Danchenko to discreetly send him a hundred rubles. There were appeals to his influence: the heartfelt pleas of an elderly woman from St. Petersburg, a timeless melodrama: an older actress is troubled by a grandson: cried, "Vladimir Ivanovich, my dear, I was indeed on the Grand Duke's payroll, but I swear to you, my grandson had nothing to do with it!"

It was remarkable how much he could achieve as a mediator. The success of Nemirovich-Danchenko's persuasiveness stemmed from his prestige and the fact that he was someone on whom so much depended. Intervening for someone he knew before someone else he also knew, Nemirovich-Danchenko believed both individuals were human beings. The trouble of the former was simply a misunderstanding that the latter would want to fix immediately. Thus, assurance was secured.

The authority of MAT and its entire direction was expanding. "Since there is no Meyerhold on the list of People's Artists of the Soviet Union—I take this to mean this announces our direction." (From a letter of September 1936.) It would be interesting to know what socio-political factors made *Anna Karenina* a favorite play in 1937, how *Cricket on the Hearth* became a favorite in 1915, and *The Green Ring* in 1917.

238 *Vladimir Nemirovich-Danchenko and the Moscow Art Theatre*

It was impossible to get tickets to a MAT play; hence, Nemirovich-Danchenko was inundated with ticket requests.

> ...You sat with your friends, Prof. Rossolimo, Prof. Gubarev, and Dr. Gubin, and you had just graduated from the Mathematics Department of Moscow University. Your friends are all dead, and you and I are alive. For these two reasons, I ask you to allow me the opportunity to see *Anna Karenina* and give me two tickets for any day. Hello to your wife. Sincerely respectful and devoted....

Signed, Professor So and So. Nemirovich-Danchenko placed question marks in the margins. He wrote, "There is no point in recalling such distant memories. We met many more times later. But it would be good to give him tickets."

Tickets were nice to give, but letters received were even more pleasant—a telegram from winter residents who were grateful for the radio broadcast of a play. After collective listening to the same broadcast in factories, messages contained a whole packet of them. There are greetings on anniversary days. A courageous spectator announced "the gratitude of the ranks" to Nemirovich-Danchenko, MAT's founder, and the entire team. "Warm greetings from the far eastern border! I wish you all good health and further creative strength for the benefit of the working people." "Work in peace! Our Soviet Union, with its far eastern borders, is strongly protected, and the key is in the safe hands of happy Soviet border guards." "Japanese samurai will never venture into the sacred Soviet Far East; they have recently experienced our power and strength at Khasan."

In July 1939, Nemirovich-Danchenko spent two weeks in Paris before moving to Evian for the rest of his vacation. Despite the war panic in Parisian newspapers, he decided to extend his stay in Evian for its pleasant weather. It was noted that he would attend the Agricultural Exhibition in Moscow upon his return in August.

Deep Emotion and Life's Mystery in *Three Sisters*

From Peter Lapshin's Notes (1930–1940).

I'm feeling just like I did back in the day before the premiere of *Three Sisters* when I was a kid. We got ready seriously, went through the play, and studied all the available material.

Vladimir Ivanovich's rehearsals for the new take on *Three Sisters* are starting soon. It's exciting to see what we'll get!

It's somewhat sad how my memory picks up random bits and pieces and piles them up. I want to remember something, even though I wouldn't trust my own words if I didn't write them down immediately after witnessing or hearing something.

How am I going to recall what Vladimir Ivanovich said at Stanislavsky's funeral? I only remember one of my notes: "I don't know Stanislavsky's

Chapter from another Book 1919–1943 (The Soviet Years) 239

deepest thoughts." Back then, you didn't ask, and you didn't know. You can't ask someone who's passed away, let alone someone immortal. I do recall the word "immortality." They said Vladimir Ivanovich went to Novodevichy Cemetery straight from the train station; he heard of Konstantin Sergeyevich's death while on a train at Negoreloe Station in Belarus.

Vladimir Ivanovich was standing, and I was observing his hands. The hands looked old and purple, even though it was warm in August.

Before he died, Konstantin Sergeyevich wondered: "Who's going to look after Nemirovich-Danchenko now? He's like a lone sailor now. Maybe he's unwell? Does he have enough money?"

Just as I always suspected: they were fond of each other. But still, "It's quite a puzzle."

Yet there are some who insist on whispering that one would have been happy to throttle the other and argue even more stubbornly that they're likeminded rivals, and that pigeons and doves never squabble; they live peacefully side by side (Figure 11.2).

I think there's some truth to my hunch. Why should we believe there were no disagreements between them except those about God? We love a pair of linked names, and here was a perfect example of minds in sync, flawless camaraderie, and continuity if one outlived the other. Acknowledging that at least one member of the famous pair had differing opinions would mean viewing other historical duos similarly.

Figure 11.2 Vladimir Nemirovich-Danchenko with designers at home. By permission of the Moscow Art Academic Theatre

240 *Vladimir Nemirovich-Danchenko and the Moscow Art Theatre*

Vladimir Ivanovich broke down in tears when he announced to the team that he'd start his first season without Stanislavsky.

You'd think that death would settle disputes and put everything to rest fair and square. But on her deathbed, Ekaterina Nikolaevna warned her husband not to give up an inch of what belonged to him. And on the first anniversary of Stanislavsky's passing, it bothered his wife, Marya Petrovna, that Moskvin didn't speak at the gravesite, so she tried to find out if someone had instructed him not to talk.

I can see why Marya Petrovna was still reflecting on those rehearsals for the new version of *Three Sisters*. Stanislavsky's involvement in this play ended in 1935, and MAT's directors then decided, "Reviving *Three Sisters* isn't the right move." She stated that Vladimir Ivanovich could never retrieve what was lost. Yet, to me, there was never a plan to bring back the past. Some time ago, I was concerned that there would be a reevaluation of Chekhov. This worry arose after Leonov's *Polovchansky Gardens*.[24] I was disturbed by the glorification of power, strong bodies, and unwavering souls. However, when I thought about *Three Sisters*, I saw Natasha as the only consistent and fruitful character. V.I.'s article in Izvestia about Gorky's MAT merging with Chekhov's MAT also puzzled me.[25]

Fortunately, all these concerns were merely in my mind. My intuition reassured me that everything would turn out fine.

I heard intriguing details that ignited my imagination: Vladimir Ivanovich initially wanted to start fresh with Chekhov's works but later abandoned the idea. The new production will retain the walls and ceilings for *Three Sisters*, but will also feature some MAT-style elements such as wave patterns at the bottom of the set and the seagull logo on the walls. The revolving stage will still rotate when the curtain rises for the first act, and the other riverbank will still emerge through the mist in the final act. Dmitriev's set design has received high praise, which pleases me as I have always admired his originality.

When I asked about the staging specifics, I was mysteriously informed that there is no defined mise-en-scene. It appears that the performers' movements and the overall staging will be in a Chekhovian style. It emphasizes rhythm over movement. The rhythm is precise, like the unusual tragic allegro pace in Act IV instead of the usual slow tempo.

Interestingly, this pace complements the subject of yearning for a better life.

In Act II, they perform Tchaikovsky's "Wild Nights." Could these lyrics hold significance for Vladimir Ivanovich? I recall the lines:

"Even if time's cruel hand has revealed your falsehood to me, I still cling to memories of you, trapped in the past, seeking an impossible answer."

The revolving stage moves with these words, followed by Chebutykin mentioning Balzac's marriage in Berdichev.

Vershinin's statement "It's a shame that youth has passed" lingers. What does this signify for Vladimir Ivanovich? Does he see it as a personal reflection?

Chapter from another Book 1919–1943 (The Soviet Years) 241

"I used to chase the impossible in the past" ... Well, I wouldn't want to replicate anything, not even the earlier production of *Three Sisters*. I prefer to cherish the memory of the past production and eagerly anticipate the new one. Vladimir Ivanovich advised Stepanova, who plays Irina: "In the first scene: joy, radiance; and eventually, through weariness, sorrow, and tears, you will arrive at the play's conclusion filled with goodness." I couldn't recall the word joy initially, but it is mentioned early in Act IV (I double-checked). So, the whole MAT approach will go on, no need for a big fuss (about Gorky's theatre absorbing Chekhov's theatre. I didn't understand it). But all my worries are "in my head," meanwhile, my intuition tells me that everything will not be as I imagine, but it's okay.

I'll save my thoughts on *Three Sisters* until I see it. I decided it's best not to write right after seeing *Anna Karenina*. My mind was all over the place, and I couldn't fully appreciate the show. Later on, having read the book kindly sent by Vasily Sakhnovsky, I pondered a lot about it. Also got really captivated by Vladimir Ivanovich's letter that came with design sketches. He's got some new idea going with his creative process, something different since the start. Remember before *The Seagull*, all it took was a bird's cry in the night, a shadowy female figure, and the rain's sound on the courtyard for inspiration. Everything sprouted from there.

Even in his *La Traviata* production, I was amazed at how those 1870s dresses and Empress Eugenia hairstyles fueled his creativity. The theatre theme is so strong in everything. There's a gold-leafed bed on stage that hints at the ending and death in the last act, covered with post-show muslin as a symbol.

The scene with the beautiful blue velvet in *Anna Karenina*, the sleek rosewood, the carefully chosen authentic items, and the theatre boxes recreated onstage got me thinking the same. It's not just about having the right objects for the play; they actually become, as someone told me, part of the story. This concept had already caught Vladimir Ivanovich's interest even before *Anna Karenina*, playing with the stage's edge, the gloom of train lights, and the interplay of light and darkness before and after all interior scenes. He set the narrative in the St. Petersburg of Alexander II and Alexander III, drawing from the past as he wrote,

the golden-embroidered uniforms, flashy horsemen, bulky religious garments, the grand costumes of barely clothed beauties, the stern look of priests, the fake smiles, with sinister undertones lurking in every part of this grand establishment. And above all, the stern face of the chief priest, Pontifex Maximus.

Anna Karenina that night with mixed feelings. I remember thinking, "I'm so fortunate. I adore theatre so much, and there's theatre magic like this out there." And soon enough, if I'm still around, I'll see *Three Sisters*.

Moscow, April 25, 1940.

242 *Vladimir Nemirovich-Danchenko and the Moscow Art Theatre*

Vladimir Ivanovich, people are going to praise your latest production and analyze its impact on Chekhov's ideas and how it brings truth to the stage. Honestly, others are better at understanding the significance of what's happening at MAT right now than I am. You've done it again, breaking through barriers like you did after *The Brothers Karamazov*. Everyone else can probably explain better than me if your colleagues are ready to embrace the bold new vision and break away from the usual. Let me just share what really moved me during *Three Sisters*.

I couldn't contain my excitement as I weaved through the crowd and kept saying, "That was amazing!" And then you said, "Let's wait for the fat letter."[26]

I've been trying to pinpoint exactly what gave me that warm feeling since I first saw Irina in the doorway and felt the soft green light filling the room. It was familiar, yes, but you didn't recreate it to evoke nostalgia. Stepping into the Prozorovs' world felt almost magical. I could almost taste the vodka, smell the flowers, and sense the chilly May air, but there was this captivating distance between me and the characters.

And that distance wasn't about the time period or our different lives. It was you, the mastermind behind the production, who created it.

I feel that when the characters' lives were being finely tuned during rehearsals, no one wondered about their current lives, how they adapted to changes, or where Vershinin would be buried. Asking about them today would've seemed out of place in the world you crafted. It's like questioning where the woman in Sistine Madonna is right now—she's on that canvas, in the clouds, holding her child.

Sure, calling something an "artistic triumph" sounds cliché, but *Three Sisters* truly was. It left me in awe, even though those moments also carried a hint of personal sadness. Dearest sisters! Remember how we used to know each other? You were like a wife to me, with your dresses, gestures, and words as familiar as my wife's. Sadly, it seems you've moved on from me and the vibrant art scene. My life and my wife's life found meaning through you.

I've come to see art as something that doesn't just capture life but transforms it, promising eternity—that's the magic of art. I was truly happy to be a part of it all. *Three Sisters* was the most complete and beautiful stage production I've ever witnessed. The harmony within it remains a mystery to me—an enigma, as a friend once described it, a riddle filled with symbols. Your performance captured that mystery, despite the liveliness and light that shone throughout (like when Masha cast off her fur coat in the second act or the snowflakes falling around her neck). I must admit, I was a bit intimidated by you. The day after the show, I visited Zagorsk and saw *The Myrrh Bearers' Wives*, so distinct in Andrei Rublev's paintings, standing together like intertwined trees. I couldn't help but recall your production upon seeing them. The image of Olga, Irina, and Masha standing next to the birch trees in your play, seemingly emerging from the same root, lingered in my mind. I don't attribute any stylization to you, and I am only talking about my arbitrary mental associations. Please, don't be upset

Chapter from another Book 1919–1943 (The Soviet Years) 243

by this "enigma" or the symbolism involved. The connections Blok made between Chekhov and the mysteries of religious art truly seduced me.

Perhaps, upon reflection, you might see a hint of the mystery in your perfectly harmonious work. We have yet to answer the question that puzzled us in our youth—can an artist create harmony from a discordant life, and should the audience revel in this created harmony?

Thank you for letting me contemplate these youthful doubts and sins in my old age and revel in the harmony of it all.

Creativity and Dedication to Art Amid Upheavals and Impending Mortality[27]

The dress rehearsals for *Three Sisters* began in April 1940, and I wrote, "It's a blessed morning MAT." This morning made me realize that we still have life to live but in a new light shown by *Three Sisters*.

"What beautiful trees…" The trees painted by the designer and the autumn scenery were truly stunning.

> May this day and all days to come be blessed.
> Life will shower us with more generosity.
> A beautiful, eternal autumn will continue crowning our lives.
> Life is truly a gift.[28]

Nemirovich-Danchenko will not experience any decline in creative power. His rehearsals of *The Kremlin Chimes* will continue to progress strongly, pleasing everyone.[29] He will be more immersed in his creative dreams, even though he chuckles a bit at the thought of dreaming like this at his age. He will set *Hamlet* aside to explore new ideas about Shakespeare, particularly regarding the intriguing woman Cleopatra, who has captivated people for two thousand years. She sparks his imagination—how she erupts in anger, throws things at Antony, then weeps and kisses his feet—and emerges victorious, a woman of great intellect. Her lavish Egypt is indulgent and tumultuous, deceitful, and unstable, embodying the seductive horizontality of her world. Egypt lies flat like the sea and the desert. Antony represents a force of nature, a whirlwind, rather than just a man. Rome possesses its own beauty, not in its porticoes, columns, and statues, as depicted in forum photographs, but in the subtle motions and rugged hills of the city. "Rome stands tall like an armored vehicle." Initially, the separate worlds observe each other for an extended period, then the scene changes become more frequent, leading to clashes.

Hamlet resides within him, just as he resides within *Hamlet*. The foreboding Elsinore castle overlooks a leaden sea, enveloped in penetrating cold, with narrow passages within its walls. The crucial events take place there, not in the grand halls. When pondering the reality of this castle, he doesn't think of "wine, meat;" instead, he thinks of "bread, porridge;" basic, unsatisfying sustenance; a dim, unheated fortress.

244 *Vladimir Nemirovich-Danchenko and the Moscow Art Theatre*

He contemplates the idea of a theatre of emotions. Similar dreams had previously brought *Katerina Izmailova* (*Lady Macbeth of Mtsensk*) to life.[30] Despite its tragic outcome, he remained loyal to Shostakovich's opera. He laments that those who penned the article "Confusion Instead of Music" did not witness his production, as he could have defended it, he believed.

He also had a directorial concept for *Romeo and Juliet*: "Southern set. She is 14, and he is 19–20? Mature fruits." A noble family?—defending their honor. "Or akin to some mountain families?" Georgians, Spaniards? "The kiss at the start of Act I. Prior to that, Romeo's melancholy without kisses is essential. Concerning Juliet, the nurse and mother only talk about Juliet's perplexing indifference." All obstacles propel the action forward (night time, initial date on the balcony). "Since church marriage is not an option, we'll have a secret wedding. Naturally, without regret, without hesitation, like two bold rebels."

"Shakespeare's language, often exquisitely beautiful, is fundamentally simple. However, at times it becomes so obscure that it masks the essence, preventing access to the clear and tangible emotions that should be the starting point." He hopes to rekindle Boris Pasternak's passion for Shakespeare, the same Boris Pasternak who translated *Hamlet* and *Antony and Cleopatra* for him. At age 84, he marveled at actress Claudia Elanskaya. She was preparing to play the Queen in *Hamlet* and was perplexed as to why the Queen did not see or pay attention; how could she not...? What did the Queen even know or understand at this point? "It is because she is so drunk with Claudius, so enamored of him that she sees nothing else." "You are passionate enough to find the right feeling, to call up thoughts you can't even reveal to your pillow. Find those dark thoughts..." Elanskaya did not understand how a woman could lose her head.[31] But he understood "what passion has done to this queen!" He will be inclined to suddenly move toward what was "terribly simple." In Hamlet's scene with the Ghost, the director encourages Hamlet's "unbearable pity for him." "He cannot forget the anguish his father is going through." All the performers miss this, but how could they? Hamlet knows they hold his frightened and guiltless father somewhere, tormented and burning in fire, by order of a specific person. Everything is real.

Nemirovich does not use phrases like "If I'm alive...." "God willing...." "If I have enough strength...." Death has its rights. Its time will come; it will not take him by surprise, but his business is to live. Fate would allow him to live. Evacuated from Moscow to Georgia in 1941, he would see his homeland again.[32] To close the vast, sixty-five-year circle so that he will again transfer in Vladikavkaz. Trains only started from here in the past, but now he was going there by train. From there, he traveled in a Soviet limousine with the owner of the Rustaveli Theatre, who came out to meet him. They drove to his home along the Georgian Military Road to Tbilisi (formerly Tiflis). He walked around the city during his first days back, looking for the places where he lived and the theatre where he performed. They were no longer there!

Chapter from another Book 1919–1943 (The Soviet Years) 245

He was back in Moscow in September 1942.[33]

Yes, I flew in. And I did not hesitate. I thought it was all the same, perishing in a hospital from pneumonia or some airplane accident. But unexpectedly, it was a genuine pleasure, new sensations, and new views of nature. It makes me want to go again.

He was pleased with the start of high-level business meetings: "The attitude towards me is excellent." He would continue rehearsing Bulgakov's

Figure 11.3 Vladimir Nemirovich-Danchenko (1942). By permission of the Moscow Art Academic Theatre.

246   *Vladimir Nemirovich-Danchenko and the Moscow Art Theatre*

The Last Days of the Turbins. When referring to the "post office" scene, he said, "We must create a shoddier atmosphere. Nothing more is needed. The entire scene is meant for those who are being driven away." After viewing the cozy apartment, the palace, and the luxurious boarding school, the performance concludes in the worst possible peasant hut. This detail showcases the extraordinary depth of Bulgakov's play. From the glitter of St. Petersburg, the magnificent apartment, the palace, and the ball, suddenly transitions to wilderness, a smoky ceiling, greasy candles, cold, and gendarmes. They carry copies of Pushkin with them. They huddle together for warmth, take a break, and then push on.

During the rehearsal of Ostrovsky's *The Last Victim*, he examined the scenery sketches.[34] He discussed the premiere of this comedy with Sakhnovsky and Khmelev. He also reminisced about his conversations with Ostrovsky. He continued contemplating *Hamlet.* "I can't shake off the idea that the cemetery is somewhere below. The tower wall, the procession, and the cemetery descending somewhere." He was superstitious and never visited the theatre on Mondays. However, it didn't bother him that one of his productions was *The Last Victim* and another *The Last Days.* Seeing a sketch of the cemetery also didn't disturb him.

He still had much potentially ahead of him. On April 25, 1943, he attended a performance of Tchaikovsky's *Swan Lake* in the evening at the Bolshoi Theatre. He passed away from a heart attack during the event (Figure 11.3).[35]

Notes

1 *Maybe that was not the only reason, however...* The timeline of this chapter corresponds to the early years of Russia's repressive Stalinist period (1919–1943). By 1979, state censorship remained pervasive and may have been especially significant at the time of the biography's publication, potentially shaping a shift in the narrative perspective.

2 "Peter Lapshin" uses Nemirovich's first name and patronymic (Vladimir Ivanovich), as is the custom when addressing professional colleagues and those of superior social standing.

3 USSR. The Soviet Union, or the Union of Soviet Socialist Republics, was nominally a federal union of socialist states covering most of Eurasia from 1922 to 1991.

4 In 1918, Stanislavsky established an Opera Studio with the support of the Bolshoi Theatre. In 1941, the Moscow State Stanislavsky and Nemirovich-Danchenko Music Theatre (MAMT) was founded. This new theatre was a combination of the Opera Studio and the Nemirovich-Danchenko Music Theatre, which had been set up in 1919 as a Studio of MAT. The artistic principles of its founders, who applied the system of the MAT to opera and ballet, were followed by the new theatre.

5 *Madame Angot's Daughter* (1872) operetta by composer Charles Lecocq (1832–1918). It tells the story of Clairette, the daughter of a famous opera singer, who falls in love with an artist named Ange Pitou. The Countess schemes to come

Chapter from another Book 1919–1943 (The Soviet Years) 247

between them, but they ultimately triumph and find love. It was produced by the MAT Music Studio in 1920.

6 *Theatre Herald* (Teatralny Vestnik) 1921, no. 87–88, pp. 2–5, 16–17.

7 The Antonov Rebellion (1920–1921) was a peasant revolt in the Tambov province of Central Russia.

8 In 1923, the MAT Music Studio premiered Aristophanes's *Lysistrata* in Moscow, under the direction of Vladimir Nemirovich-Danchenko. The performance received various reactions and sparked public discussions. It ran for 215 performances, including in Leningrad and Berlin. According to Nemirovich-Danchenko, Aristophanes' comedy explores timeless themes such as nature, war, peace, health, and the dynamics between men and women. The production took approximately two years to complete at the MAT, with Dmitry Smolin writing the script, dances in the style of Isadora Duncan, and Reinhold Glière composing the music.

9 Pavel Markov, "Lysistrata: Muzykalnaya studiya MXAT" in *About Theatre: From the History of Russian Theatre*, edited by E. P. Udalnova (Vol. 3, Moscow: Isskustvo, 1977), p. 133.

10 *Carmencita and the Soldier* (from Bizet's 1875 opera *Carmen*) was directed by Nemirovich and produced at MAT's Music Studio in 1924.

11 Here the author's text returns to the narrative style of the earlier chapters.

12 *The Ardent Heart* (1869) is a play by Alexander Ostrovsky that tells the story of Kuroslepov, a wealthy merchant who wastes his life drinking while his wife Matrona spends his money and has an affair with the bailiff.

13 *Pugachev's Rebellion* (1925, the first Soviet play staged at MAT) is a play by author and playwright Konstantin Trenev (1876–1945) about a peasant uprising led by Yemelyan Pugachev against the Russian government in the eighteenth century, and its eventual defeat.

14 Conrad Veidt (1893–1943) was a German film actor and an early star in American films.

15 Valentin Katayev (1897–1986) was an author and playwright whose specialty was satirical treatments of post-Revolutionary social conditions. *The Embezzlers* was adapted from the novel of the same name and tells the story of accountant Filipp Stepanovich, cashier Vanechka, and courier Nikita fell victim to the recent embezzlement wave that hit 90% of Moscow's businesses. They stole 12,000 rubles meant for delivery and went on an extravagant drinking spree. From Leningrad to the South of Russia, their reckless adventure left them broke and back in Moscow, leading to their immediate arrest and imprisonment.

16 The Second MAT (MAT II, 1924–1936) was an expansion of the MAT First Studio founded in 1912 by Stanislavsky and Sulerjitsky and succeeded by Michael Chekhov.

17 Ivan Bersenev (1889–1951) joined MAT as an actor in 1911 and was head of MAT II in 1933 until its closure, then became head of the newly formed Lenin Komsomol Theatre (Lenkom) until the end of his life.

18 Vasily Sakhnovsky (1886–1945) was an actor, theatre critic, director, teacher, and Doctor of Art History associated with MAT.

19 Boris Pasternak (1880–1960) was a poet, novelist, composer, and literary translator, especially Shakespeare's plays.

20 Pavel Markov, "Vl. I. Nemirovich-Danchenko" *About Theatre: From the History of Russian Theatre* (Vol. 4, Moskva: Iskusstvo, 1977), pp. 25–58.

21 Vitaly Vilenkin (1910–1997) was a philologist by education and started as a literary secretary for the MAT Directorate in 1934. He later became the personal literary secretary for both Nemirovich-Danchenko and Vasily Kachalov, eventually

248 *Vladimir Nemirovich-Danchenko and the Moscow Art Theatre*

becoming their biographer. He also worked in the literary department of MAT with Pavel Markov.

22 *Lyubov Yarovaya* (1936) by Konstantin Trenev (1876–1945) tells the story of a young woman who is forced to choose between love and duty in pre-Revolutionary Russia.

23 *Enemies* (1906) is set in the terrace and home of factory owners Bardiny and Skrobotov. The factory workers demand the removal of a cruel manager, but Skrobotov refuses, leading to a violent conflict. Skrobotov is killed, and a murder investigation begins. The accused worker, Akimov, and other workers refuse to flee and instead fight for their rights and justice.

24 *Polovchansky Gardens* (1938) is a play about heroism on the eve of the Great Patriotic War (World War II) by soviet playwright, novelist, and advocate of Socialist Realism Leonid Leonov (1898–1994).

25 Gorky's MAT. The Moscow Art Theatre has undergone several name changes since its establishment in 1898:

(Note the Russian word for artistic is Художественный, hence МХАТ)

1898: Initially named "Moscow Art and Accessible Theatre (MXDT)"
1901: Shortened to "Moscow Art Theatre" (MXT) after removing "Accessible"
1919: Received the status of "Academic Theater" and became known as "Moscow Art Academic Theatre" (MAT)
1932: Renamed "The Gorky Moscow Academic Art Theater" under Stalin's government
1987: Split into two companies:
Moscow Art Academic Theatre named after Gorky
Moscow Art Academic Theatre named after Chekhov
2004: Returned to its original name "Moscow Art Theatre" (MXT), removing "Academic"

The theatre has maintained its current name, Moscow Art Theatre (MXT), since 2004.

26 "Let's wait for the fat letter." i.e., from the government's critics.

27 Traditional birthday greetings for an older person.

28 Here author's text returns to the narrative style of the earlier chapters.

29 *The Kremlin Chimes* (1940) is a play by Nikolai Pogodin (1900–1962). The play is set in 1920s Moscow during Lenin's electrification drive. Engineer Zabelin's criticism draws the attention of the Cheka chairman. Amid famine and arbitrary arrests, the play ends optimistically with young lovers, a creative sailor finding hope, and the chimes of the Kremlin ringing again.

30 *Katerina Izmailova* (originally titled *Lady Macbeth of the Mtsensk District*), an opera by Dmitri Shostakovich (1906–1975), was banned in 1935.

31 Claudia Elanskaya (1898–1972) was an actress associated with MAT and was adept at enriching one-dimensional melodramatic roles.

32 In early October, a notification came from the Committee for the Arts about the evacuation of Nemirovich-Danchenko to Tbilisi (1200 miles south).

33 Evacuation of industries and population from the Moscow region eastward was begun in late 1940 and early 1941 as a result of Operation Barbarossa, the German military invasion of June 1941.

34 *The Last Victim* (1877). The play tells the story of a woman deeply in love and willing to sacrifice her entire fortune for the sake of her beloved's salvation. However, it remains to be seen how Vadim Dulchin, a charming but reckless man, would respond to such devotion.

Chapter from another Book 1919–1943 (The Soviet Years) 249

35 On April 26, 1943, the Council of People's Commissars of the USSR issued a decree to honor the memory of Nemirovich-Danchenko. Among other initiatives, this decree announced the establishment of the Moscow Art Theatre School named after him. The creation of a memorial museum at his apartment 5/7 Glinishchevsky Lane, where he spent the last five years of his life, was inaugurated in 1944, and the lane was renamed in honor of Vladimir Nemirovich-Danchenko. The studio school officially opened on October 20, 1943.

Index

Note: *Italic* page numbers refer to figures and page numbers followed by "n" denote endnotes.

Abramova, Maria 37, 62n5
adaptations 29, 43, 195, 209, 232; achieving unity in complex 186–188; political demands 234–238; public demands 234–238; and tension in theatre's evolution 148–151
Akimova, Sophia 12
The Alarm Clock magazine 7–8, 12, 145
Alexandrov, Alexei 11
Alexeev, K. S. 68
All-Russian Exhibition 57
All-Union Agricultural Exhibition 3
ambition: art and 98–103; and self-reflection 103–108
Anathema (Andreyev) 163, 173, 177n6
Andreyev, Leonid 177n1; *Anathema* 163, 173, 177n6; *Ekaterina Ivanovna* 176, 203, 208n6; *The Life of Man* 160–161, 176; *Thought* 203–204, 208n7
Andreyeva, Maria 112n11
anguish: and isolation 188–191; and theatrical innovation 188–191
Anna Karenina (Tolstoy) 17, 29, 237, 241
Antigone (Sophocles) 80
Antonov Rebellion 247n7
The Ardent Heart (Ostrovsky) 230, 247n12
art: and ambition 98–103; amid upheavals and impending mortality 243–246; creativity and dedication to 243–246; role amid social crisis 212–215; and World War I 212–215
Artem, Alexander 108, 113n12, 204

artistic: creativity 182, 204, 211, 215, 234, 236; reinvention/adaptability 209–211; struggle amid political turmoil 135–141; struggle amid societal turmoil 135–141
artistic expression 211; amid social upheaval 215–216; bold 215–216; power of 13
artistic innovation 29; and social resonance in *The Seagull* 76–81; tradition *vs.* 118–123
artistic legacy 146; dedication in 179–181; sacrifice in 179–181
artistic vision 41–44; *vs.* cultural changes 228–234; experiences in Hollywood 228–234; *vs.* ideological conflict 191–194; *vs.* political changes 228–234
The Ascension of Hannele (Hauptmann) 67, 79, 87n12
At the Gate of the Kingdom (Hamsun) 176
At the Graveyard Cross (Nemirovich-Danchenko) 35
At the Monastery (Yartsev) 112, 113n15, 145
At the Postal Station (Nemirovich-Danchenko) 35, 43
audience: dynamics, evolving 151–153; engagement 153–157
authenticity 81, 130, 160; domestic 77; in *The Living Corpse* 198–202
Autumn Violins (Surguchev) 215–216, 224n4
Averkiev, Vasily 19

252 *Index*

Ballets Russes (Diaghilev) 199, 208n3
Bankrupt in France
  (Nemirovich-Danchenko) 29, 109
Barry, Philip: *Without Love* 25
Bauman, Nikolai 125–126, 141n10
The Beginning of the Century (Bely)
  145, 157n5
Belinsky, Vissarion 18, 123, 141n6
Bely, Andrei 157n5; *The Beginning of
  the Century* 145
Benois, Alexander 163, 181–182, 192,
  196n4, 203, 216
Berkovsky, Naum 71
Bersenev, Ivan 222, 224n19, 233,
  247n17
Birman, Serafima 185, 196n8, 206,
  218, 228
Bizet, Georges: *Carmen* 232
Black Snow (Bulgakov) 140, 142n20
Blockade (Ivanov) 224n14
Blok, Alexander: *The Rose and the
  Cross* 217–219, 224n8; *The Song of
  Fate* 177; *The Twelve* 185
The Blue Bird (film) 109, 145, 173, 176,
  180, 214
The Blusher 34
Boborykin, Pyotr 87n11; *Classmates* 78;
  Ladies 90
Borborykin, Peter: *The Smallholders*
  115
Boris Godunov (Pushkin) 168, 170,
  177n8, 185, 230
Brenko, Anna 45, 62n9
The Brothers Karamazov (Dostoevsky)
  39, 185, 194–196, 198–199,
  203, 242
Bryusov, Valery: *Earth's Axis* 3
Bulgakov, Mikhail: *Black Snow* 140,
  142n20; *The Cabal of Hypocrites*
  177; *Days of the Turbins* 150; *The
  Last Days of the Turbins* 246; *The
  Master and Margarita* 150, 209; *The
  White Guard* 150
The Burial Mound (Ibsen) 114

The Cabal of Hypocrites (Bulgakov) 177
Capital (Marx) 6
Carmen (Bizet) 232
Carr, J. L.: *A Month in the Country* 16,
  19, 164, 166–167, 177
Chaliapin, Fyodor 163, 177n5
change: cultural 202–208, 228–234;
  generational 202–208; in life and
  legacy 108–112; nostalgia amid 114–
  118; political 228–234

Chekhov, Anton: *The Cherry Orchard*
  9, 109–110, 116–118, 123, 143, 176;
  A Dreary Story 8; *The Governor's
  Inspection* 50; *Ivanov* 11, 20, 42,
  43, 114–116, 118–123; *The Seagull*
  42, 47, 63–66, 70, 71, 76–81, 85,
  92, 100, 108, 114, 200; tradition *vs.*
  innovation in 118–123; *Uncle Vanya*
  123, 143, 175, 176, 201, 231
Chernevsky, Sergei 62n3
The Cherry Orchard (Chekhov) 9,
  109–110, 116–118, 123, 143, 176
Children of the Sun (Gorky) 138–140,
  142n18, 143
classics relevance 159–162
Classmates (Boborykin) 78
collaboration: and creative conflicts
  123–126; cultural 44–45; leadership
  through 182–185
conflicts: creative 123–126; ideological
  191–194; interpreting realism
  127–131
contemporary relevance 159–162
creative conflicts 123–126
creative crises: and ideals 217–220;
  realities amid 217–220
creativity: to art amid upheavals/
  impending mortality 243–246;
  artistic 182, 204, 211, 215, 234, 236;
  individual 10; insightful-creativity 44;
  insincere 103; and rationalism 168;
  responsive 44, 125; self-sufficient
  152; theatrical 152; true 104; vanity
  and guilt of 139–140
Cricket on the Hearth 178n19, 213,
  219, 237
cultural changes: artistic vision *vs.*
  228–234; renewal and doubt amid
  202–208
cultural collaboration 44–45

Daggers Drawn 16
The Daily Gazette 21
D'Annunzio, Gabriele 100, 112n8, 145,
  156, 159, 160; *Glory* 159–160; *La
  Gioconda* 100, 159–160
Dark Forest (Liu Cixin) 26
Dashing Force 25–26
Davydov, Vladimir 37, 205
Days of the Turbins (Bulgakov) 150
The Death of Ivan the Terrible (Tolstoy)
  66, 94–95
The Death of Pazukhin
  (Saltykov-Shchedrin) 177, 178n20,
  216, 230

dedication: in artistic legacy 179–181; to cultural collaboration 44–45; to theatre 44–45
deep emotion in *Three Sisters* 238–243
Demons (Dostoevsky) 16, 192–193, 197n12
Denikin, Anton 222, 224n18
The Desert 3
Diaghilev, Sergei 199, 208n3; *Ballets Russes* 199, 208n3
Dikiy, Alexey 186, 197n11, 218
Dilettantes (Nemirovich-Danchenko) 39–40
Do Not Tempt Me 64, 79
Dostoevsky, Fyodor: *The Brothers Karamazov* 39, 185, 194–196, 198–199, 203, 242; *Demons* 16, 192–193, 197n12; *The Gambler* 232; *The Village of Stepanchikovo* 217–219
Drama Behind the Scenes (Nemirovich-Danchenko) 47–48
The Drama of Life (Hamsun) 150–153, 156, 158n15, 159–161, 176, 194
A Dreary Story (Chekhov) 8

Earth's Axis (Bryusov) 3
education: and independence 4–7; transforming theatre through 45–54
Efros, Anatoly 10, 31n8; *The Joy of Rehearsal* 31n8
Efros, Nikolai 41, 62n7, 77, 91
Ekaterina Ivanovna (Andreyev) 176, 203, 208n6
Elanskaya, Claudia 244, 248n31
The Embezzlers (Kataev) 233, 247n15
An Enemy of the People (Ibsen) 95–96, 198, 218, 230
Enough Stupidity in Every Wise Man (Ostrovsky) 96, 164, 169, 172, 174, 177, 177n9
Eros (Ivanov) 3
ethics 17, 207; and intelligentsia 228; justifying theatre through 194–196; work 26
Eugene Onegin (Ostrovsky) 232
existential struggles 54–56
existential tragedy in Russian theatre 131–135
experimentation 145, 162–163

Falcons and Ravens (Nemirovich-Danchenko and Sumbatov-Yuzhin) 26, 29
Feast in a Time of Plague (Pushkin) 216
Fedotov, Aleksander 67, 86n5

Fedotova, Glikeria 12, 16, 25, 31n11, 33, 37, 86n5
Fet, Afanasy 53, 166, 178n10
The Field magazine 35, 56–61, 159, 161
Figrang, W. K. 68
first farewells (1904–1905) 114–141; artistic struggle amid political/societal turmoil 135–141; collaboration 123–126; conflicts interpreting realism 127–131; creative conflicts 123–126; existential tragedy in Russian theatre 131–135; nostalgia amid change 114–118; tradition *vs.* innovation in Chekhov 118–123
First World War 9, 211–212
Flammarion, Camille 40, 62n6
Flerov, Sergei 15
Fokine, Mikhail 37, 62n4
Fonzivin, Denis 72
The Forced Marriage (Moliere) 203
France, Anatole: *The Garden of Epicurus* 3
Freidkina, Lyubov 12, 31n9
French Revolution 233
From the Past (Nemirovich-Danchenko) 31n1, 143–144

The Gambler (Dostoevsky) 232
The Garden of Epicurus (France) 3
Geltser, Anatoly 36, 62n3
generational change 202–208
Gennert, Arkady 221
Germanova, Maria 112, 113n14, 123, 184–185
Giatsintov, Vladimir 206, 208n8
Giatsintova, Sofia 131, 208n8
Gilyarovsky, Vladimir 126, 141n12
Gippius, Zinaida: *The Green Ring* 219, 222, 224n9, 237
Gladkov, Alexander 150, 158n14
Gladky, Pyotr 2
Glory (D'Annunzio) 159–160
God Save the Tsar (National anthem) 74
Godunov, Boris 74–75
Gogol, Nikolai 72; *The Inspector General* 89, 164, 168–172, 177, 230; *Mirgorod* 43
Gold (Nemirovich-Danchenko) 37, 40, 181, 196n3
The Goldfish (Nemirovich-Danchenko) 34
Goldoni, Carlo: *The Mistress of the Inn* 72, 177
Goncharov, Ivan 26, 31n17

254 *Index*

A Good Case (Nemirovich-Danchenko) 34–35
Gorky, Maxim 125; *Children of the Sun* 138–140, 142n18, 143; *The Lower Depths* 90, 126–127, 130, 133–135, 176, 209; *Philistines* 126–127, 130, 142n14; *Summerfolk* 135–136, 142n16, 145
The Governor's Inspection (Chekhov) 50, 102
Grabar, Igor 30, 31n20
Green, Alexander 141n3; *Voice and Eye* 141n3
The Green Ring (Gippius) 219, 222, 224n9, 237
Greta's Happiness (Mariott) 72, 79, 99–100, 112n7
Griboyedov, Alexander 72; *Woe from Wit* 17, 18, 22, 109, 123, 140, 159, 164, 166, 169, 177
Grigorovich, Dmitry 30, 31n18, 31n19
Guilty without Guilt (Ostrovskiy) 16
Gukhale, K. A. 68
Gutzkow, Karl: *Uriel Acosta* 12, 18, 70, 87n6

Hamlet (Shakespeare) 2, 6, 12, 164, 243–244
Hamsun, Knut: *The Drama of Life* 150–153, 156, 158n15, 159–161, 176, 194; *At the Gate of the Kingdom* 176; *In the Grip of Life* 189, 203
Hauptmann, Gerhart: *The Ascension of Hannele* 67, 79, 87n12; *Lonely People* 95, 158n21; *Michael Kramer* 71, 87n8; *Schluck and Jau* 1900 157n10; *The Sunken Bell* 70–71, 134
The Heart is Not a Stone (Ostrovsky) 16
Hedda Gabler (Ibsen) 91
Heijermans, Herman 160–161, 177n4
Hennert, A. E. 68
Herzen, Alexander: *My Past and Thoughts* 198
history: and poetry 167–168; and realism 167–168
Hofmannsthal, Hugo von 159–161, 177n3
Hollywood 228–234
Homer: *The Iliad* 53
The Huguenots (Meyerbeer) 38
human genius, and theatre 194–196

humor: in Russian theatre 172–174; self-aware 172–174; self-reflective 174–176
Hymns to Claudian (Sudermann) 90, 112n1

Ibsen, Henrik: *The Burial Mound* 114; *An Enemy of the People* 95–96, 198, 218, 230; *Hedda Gabler* 91; *The Master Builder* 92; *Peer Gynt* 93, 154; *Pillars of Society* 137; *The Warrior's Barrow* 104, 112n11; *When We Dead Awaken* 100, 102
ideals amid creative/personal crises 217–220
ideological conflict *vs.* artistic vision 191–194
The Iliad (Homer) 53
individual creativity 10
In Dreams (Nemirovich-Danchenko) 39, 40, 55, 102, 103
Inferno (Nemirovich-Danchenko) 124–125
influence: and adaptation to public/political demands 234–238; and theatre ideology 234–238
innovation: artistic 76–81; musical theatre 226–228; theatrical 153–157, 188–191; *vs.* tradition in Chekhov 118–123
insincere creativity 103
The Inspector General (Gogol) 89, 164, 168–172, 177, 230
intellect: and societal expectations 7–11; and theatre 7–11
Interior (Maeterlinck) 159, 161
In the Grip of Life (Hamsun) 189, 203
In the Steppe (Nemirovich-Danchenko) 39, 40
In the Storm (Khrennikov) 221
isolation: and anguish 188–191; and theatrical innovation 188–191
Ivanov (Chekhov) 11, 20, 42, 43, 114–116, 118–123
Ivanov, Vladimir 23
Ivanov, Vyacheslav: *Blockade* 224n14; *Eros* 3

Jamgarov Bank 80
John of Damascus (Tolstoy) 65, 86n4
The Joy of Rehearsal (Efros) 31n8
Joy Will Come (Merezhkovsky) 221, 224n13

Julius Caesar (Shakespeare) 18, 137–138, 164
Jungmann, Albert 37

Kachalov, Vasily 84, 87n14
Kalguyev, Andrei 40
Kālidāsa: *Sakuntala* 204
Karamazov, Alyosha 39
Karsavina, Tamara 199, 208n4
Karyshev, Nikolai 43–44, 62n8
Katayev, Valentin 247n15; *The Embezzlers* 233, 247n15
Katkov, Mikhail 15
Kern, Anna 30
Khalyutina, Sophia 92–93, 112n3
Khodynka Field 62n16
Khodynka Tragedy 56–62
Khrennikov, Tikhon: *In the Storm* 221
Kicheev, Nikolai 12
Kicheev, Pyotr 145, 157n4
Kirshon, Vladimir: *North Wind* 221
Knipper, Olga 47, 62n11
Koonen, Alisa 93, 112n5
Korf, Baron Nikolai 32–33
Kotlyarevsky, Nestor 199, 208n2
Koznov, N. P. 68
The Kremlin Chimes (Pogodin) 224n15, 243, 248n29
Krylov, Viktor 38
Kuprin, Alexander 3

Ladies (Boborykin) 90
The Ladies' Battle (Scribe) 230
La Gioconda (D'Annunzio) 100, 159–160
Lanin, Nikolai 14, 21
Lassalle, Ferdinand 23, 31n16
The Last Days of the Turbins (Bulgakov) 246
The Last Meeting (Nemirovich-Danchenko) 46, 47, 49
The Last Victim (Ostrovsky) 246, 248n34
Last Will (Nemirovich-Danchenko) 36–37
leadership: and theatre's role amid revolutionary upheaval 220–223; through collaboration 182–185; through resilience 182–185
Lecocq, Charles: *Madame Angot's Daughter* 246n5
legacy: artistic 146, 179–181; and change 108–112; professional 1–4;

resilience in 108–112; and tradition 108–112
Lenin, Vladimir 44, 224n15, 230, 248n29
Leningrad Prospect 62n16
Lenin Komsomol Theatre (Lenkom) 224n19, 247n17
Lenin Library 12
Lensky, Alexander 32, 50, 62n2
Leonidov, Leonid 112n2, 195
Leonidov, Yuri 92, 148
Leonov, Leonid: *Polovchansky Gardens* 240, 248n24
Lermontov, Mikhail: *Masquerade* 216
Leskov, Nikolai 16; *No Way Out* 16
liberalism 14–21
life: change in 108–112; mystery in *Three Sisters* 238–243; resilience in 108–112; tradition in 108–112
The Life of Man (Andreyev) 160–161, 176
Lilina, Maria 78, 87n10
Liszt, Franz 46
Literary Bread (Nemirovich-Danchenko) 14, 16, 21, 23, 28, 29
Little Tragedies (Pushkin) 216
Liu Cixin: *Dark Forest* 26
The Living Corpse (Tolstoy) 93, 185, 197n9, 200–202; authenticity in 198–202; self-fulfillment in 198–202
Lonely People (Hauptmann) 95, 158n21, 160, 161
The Lower Depths (Gorky) 90, 126–127, 130, 133–135, 176, 209
Lucky Man (Nemirovich-Danchenko) 27–28, 36
Lukutin, I. A. 68
Lunacharsky, Anatoly 3, 31n4
Luzhsky, Vasily 19, 31n14
Lyubov Yarovaya (Trenyev) 221, 235, 248n22

Madame Angot's Daughter (Lecocq) 246n5
Maeterlinck, Maurice 87n13; *Interior* 159, 161; *Pelleas and Melisande* 159–160, 166
Maly Theatre (Small Theatre) 4, 8, 13, 16, 18–19, 23–24, 26, 31n5, 31n11, 33, 36, 38, 42, 45, 53, 62n2, 69, 72, 86n5, 93, 147–148, 180, 183, 198, 230
Mamontov, Konstantin 225n21

256 *Index*

Mamontov, Savva 109, 113n13, 222
Maria Tudor (Hugo) 16, 24
Mariott, Emil: *Greta's Happiness* 72,
 79, 99–100, 112n7
Markov, Pavel 171, 194
Marx, A. F. 2, 31n3
Marx, Karl 31n16; *Capital* 6
The Mask of the Red Death
 (Tcherepnin) 227
Masquerade (Lermontov) 216
The Master and Margarita (Bulgakov)
 150, 209
The Master Builder (Ibsen) 92
Men Above the Law (Pisemsky) 73
The Merchant of Venice (Shakespeare)
 74, 164
Merezhkovsky, Dmitry 224n13; *Joy
 Will Come* 221, 224n13
merlichlundria 121, 141n1
Meyerbeer, Giacomo: *The Huguenots* 38
Mgebrov, Alexander 2
Michael Kramer (Hauptmann) 71, 87n8
Milton, John: *Paradise Lost* 148
Mirgorod (Gogol) 43
Miserere (Yushkevich) 93, 163, 177n7,
 189, 203
The Mist (Nemirovich-Danchenko) 34,
 39, 46, 91
The Mistress of the Inn (Goldoni) 72,
 177
Mochalov, Pavel 18, 31n10
modernity 36–41, 142n14
Modern Times 13
Moliere: *The Forced Marriage* 203
A Month in the Country (Turgenev) 16,
 19, 164, 166–167, 177
Morozov, Savva 68, 142n22
Morozov, Sergei. T. 68
mortality: creativity and dedication
 to art amid 243–246; creativity/
 dedication to art amid 243–246;
 impending 243–246
The Moscow Illustrated Gazette
 (newspaper) 44
Moscow Art Theatre (MAT) 2, 4,
 4, 9, 17, 19, 22, 31n14; audience
 dynamics, evolving 151–153;
 continuity of life in productions of
 174–176; creative tension 151–153;
 first season 64–67; foundation and
 early trials of 67–74; founding
 meeting of 63–64; and principles of
 nobility 44–45; self-reflective humor
 in productions of 174–176

Moscow Art Theatre Museum 2
Moscow Gazette (newspaper) 15
Moskvin, Ivan 53, 62n13
Mozart and Salieri (Pushkin) 216
musical theatre innovations 226–228
My Life in the Russian Theatre
 (Nemirovich-Danchenko) 31n1
My Past and Thoughts (Herzen) 198

Naidanov, Sergey: *The Walls* 151,
 158n17, 162
Nefedov, Philip 14
Nekrasov, Nikolay 156, 158n20, 166,
 178n11
Nemirovich-Danchenko, Vasily 7, 31n6,
 32, 181
Nemirovich-Danchenko, Vladimir
 1–3, *4*, *5*, 6, 8–13, *15*, 18, 20–21,
 24–26, 30, 32, 68, *73*, 88–89, 99,
 245; *At the Graveyard Cross* 35; *At
 the Postal Station* 35, 43; *Bankrupt
 in France* 29, 109; and classics/
 contemporary relevance 159–162;
 Dilettantes 39–40; *Drama Behind
 the Scenes* 47–48; *In Dreams* 39, 40,
 55, 102–103; *Falcons and Ravens* 26,
 29; *Gold* 37, 40, 181, 196n3; *The
 Goldfish* 34; *A Good Case* 34–35;
 Inferno 124–125; *The Inspector
 General* 230; *The Inspector General*
 89, 164, 168–172, 177, 230; *In the
 Steppe* 39, 40; *The Last Meeting*
 46–47, 49; *Last Will* 36, 37; *Literary
 Bread* 14, 16, 21, 23, 28, 29; *Lucky
 Man* 27–28, 36; marriage and
 creative fulfillment 32; *The Mist* 34,
 39, 46, 91; *My Life in the Russian
 Theatre* 31n1; *New Business* 37,
 40; *Our Americans* 24–26; *From
 the Past* 143–144; *Police Inspector
 Stanovoy* 40; *Poor Noel Rambert* 2;
 Porcelain Dolls 34; *The Price of Life*
 42, 54, 99; self-improvement through
 continuous effort 23–30; *The Textile
 Worker* 33; theatrical journalism and
 evolving ideals 11–13; and tradition/
 relevance 168–169; *Under the
 Wife* 38
New Business (Nemirovich-Danchenko)
 37, 40
News and Exchange (newspaper) 97
News of the Day (newspaper) 67
News of the Season (newspaper)
 172, 174

Index 257

The New Times (newspaper) 10, 20, 80, 84–85, 132
Nijinsky, Vaslav 199, 208n5
Nikolaev, Alexander 2
Nikolaevna, Ekaterina 240
Nikolai, Korf 32, 62n1
The Northern Herald (newspaper) 42
North Wind (Kirshon) 221
nostalgia amid change 114–118
No Way Out (Leskov) 16

Onisimovich, Vasily 40
Osipov, K. V. 68
Ostrovsky, Alexander: *The Ardent Heart* 230, 247n12; *Enough Stupidity in Every Wise Man* 96, 164, 169, 172, 174, 177, 177n9; *Guilty without Guilt* 16; *The Heart is Not a Stone* 16; *The Last Victim* 246, 248n34; *The Poor Bride* 17, 73
Othello (Shakespeare) 18, 70
Our Americans (Nemirovich-Danchenko) 24–26

Paradise Lost (Milton) 148
The Parasite (Turgenev) 203
passion and responsibility 21–23
Pasternak, Boris 234, 244, 247n19
Pchelnikov, Pavel 21
Peer Gynt (Ibsen) 93, 154, 203
Pelleas and Melisande (Maeterlinck) 159–160, 166
personal crises 217–220
personal revelations and professional legacy 1–4
Petrushka (Stravinsky) 199–200
Philistines (Gorky) 126–127, 130, 142n14
Pillars of Society (Ibsen) 137
Pisemsky, Aleksei 45, 62n10, 73; *Men Above the Law* 73; *Self-Governance* 45
Podgorny, Nikolai 157n12
poetry 53, 110, 115–117, 144, 162; of Afanasy Fet 166; of everyday life 188; and history 167–168; neoromantic 141n3; and realism 167–168; stage life-poetry 81; symbolist 79
Pogodin, Nikolai: *The Kremlin Chimes* 224n15, 243, 248n29
Police Inspector Stanovoy (Nemirovich-Danchenko) 40
political changes 228–234
political turmoil 135–141

Polovchansky Gardens (Leonov) 240, 248n24
The Poor Bride (Ostrovsky) 17, 73
Poor Noel Rambert (Nemirovich-Danchenko) 2
Popov, Alexei 2
Porcelain Dolls (Nemirovich-Danchenko) 34
Potekhin, Alexei 26, 30, 31n18, 36
The Power of Darkness (Tolstoy) 51, 92
The Price of Life (Nemirovich-Danchenko) 42, 54, 99
professional legacy 1–4
Prokofiev, I. A. 68
Przybyszewski, Stanislaw 3, 177n2
Pugachev's Rebellion (Trenev) 230, 247n13
Pushkin, Alexander: *Boris Godunov* 168, 170, 177n8, 185, 230; *Feast in a Time of Plague* 216; *Little Tragedies* 216; *Mozart and Salieri* 216

Quiet Flows the Don (Sholokhov) 221

radicalism 153–157
rationalism and creativity 168
realism: conflicts interpreting 127–131; and history 167–168; and poetry 167–168; shifts in 162–163; vivid 33–36
realities: amid creative crises 217–220; amid personal crises 217–220
relevance in theatre 168–169
renewal/doubt: amid cultural change 202–208; amid generational change 202–208
resilience: amid societal and financial upheaval 143–148; leadership through 182–185; in life and legacy 108–112
responsibility 21–23, 39, 168, 180, 182, 186
responsive creativity 44, 125
Resurrection (Tolstoy) 223n1, 235
revolutionary upheaval: and leadership 220–223; theatre's role amid 220–223
Rimsky-Korsakov, Nikolai: *The Snow Maiden* 86, 108, 129, 146, 227
The Rose and the Cross (Blok) 217–219, 224n8
Roshchin-Insarov, Nikolai 68
Russian classics 123, 163–167

258 *Index*

The Russian Courier (newspaper) 12, 14–16, 18, 20–21, 23, 30, 44, 118
The Russian Gazette (newspaper) 44, 118
Russian Land (newspaper) 186, 198
Russian News (newspaper) 11
Russian theatre: existential tragedy in 131–135; self-aware humor in 172–174
Russian tragedy 135, 179–196; and anguish 188–191; artistic vision *vs.* ideological conflict 191–194; collaboration/resilience, leadership through 182–185; dedication/sacrifice in artistic legacy 179–181; and isolation 188–191; theatre and truth/ethics/human genius 194–196; theatrical innovation 188–191; unity in complex adaptations 186–188
Russian Word (newspaper) 182
Russo-Japanese War 141n7
Rybakov, Nikolai 53

sacrifice in artistic legacy 179–181
Sakhnovsky, Vasily 233, 241, 247n18
Sakuntala (Kālidāsa) 204
Saltykov-Shchedrin, Mikhail: *The Death of Pazukhin* 177, 178n20, 230
satire in theatre 169–172
Savina, Iya 40
Savina, Maria 37
Savitskaya, Margarita 47, 84
Schiller, Friedrich 38
Schluck and Jau 1900 (Hauptmann) 157n10
Scribe, Eugene: *The Ladies' Battle* 230
The Seagull (Chekhov) 42, 45, 47, 63–66, 70, 71, 76–81, 85, 92, 100, 108, 114, 200; artistic innovation in 76–81; social resonance in 76–81
self-aware humor in Russian theatre 172–174
self-fulfillment in *The Living Corpse* 198–202
Self-Governance (Pisemsky) 45
self-reflection: ambition and 103–108; in theatre 169–172
self-reflective humor 174–176
self-sufficient creativity 152
Sergei Palm 13, 31n12
Severov, Nikolai 4, 11
Sezenevsky, Boris 9–10
Shakespeare, William 12; *Hamlet* 2, 6, 12, 164, 243–244; *Julius Caesar*

18, 137, 138, 164; *The Merchant of Venice* 74, 164; *Othello* 18, 70
Shmenev, Johann 2
Sholokhov, Mikhail: *Quiet Flows the Don* 221
Shostakovsky, Pyotr 46
Shuvalov, Ivan 68
The Smallholders (Borborykin) 115
The Snow Maiden (Rimsky-Korsakov) 86, 108, 129, 134, 146, 227
Sobolev, Yuri 9
social crisis: role of art 212–215; and World War I 212–215
social upheaval 143–148, 215–216
societal expectations: and intellect 7–11; and theatre 7–11
societal turmoil 135–141
Soloviev, Sergei 7
The Song of Fate (Blok) 177
Sophocles: *Antigone* 80
The Spassky Gate 62n14
Stakhovich, Alexey 144, 146, 157n9, 181–183
Stanislavsky, Konstantin 4, 12, 17–18, 45, 63–72, 74–75, 79, 82–85, 86n2, 87n10, 88–90, 93–98, 100–101, 103–104, 108–109, 117, 123, 126–140, 141n9, 145–153, 157, 157n6, 159–163, 166–177, 178n19, 179–180, 182–185, 188–189, 194–196, 200, 202–203, 205–207, 210, 212–213, 216–219, 222–223, 224n2, 233–234, 237–240, 246n4, 247n16; *My Life in Art* 83, 89, 167, 210
storytelling 33–36
Stravinsky, Igor: *Petrushka* 199–200
Strepetova, Polina 17
Sudermann, Hermann: *Hymns to Claudian* 90, 112n1
Sulerzhitsky, Leopold 83, 125, 141n9
Sumbatov, Alexander 4, 11, 32
Summerfolk (Gorky) 135–136, 142n16, 145
The Sunken Bell (Hauptmann) 70–71, 134
Surguchev, Ilya 215; *Autumn Violins* 215–216, 224n4
Swan Song 42

Tarasov, Nikolai 143–144, 157n2
Tarasova, Alla 17, 222
The Textile Worker (Nemirovich-Danchenko) 33

theatre: adaptation/tension in evolution of 148–151; balancing tradition/relevance in 168–169; creative tension 151–153; dedication to 44–45; and intellect 7–11; justifying through truth/ethics/human genius 194–196; as medium for transformative truth 91–98; organization and creative excellence 88–90; role amid revolutionary upheaval 220–223; satire and self-reflection in 169–172; and societal expectations 7–11; transforming through education 45–54

Theatre magazine 12

theatrical creativity 152

theatrical innovation 153–157; and anguish 188–191; and isolation 188–191

theatrical journalism 11–13

Thought (Andreyev) 203–204, 208n7

Three Sisters 3, 81–82, 84–86, 108, 123, 127, 175, 176, 204, 209, 240–243; deep emotion in 238–243; life's mystery in 238–243; yearning for purpose amid societal/personal challenges in 81–86

Tolstoy, Alexei: *The Death of Ivan the Terrible* 66; *John of Damascus* 86n4; *Tsar Fyodor Ivanovich* 51, 63–67, 74, 81, 86n3, 164, 167, 208, 230

Tolstoy, Leo: *Anna Karenina* 17, 29, 237, 241; *The Living Corpse* 93, 185, 197n9, 198–202; *The Power of Darkness* 51, 92; *Resurrection* 223n1

tradition: *vs.* innovation in Chekhov 118–123; in life and legacy 108–112; struggle with 36–41; in theatre 168–169

Trenev, Konstantin: *Lyubov Yarovaya* 221, 235, 248n22; *Pugachev's Rebellion* 247n13

truth: justifying theatre through 194–196; theatre as medium for transformative 91–98

Tsar Fyodor Ivanovich (Tolstoy) 51, 63–67, 74, 81, 86n3, 164, 167, 208, 230; national struggles 74–76; personal struggles 74–76

Tsulukidzeva, Maria 2

Turgenev, Ivan 26; *A Month in the Country* 16, 19, 164, 166–167, 177; *The Parasite* 203

The Twelve (Blok) 185

Uncle Vanya (Chekhov) 123, 143, 175, 176, 201, 231

Under the Wife (Nemirovich-Danchenko) 38

Union of Soviet Socialist Republics (USSR) 2, 3, 226, 246n3, 249n35

unresolved ideals 54–56

upheaval: creativity and dedication to art amid 243–246; financial 143–148; revolutionary 220–223; social 143–148, 215–216

Uriel Acosta (Gutzkow) 12, 18, 70

Ushkov, K. K. 68

Vakhtangov, Evgeny 191, 197n16, 206–207, 228

Veidt, Conrad 232, 247n14

Vilenkin, Vitaly 39, 94, 234, 247n21

The Village of Stepanchikovo (Dostoevsky) 217–219

Vishnevsky, Alexander 133, 143, 146, 157n1, 162, 173, 196, 217

vivid realism in storytelling 33–36

Voice and Eye (Green) 141n3

The Voice (newspaper) 13, 35, 118

Vostriakov, D. P. 68

The Walls (Naidanov) 151, 158n17, 162, 176

Wandering Fires 22

The Warrior's Barrow (Ibsen) 104, 112n11

Webster, John: *White Devil* 164

Wenger, Semyon 16

Wenger's Biographical Dictionary 23

When We Dead Awaken (Ibsen) 100, 102

White Devil (Webster) 164

The White Guard (Bulgakov) 150

Wild Rose 23–24, 26

Without a Position 27, 28

Without Love (Barry) 25, 27

Witte, Sergei Yulyevich 143, 157n3

Woe from Wit (Griboyedov) 17, 18, 22, 109, 123, 140, 159, 164, 166, 169, 177, 204–205, 231

World of Art movement 115

World War I 112, 212–215

260 Index

Yablochkina, Alexandra 17
Yakovlev, Kondrat 68
Yartsev, Pyotr: *At the Monastery* 112, 113n15, 145
Yegor Bulychov and Others (film) 134, 221
Yermolova, Maria 12, 17

Yushkevich, Semyon: *Miserere* 93, 163, 177n7, 189, 203
Yuzhin, Alexander 4, 5

Zemshchina (newspaper) 198
Znanievtsy's Book of Facts 3

Printed in the United States
by Baker & Taylor Publisher Services